Mental Health Promotion in Schools

(Volume 2)

Edited by

Raymond J. Waller

Troy University

Dothan

United States

Bentham Science Publishers Ltd.
Executive Suite Y - 2
PO Box 7917, Saif Zone
Sharjah, U.A.E.
Email: subscriptions@benthamscience.org

CONTENTS

FOREWORD

As a leader in the field of school mental health for nearly 20 years, I continue to be alarmed by the number of youth falling behind academically in the United States. Achievement rates are abysmal, as only 42% of 4th graders are proficient in math and 34% in reading; whereas only 36% of 8th graders are proficient in math and reading (NAEP, 2014). Nearly 20% of youth today do not graduate from high school (DePaoli *et al.*, 2015) and estimates suggest that 7,000 youth drop out of school each day (Balfanz *et al.*, 2009). Youth living in poverty, of color, involved in special education, and those who are English-Language-Learners are at highest risk for dropping out and in turn poor outcomes (DePaoli *et al.*, 2015).

The implications are clear. Many youth, especially those most vulnerable, are inadequately prepared to be employable in today's global economy. As a result, these young people often succumb to the pressures of gangs and other social ills, suffer the consequences of the pipeline-to-prison, and often become over-reliant on government-funded social programs. In addition to the loss of human capital, there also are broader implications for society-at-large. A high school dropout costs the public over $200,000 in government spending over the course of their life (Levin *et al.*, 2007). Further, poor educational outcomes overall make it difficult to attract and retain corporate investments, further lowering tax revenues thereby decreasing public investments in neighborhoods and escalating risk and marginalization (Amos, 2008; Cardichon & Lovell, 2015).

So why are so many youth falling behind?

Many students come to school with multiple barriers to learning that impede their academic achievement and healthy development. For instance, between 14-20% of children and adolescents experience a mental, emotional, or behavioral disorder each year (National Research Council and Institute of Medicine, 2009). One of every 88 children (and 1 in 54 boys) in the United States have autism spectrum disorders (CDC, 2012). Estimates suggest that 1 in 5 youth are lacking in age-appropriate life/social skills (Blumberg, Carle, O'Connor, Moore, & Lippman, 2008). As a result, many youth are lacking in the social and behavioral pre-requisite skills necessary for success in school and life.

Still others suffer from additional risk factors that increase the likelihood for poor outcomes. Over half of all students in the public education system are living in poverty (DePaoli *et al.*, 2015). One of every 58 children is a victim of child abuse and/or neglect each year (Sedlak *et al.*, 2010). Sixty percent of youth have been exposed to violence in their homes and communities in the past year (Finkelhor *et al.*, 2009). Poverty, trauma, and its correlates impact student learning, and also are known to have detrimental long-term negative employment, health, and mental health impacts (Felitti & Anda, 2009; Felitti *et al.*, 1997). Youth today simply are exposed to too much risk.

Given the rising prevalence of needs among youth and associated demands placed on the education system, there has been a significant movement toward the adoption of school-family-community partnership models that maximize resources in support of school success (Anderson-Butcher, 2004; Anderson-Butcher *et al.*, 2008). In particular, school mental health (SMH) programs and approaches have become increasingly common (*e.g.*, Weist, Lindsey, Moore, & Slade, 2006; Weist, 2003; Weist *et al.*, 2003; Mellin & Weist, 2011), and have shown promise toward promoting positive academic, health, and mental health outcomes among youth (*e.g.*, Hoagwood, Olin, Kerker, Kratochwill, Crowe, & Saka, 2007; Kutash & Duchnowski, 2011; Suldo *et al.*, 2014; Wilson & Lipsky, 2007). SMH approaches involve universal, school-wide mental health promotion and prevention, assessment, early intervention, and linkage, and intensive interventions/treatment to support the health, mental health, and academic learning of youth today.

The evolution of SMH and other approaches, along with the growing needs among youth today, both necessitate that professionals working in and with schools develop new and expanded competencies to support student learning and development. In fact, the Mental Health-Education Integration Consortium (MHEDIC), a national network of academicians, state and agency-level administrators, and practitioners of which I Chair, has called for enhancement of both pre-service preparation programs and professional development opportunities across multiple disciplines. MHEDIC leaders also are envisioning new SMH competencies for educators (Ball & Anderson-Butcher, 2014; Western *et al.*, 2010), school mental health professionals (Anderson-Butcher *et al.*, 2014; Ball *et al.*, 2010), and others working in interdisciplinary school teams and settings (Iachini *et al.*, 2013; Mellin *et al.*, 2011; Michael *et al.*, 2014).

Priorities are clear. Educators and others working in and with schools simply need to be better prepared to support young people today who come from increasing levels of risk, often have unaddressed health and mental health needs, and often are falling behind. They need to understand the challenges and issues facing young people today (especially those from diverse backgrounds), be knowledgeable of and skilled in evidence-based practices across the learning support continuum, and be motivated to work collectively on behalf of young people today.

To do this work, the field needs resources to utilize in pre-service preparation and training programs, as well as resources to support professional development and capacity-building efforts for those already working in and with schools. This book, Volume II of Mental Health Promotion in Schools (Special Topics, Special Challenges) published by Bentham Science and edited by Raymond J. Waller, builds upon the first Volume (Foundations) and serves as a primary resource to promote competencies among those working in school mental health. He discusses this more specifically below.

As such, I am honored to provide the introduction to this book, as it promises to serve as an excellent and unique resource for educators and others who wish to broaden their impact on student learning and development (especially among those with "special challenges'), who aspire to ensure all youth graduate from high school and successfully transition to adulthood, and who hope to further make a difference in the lives of youth today especially those that are most vulnerable.

Dawn Anderson-Butcher
Professor-College of Social Work
The Ohio State University
Director-Community and Youth Collaborative Institute
Chair-Mental Health-Education Integration Council
USA

REFERENCES

Amos, J. (2008). *Dropouts, Diplomas, and Dollars: U.S. High Schools and the Nation's Economy..* Alliance for Excellent Education.

Anderson-Butcher, D. (2004). Transforming schools into 21st Century Community Learning Centers. *Child. Schools, 26*(4), 248-252.
[http://dx.doi.org/10.1093/cs/26.4.248]

Anderson-Butcher, D., Lawson, H.A., Bean, J., Flaspohler, P., Boone, B., Kwiatkowski, A. (2008). Community collaboration to improve schools: Introducing a new model from Ohio. *Child. Schools, 30*(3), 161-172.
[http://dx.doi.org/10.1093/cs/30.3.161]

Anderson-Butcher, D., Mellin, E., Iachini, A., Ball, A. (2014). Promoting mental health in schools. In: Melnyk B, Jensen P, (Eds.), *A practical guide to child and adolescent mental health screening, early intervention, and health promotion..* (2nd ed., pp. 357-373). Cherry Hill, NJ: National Association of Pediatric Nurse Practitioners.

Balfanz, R., Fox, J.H., Bridgeland, J.M., McNaught, M. (2009). *Grad nation. A guidebook to help communities tackle the dropout crisis..* Washington, DC: America's Promise.

Ball, A., Anderson-Butcher, D. (2014). Perceived student mental health needs, strengths in the student support system, and teacher stress. *Child. Schools, 36*(4), 221-229.
[http://dx.doi.org/10.1093/cs/cdu017]

Ball, A., Anderson-Butcher, D., Mellin, E.A., Green, J.H. (2010). A cross-walk of professional competencies involved in expanded school mental health: An exploratory study. *School Ment. Health, 2*, 114-124.
[http://dx.doi.org/10.1007/s12310-010-9039-0]

Ball, A., Anderson-Butcher, D., Mellin, E., Green, J. (2010). Developing interdisciplinary competencies for expanded school mental health practice: An exploratory study. *School Ment. Health, 2*(3), 114-125. [http://dx.doi.org/10.1007/s12310-010-9039-0]

Blumberg, S., Carle, A., O'Connor, K., Moore, K., Lippman, L. (2008). Social competence: Development of an indicator for children and adolescents. *Child Indic. Res., 1*(2), 176-197. [http://dx.doi.org/10.1007/s12187-007-9007-x]

Boling, C., Evans, W. (2008). Reading Success in the Secondary Classroom. *Prev. Sch. Fail., 52*(2), 59-66.
[http://dx.doi.org/10.3200/PSFL.52.2.59-66]

Centers for Disease Control and Prevention. (2012). Prevalence of autism spectrum disorders-autism and developmental disabilities monitoring network, 14 sites, United States, 2008. *Morbidity and Mortality Weekly Report Surveillance Summary, 61*(3)

Cardichon, J., Lovell, P. (2015). *Below the surface: Solving the hidden graduation rate crisis.*. Washington, DC: Alliance for Excellent Education.

DePaoli, J.L., Hornig Fox, J., Ingram, E.S., Maushard, M., Bridgeland, J.M., Balfanz, R. (2015). *Building a Grad nation: Progress and challenge in ending the high school graduation epidemic.*. Baltimore, MD: Enterprises Everyone Graduates Center, School of Education, Johns Hopkins University.

Felitti, V.J., Anda, R.F. (2009). The relationship of adverse childhood experiences to adult medical disease, psychiatric disorders, and sexual behavior: Implications for healthcare. In: Lanius R, Vermetten E, (Eds.), *The Hidden Epidemic: The Impact of Early life Trauma on Health and Disparities.*. (pp. 2-18). Cambridge, MA: Cambridge University Press.

Kutash, K., Duchnowski, A.J. (2011). School-based mental health programs for students who have emotional disturbances: Academic and social-emotional outcomes. *School Ment. Health, 3*, 191-208. [http://dx.doi.org/10.1007/s12310-011-9062-9]

Felitti, V.J., Anda, R.F., Nordenberg, D., Williamson, D.F., Spitz, A.M., Edwards, V., Koss, M.P., Marks, J.S. (1998). Relationship of childhood abuse and household dysfunction to many of the leading causes of death in adults. The Adverse Childhood Experiences (ACE) Study. *Am. J. Prev. Med., 14*(4), 245-258.
[http://dx.doi.org/10.1016/S0749-3797(98)00017-8] [PMID: 9635069]

Finkelhor, D., Turner, H., Ormrod, R., Hamby, S.L. (2009). Violence, abuse, and crime exposure in a national sample of children and youth. *Pediatrics, 124*(5), 1411-1423.
[http://dx.doi.org/10.1542/peds.2009-0467] [PMID: 19805459]

Hoagwood, K.E., Olin, S.S., Kerker, B.D., Kratochwill, T.R., Crowe, M., Saka, N. (2007). Empirically based school interventions targeted at academic and mental health functioning. *J. Emot. Behav. Disord., 15*, 66-92.
[http://dx.doi.org/10.1177/10634266070150020301]

Iachini, A.L., Anderson-Butcher, D., Mellin, E.A. (2013). Exploring best practice teaming strategies: Implications for school mental health practice and research. *Adv. Sch. Ment. Health Promot., 6*(2), 139-154.
[http://dx.doi.org/10.1080/1754730X.2013.784618]

Levin, H., Belfield, C., Muennig, P., Rouse, C. (2007). *The costs and benefits of an excellent education for all of America's children.*. New York, NY: Center for Cost-Benefit Studies of Education Teachers College, Columbia University.

Mellin, E.A., Bronstein, L., Anderson-Butcher, D., Amorose, A.J., Ball, A., Green, J. (2010). Measuring interprofessional team collaboration in expanded school mental health: Model refinement and scale development. *J. Interprof. Care, 24*(5), 514-523.
[http://dx.doi.org/10.3109/13561821003624622] [PMID: 20594069]

Michael, K., Bernstein, S., Owens, J., Albright, A., Anderson-Butcher, D. (2014). Preparing school mental health professionals: Competencies in interdisciplinary and cross-systems collaboration. In: Weist M, Lever N, Bradshaw C, Owens J, (Eds.), *Handbook of school mental health.*. (2nd ed.). New York: Springer.
[http://dx.doi.org/10.1007/978-1-4614-7624-5_3]

National Assessment of Educational Progress. (2013). *A first look: 2013 Mathematics and reading: National assessment of educational progress at grades 4 and 8.*. Washington, DC: U.S. Department of Education, Institute of Education Sciences, National Center for Education Statistics.

Sedlak, A.J., Mettenburg, J., Basena, M., Petta, I., McPherson, K., Greene, A., Li, S. (2010). *Fourth National Incidence Study of Child Abuse and Neglect (NIS–4): Report to Congress, Executive Summary.*. Washington, DC: U.S. Department of Health and Human Services, Administration for Children and Families.

Suldo, S., Gormley, M., DuPaul, G., Anderson-Butcher, D. (2014). Connecting school mental health to students' and schools' academic outcomes. *School Ment. Health, 6*(2), 84-98.
[http://dx.doi.org/10.1007/s12310-013-9116-2]

Weist, M.D., Evans, S.W., Lever, N.A. (2003). *Handbook of school mental health: Advancing practice and research.*. (pp. 149-162). New York, NY: Springer.

Weist, M.D., Lindsey, M., Moore, E., Slade, E. (2006). Building capacity in school mental health. *Int. J. Ment. Health Promot., 8*, 30-36.
[http://dx.doi.org/10.1080/14623730.2006.9721743]

Weist, M.D., Goldstein, A., Morris, L., Bryant, T. (2003). Integrating expanded school mental health programs and school-based health centers. *Psychol. Sch., 40*(3), 297-308.
[http://dx.doi.org/10.1002/pits.10089]

Wilson, S.J., Lipsey, M.W. (2007). School-based interventions for aggressive and disruptive behavior: update of a meta-analysis. *Am. J. Prev. Med., 33*(2) (Suppl.), S130-S143.
[http://dx.doi.org/10.1016/j.amepre.2007.04.011] [PMID: 17675014]

PREFACE

School mental health promotion has grown rapidly from an idea and acknowledgement that schools, by virtue of the eminent role they hold in children's education, development, and socialization, had the potential to serve as a foundational locus for active programming in which policies and practices in schools purposefully engaged in promoting student mental health. This emerged from several observations among those of us working in K-12 settings including:

- **Some practices commonly seen in schools imposed psychological risk, such as some punitive disciplinary approaches,**
- **Schools have been identified as a best practice forum in health promotion,**
- **The dichotomy between mental health and physical health is nonexistent-so in order to improve one, you must address people holistically and include both, and**
- **Intentionally promoting mental health is highly correlated with positive school outcomes such as reducing undesirable behaviors, increasing engagement with the school community, and improving academic outcomes.**

School mental health promotion has evolved to the current standing of an international practice and academic emphasis in its own right, with texts (*e.g.* Waller, 2006 & Waller, 2012) and academic journals (e. g. *Advances in School Mental Health Promotion*) as well as support by prestigious centers of research and practice (National Center for Mental Health in Schools at UCLA and Clifford Beers Foundation).

Several approaches were contemplated pertaining to the direction and outcome desired with the second volume in this series, *Mental Health Promotion in Schools,* before concluding that the logical follow-up to the first volume, *Foundations,* as well as the best contribution would be *Special Topics, Special Challenges.*

This volume is intended to provide the reader with unique situations and student groups that were selected based on three desired outcomes. These were offering the reader discussion and school mental health promotion topics that:

- **Were universal in scope,**
- **Could be easily generalized to broader educational practice, and/or**
- **Involved situations or student groups that are not typically considered as potential benefactors of school mental health promotion practices.**

I would like to express sincere and deep gratitude for the overwhelmingly positive response and participation of the experts who contributed their time and knowledge in generously supporting this work. Distinguished international scholars from Volume I including Howard Adelman, Linda Taylor, Mark Weist, Dawn Anderson-Butcher, Elise Capella, and Steven Little are joined in Volume II by the expertise of, among others, John Miller, Kathleen Rudasill, Bruce Thyer, S.A. Moore and R.C. Mitchell, and Elizabeth Mellin.

To the reader, I convey the collective knowledge and experience of the contributing authors. I also extend the invitation of feedback on the volumes already available as well as identified areas of inquiry that you would find essential as we complete subsequent volumes.

Most importantly, I hope that the material in Volumes I and II have buttressed in some way your practice interest and efforts in this important topic.

Raymond J. Waller
MSW Program
Troy University
Dothan
USA

REFERENCES

Waller, R.J. (2006). *Fostering child and adolescent mental health in the classroom.*. Thousand Oaks, CA: Sage.

Waller, R.J. (2012). *Mental health promotion in schools volume I: Foundations.*. Bentham Science eBooks.

DEDICATION

For Amy E. Cox, friend and co-worker, who so rapidly has become an indispensable team member-a role that just as rapidly may lose its lustre with dawning awareness that she is, essentially, the team;

For the ongoing generosity of so much expertise from such esteemed colleagues, who are both near and far in proximity, but who are always near in mission;

For the patient perseverance of Asma Ahmed and Bentham Science;

For my very good friends William Warnock and Greg Ruediger, for the pricelessness of having their friendship and counsel;

For Sarah and Emily, who bring so much to the world that six book dedications is the minimum acceptable;

For Jackson and Charlotte, because a person has never achieved a level of growth so optimal that they are not improved by coercion to develop higher levels of patience and humility; and

For Moki and Toby, because they are better than I am and know it and share it charitably and frequently, but even so, accept me with unflagging acceptance and enthusiasm at no more personal expense than a bite of chicken jerky.

List of Contributors

Wendi Albert	University of Memphis, Memphis, USA
Dawn Anderson-Butcher	The Ohio State University, Columbus, USA
Amy E. Cox	Troy University, Dothan, USA
Sherrionda H. Crawford	Troy University, Dothan, USA
Rebecca Fensler	Wright State University, Dayton, USA
Denise M. Green	Troy University, Dothan, USA
Katherine King	University of Georgia, Athens, USA
Mary Kralemann	University of Nebraska-Lincoln, Lincoln, USA
Kenji Madison	University of Nebraska-Lincoln, Lincoln, USA
Sheryl Matney	Troy University, Dothan, USA
Elizabeth A. Mellin	Binghamton University, Binghamton, USA
John J. Miller	Troy University, Dothan, USA
Richard C. Mitchell	Brock University, Ontario, Canada
Victoria J. Molfese	University of Nebraska-Lincoln, Lincoln, USA
Shannon Moore	Brock University, Ontario, Canada
Laura Myers	Florida A&M University, Tallahassee, USA
Amanda Prokasky	University of Nebraska-Lincoln, Lincoln, USA
Stephanie Grace Prost	Florida State University, Tallahassee, USA
Kathleen Moritz Rudasill	University of Nebraska-Lincoln, Lincoln, USA
Carly A. Scarton	The Pennsylvania State University, University Park, USA
Kate Sirota	University of Nebraska-Lincoln, Lincoln, USA
Steven Soifer	University of Memphis, Memphis, USA
Bruce A. Thyer	Florida State University, Tallahassee, USA
Sarah Twill	Wright State University, Dayton, USA
Betsy Vonk	University of Georgia, Athens, USA
Raymond J. Waller	Troy University, Dothan, USA
Suzanne Tew-Washburn	Troy University, Phenix City, USA

Kimber Wickersham Troy University, Phenix City, USA

Joel Willis Troy University, Phenix City, USA

Mental Health Promotion in Schools

(Volume 2)

CHAPTER 1

Restorative Justice and Transdisciplinary Praxis: An Investigation in Ontario Schools and a Framework for Moving Forward in School Mental Health Promotion

S. A. Moore and **R. C. Mitchell**[*]

[*] *Brock University, Ontario, Canada*

Abstract: Schools are, for many nations, among the most enduring societal institutions. As such, they serve as repositories of wisdom, learning, and tradition. Tradition can be of incalculable cultural value, but can also serve as a functional barrier in some cases. Promotion of mental health in schools is a violation of traditional thought for many. This chapter discusses transdisciplinary praxis as a functional framework within which needs of contemporary students can be effectively addressed. This framework involves abandonment of the punitive practices, exclusion, and deficiency based assessment traditional in many schools and in juvenile justice in favour of restorative justice, community building, and considering behaviour within environmental context. Restorative practices have garnered such support so rapidly that some leading universities now offer graduate degrees in their study and implementation.

Keywords: *Diagnostic and Statistical Manual of Mental Disorders* (DSM), Medical model, Praxis, Resilience, Restorative practices, Transdisciplinarity.

INTRODUCTION AND CONTEXT

This chapter presents a thematic analysis of preliminary findings from a 2013 school-based restorative justice study in Ontario, Canada. The dataset included a systematic review of legal, policy documents, qualitative and quantitative results

[*] **Corresponding author R. C. Mitchell** Brock University, Ontario, Canada; Tel:/Fax: 905-688-5550/905-641-2509; Email: rmitchell@brocku.ca.

Raymond J. Waller (Ed.)

contributed by 300 participants from 60 schools in 14 rural and urban districts across southern Ontario near the capital city of Toronto. In 2012, the *Safe and Accepting Schools Branch* of Ontario's Ministry of Education invited a provincially based organization known as the Restorative Practices Consortium to suggest means to expand their discourse with multiple school boards in their region, and one of us (Moore) was invited as a consultant to carry out the study. The challenges were accepted and involved the designing of a multi-faceted, evidence-based investigation that articulated the following main aims:

- **To ascertain foremost practices for fruitful application of restorative practices within schools congruently, accurately, and systematically,**
- **To ascertain impediments to engagement of these practices congruently, accurately, and systematically, and**
- **Wide dissemination of empirical findings to facilitate greater and more effective implementation of restorative practices province-wide.**

In previous careers, we had engaged with children, young people, their families and caregivers in frontline practice within British Columbia's mental health, youth justice, educational and child welfare systems before moving to research, teaching and tenure at a mid-sized Ontario university. A number of scholarly outcomes ensued for us as we translated professionally based knowledge into theoretically and pedagogically congruent research and teaching programs.

First and foremost we adopted the Greek term praxis to delimit our work, a term commonly adopted by critical educators inspired by Paulo Freire's (1970, 1999) teaching and learning philosophy. This term is defined as any endeavour that coalesces theorizing and application, and deliberation with deed, for emancipatory purposes. Secondly, a *transdisciplinary* point-of-view has shaped our research projects in response to the fragmentation and disciplinary myopia we encountered over the course of our careers with thousands of young people (Mitchell, 2003, 2007, 2013; Mitchell and Moore, 2012; Moore and Mitchell, 2008, 2009, 2011a, b; Moore, 2004, 2008, Moore, Tulk, and Mitchell, 2005). Leavy (2011) astutely acknowledges that transdisciplinary research practices have emerged within the context of "a confluence of extraordinary changes within and beyond the academy" (p. 36; also Pinker, 2011 and his counterintuitive thesis), and many of these changes are reflected in our chapter.

The chapter has taken shape during a time of increasing uncertainty for the promotion of well-being of children and young people in Canadian schools - one being fanned in no small part by numerous high-profile suicides of young people after social media 'cyber-bullying' and related events (CBC News, 2013a, b). A public inquiry into the custodial suicide of nineteen-year-old Ashley Smith (Richard, 2008) - first incarcerated when she was fourteen years old - as well as the recent release of the Diagnostic and Statistical Manual of Mental Disorders, Fifth Edition (DSM-5) have further fomented the controversy surrounding how various professionals can further well-being within and beyond schools (American Psychiatric Association, 2013).

The DSM-5 was 16 years in the making, comprising more than 800 pages in length (Moffitt, Arseneault, Jaffee, Kim-Cohen, Koenen, Odgers, Slutske, and Viding, 2008) and framing the dominant discourse within child and youth mental health across educational and youth justice settings in both Canada and the US. Released in May of 2013, a shift was made from a multiaxial system to a dimensional structure for assessment, and the aim of this new modus is to encourage additional specific communication regarding diagnoses and to consider clients in the context of a system or continuum of functioning.

The transformation was argued as a move away from a previous DSM focus on pre-existing categories within which to cast clients (*i.e.* to fit clients in a therapeutic box rather than understanding the person's experiences in context). This evolution includes a greater developmental sensitivity and a consideration of differences due to the intersections of culture, psychosocial, and environmental factors affecting functioning, contended Leigh (2009). This widespread framework for understanding behavioural difficulties and affective challenges occurring within young people's lives is also being roundly but fairly critiqued for displaying numerous theoretical and cultural shortcomings.

Resource	http://www.dsm5.org/Pages/Default.aspx

US-based psychologist Kenneth Gergen (2000) has previously taken aim at the ambiguity within the DSM framework arguing forcefully that we must begin by...

> ...removing the existing demands for diagnostic categorization and enabling clients to receive therapeutic help without deficit labelling. Current practices of psychodiagnostics (*i.e.* DSM categorization) represent the conceptions of psychological process shared by a small and rarefied sector of the population; they function without empirical warrant....Increasingly these standards are being questioned within the population at large - consider for example the spate of books criticizing the burdening of our children with the Attention Deficit Hyperactivity Diagnosis (para. 2, cited in Mitchell, 2003, p. 283).

Where therapeutic interventions for those of school age is involved, *diagnostic-free* therapy such as Gergen promotes would be seen as activist within most mental health systems, and for that matter, in the majority of schools or youth justice services presently influenced by strictly medical-model thinking (see British educators Moss and Petrie, 2002 for comparison). When cogitating replacements that may be more effective, it seems judicious to pursue a more judicious, inclusive philosophy based upon congruent conjectural and experimental appreciation of child development through productive interactions within families and communities (Bronfenbrenner, 1977; Christensen and James, 2000; James and Prout, 1997).

British-based educator Martin Woodhead (1999) "has taken some "first steps" towards a construction of developmental psychology" (Mitchell, 2003 p. 283) devoid of deficit categorization of previous DSM adaptations might be further achieved. He discusses the escalating pursuits among psychologists considering development as a socio-cultural progression:

> Psychologists are beginning to embrace the possibility that liberal individualistic Western models of child development (including Piagetian cognitive development as well as theories specifically about personal and social development) might be founded on a culture-specific and epoch-specific image of human boundedness (Woodhead, 1999, pp. 9, 11).

With regard to diagnoses for attention and conduct challenges, Richters and Cicchetti (1993, p. 20) similarly emphasized the "need for an integrative framework within which individual functions and their failures can be conceptualized in the broader context of development and functioning." They, too, disputed the DSM's ontological assumptions that a mental disorder inevitably underlies young people's complex behavioral concerns (see also Fewster, 2002). Their earlier contentions still stand in light of the continued complex questions raised in the climate of the current DSM-5 debate.

> It is useful to remind ourselves occasionally that the DSM is fundamentally an administrative classification system for the human problems and conditions treated by mental health professionals . . . [to] provide a common language for communicating about these conditions (*ibid.*, p. 21; see also Cicchetti, 1990, 1991).

Indeed, the paradigm assuming child and adolescent psychosocial distresses and disruptive behaviors must of necessity be 'disordered' seems flawed when scrutinized analytically. Using both historical and critical analyses, the DSM's 'common language' is identified as a translation of deterministic models viewing people as objects of rather than participants in research, as lacking competence instead of able, and as 'adults-in-miniature' instead of people on their developmental path. While not intended specifically at entering into this contentious debate, the initiative reviewed in this chapter does offer:

- **a number of alternative entry points for creating positive school cultures and mediating violence-related behaviours, and**
- **creating conditions for agency and well-being for students rather than criminal trajectories and drastic mental health outcomes.**

The increasingly globalized debate about mental health interventions among all professionals working with children offers us perhaps the most salient context for arguing for a continued evolution of school-based interventions for resolving conflict, particularly when educational systems begin to intersect with youth criminal justice systems in either of our North American contexts. By furthering a diverse, multi-systemic comprehension of adult–child authority interactions within and across education and justice milieus, advancement favoring more effectual interventions is hypothesized for all programs framed with pro-social principles for mediating mental health and youth criminal behaviors (Moore and Mitchell, 2009, p. 28-29).

Resource	http://www.utexas.edu/research/cswr/rji/rdinschools.html

Transdisciplinary Standpoint

The authors' transdisciplinary Restorative Practice ToolKit (Moore, 2008; Moore and Mitchell, 2009; Moore and Mitchell, 2011a) provided the research team with a framework for engaging directly and taking their objectives forward. Its integrated conceptual approach also holds *praxis* and *transdisciplinarity* as the *sine qua non* – the latter "a way of knowing that will be essential in the 21st and later centuries" argued Japanese neuroscientist Hideaki Koizumi (2001, p. 219).

"The most critical problems humanity faces today are complex problems", observed Apgar, Argumedo and Allen (2009, p. 255), contending our times are "characterized by high levels of uncertainty, multiple perspectives and multiple interlinked processes from local to global scales". British sociologist and childhood theorist Alan Prout (2001, p. 19) echoed these concerns when he observed we

> live with the knowledge that modernity's project of rational control has limits....The mood is more cautious and reflexive about the status of our understanding, more aware of the complexity of nature and society, more alert to the unintended consequences of our social actions and less sure of our social institutions.

Resource	http://p2pfoundation.net/Transdisciplinarity

As highlighted in our previous work, research with and for children can capture these epistemological and methodological shifts while aiming to resolve some of the complexity in schools. Such approaches occupy increasing prominence in academic publishing related to:

- **the social science fields,**
- **climate change,**
- **humanities,**
- **healthcare, and**
- **conventional empirical journals**

beneath this banner of 'transdisciplinarity' (Brown, Harris and Russell, 2010; Giroux and Searls-Giroux, 2004; Holmes & Gastaldo, 2004; Koizumi, 2001; Leavy, 2011; Mitchell, 2013; Nicolescu, 2002; Russell, 2000). Arguing in this discourse, Freirean's critical pedagogues Giroux and Searls-Giroux (2004) observed that transdisciplinary work offers an alternative discourse relating to the historical propagation, hierarchical structure, and use of knowledge within disciplines to endorse the enforcement of authority and marginalization.

Trans- disciplinary work represents the most innovative paradigm of knowledge acquisition and use, they went on to observe, serving as an impetus for everyone in the learning environment to actively formulate inquiry and generate new models of consideration beyond widespread methods of knowing presumed inerrant and to extrapolate and theorize beyond the conventional disciplines that constraint thinking. Restorative practices appear wholly congruent with these aims, as well as with the new pedagogical "tools" these authors claim are necessary for educators to navigate the 21st century. In an exhaustive, three-volume literature review of the range of this dialogue, two Canadian health scientists highlight this definition:

> Transdisciplinarity integrates the natural, social and health sciences in a humanities context, and transcends their traditional boundaries. The objectives of multiple disciplinary approaches are to resolve real world or complex problems, to provide different perspectives on problems, to create comprehensive research questions, to develop consensus clinical definitions

> and guidelines, and to provide comprehensive health services. Multiple disciplinary teamwork has both benefits and drawbacks (Choi and Pak, 2006 p. 351).

Benchmark descriptors for multidisciplinary, interdisciplinary and trans-disciplinary are "additive, interactive, and holistic", they observed respectively (*ibid.*). They further noted the holistic typologies underlying transdisciplinary research, and referred to the term "as involving any application of multiple disciplines to varying degrees on the same continuum" p. 351). However, transdisciplinary approaches to research and teaching are inherently critical, and, as we have suggested, approaching practice with young people from this perspective offers new ways forward; moving away from the entrenched "tower of babble" in so many of our institutions and systems where young people's views and experiences are often silenced or devalued (Moore and Mitchell, 2009, p. 30; also Senate of Canada, 2007).

This epistemological standpoint also builds upon Rumanian quantum physicist Basarab Nicolescu's body of work defining transdisciplinarity (2002). He observed the concept "retains a certain pristine charm, mostly because it has not yet been corrupted by time" (p. 1), although that moment might be imminent. Swiss developmental psychologist Jean Piaget is commonly attributed to first use of the idiom in 1970, simultaneously with Austrian astrophysicist Erich Jantsch and French sociologist Edgar Morin, "to give expression to a need that was perceived – especially in the area of education – to celebrate the transgression of disciplinary boundaries" (*ibid.*). Drawing upon a wide range of contributors during a 1999 Montreal symposium, Visser (1999) described the integrative, transdisciplinary view of education in the coming era:

- **Learning is still an underdeveloped concept, but it is necessary for all humans to be able to adapt to continuous and ever-faster change in an increasingly complex world. Fundamental changes are urgently required in the way school systems throughout the world are organized that must include more holistic conceptualizations of schools themselves as only one part of a comprehensive learning environment.**
- **Learning is a transdisciplinary concept related to overarching concerns**

such as change and growth; community-based processes and development; complex, diverse, and emerging adaptive expressions; new designs for systems of knowledge construction interacting with, and building upon, existing knowledge bases; lifelong learning at different levels of organizational complexity; neuroscience and lifespan cognitive development; the interconnections and distinctions between and among data, information, knowledge and wisdom; and new technologies for learning, languages, cognition, and meta-cognition. Efforts to transcend these currently separated views will acquire a transdisciplinary, integrative vision of learning.

- **Learning has to do with the capacity to interact creatively and constructively with problems. In most of our current pedagogical practices throughout the minority and majority worlds, such problems are often concealed or ignored altogether. [In a manner similar to Freire, 1970, 1999] learning therefore needs to be re-focused on problems, including their historical and epistemological contexts (p. 1).**

Resource	http://www.oijj.org/en/docs/general/rights-based-restorative-practice-evaluation-toolkit

Defined by transcending traditional boundaries of thought, therefore influenced by diverse theoretical frameworks such as feminist, postmodern and critical race theorists who place great value on participatory research approaches, transdisciplinary researchers and practitioners acknowledge the deep complexity of the world and her inhabitants, who are responding to relationships and variables of power rather than pathology, and as a result, that traditional empirical inquiry may be insufficient or inappropriate in application to some endeavors (Leavy, 2011). One of the main aspirations of its adherents is the application of this understanding in education. Slowly but resolutely, transdisciplinarity has achieved acknowledgement in many areas of inquiry and achieved international impact, particularly in top-quality educational venues in the wake of universities worldwide opening themselves to appraising transdisciplinary programs, empirical undertakings, and symposia (Dincă, 2011). Nicolescu (1999, p. 4) articulated the stance succinctly: "The emergence of a new culture, capable of contributing to the elimination of tensions menacing life on our planet will be impossible without a new type of education which takes into account all the dimensions of the human being". This standpoint offered the greatest understanding and capacity for critical analysis during the intersections of research, theory, and praxis in this project, and is reflected in the following sections.

Restorative Praxis in Ontario Schools: From Local to Global

As researchers, we also concur with British criminologist John Muncie (2005, p. 35) who noted, "the concept of globalization has gradually permeated criminology… and widespread experimentation with restorative justice offers possibilities for rehabilitation".

Recalling French philosopher Michel Foucault's 'relations of power' (1977), restorative justice pursues positive change through relational efforts rather than presuming restitution and justice occur by mandate, placing pre-eminence on individual relationships - those from national and international legal, pedagogical and political centers directly impacting educational and youth justice diversionary programs (Van Ness, 2005).

In our Canadian province of Ontario, restorative practices are recurrently used in school locations redress discord, bodily or violent relational interactions (such as bullying), and to temper rates of suspension and exclusion (Vanderling, 2011). These targets for intervention have fostered "misconceptions that the concept of restorative practices is merely a disciplinary approach" for schools (Costello, Wachtel and Wachtel, 2009, pp. 7-8). Rather, restorative approaches in schools have been discovered to assist students in exercising responsibility for their deeds within and without school and to be vigorously involved in their schools, which can advance the practise of both teaching and learning and promote mental health. The aspiration is to improve social relations among all adherents of the school community. It is often challenging for schools to focus on their primary organizational and societal mandates of instructing rather than governing behaviour. Contemporary, ongoing exploration supporting the use of restorative practices in not only supports but necessitates concentrating on relationships *and* fundamental social justice rather than addressing specific objectionable behaviors (Vanderling, 2011).

Restorative practices have evolved historically under the similar notion of restorative justice, which has been situated within both olden and modern cultures and distinguished within more than 100 nations, including both Canada and the US (Moore, 2008). Restorative practices are also constructed upon "indigenous epistemologies" (Arabena, 2008, 2010) and a communitarian worldview (see also Apgar, Argumedo and Allen, 2009) with emphasis on the comprehensive involvement of all pertinent members from the community in disentangling problems, and remedying detriment, transgression, or offense.

These concepts are buttressed by the conceptual circle as a representation and fundamental practice apparatus denoting "community, connection, inclusion, fairness, equity and wholeness…which is a common thread" foundational to restorative practices (Costello, Wachtel and Wachtel, 2010, p.5). A dedication to value social and interpersonal relations (Moore and Mitchell, 2011b) and the self-worth of each party are established values in restorative practice (Vanderling, 2010, 2011). Consistent with transdisciplinary discourses, the expressions of youth with vulnerability due to:

- **age,**
- **minority status,**
- **ability,**
- **social circumstance, or**
- **victimization**

are accentuated here (Moore, 2008).

Thus, while engaging in restorative circles, all persons impacted by injury are brought into a conversation targeting the enhancement of "healthy relationships, making good choices, continuing their learning" (Government of Ontario, 2012a). Restorative practices are built on the assumptions of child and youth agency and competency, along with gendered and cultural respect and subjectivities, and are gaining momentum in US communities as well as numerous Canadian settings.

Dr. Lauren Abramson is Executive Director of the Community Conferencing Center (CCC) in Baltimore, Maryland, and a part-time assistant professor of child psychiatry at Johns Hopkins University School of Medicine. In the 2013 Public Broadcasting documentary shown throughout the US, she argued the work of the Center is making a difference in Baltimore (PBS, 2013, Fixing Juvie Justice). "I think one of the important things about what we're doing is that this is being done in some of the most disinvested and distressed neighborhoods in Baltimore, the second most violent city in the United States."

Resource	http://www.communityconferencing.org

The CCC has mediated over 500 conferences as court diversion in cases of nonviolent juvenile offenders as well as juvenile first felony offenders, as a substitute for traditional coercive approaches emphasizing school exclusion practices such as suspension in order to mend ongoing community quarrels and to cultivate re-entry and engagement into the broad social network subsequent to incarceration (see also Matsinhe, 2008). The process used by the CCC draws upon traditional indigenous Maori practices, and Abramson reports their local version is a "three-part restorative conference structure: hearing what happened, letting everybody say how they have been affected by the situation and then having the group come up with ways to repair the harm and prevent it from happening again." Abramson observed:

> Out of over 500 conferences, 99% have resulted in agreements with over 90% in compliance with those agreements…So much of the research is about recidivism and participant satisfaction. Collateral impact refers to the effect conferences have on communities….I think it's really all about relationships and building social capital. That's where the incredible benefit comes from this process.
>
> What we're faced with in this world is that the final frontier is probably

> human relationships - how we figure out to get along with each other. This process is amazingly powerful at giving people a way to realize that if they work together they can do amazing things. Very specific things come out of conferences that people do work on collectively. Social scientists talk about the importance of collective efficacy and social capital and that's what this is really about: it's using conflict to build communities (International Institute for Restorative Practices, 2004, para. one).

Abramson's interventions in Baltimore appear wholly congruent with our proposition that diverse professional and scholastic specialties understand and manage their interactions with youth from vastly distinctive viewpoints, and this is another way of appreciating transdisciplinary perspectives in the framework of restorative practices. Recognizing and reinforcing similar themes, the International Association of Youth and Family Judges and Magistrates VVII World Congress produced the Belfast Declaration (International Association of Youth and Family Judges and Magistrates, 2006) which articulated a "set of internationally derived standards to guide juvenile justice while at the same time recognizing vulnerabilities of children in contact with criminal justice systems" (Moore & Mitchell, 2009 p. 29) which are:

> In compliance with…internationally agreed upon standards including the Beijing Rules, the Havana Rules, the Riyadh Guidelines, the UN guidelines on child and victims and witnesses of crime, a holistic youth justice system that prioritizes and properly resources (International Association of Youth and Family Judges and Magistrates, 2006 p. 4–5):

- **Alternative diversion measures for children who come into contact with the criminal justice system;**
- **An interdisciplinary approach which also fully involves children, the family and community;**
- **A restorative justice system which should include a meaningful partial transfer of power to communities, victims, offenders and their families to produce a restorative response to offending. (International Association of Youth/ Family Judges and Magistrates, 2006, pp. 4–5).**

Recurrently, the first indications of struggle for children with mental health, physical health, and behavioral or relational health are distinguished in school, and educational professionals require an expansive web of collaborations to assure efficacious results for students (CBC News 2013a, b). It is correspondingly manifest that educators abide a ceaseless tide of pressures associated to both scholastic attainment and accountability. Costello, Wachtel and Wachtel (2009) observed there are significantly more exigencies placed on contemporary classroom teachers and school administrators than was the case historically, with the undesirable result of less time for developing bonds and links with youth. Unfortunately, devoid of those associations and relational skills, students are less engaged with school and at increased risk of school failure and associated outcomes.

The use of restorative practices in schools is a shift from "rule-based to relationship-based school cultures" (p. 8). Cooley and Borgida (2005) noted that by honouring the worthiness of all parties and all social connections impacted by maltreatment, it becomes feasible to entice students away from the threshold of jeopardy and exclusion. It should be ever considered that employing traditional, coercive, practices such as suspension for deviation from school expectations, formal instruction is ordinarily supplanted by the lessons that will be taught from sources that are often undesirable. A consequent rupture occurs to the safety net, offsetting resilience associated with school engagement for the risks linked to ostracism.

Hindrances to communication among people and programs with different foci from divergent perspectives attempt to meet the needs of the excluded student in domains such as health, education, supervision and protection form schisms that widen by continuing expulsion. Students require the foundation of their social bonds nurtured through engagement with the school community to develop resilience and preclude their enmeshment with public assistance, social services, and the juvenile justice system (Moore and Mitchell, 2009), whose mission statements speak of helpfulness but unfortunately can promote the opposite.

In this context, effective and lasting transformation will only be inaugurated when it is fathomed that a lone pupil deed may not inevitably be the commencement of permanent harm, character flaw, or enduring mental disturbance. Such action may be simply an indicator of deleterious interpersonal and structural relations between student and power dynamics in the school and the larger communities to which we all belong (Moore, 2004). Effectively bringing frontward restorative practices and values in schools, educators are increasingly being implored to be analytically cognizant of their interconnection to one another and with the school community.

This emphasis on social interconnectedness is correspondingly the foundation of Canadian-based PREV-Net's Healthy Relationships Model, which offers another entry point into progressive schooling within which the undertaking of teaching community can be valued and flourish (Craig, Peplar, Cummings, Quigley and Daniels, 2012). As US-based black feminist and critical educator Bell Hooks (2003) has suggested, such schools might provide a focal point of "liberating mutuality" that is "life-sustaining" and "mind-expanding" for administrators, teachers, and students alike.

Thus, resilience, well-being, and mental health for young people are valued here as inextricably and synergistically entwined with their social world, social network, and social contexts (see also Bronfenbrenner's 1977 analysis). This model of connectivity as an interface between people and their social and political environments exposes the crucial roles of communication and community in building mentally and emotionally healthful relationships for students. Consistent with this whole school method, a restorative justice concentration on accountability to building positive school climates among all stakeholders – including provincial or state governance structures, the various boards, individual schools, classes, educators, pupils, their families, and communities.

Methodology and Design

In order to address the research aims and determine both leading practices and barriers to implementing restorative practices in Ontario schools, the design invoked a mixed methodological approach and an iterative process with the bulk of data gathered during a one-day conference. The dataset drawn upon for this chapter includes legal and policy literature and both qualitative and quantitative results gathered from 300 participants at a restorative justice symposium conducted in the southern Ontario area of Cobourg in May 2013 with emissaries from 60 schools representing 14 rural and urban Ontario school boards in attendance.

The project evolved with an inductive, emergent strategy and a commitment to participatory equity among all informants, who engaged in a facilitated dialogue from the opening stages to the final write-up and articulation of recommendations from the research. The choice of an exploratory methodology and related procedures for collection and analysis were adopted as the most congruent with international principles of restorative practice (Moore and Mitchell, 2009; Van Ness, 2005).

Data collection began with a pre-conference survey gathered through e-mailed documents for registrants. Participants included:

- **teaching and non-teaching staff,**
- **educational assistant youth workers,**
- **social service staff,**
- **principals and vice-principals,**
- **curriculum developers,**
- **district superintendents, and most notably, and**
- **ninety students from elementary and secondary levels.**

In addition, personnel from Ontario's Ministry of Education and researchers representing other jurisdictions attended, and but for a small number of guest observers, all representatives were engaged as study participants. While the approach presented initial challenges to the research team, the need for a scrupulous and organized design was considered within the objective of fostering accord among governmental, administrative, teaching and student participants, as well as with the researchers engaged with the Restorative Practice Consortium of Ontario.

The mixed methodology also drew upon modified Delphi methods for data collection (Hsu and Sandford, 2007), and these were actively exercised with the study participants throughout. The Delphi technique is a group communication system of inquiry utilizing methods valuable in data collection when the desired outcome is to reach a convergence of opinions from an identified group with members representing disparate backgrounds who have knowledge in the area of inquiry. The most noteworthy thematic evidence presented herein was accumulated during the symposium. In accordance with Delphi methods, participants were organized into groups commensurate with their knowledge and backgrounds as students, administrators, or educators/staff.

An acknowledged consensus-building method, this methodology is also compatible with restorative doctrines and thinking as well as the iterative process adopted in the opening junctures of the venture. While restorative practices comprise a considerable gamut in terms of methods of facilitation and domains of application, the development, rejuvenation and preservation of healthy relationships are fundamental. This point serves as the pinnacle when facing challenges confronted by educationists as they endeavor to cultivate and sustain safe and compassionate school communities.

The policy and legal literature cited within this chapter presents a solid underpinning for nurturing and propagating restorative practice by establishing links with principles of social justice and children's human rights amongst: Bill 13 (*Safe and Accepting Schools Act, 2012*); Ontario's Equity and Inclusive Education Strategy; Mental Health and Addiction Strategy; Whole School Approach & Progressive Disciplines; PREV-Net's Healthy Relationships Model (also Government of Ontario, 2008, 2009, 2011, 2012b, 2013a).

Summarized Findings and Conclusions

As participants in our study authenticated, restorative *"practices are congruent with the Ontario College of Teachers code of ethics and school code of conduct...standards of practice, and care ethics like dignity of the student"* (Educational Staff Participant Voice; also see Ontario College of Teachers [OCT], 2013). Restorative practices establish an atmosphere of egalitarianism and integrity where it change becomes a viable option in students as they

"let adults in and develop trust... as they accept support from adults". This

> *is achieved "through an inclusive dialogue that repairs harm and builds relational trust in a community that values the voices of all involved".*

Consequently, educators discover "*building and strengthening relationships improves learning*" (Educational Staff Participant Voice). For students, participatory equity and justice is experienced by means of restorative dialogues and engagement in the process from beginning through end:

> *"negotiated settlements with principal, staff and students all in agreement...all parties listening...hearing all sides...with positive and equal communication"* (Student Participant Voice).

The engrossment as key participants promotes affirmative viewpoints of being *"accepted, appreciated, respected...and a sense of safety...empathy and respect of all those involved"* (Student Participant Voice). Unsurprisingly, when people of any age confront the absence of due process with subsequent imposition of penalties without being given a voice before judgement is rendered, the result is associated with the undesirable outcomes of *"isolation", "discouragement"* and a sense of being overpowered... [such that students] *"shut down...it is tough to open up in an untrustworthy circle"* (Student Participant Voice). Other recipients of this form of process feel a desire to *"retaliate",* as well as ongoing *"anger", "distrust" and "defensiveness"* (Student Participant Voice). By means of comprehension, teaching, and nurturing critical consciousness, constructive participant affect and behavior are promoted whilst immunizing against future dispute. These very doctrines are endorsed by Ontario's Bill 13 (*Safe and Accepting Schools Act*, 2012):

> Students need to be equipped with the knowledge, skills, attitude and values to engage the world and others critically, which means developing a critical consciousness that allows them to take action on making their schools and communities more equitable and inclusive for all people, including LGBTTIQ ... Recognize that a whole-school approach is required, and that everyone— government, educators, school staff, parents, students and the wider community— has a role to play...acknowledge that an open and ongoing dialogue among the principal, school staff, parents and students is an important component in creating a positive school climate in which

everyone feels safe and respected (Government of Ontario, 2012a).

These statutory obligations provide an additional, congruent framework for engaging in restorative practices within schools in the creation of safe and inclusive environments. The potential supported from findings in this exploratory phase is for restorative practices to cultivate a complete paradigm modification *to* relationship-focused school climates *from* the toxifying and impeding school climates built upon punitive cultures. To achieve this, all members of a school community must be afforded opportunities and means to acquire the skills needed to:

- **maintain healthy relationships,**
- **cope with mental health and special needs, and**
- **account for the complex intersections of identity relations as indelible attributes of school communities.**

With these components established, it is reasonable to anticipate the development of more school citizens to be accountable and involved both within and without the school, and for educators to witness the evolution to safer, healthier, more empathetic school communities by means of employment of restorative strategies as crucial teaching, learning, and intervention philosophy. "*We prepare for fires with fire drills. Why not conflict? It will be encountered regularly throughout our lives and our curriculum should reflect this by preparing us*" (Student Participant Voice).

Through grounded theory coding and constant comparative analysis of data (Glaser, 2005; Glaser and Strauss, 1967), three thematic concentrations occurred that informed the implementation of sustainable restorative practice strategies in this sample of schools while also supporting a basis for comprehending both leading restorative practices and obstacles to efficacious implementation of restorative strategies in Ontario schools:

- **Complete School Application,**
- **Paradigm Change *from* Castigatory Methods to *Relationship* Fostering, and,**

- **Secure and Nurturing Schools Comprised of Engaged Citizens.**

Educational professionals and practices are informed by legislative statutes, textbooks, and examples of skilled evidence-based programming to create just and safe schools, and restorative practices are emerging as among the most viable means by which the goals can be achieved. Restorative practice will only be implemented when sufficient time training, time, and priorities for integration are consistently evident and longitudinal assurances ensured both horizontally and vertically throughout the organization to allow assimilation of the ideologies of restorative practice in an educational venue. As a universal standard of evidence based practices, all investiture in restorative practices should also be measured by means of ongoing evaluation to assure only the most consistent, productive practices are perpetuated as school communities evolve. Howard Zehr (2005), a criminologist and innovator of restorative justice in the contemporary arena, reinforced the necessity that we relentlessly assess restorative approaches to ensure accountability to the principles and effectiveness of restorative practices transcending all components of implementation:

> We need evaluation, and we need to pay attention to the results....and evaluation needs to be multi-method and multi-focus. We need to evaluate processes and outcomes, and need to evaluate the goals and functioning of our organizations. We need to evaluate what we are doing and how this compares to what we think we are doing....[evaluation needs to include] a set of transformative guidelines that call for a more restorative stance towards knowledge, our subjects and our roles (p. 300).

Moving forward, more quantitative and qualitative data should be obtained through comprehensive interviews that identify ongoing practices as well as obstructions to the application of restorative strategies, supported by diverse sources of qualitative and quantitative data, could similarly be mustered at all stakeholder levels to understand further the notion of teaching and developing community while fostering restorative cultures in educational contexts. Rigorous assessment including follow-up confirms that strategies are not only compatible with restorative doctrines and philosophy (Hsu and Sanford, 2007) but that the ongoing initiative is justifiable. Compatible to transdisciplinary facets of restorative planning previously mentioned, accurate, useful evidence must be gathered through dialogue with all stakeholders is obligatory to both transdisciplinarity and restorative principles.

One finding from our investigation was the need for greater care and exerted attention to hearing the softer voices participating in restorative programing (*e.g.* students who are casualties of hurt, such as those physically and cognitively challenged, and racialized, sexual, and religious minorities). Finally, this active listening and hearing process is also posited as a basis for more effective mental health interventions in the early stages of manifestation rather than a repeated series of ineffective-or directly harmful-disciplinary tactics. In this way, rather than allowing or contributing to behavioural and affective challenges evolving into stereotyped, recalcitrant issues less compatible with efficient resolution. It is hoped that these findings, and the framework discussed in this chapter, provide a conceptual framework that will be useful as you progress through the text, encouraging creativity in means of building justice, community, skill sets, and well-being.

CONFLICT OF INTEREST

The authors confirm that they have no conflict of interest to declare for this publication.

ACKNOWLEDGEMENTS

Declared none.

REFERENCES

American Psychiatric Association. (2013). *Diagnostic and statistical manual of mental disorders.*

Apgar, J.M., Argumedo, A., Allen, W. (2009). Building transdisciplinarity for managing complexity: Lessons from indigenous practice. *International Journal of Interdisciplinary Social Sciences, 4*(5), 225-270.

Arabena, K. (2008). *Indigenous epistemology and well-being: Universe referent citizenship (Australian Institute of Aboriginal and Torres Strait Is lander Studies Discussion Paper, Number 22).* Canberra: Government of Australia. Retrieved January 14, 2014, from www.aiatsis.gov.au/research/docs/dp/DP22.pdf

Arabena, K. (2010). All knowledge is Indigenous. In: Brown, V.A., Harris, J.A., Russell, J.Y., (Eds.), *Tackling wicked problems through the transdisciplinary imagination.* (pp. 260-267). London, Washington:

Earthscan.

Bronfenbrenner, U. (1977). Toward an experimental ecology of human development. *Am. Psychol., 32*(7), 513-531.
[http://dx.doi.org/10.1037/0003-066X.32.7.513]

Brown, V.A., Harris, J.A., Russell, J.A. (2010). *Tackling wicked problems through the transdisciplinary imagination.*. London, Washington: Earthscan Publications.

CBC News. (2013). *Police role in Rehtaeh Parsons case to be reviewed.* Retrieved February 5, 2014, from http://www.cbc.ca/news/canada/novascotia/ police-role-in-rehtaeh-parsons-case-to-be-reviewed-1.1380992

CBC News. (2013). *Amanda Todd suicide: RCMP repeatedly told of blackmailer's attempts.* Retrieved February 5, 2014, from http://www.cbc.ca/news/canada/amanda-todd-suicide-rcmp-repeatedly-told-ofblackmailers-attempts-1.2427097

Choi, B.C., Pak, A.W. (2006). Multidisciplinarity, interdisciplinarity and transdisciplinarity in health research, services, education and policy: 1. Definitions, objectives, and evidence of effectiveness. *Clin. Invest. Med., 29*(6), 351-364.
[PMID: 17330451]

Christensen, P., James, A. (2000). *Research with children: Perspectives and Practices.*. London: Falmer Press.

Cicchetti, D. (1990). Perspectives on the interface between normal and atypical development. *Dev. Psychopathol., 2*(4), 329-333.
[http://dx.doi.org/10.1017/S0954579400005757]

Cicchetti, D. (1991). Fractures in the crystal: Developmental psychopathology and the emergence of self. *Dev. Rev., 1*(1), 271-287.
[http://dx.doi.org/10.1016/0273-2297(91)90014-F]

Cooley, D., Borgida, A. (2005). *It takes a community: Report of the stak eholder consultation on alternatives to custody for young people (Youth Jus tice Services).*. Toronto: Ministry of Children and Youth Services, Ontario.

Costello, B., Wachtel, J., Wachtel, T. (2009). *The restorative practices handbook: For teachers, disciplinarians and administrators.*. Bethlehem, PA: International Institute for Restorative Practices.

Costello, B., Wachtel, J., Wachtel, T. (2010). *Restorative circles in schools: Building community and enhancing learning.*. Bethlehem, PA: International Institute for Restorative Practices.

Craig, W.M., Pepler, D.J. (2003). Identifying and targeting risk for involvement in bullying and victimization. *Can. J. Psychiatry, 48*(9), 577-582.
[PMID: 14631877]

Craig, W., Pepler, D., Cummings, J., Quigley, D., Daniels, T. (2012). *Prev-net healthy relationships training module. Facilitator's guide.*Kingston, ON: Queen's University. Retrieved February 10, 2014, from http://www.prevnet.ca

Dincă, I. (2011). Stages in the configuration of Bararab Nicolescu's transdisciplinary project. *Transdisciplinary Studies – Science, Spirituality, Society No. 2,* 1-20.Bucharest: Curtea Veche Publishing. Retrieved February 10, 2014, from http://www.slashdocs.com/itqqnk/irina-dinca-stages-in-the-configuration-of-thetransdisciplinary- project-o--basarab-nicolescu.html

Fewster, G. (2002). The DSM IV you but not IV me. *Child Youth Care Forum, 31*(6), 365-380. [http://dx.doi.org/10.1023/A:1021118432140]

Foucault, M. (1977). *Discipline and punish: The birth of the prison..* London: Penguin.

Freire, P. (1970). *Pedagogy of the oppressed..* New York: Herder and Herder.

Freire, P. (1999). Education and community involvement. In: Castells, M., Flecha, R., Freire, P., Giroux, H.A., Macedo, D., Willis, P., (Eds.), *Critical education in the new information age.* (pp. 83-92). Boston: Rowman & Littlefield Publishers, Inc..

Gergen, K. (2000). Ghost in the therapy machine - An interview with Kenneth Gergen. *TransThe New Therapist.* Retrieved February 10, 2014, from http://www.newtherapist.com

Giroux, H.A., Searls-Giroux, S. (2004). *Take back higher education: Race, youth and the crisis of democracy in the post-civil rights era. New York..* Algrave: Macmillan. [http://dx.doi.org/10.1057/9781403982667]

Glaser, B. (2005). *The grounded theory perspective III: Theoretical coding..* Mill Valley, CA: Sociology Press.

Glaser, B., Strauss, A. (1967). *The discovery of grounded theory: Strategies for qualitative research..* Chicago: Aldine.

Government of Ontario. (2008). *Progressive discipline: A new approach to help make schools safer.*Toronto: Ministry of Education, Ontario. Retrieved February 5, 2014, from http://www.edu.gov.on.ca/eng/safeschools/discipline.html

Government of Ontario. (2009). *Equity and inclusive education strategy, 2009.*Toronto: Minis try of Education, Ontario. Retrieved February 5, 2014, from http://cal2.edu.gov.on.ca/april2009/EquityEducationStrategy.pdf

(2011). *Open minds, healthy minds: Ontario's comprehensive mental health and addictions strategy.*Toronto: Ministry of Health, Ontario. Retrieved February 10, 2014, from http://www.health.gov.on.ca/en/common/ministry/publications/reports/mental_health2011/mentalhealth_rep2011.pdf

(2012a). Toronto: Author. Retrieved February 5, 2014, from http://ontla.on.ca/web/bills/bills_detail.do?locale=en&BillID=2549

(2012b). Toronto: Ministry of Education. Retrieved February 5, 2014, from http://www.edu.gov.on.ca/extra/eng/ppm/145.pdf

Holmes, D., Gastaldo, D. (2004). Rhizomatic thought in nursing: an alternative path for the development of the discipline. *Nurs. Philos., 5*(3), 258-267.
[http://dx.doi.org/10.1111/j.1466-769X.2004.00184.x] [PMID: 15385036]

Hooks, B. (2003). *Teaching community: A pedagogy of hope..* London: Routledge.

Hsu, C., Sandford, B. (2007). The Delphi technique: Making sense of consensus. *Pract. Assess., Res. Eval., 12*(10), 1-7.

International Association of Youth and Family Judges and Magistrates. (2006). *Belfast Declaration, XVII world congress in Belfast, Northern Ireland, from August 27 –September 1, 2006,* 1-5. Retrieved February 10, 2014, from http://www2.ohchr.org/english/bodies/crc/docs/D%C3%A9clarationBelfast%20_ En.pdf

James, A., Prout, A. (1997). *Constructing and reconstructing childhood - Contemporary issues in the sociological study of childhood.* (2nd ed.). Hampshire, UK: Routledge/Falmer Press.

Koizumi, H. (2001). Trans-disciplinarity. *Neuroendocrinol. Lett., 22*(4), 219-221.
[PMID: 11524626]

Leavy, P. (2010). *Essentials of transdisciplinary research: Using problem-centered methodologies..* Walnut Creek, CA: Left Coast Press.

Leigh, H. (2009). A proposal for a new multiaxial model of psychiatric diagnosis. A continuum-based patient model derived from evolutionary developmental gene-environment interaction. *Psychopathology, 42*(1), 1-10.
[http://dx.doi.org/10.1159/000173698] [PMID: 19023229]

Matsinhe, D.M. (2008). *Community conferencing: A review of restorative practices..* Edmonton, AB: Conflict Transformation Society.

Mitchell, R.C. (2003). Ideological reflections on the DSM-IV-R (or Pay no attention to that man behind the curtain, Dorothy!). *Child Youth Care Forum, 32*(5), 281-298.
[http://dx.doi.org/10.1023/A:1025887827899]

Mitchell, R.C. (2007). Grounded theory and autopoietic social systems: Are they methodologically compatible? *Qualitative Sociological Review, 3*(2), 5-18.

Mitchell, R.C. (2013). Reflections on the UNCRC's future from a transdisciplinary bricoleur. *Int. J. Child. Rights, 21*(1), 510-522.
[http://dx.doi.org/10.1163/15718182-02103002]

Mitchell, R.C., Moore, S.A. (2012). *Politics, Participation & Power Relations: Transdisciplinary Approaches to Critical Citizenship in the Classroom and Community..* Rotterdam, Boston, Taipei: Sense Publishers.

[http://dx.doi.org/10.1007/978-94-6091-743-1]

Moffitt, T.E., Arseneault, L., Jaffee, S.R., Kim-Cohen, J., Koenen, K.C., Odgers, C.L., Slutske, W.S., Viding, E. (2008). Research review: DSM-V conduct disorder: research needs for an evidence base. *J. Child Psychol. Psychiatry, 49*(1), 3-33.
[http://dx.doi.org/10.1111/j.1469-7610.2007.01823.x] [PMID: 18181878]

Moore, S.A. (2004). Towards an integrated perspective: Restorative justice, cross-cultural counselling and school-based programming. In: France, M.H., Rodriguez, M.C., Hett, G.G., (Eds.), *Diversity, culture and counselling: A Canadian perspective.* (pp. 347-355). Calgary, AB: Detselig.

Moore, S.A. (2008). Social justice and education in a world fit for children? In: Kentel, J.A., Short, A., (Eds.), *Totems and taboos: Risk and relevance in research on teachers and teaching.* (pp. 17-29). Rotterdam: Sense Publishers.

Moore, S.A. (2011). Preface: Social justice in child, youth and family studies. *Int. J. Child Youth Fam. Stud., 2*(3/4), 353-360.

Moore, S.A., Gegieckas, T., Marval, L., McCauley, H., Peloquin, S. (2011). Constructing critical citizenship education with young people: Alternative pedagogies. *Int. J. Child Youth Fam. Stud., 2*(3/4), 494-509.

Moore, S. A., Mitchell, R. C. (2007). Hers telrecht volgens de mensenrechten principes [Rights -based restorative justice]. *Het Tijdschrift voor Jeugdrecht en Kinderrechten [TJK - Flemish Journal for Youth and Children's Law], 5*(4), 251-259.

Moore, S.A., Mitchell, R.C. (2008). *Power, pedagogy and praxis: Social justice in the globalized classroom..* Rotterdam: Sense Publishers.

Moore, S.A., Mitchell, R.C. (2009). Rights-based restorative justice: Evaluating compliance with international standards. *Youth Justice, 9*(1), 27-43.
[http://dx.doi.org/10.1177/1473225408101430]

Moore, S.A., Mitchell, R.C. (2011). Theorising rights-based restorative justice: The Canadian context. *Int. J. Child. Rights, 19*(1), 81-105. a
[http://dx.doi.org/10.1163/157181810X508483]

Moore, S.A., Mitchell, R.C. (2011). Rights-based restorative justice in Canada: From silence to citizenship. In: Freeman, M., (Ed.), *Current legal issues.* (pp. 202-218). Oxford, UK: Oxford University Press. b

Moss, P., Petrie, P. (2002). *From children's services to children's spaces—Public policy, children and childhood. London..* Falmer: Routledge.

Muncie, J. (2005). The globalization of crime control – The case of youth and juvenile justice: Neoliberalism, policy convergence and international conventions. *Theor. Criminol., 9*(1), 35-64.
[http://dx.doi.org/10.1177/1362480605048942]

Nicolescu, B. (1999). The transdisciplinary evolution of learning. *Symposium on Overcoming Underdevelopment of Learning held at the annual meeting of the American Educational Research*

*Association.*Montreal, Canada

Ontario College of Teachers. (2013). *Ethical standards*. Retrieved February 5, 2014, from http://www.oct.ca/public/professional-standards/ethical-standards

Pinker, S. (2011). *The better angels of our nature – Why violence has declined.*. New York: Viking Press.

Prout, A. (2001). *The future of childhood. First annual lecture of the Children's Research Centre.*. Dublin: Trinity College.

Richard, B. (2008). *Ashley Smith: A report of the New Brunswick Ombudsman and Child and Youth Advocate on the services provided to a youth involved in the youth criminal justice system.*. Fredericton, NB: Office of the Ombudsman & Child and Youth Advocate.

Richters, J.E., Cicchetti, D. (1993). Mark Twain meets DSM-III-R: Conduct disorder, development, and the concept of harmful dysfunction. *Dev. Psychopathol., 5*, 5-29. [http://dx.doi.org/10.1017/S0954579400004235]

Russell, W. (2000). Forging new paths: Transdisciplinarity in universities. Wisenet Journal. *Australia's Women in Science Inquiry Network, 53*, 1-4.

Senate of Canada. (2007). Children: The silenced citizens. Ottawa: Standing Senate Committee on Human Rights, Government of Canada.. Retrieved February 10, 2014, from http://www.parl.gc.ca/Content/SEN/Committee/391/huma/rep/rep10apr07-e.pdf

United Nations. (1989). *Convention on the rights of the child.*. New York: UN General Assembly.

United Nations Economic and Social Council. (2002). *UN basic principles on the use of restorative justice programmes in criminal matters.*New York and Geneva: ECOSOC.. Retrieved February 10, 2014, from http://www.unodc.org/pdf/crine/terrorism/2002/19eb.pdf

Vaanderling, D. (2010). The significance of critical theory for restorative justice in education. *Rev. Educ. Pedagog. Cult. Stud., 32*(2), 145-176. [http://dx.doi.org/10.1080/10714411003799165]

Van Ness, D. (2005). *An overview of restorative justice around the world.*Eleventh United Nations Congress on Crime Prevention and Criminal JusticeBangkok, Thailand, April 18 to 25, 2005 Retrieved February 5, 2014, from http://www.icclr.law.ubc.ca/publications/reports/11_un/dan%20van%20ness%20f inal%20 paper.pdf

Visser, J. (1999). *Overcoming the underdevelopment of learning: A transdisciplinary view.*presented at the Symposium on Overcoming the Underdevelopment of Learning held at the annual meeting of the American Educational Research AssociationMontreal, Canada, April 19 to 23, 1999 Retrieved February 10, 2014, from http://www.unesco.org/education/lwf/doc/aera1999.html#visser

Woodhead, M. (1999). Reconstructing developmental psychology—some first steps. *Child. Soc., 13*(1), 3-19. [http://dx.doi.org/10.1002/(SICI)1099-0860(199902)13:1<3::AID-CHI152>3.3.CO;2-2]

Zehr, H. (2005). Evaluation and restorative justice principles. In: Elliot, E., Gordon, R., (Eds.), *New directions in restorative justice.* (pp. 296-303). London: Willan Publishing.

CHAPTER 2

Students with Disabilities: Reversing a History of School as a Risk to Mental Health

Sheryl R. Matney* and **Joel P. Willis**

Troy University, Troy, AL 36082, United States

Abstract: Persons with disabilities have, throughout history, been exposed to segregation, harassment, and brutal maltreatment. Few opportunities existed whereby meaningful community involvement was a viable option. Over the course of centuries, little changed for far too many. Legislation rapidly snowballed over the past hundred years, decreasing persecution and, even more recently promoting individual rights and access rather than minimizing mistreatment. School legislation and compulsory education have arguably had more impact on improving outcomes for youth with disabilities than any other political or social realm, and have recently moved from the older philosophy of mainstreaming to the current model of inclusion. This reflects a significant improvement, but has to be fully implemented *in vivo* or *in vitro*.

Keywords: Compulsory education, Inclusion, Least restrictive environment, Mainstreaming, Medical model, Normality, Self-efficacy.

INTRODUCTION

Students with disabilities often experience low self-esteem, apprehension and depression among other psychosocial issues (Hurwitz & Weston, 2010). Emotional, behavioral, and social problems create conditions that can impede the child's ability to be successful in the academic setting. Schools that intentionally provide a positive environment for all students benefit in ways that include increased academic achievement, decreases in problem behaviors, improved

* **Corresponding author Sheryl R. Matney:** Troy University, Troy, AL 36082, United States; Tel:/Fax: 334-670 - 3352; Email: smatney@troy.edu

Raymond J. Waller (Ed.)

relationships connectedness among school community members, and increased positive school and classroom climates (Hurwitz & Weston, 2010).

The School Environment – Climate and Community

A school is more than a building where teaching and learning are the only activities taking place. Schools provide social and emotional growth opportunities nestled within a community of its own. Educators, administrators, students and other personnel can be engaged in activities designed to improve the overall culture of a school. These activities may strengthen relationships between students and teachers, foster feelings of shared purpose, inclusion, caring and mutual investment (Great Schools Partnerships, 2013). In our view, the term school community is affected by all experiences afforded to stakeholders such as learning, playing, eating, resting, helping, governing, competing, and other activities taking place in a school setting.

It is imperative for students with disabilities to feel a sense of belonging and acceptance within their school community. When describing a school community, often the defining criteria involves a group of people who are associated with each other and share common values about the education of children (Redding, 1991).

Of course, a school community promotes academic learning, but it also provides an environment where social, emotional, ethical and community development of students occurs. School communities should create an environment where everyone is welcomed and supported socially, emotionally, physically, and intellectually (National School Climate Center, 2013). School climate has been described as the quality and character of school life and is based on norms, values and expectations that support people:

- **feeling socially, emotionally, and physically safe,**
- **being engaged and respected,**
- **working together to develop, live and contribute to a shared vision,**
- **modelling and nurturing attitudes that emphasize benefits and satisfaction gained from learning, and**
- **each person contributing to the operations of the school and the care of the**

physical environment (Definition developed by the National School Climate Council).

Resource	http://www.schoolclimate.org/climate/ http://www.schoolclimate.org/climate/ http://www.schoolclimate.org/climate/process.php

Of what ultimate benefit is discussion about the school community, school climate and overall environment of the school and how does this relate to children with disabilities and mental health? In the quest for understanding the experiences of people with disabilities, it is important to review the history and cultural background of disability. Many disability advocates value the teaching of disability history and culture because, as George Santayana (1905) asserted, people who cannot remember the past are condemned to repeat the past. A brief historical synopsis of separateness and exclusion is presented and sets the stage for examining the attitudinal barriers students with disabilities face in a school community and the community at large.

Historical Overview: The Legacy of Discrimination and Ostracism

Throughout history, individuals with disabilities have been the subject of discrimination resulting from negative attitudes within society. Many of these negative attitudes stem from subtle cultural factors that determine standards of normality within a society. Individuals who do not meet the preferred standards are marginalized if not excluded from participation within society (Boswell, Hamner, Knight, Glacoff, & McChesney, 2012; Braddock & Parrish, 2001; Fox, & Marini, 2012; Taylor & Searl, 2001).

Examples of this exclusion and marginalization are well documented in literature throughout history and describe the unfair and sometimes inhumane treatment of those with disabilities. In his 1684 book The Practice of Physick: Two Discourses Concerning the Soul of Brutes, Thomas Willis described the 'insane' as animal-like, humans who had descended to a brutish state. The most effective treatment for the insane, according to Willis, was torture and torment (Scull, 1989).

Throughout the 18th century, disabilities were explained as being the result of punishment by God or the result of demonic possession. The assumption of possession and divine punishment continue to occur in modern societies (Deutsch, 1967; Boswell *et al.*, 2012; Porter, 2002; Scull, 2011; Winzer 1997). Many during this period in history believed a child with a congenital disability to be a changeling, or the offspring of a fairy, troll or other creature who had been exchanged for the normal child shortly after birth (Eberly, 1998).

The latter half of the 19th century and early years of the 20th century were marked by three major social trends that would greatly affect those with disabilities. The first major trend was a shift from a rural agrarian society to an urban industrial society. Urbanization in the mid to late 1800s continued well into the early 1900s. This shift resulted in a significant increase in urban population across the United States. The percentage of Americans living in urban areas increased from 6.1% in 1800 to 51.2% in 1920. By the turn of the century the value of manufactured products were 2.5 times the total values of farm products (Taylor & Seal, 2001; Platt, 1969; Stockwell, 1968; Trattner, 1999).

The second major societal trend was industrialization, a catalyst for urbanization. The period between the last half of the 18th century and the first half of the 19th century witnessed advances in technology that transformed the production of goods. New manufacturing processes took advantage of the abundance of natural resources and cheap energy, as well as available capital and labor (Trattner, 1999). The promise of employment in industrial factories drew many to urban areas, necessitating the restructuring of the family system. Unfortunately, not everyone fit favorably into this new economic system. Within the agrarian society the young, the elderly, and those with disabilities were able, to some extent, to perform some useful role that would contribute to the household. In the urban industrial setting this was not the case; a person's social role and worth were determined by how well he/she performed in a competitive labor market. This shift in social roles relegated those thought to be unfit to participate in the new economic system to the streets and institutions, (*e.g.* children, the elderly, and those with disabilities) (Taylor & Seal, 2001).

The final trend affecting America's social and economic environment during the latter half of the 18th and first half of the 19th centuries was immigration. Although America was a nation of immigrants, the number of foreign-born individuals coming to United States increased by approximately 38 million immigrants between 1830 and 1920. This population growth peaked with 8 million foreign-born persons coming to America during the first decade of the 20th century. The considerable infusion of immigrants brought a wide range of communal diversity to an ever-expanding urban population. The different languages, cultures, and ethnic backgrounds of foreigners, however were often met with suspicion, resentment and hostility (Stockwell, 1968; Trattner, 1999).

Products of industrialization, urbanization and immigration were accompanied by the rise of the first large-scale social problems in American society, (*i.e.*, slums, unemployment, homelessness, crime, delinquency, and according to many, vice and immorality). The social ills that emerged during the latter half of the 19th century were rationalized by social theorists who applied evolutionary theory to the development of societies. The foundation of this rationalization was based on the concept of a genetic weakness within the human race. Two theories were developed in an attempt to explain and marginalize the newly proposed conundrums of 'human defect', Sir Francis Galton's theory of eugenics and Herbert Spencer's theory of Social Darwinism (Galton, 1904; Taylor & Seal, 2001; Rubin & Roessler, 2008).

Sir Francis Galton, first cousin to Charles Darwin, coined the term 'eugenics' in 1883. Galton (1904) defined eugenics as "the science which deals with all influences that improve the inborn qualities of a race" (p. 1). He postulated that humans inherited many characteristics including mental, physical, and moral traits. According to Galton, "human defectives [were] increasing at such an alarming rate that, unless some efficient methods [were] devised for keeping them in check, they [would] endanger the welfare of the entire race" (p. 2). He believed that through selective breeding, a race could manipulate and control future generations, making them of superior stock. Galton hypothesized that "all creatures would agree that it is better to be healthy than sick, vigorous than weak, well-fitted than ill-fitted for their part in life; in short, that it was better to be good rather than bad specimens of their kind, whatever that kind might be. So with men" (p. 2).

Herbert Spencer, an English philosopher, developed the theory of Social Darwinism and coined the phrase survival of the fittest. This theory found much acceptance in the United States during the latter part of the 19th century. Spencer saw society as advancing toward a higher level of morality *via* natural selection. For example, only those capable of adapting to a changing society would survive. He believed that any form of government intercession or succour on behalf of the impoverished or disadvantaged would interfere with the 'natural' order, thus threatening a society's existence. Spencer felt it far better for a society to allow those who were poor and weak to perish than to sustain their existence through beneficent support (Fine, 1956; Morison, 1965). According to Wolfensberger (1975) by the end of the 1920s, the impact of these theories on policy and practice began to wane. But the overreaching context of these and other social theories continued to play a major role in shaping public thought and policy toward people with disabilities for decades to come (Taylor & Seal, 2001, 2001; Trattner, 1999).

In addition to neglect, another attempt to deal with the social problems brought on by industrialization, urbanization, and immigration was the concept of segregation, a process of isolating those who were deemed unfit for mainstream society by placing them in institutions. Thus, those deemed unable to be productive citizens were relegated to asylums. This form of isolation continued to expand from the 1920s into the 1960s. The prevalence of institutions during this time was born out of the prevailing segregationist attitude driven by a desire to separate the "deviant" from the "normal". Many of those who were segregated and excluded from society were children with disabilities.

Catalyst for Inclusion

The same social forces that produced America's first challenges with social issues also set the stage for compulsory education laws, which mandated the education of all children (Taylor & Seal, 2001). According to Coulson (1999), compulsory education laws were enacted, in part, as a response to changes occurring in American society. It is also important to remember that compulsory education was legislated in part to satisfy new child labor laws that, when enforced, put many previously employed children on the streets. Within the context of social issues brought about by the expansion and urbanization of industrial cities, the schools would serve a vital social function. Katz (1983) suggested that compulsory education was established for providing a way to socialize students and train them to be better, more productive workers. He argued that not only were the schools to teach and train future workforce participants, but also to instil the values and beliefs necessary for the maintenance of an urban working class.

By 1890, most states had passed compulsory education laws and by the early years of the 20th century, enforcement of these laws had strengthened. This contributed to the potentiality of special education programs in the public schools (Rubin & Roessler, 2008; Sarason & Doris, 1979). The challenge of compulsory education became evident as teachers began having difficulties with some students, especially as the social problems of the cities grew with culturally diverse populations and their concentration in multilingual slums. Addressing this issue, in 1908, the superintendent of Baltimore public schools, James Van Sickle stated, in part, that the presence of "one or two mentally or morally defective children" (p. 5) in the classroom required too much attention from the teacher at the expense of those "commonly enrolled in a class" (p. 5) (Sarason & Doris, 1979).

According to Winzer (1993), in order to satisfy the requirements of the law and the wishes of the schools, school districts created the community equivalent of institutions in the form of special segregated classes. These segregated classrooms became a dumping ground for a broad range of students who did not fit into typical classes including students with emotional or behavioral problems as well as those students with intellectual, cognitive, or physical disabilities (Sarason & Doris, 1979). Public educators justified the use of separate classrooms and believed them to be beneficial to students with disabilities because

- **smaller class sizes would permit more individualized teaching,**
- **homogenous grouping would expedite instruction, and**
- **the less competitive spirit would enhance the student's self-esteem (Winzer, 1993).**

This form of segregation went, for most part, unchallenged for the next three to four decades, facilitating the expansion of special education programs (Lakin,

1979; Sarason & Doris, 1979; Scheerenberger, 1983).

Legislative Impact on Education

The decade of the 1950s ushered in a new era in the history of society's treatment of those with disabilities. A more positive attitude began to emerge brought about, in part, by civil rights legislation. In 1954, the *Brown v. Board of Education* case was disputed before the Supreme Court and which resulted in a landmark decision that outlawed racial segregation in schools. This judgement opened numerous legal avenues for those seeking reform in special education. It was argued that the practice of segregating schools was inherently damaging to the educational prospects for minorities, or succinctly ruling separate but equal is inherently unequal.

Furthermore, the segregation of public schools was deemed in direct violation of black students' constitutional right under the 14th Amendment of the Constitution, which mandates "equal protection under the law" (Turnbull, 1993). The resulted in the *Brown v. Board of Education* case becoming an impetus for special education in America and facilitated extensive changes in public school policies and approaches to educating students with disabilities. It became more obvious that equal protection under the law applied to all citizens, including those with disabilities.

Eighteen years after the *Brown v. Board of Education* decision, two court cases in 1972 applied the same argument for equal protection/opportunity for children with disabilities. These cases (a) *Pennsylvania Association for Retarded Citizens (PARC) v. Commonwealth of Pennsylvania* and (b) *Mills v the District of Columbia* were brought against state laws and guidelines that excluded students with disabilities from an appropriate education in school.

In the PARC case, the plaintiffs argued that students with intellectual disabilities were not receiving a publicly supported education because the state was delaying or ignoring its constitutional obligation to do so. This case was settled by a consent agreement stipulating that all children with intellectual disabilities between the ages of 6 and 21 must be afforded a free public education and that it is was most desirable to educate children with intellectual disabilities in a program like the one the programs provided for their peers without disabilities (Yell, 2015).

Soon after the PARC case was handed down, a class action suit was filed against the board of education in the District of Columbia by the parents of seven children with disabilities. The children's disabilities included behavioral problems, hyperactivity, epilepsy, intellectual disabilities and physical impairments. These seven children represented more than 18,000 students who were forbad access to public education in Washington, D.C. It was argued that children with disabilities were being improperly excluded from school without due process, in direct violation of their constitutional rights under the 14th Amendment. The court ruled that, because segregation of public education on the bases of race was unconstitutional, the exclusion of students with disabilities was also unconstitutional. Among other things, the court decision mandated that the board of education provide all children with disabilities a publicly supported education.

The landmark rulings in these two cases laid the foundation on which future successful cases would be filed. Less than four years after the PARC and Mills decisions, approximately 46 right-to-educate cases were filed in 28 states on behalf of children with disabilities (Zettel & Ballard, 1982). By the mid-1970s, the educational needs of children with disabilities were being addressed by the courts as never before, thus providing students with disabilities similar protections under the law as those long afforded to students without disabilities.

The Culmination of Decades of Effort

On November 29, 1975, President Gerald Ford signed the *Education for All Handicapped Children Act* (EAHCA), often referred to as P.L. 91-142. This piece of federal legislation provided financial incentives to states that agreed to develop policies that would assure all qualified children with disabilities a special education. Prior to EAHCA, educational opportunities for children with disabilities were limited in two ways.

First, as mentioned earlier, many students with disabilities were excluded from public schools (as evidenced by Congressional findings in 1974) that revealed that more than 1.75 million pupils with disabilities did not receive educational services. Second, more than 3 million students with disabilities who were enrolled in school did not receive an education that was commensurate to their needs (Katsiyannis, Yell, & Bradley, 2001). Access to an education that was appropriate was addressed in P.L. 91-142, providing, in essence, an educational bill of rights. Included in this were six guiding principles, which mandated:

- **a free appropriate education;**
- **unbiased testing, assessment, and placement procedures;**
- **education in the least restrictive environment (LRE);**
- **an individualized education program (IEP);**
- **parent and student participation in decision making; and**
- **procedural safeguards.**

In 1990, amendments to the *Education for All Handicapped Children Act*, among other things, changed the title of the law from the *Education for All Handicapped Children Act* to the *Individuals with Disabilities Education Act* (IDEA). The amendment also mandated that transition services be incorporated in a student's individualized educational program (IEP) by the time he/she reached 16 years of age. According to the IDEA, transition services refer to:

> a coordinated set of activities for a child with a disability that (a) is designed to be within a results oriented process, that is focused on improving the academic and functional achievement of the child with a disability to facilitate the child's movement from school to post-school activities, including postsecondary education, vocational education, integrated employment (including supported employment), continuing and adult education, adult services, independent living, or community participation; and (b) are based on the individual child's needs, taking into account the child's strengths, preferences, and interests; and includes instruction, related services, community experiences, development of employment and other post-school adult living objectives, and, if appropriate, acquisition of daily living skills and provision of a functional vocational evaluation (IDEA, 2004; 20 U.S.C. 1401(34)).

In 2002, President Bush signed *No Child Left Behind* (NCLB) in response to low academic achievement of American students. This legislation was designed to improve teacher accountability and student performance (U.S. Department of Education, 2005; Yell & Drasgow, 2005). The focus of NCLB was to bring every student up to state standards in reading, math, and science by the end of the 2013-2014 academic school years. In order to measure performance, school districts were mandated to use quantitative data as evidence of improved learner outcomes. In order to achieve higher student performance, NCLB mandated improvement in teacher quality by regulating teacher certification requirements and stipulating specific qualifications required to be considered a High Quality Teacher (Yell, Drasgow & Lowery, 2005).

Students with disabilities were not discounted in this law. In fact, inclusion-a component of NCLB, was hoped to guarantee that education and accomplishment for students with disabilities would improve, and those with disabilities would not be "left behind". It was felt if students with disabilities were excluded from the same accountability measures as their counterparts then they would be ignored and not receive the academic attention deserved. By including students with disabilities in NCLB's assessment and accountability systems, Congress hoped to assure that schools would be held accountable for the educational accomplishment of these students (Yell, 2006).

Summary of the Legislative Journey

Over the last six decades, disability legislation has been enacted and expanded in an attempt to provide civil rights protection for all people with disabilities. Many of the laws passed have primarily focused on providing basic rights to education for children with disabilities such as the *Individuals with Disabilities Education Act* and *No Child Left Behind.* Although far from perfect, these as well as other disability legislation serve as a platform to help change discriminatory attitudes towards those with disabilities.

Schools Today

In an educational setting, schools that provide a welcoming environment for students with disabilities demonstrate active engagement in fostering an inclusive society. School environments committed to respecting and valuing diversity and promoting democratic principles related to equality and social justice are key elements for ensuring a positive environment for students with disabilities (National School Climate Center, 2013). Miles and Singal (2009) asserted education is an essential element to individual well-being. School environments that value children with disabilities will help shift attitudes about how people view others with disabilities and is an essential element to further the development of more inclusive societies at large (UNICEF, 2011) and demonstrate the fundamental veracity that valuing diverse students is essential in fully valuing any students.

Antipathy towards Those with Disabilities: "There, but for the grace of God go I."

As noted earlier, compulsory education was established, at least in part, as a means to supply the ever-growing industrial environment with better and more productive workers. Schools would not only supply workers but also provide a forum to socialize students and instil the values and beliefs necessary to maintain an urban working class (Katz, 1983). In this capacity, is it possible that, over the generations, public schools have instilled or perpetuated a sense of disinclination towards those with disabilities by modelling behavior that devalues those students considered incapable of succeeding in life?

It is important to remember that the many values and social skills learned in school may be perpetuated in adulthood. It should also be considered that avoiding, separating, or segregating those who are deemed different has been attributed to two critical societal values-personal appearance and individual autonomy. People failing to meet the prescribed standard of physical desirability and functional self-sufficiency are frequently judged biologically subordinate and pilloried as something less than human (Goffman, 2009; Hahn, 1988).

Besides aversion to people with disabilities, it is possible that observed bias occurs because of anxiety in those without disabilities. Livneh (1982) described aesthetic and existential anxiety attributable to public aversion toward those with disabilities. The term aesthetic anxiety refers to the fear experienced by people whose appearance diverges significantly from the accustomed human form, such that the individual without a disability worries about their own appearance or the potential loss of attractiveness (Livneh, 1982). Studies support outcomes that are more favorable for individuals meeting ideals of cultural attractiveness.

For example, those who are considered physically attractive are more likely to be offered jobs with higher starting salaries; attractive employees receive more favorable job performance evaluations; and are more likely to be selected for management training and promoted to managerial positions (Drogosz & Leve, 1996; Jackson, 1983; Riniolo, 2006). Research appears to support belief in the concept that the attractive among us are more capable and intelligent than those of us who are not as attractive – or receive social rewards suggesting that they are. Unfortunately for the beautiful, when empirical evidence is the standard for measuring outcome rather than popular presumption of physical aesthetics (*e.g.* Feingold, 1992) attractiveness has proven to be a poor predictor for measuring ability.

Existential anxiety is the realization that the body is truly fragile and the possibility of the loss of our own functional capacities caused by an unforeseen disabling condition occurs because of observing others with disabilities (Hahn, 1988; Livneh, 1982; Wendell, 1989). According to Hahn, existential anxiety is probably the most frequent source of affective unease experienced by some who interact with persons with disabilities. The anxiety evoked while in the presence of those with disabilities might best be summed up by the words of the 16th century English Reformer John Bradford who said, "There, but by the grace of God go I."

Many contemplate these words when seeing someone whose condition is perceived as worse than their own. Disabilities are presumed as having a personal tragedy by those now unable to participate in or enjoy life. Viewing disabilities from the perspective of a personal tragedy is perhaps the most devaluing presumptions made. The tragedy is to be avoided, eradicated, or "normalized" by all possible means (French & Swain, 2000). Perhaps John Bradford, and contemporary proponents of his maxim fail to see the logical inconsistency of their words and belief – surely the grace of God applies to everyone, not just the perpetuators of incongruous adages.

Medical and Social Models of Disabilities

As history has demonstrated, individuals with disabilities have been considered the victims of tragic outcomes and a perceived burden on both society and the family. Such views are largely based on the medical model of disability. The medical model derives from the traditional approach to medicine, which is seen as the restorative process of returning a patient to a previous or optimal state of health. Like a mechanical device, physicians view the human body as a finely tuned instrument with many different parts.

If there is a "problem", the physician looks for the broken or dysfunctional part with goal of "fixing" it. These repairs to the body can be accomplished through surgery or with medications. A mechanical concept is based in part on the postulation that there is a 'normal' body with which the "broken" body can be compared. Such conceptualization implies the existence of certain 'norms' against which the person is judged, that is to say the, focus is what the person cannot do, rather than what they can do. According to the medical model, a disability is a structural or functional deficiency that deviates negatively form the 'norm'.

The medical model has led to the dehumanizing of those with disabilities by viewing them as abnormal or deficient. The disability is viewed as an individual problem, not a societal or perceptual problem. Viewing disabilities through the lens of the medical model has had enormous consequences for those with disabilities. Since the 'problem' lies within the person, reflecting inadequacy of personhood, many societies have neglected to accommodate those with disabilities in all areas of life such as transportation, housing, recreation, and education.

In recent years, an alternate model for disabilities has emerged and is a direct challenge to the medical model. The social model of disability, conceived by Carol Gill at the Chicago Institute of Disability Research, places the locus of the 'problem' with disabilities on society rather than the individual. Proponents of the social model argue that rather than impairment causing the disability, it is society's failure to provide for all its citizens from which differential functionality transpires. The corollary is that any correction of disability-related problems is no longer the sole responsibility of the health care profession but the responsibility is shared with society and expressed through advocacy, political activism, and public support (Fernandez, South-Paul & Matheny, 2005; Gill, 1987 & 2001; Moore, 2002; Wasserman, 2001). Articulated another, perhaps stereotypical way: rather than expecting a person with visual impairment to see better, society should.

According to Asch (2001), those who support the social model of disability believe the medical model contains two flawed assumptions. The first is that someone with a disability will always have issues that are disruptive to living a 'normal' life. This assumption may be based in part on generalizing the experiences of those with disabilities at the initial stages of observed functional impairment, which fail to reflect adaptation, rehabilitation, and changes in one's life plans and skills. The second flawed assumption is that the inevitable results of a disability are powerlessness, poverty, unemployment, and low social status. Thus, those who embrace the medical model fail to recognize that functional consequences of disability cannot solely be attributed to the condition but to society's lack of accommodation for the disability and for discriminatory perceptual assumptions of society members.

Asch (2001) goes on to assert that these flawed assumptions can be disproven by disability studies, which indicate:

- **life with a disability is not one of tragedy and disruptions portrayed sometimes in medical literature, and**
- **the true problem is not biological, psychological, or cognitive flaws of the individual but the social, institutional, and physical environments in which those with disabilities must function.**

Inclusion, Acceptance, and Value: MH Promotion

The quest to provide an inclusive education for children with disabilities gives the student access to non-segregated educational settings; however, including a student with disabilities in a classroom - resulting in physical presence in the classroom - does not guarantee acceptance by other students (Sherwin, 2011).

School-age students with disabilities continue to be stigmatized, which translates into negative school experiences (Milsom, 2006). Negative attitudes and correlated behaviors of others negatively effects the education, employment, social relationships, behavior, and health of students with disabilities – all of which can be categorized as elements that can be a detriment to the mental health status of these students.

The social exclusion of a student with disabilities prevents that student from taking advantage of opportunities to be productive and contributing school community members (Green, Moore & O'Brien, 2009). By providing students with disabilities opportunities for meaningful participation, an increased sense of belonging and acceptance may occur because increased opportunities for personal relationships beyond paid staff, immediate family members or other students with disabilities are afforded to the student (Sherwin, 2011). Active participation by students with disabilities in classroom and the school community at large allows others to see students with disabilities as valued, participating members of the community at-large who are capable of contributing (Roberts, Beadle-Brown, & Youell, 2011).

The Example of Intellectual Disability

Historically, we have plenty of evidence that people with intellectual disabilities have been treated with less concern and dignity than other citizens (Prilleltensky, 2010). In schools, past research indicated students with intellectual disabilities:

- **were viewed as having little credibility,**
- **lacked opportunities to exercise self-determination,**
- **depended on others to meet their needs,**
- **had limited access to resources,**
- **were economically deprived, and**
- **were taught to be compliant (Wolfesnberger, 2010).**

Mayer (2012) found that results of such perceptions encouraged children with disabilities to see themselves from a deficit perspective, lest there be doubt that environment and attitudes significantly affect the individual child. Teachers and other school personnel who ignore or exclude students with disabilities send a clear message to the student with the disability as well as to students without disabilities about who is valued and who is not, who is expected to achieve and who is not, and who can participate and who cannot or should not (Swedeen, 2009).

Being "Special": Feelings of Belonging and Inclusion

Engagement and connectedness result in academic success and positive outcomes. Singling out of students with disabilities as "special" can create a situation where negative messaging about students with disabilities is fostered. Schools that single out students with disabilities as different and special (special classrooms, special diplomas, special transportation, special everything) can unintentionally communicate to students with disabilities that they are less worthy than students without disabilities.

Encouraging students with disabilities to participate in college fairs, college admissions exams and other opportunities will reinforce high expectations and support hopes and dreams (Milsom, 2006). School personnel such as school counsellors can exert leadership ensuring or improving a positive school experience that will facilitate developing skills for future academic and career success, developing social skills, and enjoying emotional health through *inclusion* of students with disabilities.

Inclusion

Inclusion, the philosophy that students with disabilities have the right to participate to the fullest extent possible with students without disabilities, provides a key component of promoting mental health.

Resource	http://centeroninclusion.org/Research.htm

Inclusion has replaced mainstreaming as the philosophy of educating students with disabilities. These terms are often heard used interchangeably, though doing so is inaccurate. Mainstreaming is the more antiquated term relating to the idea that the educational 'home' of these 'special' students is in a restricted 'special ed' classroom, whereas inclusion is the current philosophy that all students should be educated together to the maximum extent educationally productive (see http://faculty.knox.edu/jvanderg/201_Website_S_08/Inclusion.html). Conceptualized differently, students with disabilities 'belong in special' under the former philosophy and are 'mainstreamed' to settings with peers when appropriate (often rarely). Thus, special education is a location. With inclusion, all students are taught together, and, based on need, receive accommodations. Thus, special education is a set of services.

Inclusion, as of yet, has failed to achieve true universal implementation. Reasons for this resistance include reports such as the one made by Roberts and colleagues (2011), who found that inclusion continues to be difficult due to a lack of adequate training and resources for teachers and students. Though periods of economic constraint occur, school personnel can take action to create a school climate that is welcoming of all students and offers participant opportunities for everyone. A series of deliberations by school personnel can help identify ways to enhance inclusive learning and foster acceptance of students with disabilities.

For example, classroom and/or other school spaces should be considered – when thinking about a classroom, are students with disabilities present but isolated from other students in a 'special' area, or sitting with away from peers with an adult? Social considerations should be made – for example, are students with disabilities looked over and not called on or not expected to contribute during student activities? Are students with and without disabilities encouraged to support *each other* or is a prevailing competitive fervour prevalent?

> "Mainstreaming is like visiting. Inclusion is belonging."
>
> Dan Wilkins (n.d.)

Social Role Valorization: An Extension of the Normalization Principle

The basis and logic of the normalization principle was grounded in the concept that a system or society makes accessible to people with disabilities opportunities and circumstances of everyday living which are as close as possible to customary conditions and ways of life in society (Nirje, 1982). Wolf Wolfensberger, a German-American academic, extended the normalization principle with a concept called *Social Role Valorization* (SRV). SRV focused on the need to emphasize personal relationships between valued and devalued people.

Today, our society acknowledges through policies and laws the concepts of equal access and rights to offer all people, regardless of disability, the opportunity to participate in all facets of community life. Wolfensberger recognized that people in society often ascribe labels to groups of people deemed different, and, based on these labels, deem different individuals to be of less value than others (Thomas, 2011). Wolfensberger (2010) asserted that people who do not have valued social roles would be considered by others as having low value. As a result, devalued people will be treated poorly and rejected by others. They will also be treated in ways that reduce their dignity, growth, welfare, and competence.

Further, Wolfensberger (2010) believed an individual's behavior is directly correlated with how he/she is treated. Wolfensberger (2010) described two core action strategies that can be used to address the devalued roles society places on an individual. The first is to reduce or prevent the differentness or stigma, which devalues a person in the eyes of others and the second is to change the way society perceives and values community members.

This involves a reciprocal exchange – both positively and negatively. A student who has a disability is at risk of being seen and assessed as a person with low value – this perception leads to image-impairment (Wolfensberger, 2010). Children who are perceived as having a positive value are provided with opportunities and experiences that lead to greater expectations from society and as a result will achieve more positive outcomes. What does this have to do with a child's mental health? Everything! The structural considerations within a school community along with attitudinal factors among school personnel affect students with disabilities in global ways, just as these affect students without disabilities.

Existing research reveals that students and teachers too frequently view children with disabilities as inferior to children without disabilities (Milsom, 2006). Research further indicates a differential effect of negative attitudes based on the type of disability experienced. For example, emotional or behavioral problems are viewed more negatively than other disabilities. Encouraging research indicates that the amount of education and training provided to school personnel in the areas of disabilities and special education is causal in positively influencing attitudes towards students with disabilities.

The more education provided to teachers and school personnel, the more positive are the attitudes displayed. Educators with higher levels of negative attitudes towards students with disabilities tended to expect lower achievement from these students (Milsom, 2006). Results of such studies reinforce the concept of SRV and provide additional evidence that students without valued social roles have low value and are treated poorly.

Why is attitude a big deal? Internal beliefs and values compel thoughts, which in turn drive behaviors. Negative attitudes toward students with disabilities can manifest in a variety of ways including reluctance to teach students with disabilities, avoidance or neglecting opportunities to further develop a child, discouraging a student to complete coursework required for post-secondary education and avoidance of participation in addressing academic, career, personal or social needs (Milsom, 2006). Students with disabilities who endure in a negative environment are at risk for developing a negative internal self-concept.

A social work practice orientation called *person-in-environment* offers the perspective that an individual and his/her behavior cannot be adequately understood without considering the diverse aspects of the person's environment (Mizrahi, Terry & Davis, 2008). One could conclude that a student encompassed by a negative school environment could, as a result, exhibit behaviors such as disinterest and apathy, which reciprocally could lead school personnel to believe a student has low competence when in reality, the environment is not healthy and a student with a disability is not afforded the opportunity to thrive.

School personnel can affect change at the fundamental level of social construction in the school community. Creating an environment in which a school goal of providing a positive academic environment and experience for all students can dramatically affect the individual experience of each student. This type of change challenges a school and its personnel to understand and adopt the social model of disability discussed earlier in the chapter. School personnel can take steps to improve the environment for students with disabilities by examining their own efficacy as well as beliefs, values, and education.

Teacher Self-Efficacy

According to Bandura (1977), a person's self-efficacy is the perceived capacity to complete necessary tasks involved in achieving goals. An individual's level of self-efficacy also determines which tasks are chosen, the level of performance found in goal-directed activities, the amount of effort expended, and the persistence used to ensure task completion.

Teacher effectiveness has been shown to be directly related to the level of teacher self-efficacy. Berman and McLaughlin (1997) found that teachers' sense of efficacy was a major characteristic for determining the effectiveness of Title III projects of the 1965 *Elementary and Secondary Education Act.* Similar results were reported by Armor and colleagues (1976) after evaluating the effectiveness of reading programs in Los Angeles. They found that advances in reading achievement were positively correlated with teacher efficacy.

Within the context of inclusion there continues to be mixed feelings among teachers as to their preparedness to educate students with disabilities (Taylor & Ringlaben, 2012). This overall lack of confidence in self-efficacy (*i.e.*, behavior is determined, in part, by the belief that one has the requisite skills to bring about a specific outcome) has important implications. Issues with self-efficacy can affect the learning experience because, "Teachers set the tone of classrooms, and as such, the success of inclusion may well depend upon the prevailing attitudes of teachers as they interact with students with disabilities in their classroom" (Carroll, Forlin, and Jobling, 2003, p. 65).

According to Lago-Delello (1998), the extent to which an educator understands the learning and behavioral characteristics of students with disabilities appears to have an influence on classroom dynamics. Therefore, higher levels of self-efficacy among general education teachers is directly related to the success of students with disabilities and the accommodations the teacher is willing to provide (Yesseldyke, Thurlow, Christenson, & McVicar, 1998). This issue was addressed in a study that found that practicing general education teachers were concerned with the limited exposure they had to special education in their academic training (DeBettercourt, 1999).

This concern is expressed among pre-service general education teachers as well (Shippen, Crites, Houchins, Ramsey, & Simon, 2005). The perceived lack of skills in special education may explain why general educators are less supportive of inclusion than special educators (Minke & Bear, 1996). The response to deficits in self-efficacy was also discussed by Bandura (1982) who postulated that even though individuals might recognize some specific action should be taken, they are still unwilling to attempt the specific action if they do not have the knowledge of how to carry it out completely.

The *No Child Left Behind Act* of 2001 required each state have highly qualified teachers in all classrooms by the end of the 2005-06 academic years. As a result, there was a resultant shortage of qualified special education teachers, which produced fewer opportunities for students to receive individualized supports to accommodate academic needs (Shippen, Flores, Crites, Patterson, Ramsey, Houchins & Jolivette, 2011). Since general and special educators are direct service providers for students with disabilities, they are the critical link to successful academic and behavioral outcomes (Shippen *et al.*, 2011).

It is important for school districts to provide sufficient professional development opportunities to assist with instructing students with disabilities. Teacher training and staff development activities can improve and foster confidence and positive attitudes towards students with disabilities (Shippen *et al.*, 2011) and promote self-efficacy.

Looking Within… The Risky Need for *Self-assessment*

School personnel can benefit from honestly assessing their own beliefs about and attitudes toward students with disabilities (Milsom, 2006). This assessment can be described as becoming self-aware of one's biases, perceptions and stereotypes.

Professional development activities that redress biases challenge school personnel to examine their beliefs and attitudes and both understand and accept differences in children from cultures and with strengths unlike their own – to include disabilities (National Association for the Education of Young Children (NAEYC), 2010). The anti-bias movement also provides opportunities to work with parents of children from a variety of religious and ethnic groups for learning about different practices. These types of professional development opportunities result in enriching curriculum, preventing harm to a child's self-concept, and fostering a better understanding of diverse populations (Gordan & Browne, 2013).

To assist teachers and other school personnel with recognizing their assumptions and ideological frameworks, Frank Fitch (2003) provided ideologies representing traditionalist beliefs and inclusive beliefs:

Traditionalist Beliefs/Ideology

1. Diversity in schools and society is problematic.
2. Disabilities are innate conditions of certain human beings. Those "with disabilities" are essentially different. Disability labels are inevitable, objective, fair, and beneficial.
3. Special education experts most appropriately and effectively provide support and interventions in separate settings. Progress is accomplished by professional expertise, technology, diagnosis, and intervention.
4. Special education and lower-achieving students will improve ("catch up") to their peers if they receive specialized, skill-based, intensive, individualized instruction in separate settings.
5. Learning is primarily developmentally linear; it takes place one sequential step at a time.
6. Competitive school structures are natural, fair, and expected; therefore, homogeneous grouping of students is inevitable.
7. Special education is a rational system of services that helps those individuals labelled or identified.

Inclusive Beliefs/Ideology

1. Diversity is expected and valued. Individual and group diversity contributes

positively to classroom climate, learning outcomes, and community quality.

2. Human commonalities cut across socially constructed categories of race, class, gender, sexual orientation, and disability. It is unnecessary and damaging to publicly label and group people according to how they differ from the norm.
3. It is in the interest of everyone to be in socially inclusive learning environments in which all individuals are valued. Teachers with different expertise can co-teach in inclusive settings while providing optimal social and academic results for all students.
4. Knowledge and competence are purposely constructed in a variety of ways.
5. Competitive structures and activities are socially constructed and not inevitable.
6. Collaboration, cooperation, and mutual support are preferred forms of interpersonal interaction.

Ideologies were identified as systems of beliefs, ideas, commitments or values about social reality and representations such as images, myths and ideas that help someone resolve their understanding of the world around them.

On an individual level, ideology helps one understand the way they think about the world and reflects their ideal concepts of how to live the world. Ideologies can also describe the shared beliefs of a group of people, and understanding ideologies allows for more insight into how to address different cultural norms. An improved understanding about individual and school ideologies related to disability will help provide an environment where students with disability have a voice and are valued school community participants (Groce, 1999).

Disability as an Issue of Diverse Cultures

Viewing the disability community as a culture can help ensure productive professional development activities, include information and awareness about disabilities, and promote a multi-culturally competent professional workforce. Additionally, school-wide initiatives such as promoting and celebrating diversity can be encouraged – oftentimes, diversity is thought of as a racial and ethnic experience, but including disability and other differences as diverse population among students in a school can increase awareness. Fitch (2002) advocated for the integration of disability studies in multiculturalism programs. Cultural stereotypes surrounding disabilities exist and, through education and awareness, the social constructs and relations of power that enable segregation and inequality for people with disabilities can be assuaged through awareness activities.

Environment and Impact on Mental Health Status of Students

Mental health needs for students with disabilities include two primary factors – emotional and social needs. Child wellness has been described as the satisfaction regarding personal, relational and collective needs of children and youth (Prilleltensky, 2010). Studies have shown inclusion in society contributes to a person's wellness. However, children need to have material and emotional needs fulfilled – and these elements are not exclusive of one or the other (Pilleltensky, 2010).

To help illustrate this point, Fitch (2003) examined the impact of segregation on student's psychological well-being. He looked at this issue over a 6-year period from the perspective of the student with disabilities who were included and excluded in school community. Students were followed in elementary school and then into junior high school. Findings from this study indicated that when included students became involved participants of inclusive classroom communities, she formed a confident, sanguine sense of herself as a legitimate participant in the mainstream of school culture. In classrooms that did not promote a sense of belonging, students expressed a sense of denunciation, submission, and a yearning to "escape" the classroom. Fitch also observed students who were integrated in the elementary school were eventually re-segregated in junior high schools. A final observation was that the longer students remained in segregated educational settings, the more the student assumed the role of ostracism from the broader community.

Jones (2012) stated self-concept, self-esteem, and self-perception is critical to long-term development of students with disabilities. How can teachers and other school personnel make an impact on the school environment to positively impact these learners? There are two structural activities that serve to enhance a positive view of self and increase confidence levels in students with disabilities – self-advocacy and self-determination.

Self-Advocacy and Self-Determination

The term self-advocacy is based on the concept that people can make decisions, exert control over their lives, and speak on their own behalf. Hall (2010) described self-advocacy as independent people with disabilities working together for justice, helping other people with disabilities learn empowerment, fight inequity, and learn from one another. These are core concepts that are reinforced and taught to students without disabilities, but recognizing the importance of including students with disabilities in teaching these types of competencies is necessary to ensure we are providing a foundation for all students to achieve. Self-advocacy is also described as a grassroots, civil rights movement comprised of associations and groups (Caldwell, Arnold & Rizzolo, 2012; Hall, 2010; Hayden & Nelis, 2002; Test, Fowler, Wood, Brewer & Eddy, 2005).

Self-determination involves the right to independence, control, and the satisfaction of needs. Prilleltensky (2010) believed self-determination is the cornerstone of individual rights, involving concepts such as fairness, equality, social justice, and personal rights - as well as obligations - further promoting positive mental health in children with disabilities. Self-determination is not a program but a process that is different for each person because it is person-centered and person-directed. Self-determination recognizes that each person has rights and can take charge of responsibility for their own lives. There are four principles associated with self-determination:

- **freedom,**
- **authority,**
- **autonomy, and**
- **responsibility.**

In addition, there are five values supported by self-determination including:

- **respect,**
- **choice,**
- **ownership,**
- **support, and**

- **opportunity (Center on Human Policy, 2007).**

Youth Self-Advocacy

Youth self-advocacy involves the students learning how to find their own voice and being able to speak up for themselves, being able to make their own decisions about their lives, knowing their rights and responsibilities, being able to problem-solve, listen, learn, and reach out to others when help is needed (Wrightslaw, 2014). Providing opportunities for students with disabilities to learn how to advocate for themselves can result in life-long benefits. Teachers can actively seek out leadership and advocacy training opportunities as well as provide access to a number of self-advocacy organizations specifically targeted to youth with disabilities. Local, state, and national organizations exist and are great resources for educators, parents, and students.

Many states provide adolescents with disabilities opportunity to participate in leadership training programs such as Partners in Policymaking™ and Youth Leadership Forum. These programs help further develop leadership skills for enhancing personal empowerment.

Resource	Self-Advocacy Resources! Self-Advocates Becoming Empowered (SABE): www.sabeusa.org National Youth Leadership Network (NYLN): www.nyln.org Autistic Self-Advocacy Network (ASAN): www.autisticadvocacy.org National Gateway to Self-Determination: www.ngsd.org The Riot! Self-Advocacy Newsletter: www.theriotrocks.org Self-Advocacy Online: www.selfadvocacyonline.org National Council on Independent Living: www.ncil.org Allies in Self-Advocacy: www.alliesinselfadvocacy.org

Self-Determination

In order for self-determination to be successful, teachers and other school personnel are obliged to make changes in the way they think about students with disabilities and the way they provide education and other support services. Seeing students with disabilities as valuable people with gifts, talents, strengths and abilities that strengthen their school communities is one small way to shift the educational viewpoint and ultimately lead to empowerment for the student with disabilities (Center on Human Policy, 2007).

Supporting and creating opportunities for students to exercise self-determination contributes to inclusion because self-determination includes a person's ability and opportunity to interconnect and make personal choices, to participate in and contribute to their communities, to support advocacy for self and others, and to develop leadership skills through self-advocacy training (Developmental Disabilities Assistance and Bill of Rights Act of 2000; Prillenltensky, 2010).

CONCLUSIONS

Understanding the history of disability and its impact over time on the personal development of students with disabilities offers teachers and other school personnel the opportunity to reflect on their school environment and its climate *vis a vis* positive and negative mental health outcomes. Teacher efficacy was explored regarding the ability to be competent with implementing inclusionary concepts in the school community. Included in this exploration was a review of the concepts of medical model contrasted with the social model of disability and encouraged a self-assessment review of traditional ideology compared to inclusion ideology.

Finally, this chapter explored value and acceptance concepts with a highlight on self-advocacy and self-determination as key foundational strategies to foster when creating an environment that is conducive to positive mental health outcomes for students with disabilities. Schools, as among the most fundamental of social institutions regarding participation and influencing children, are instrumental as a mechanism of social and cultural inclusion for students with disabilities. Though full benefits of optimal inclusion of students with disabilities is yet unachieved, schools remain paramount in societal advancement of promoting diversity, inclusion, and numerous quality of life outcomes. Acceptance of this verity, while sobering, offers opportunities that should find universal appeal with educators.

CONFLICT OF INTEREST

The authors confirm that they have no conflict of interest to declare for this publication.

ACKNOWLEDGEMENTS

Declared none.

REFERENCES

Advocacy. (2009). American Heritage Dictionary. Retrieved from: http://www.thefreedictionary.com/advocacy

Boswell, B., Hamner, M., Knight, S., Glacoff, M., McChesney, J. (2012). Dance of disability and spirituality. In: Marini, I., Stebnicki, M., (Eds.), *The psychological and social impact of illness and disability.* (pp. 341-344). NY: Springer Publishing Company, LLC.

Braddock, D.L., Parrish, S. (2001). An institutional history of disability. In: Albrecht, G.l., Seelman, K.D., Bury, M., (Eds.), *Handbook of disability studies.* (pp. 11-68). Thousand Oaks, CA: Sage Publications, Inc.. [http://dx.doi.org/10.4135/9781412976251.n2]

Caldwell, J., Arnold, K.K., Rizzolo, M.K. (2012). *Envisioning the future: Allies in self-advocacy final report..* Silver Springs, MD: Association of University Centers on Disabilities.

Center on Human Policy. (2007). National Resource Center on Supported Living and Choice, Syracuse University. Supported by the U.S. Department of Education, Office of Special Education and Rehabilitative Services, National Institute on Disability and Rehabilitation Research (NIDRR), through Contract No. H133B980047, and in part by the National Resource Center on Supported Living and Choice, Center on Human Policy, School of Education, Syracuse University, through the U.S. Department of Education, Office of Special Education and Rehabilitative Services, National Institute on Disability and Rehabilitation Research (NIDRR), through Contract No. H133A990001.

Developmental Disabilities Assistance and Bill of Rights Act of 2000. Public Law 106-402, 114 Stat. 1677.

Deutsch, A. (1967). *The mentally ill in America: A history of their care and treatment from colonial times..* Columbia University Press.

Eberly, S.S. (1998). Fairies and the folklore of disability: Changelings, hybrids and the solitary fairy. *Folklore, 99*, 58-77.
[http://dx.doi.org/10.1080/0015587X.1988.9716425]

Fitch, F. (2003). Inclusion, exclusion, and ideology: Special education students' changing sense of self. *Urban Rev., 3*(35), 233-252.
[http://dx.doi.org/10.1023/A:1025733719935]

Fox, D.D., Marini, I. (2012). History and treatment toward persons with disabilities in America. In: Marini, I., Stebnicki, M., (Eds.), *The psychological and social impact of illness and disability.* (pp. 341-344). NY: Springer Publishing Company, LLC.

Great Schools Partnership. (2013). *Glossary of school reform.* Retrieved from: http://www.greatschoolspartnership.org/about/

Green, M., Moore, H., O'Brien, J. (2006). *When people care enough to act: Asset based community development.*. Toronto: Inclusion Press.

Groce, N.E. (2013). Disability issues in local concepts and beliefs. *Asia Disability Rehabilitation Journal, 10*(1) Retrieved from: http://www.dinf.ne.jp/doc/english/asia/resource/apdrj/z13jo0300/z13jo0303.html

Hall, S.A. (2010). *The social inclusion of young adults with intellectual disabilities: A phenomenology of their experiences (Doctoral dissertation).* Available from ProQuest Dissertations and Theses, 133

Hurwitz, L., Weston, K. (2010). *Using coordinated school health to promote mental health for all students.* Retrieved from: http://cshca.wpengine.netdna-cdn.com/wp-content/uploads/2011/07/NASBHC.CSH-Mental-Health.pdf

Jones, J.L. (2012). Factors associated with self-concept: adolescents with intellectual and development disabilities share their perspectives. *Intellect. Dev. Disabil., 50*(1), 31-40. [http://dx.doi.org/10.1352/1934-9556-50.1.31] [PMID: 22316224]

Katsiyannis, A., Yell, M.L., Bradley, R. (2001). Reflections on the 25th anniversary of the Individuals with Disabilities Act. *Remedial Spec. Educ., 22*(6), 324-334. [http://dx.doi.org/10.1177/074193250102200602]

Miles, S., Singal, N. (2010). The education for all and inclusive education debate: Conflict, contradiction or opportunity? *Int. J. Incl. Educ., 14*(1), 1-15. [http://dx.doi.org/10.1080/13603110802265125]

Mayer, L.M. (2012). Social work practice with people with disabilities: Enhancing practice through Catholic social teaching. *Soc. Work Christ., 39*(2), 172-188.

Mizrahi, T., Davis, L.E. (2008). *Encyclopedia of Social Work.* (20th ed.). Oxford: Oxford Univ. Press. [http://dx.doi.org/10.1093/acref/9780195306613.001.0001]

National School Climate Center. (2013). *School climate.*

Porter, R. (2002). *Madness: A brief history.*. NY: Oxford University Press Inc..

Prilleltensky, I. (2010). Child wellness and social inclusion: values for action. *Am. J. Community Psychol., 46*(1-2), 238-249. [http://dx.doi.org/10.1007/s10464-010-9318-9] [PMID: 20532614]

Redding, S. (1991). What is a school community anyway? *Sch. Community J., 1*(2), 7-9.

Roberts, R., Beadle-Brown, J., Youell, D. (2011). Promoting social inclusion for children and adults on the autism spectrum - reflections on policy and practice. *Tizard Learning Disability Review, 16*(4), 45-52. [http://dx.doi.org/10.1108/13595471111172840]

Scull, A. (1989). *Social order/mental disorder: Anglo-American psychiatry in historical perspective.*. University of California Press.

Scull, A. (2011). *Madness: A very short introduction.*. NY: Oxford University Press Inc.. [http://dx.doi.org/10.1093/actrade/9780199608034.001.0001]

Sherwin, J. (2010). Leadership for social inclusion in the lives of people with disabilities. *The International Journal of Leadership in Public Services.,* (6), 84-93. [http://dx.doi.org/10.5042/ijlps.2010.0577]

Shippen, M.E., Flores, M.M., Crites, S.A., Patterson, D., Ramsey, M.L., Houchins, D.E., Jolivette, K. (2011). Classroom structure and teacher efficacy in serving students with disabilities: Differences in elementary and secondary teachers. *Int. J. Spec. Educ., 26*(3), 36-44.

Swedeen, B.L. Signs of an inclusive school: A parent's perspective on the meaning and value of authentic inclusion. (2009). *TEACHING Exceptional Children Plus.,* *5*(3) Article 1. Retrieved from: http://escholarship.bc.edu/education/tecplus/vol5/iss3/art1/

Taylor, S.T., Searl, S.J. (2001). Disability in America: A history of policies and trends. In: Martin, E.D., Jr, (Ed.), *Significant disability: Issues affecting people with significant disabilities from a historical, policy, leadership, and systems perspective.* (pp. 16-64). Springfield, IL: Charles C. Thomas Publisher, LTD.

Test, D.W., Fowler, C.H., Wood, W.M., Brewer, D.M., Eddy, S. (2005). A conceptual framework of self-advocacy for students with disabilities. *Remedial Spec. Educ., 26*(1), 43-54. [http://dx.doi.org/10.1177/07419325050260010601]

Wolfensberger, W. (2010). Social role valorization: a proposed new term for the principle of normalization. *Intellect. Dev. Disabil., 49*(6), 435-440. [http://dx.doi.org/10.1352/1934-9556-49.6.435] [PMID: 22126271]

Wolfensberger, W. (2011). An "if this, then that" formulation of decisions related to Social Role Valorization as a better way of interpreting it to people. *Intellect. Dev. Disabil., 49*(6), 456-462. [http://dx.doi.org/10.1352/1934-9556-49.6.456] [PMID: 22126273]

Wrightslaw. (2014). *Self-Advocacy.* Retrieved from: http://www.wrightslaw.com/info/self.advocacy.htm/

Yell, M.L., Drasgow, E. (2005). *No child left behind: A guide for professionals.*. Upper Saddle River, NJ: Pearson/Merrill/Prentice-Hall.

Yell, M.L. (2015). Special education in the United States: Legal history. In: Wright, J.D., (Ed.), *International encyclodedia of the social & behavioural sciences.* Elsevier. [http://dx.doi.org/10.1016/B978-0-08-097086-8.86113-9]

CHAPTER 3

Children's Temperament at School and in the Classroom

Kathleen Moritz Rudasill[*], **Kate Sirota, Mary Kralemann, Amanda Prokasky, Kenji Madison** and **Victoria J. Molfese**

University of Nebraska-Lincoln, Lincoln, NE 68588, United States

Abstract: Temperament is arguably one of the most important childhood traits about which educators should be thoroughly versed. Childhood temperament is linked with, among other outcomes, three that are essential to school success: behavioral responses, academic performance, and social interaction. It also plays a compelling role in long-term mental health. This chapter describes the range of temperamental manifestations and offers suggestions for promoting temperamental factors to support resilience rather than foster risk.

Keywords: Activity, Adaptability, Behavioral inhibition, Distractibility, Externalizing behavior, Goodness-of-fit, Internalizing behavior, Reactivity, Regulation.

INTRODUCTION

Variations in children's characteristics are universally acknowledged by teachers. In addition to widely supported differences in cognitive ability, children differ in the ways that they approach learning, follow directions, are interested in and attend to class activities, engage with peers, and interact with teachers. These differences are often rooted in temperament, defined as biologically based individual differences in thinking, feeling, and behaving in the environment (Duckworth & Allred, 2012). Although developmentally dynamic (*i.e.*, tempera-

[*] **Corresponding author Kathleen Moritz Rudasill:** University of Nebraska-Lincoln, Lincoln, NE 68588, United States; Tel:/Fax: 402-472-2455; Email: krudasill2@unl.edu

Raymond J. Waller (Ed.)

mental reactions to the environment change with advancing development), temperament is relatively stable through childhood and adolescence (Caspi & Silva, 1995; Kagan, Resnick *et al.*, 1988; Resnick *et al.*, 1986; Rimm-Kaufman & Kagan, 2005; Rothbart & Posner, 2005). Temperament is also multi-dimensional, encompassing characteristics such as activity, persistence, shyness, inhibition, and attention, and provides the foundation for personality, which extends to values, morals, beliefs and social cognition (Rothbart & Bates, 2006).

Like personality, temperament both influences and is influenced by the environment, making it an important aspect to consider when studying school environments. Indeed, children's temperament has been linked to their mental health, academic success, and social outcomes, both directly and indirectly *via* forces in schools (such as peers and teachers) that facilitate or prevent certain outcomes (*e.g.*, Degnan, Almas, & Fox, 2010; Martin & Holbrook, 1985; Rudasill & Rimm-Kaufman, 2009).

The modern era of temperament research began in the 1970s with the landmark New York Longitudinal Study by Alexander Thomas and Stella Chess. Inspired by their own children, Thomas and Chess (1977) conducted in-depth observations of infants, noting the individual differences in their behavior. They identified nine temperament dimensions: activity, rhythmicity, adaptability, approach-withdrawal, threshold to responsiveness, intensity, mood, distractibility, and attention/task persistence. Using these dimensions, Thomas and Chess were able to classify approximately 60% of children into one of three types: easy, difficult, and slow to warm up. Easy children were characterized by positive mood, high regulation, low to moderate intensity of reaction, high adaptability, and positive approach. In contrast, difficult children were described as being high in intensity of reaction, withdrawn in new situations, and slow to adapt and adjust to new routines.

Finally, slow to warm up children were characterized as displaying low levels of activity, withdrawing from new or unfamiliar stimuli, being slow to adapt and negative in mood, and responding to situations with low intensity of reaction (Thomas, Chess, & Birch, 1970). Thomas and Chess (1977) were quick to stress that no temperament type was better or worse than another; rather, positive adjustment depended on the *goodness-of-fit* between a child's temperament and environment. For example, a difficult child may thrive in a supportive environment with sensitive and responsive parenting, whereas an easy child may be overlooked because he or she does not demand much from parents or the environment.

Resource	http://childdevelopmentinfo.com/child-development/temperament_and_your_child/temp2/

Other scholars have explored temperament, resulting in variations and refinements in its conceptualization. For example, Buss and Plomin (1975) identified four dimensions of temperament: emotionality, activity, sociability and impulsivity, while Goldsmith conceptualized temperament as differences in emotionality, and Kagan examined behavioral inhibition in toddlers and connections to later shyness (Merivelde & De Pauw, 2012). Rothbart and colleagues developed one of the most widely used frameworks for temperament, conceptualizing it as being comprised of reactive and regulatory components (Rothbart & Bates, 2006). The notion of temperament as both reactive and regulatory has been useful for reconciling nuances in conceptualizations of temperament, as well as for applying temperament concepts in settings such as school. For these reasons, Rothbart's temperament framework is described in detail below.

Reactivity

Reactivity refers to the intensity of an individual's reaction to environmental stimuli; a highly reactive child may be more prone to excitement, fear, or frustration than a less reactive child (Rothbart & Jones, 1998). In short, highly reactive children experience life intensely; they may become very excited about an upcoming event, get easily frustrated from a small setback, or seem anxious when meeting someone new. An individual's level of reactivity is manifested both emotionally and behaviorally (Rothbart & Bates, 2006). Emotional reactivity describes feelings (*e.g.*, anxiety, fear, joy) associated with an environmental stimulus, and behavioral reactivity describes the response to that feeling (*e.g.*, crying, social reticence, approach). Reactivity is evident in infancy and predicts behavior in children up to age 7 and older (Rothbart, *et al.*, 2000). Rothbart's work has revealed two broad temperament dimensions indicative of reactivity: negative emotionality and surgency/extraversion (Rothbart & Bates, 2006). However, there are other temperament traits also indicative of reactivity, such as anger/frustration, shyness, and activity.

Negative emotionality, also called negative reactivity, negative affectivity, and distress proneness, refers to an individual's tendency toward "fear, anxiety, sadness, frustration/anger, guilt, and discomfort" reactions (Rothbart & Bates, 2006; p. 111). Negative emotionality has implications for children's success in school to the extent that it is associated with expressions of frustration, learned helplessness, failure, and aggression directed toward peers and teachers (Keogh, 2003; Rothbart & Jones, 1998). Surgency/extraversion, also called positive emotionality, sociability, and approach/withdrawal, refers to an individual's tendency toward pleasure, positive anticipation, extraversion, sociability, and eagerness (Rothbart & Bates, 2006). Surgency/extraversion has implications for children's academic and social success in school to the extent that is associated with "curiosity, eagerness, and energy toward goal satisfaction" (p. 3, Rothbart & Jones, 1998).

Regulation

A child's regulatory capacity acts upon his or her reactivity. That is, children's natural tendencies to react to environmental stimuli (*e.g.*, withdraw from or approach someone unfamiliar) are moderated by their abilities to regulate these reactions (Rothbart & Posner, 2005; Rothbart & Bates, 2006). Children's regulation does not begin to develop until the second or third year of life, with the greatest development occurring between ages four and seven; at that point, a child's regulatory capacity remains somewhat stable through childhood and beyond (Rothbart & Bates, 2006). Rothbart and Bates (1998) suggest that the ability to both focus and shift attention is paramount in the ability to inhibit reactions that are not appropriate. In addition, there is evidence that training can improve attention (reflecting the neural base of effortful control) in children when attentional networks are developing (between ages 4 and 7) (Rothbart & Posner, 2005). Rothbart and colleagues refer to regulation as effortful control.

Effortful control, also called task persistence, inhibitory control, and constraint, refers to an individual's tendency toward and ability to attend to important or relevant stimuli, stay focused, inhibit inappropriate behaviors, and persist in the face of difficulty or distraction; it is defined as "the ability to inhibit a dominant response to perform a subdominant response" (Rothbart & Bates, 1998, p. 137). For example, a child who is angry with a peer and wants to hit, but instead moves to a quiet activity to "cool down," is displaying effortful control. As such, effortful control is a process that allows children to reach desired goals of alleviating distress and to "behave in accordance with certain rules and expectations" (Fox & Calkins, 2003, p. 16). Effortful control thus operates upon temperamental traits indicative of reactivity, such as negative emotionality and surgency/extraversion.

Indeed, a child's responses to environmental stimuli depend on interactions between temperamental reactivity and the ability to regulate that reactivity (Rothbart & Jones, 1998). For example, a child's natural tendency to approach or withdraw from a new person or situation (*i.e.*, shyness) is tempered by the child's internal mechanism to control that tendency (*i.e.*, effortful control). Regulation explains why a child who is anger-prone might walk away from a frustrating situation to calm down, rather than lash out verbally or physically. Indeed, reactivity and regulation are complementary systems within the individual. Without reactivity, regulation is unnecessary (Eisenberg & Spinrad, 2004). Rothbart conceptualizes four types of people as determined by the combination of regulation and reactivity. Those with low regulation and low reactivity are impulsive and under controlled. Those with low regulation and high reactivity are anxious and fearful, those with high regulation and low reactivity are curious and bold, and those with high regulation and high reactivity are cautious and restrained (Rothbart & Jones, 1998).

Certain temperament characteristics indicative of reactivity and regulation are most salient to academic settings because they are linked to children's skill and comfort with social interaction (*i.e.*, shyness, effortful control) and shifting to new activities and situations (*i.e.*, adaptability), tendency toward negative feelings (*i.e.*, anger, negative emotionality), or ability to focus attention and inhibit inappropriate behaviors (*i.e.*, effortful control). In addition, children displaying a constellation of temperament characteristics indicative of higher reactivity and lower regulation (*i.e.*, difficult or aversive temperament) often have difficulty in the school and classroom environment because their behavior places more demands on teachers and peers.

Temperament and Development: Gene by Environment Models

Although temperament is relatively stable across childhood, temperament and the behavioral display of temperament result from *interactions between genetics and the environment*. Indeed, temperament influences an individual's behavioral response; that is, temperament has an impact on how an individual may respond in a given situation, and this temperament-influenced response may be, in part, influenced by an individual's genetic makeup (Saudino & Wang, 2012). In addition, an individual's temperament can influence the environment. For example, a child who displays high levels of negative emotion, such as anger and fear, may promote stress in caregivers and teachers, thus resulting in a more negative environment that is less likely to be nurturing and responsive to the child. Much of the work on temperament by environment interactions has focused on how children's temperament may influence parenting behavior. For example, Lengua and Kovacs (2005) found that children's positive emotionality predicted more maternal acceptance, and Lee and Bates (1985) found that children's negative reactivity predicted more maternal control. Others have found that a child's self-regulation predicts maternal supportive parenting (Kennedy, Rubin, Hastings & Maisel, 2004).

Gene by environment interaction patterns are particularly salient to teachers and classrooms since most children spend a large portion of their day in school. Indeed, Pluess and Belsky (2009) found that childcare quality in preschool interacts with child temperament to predict behavior problems and social competence. Children's temperament influences their behavior and how they interact with teachers and peers around them; by the same token, children's temperament can have an effect on the classroom environment (*e.g.*, Coplan & Prakash, 2003; Rudasill & Rimm-Kaufman, 2009). For example, first graders with lower levels of effortful control elicit more interactions from teachers than their more regulated peers. Relatedly, Evans (1992) reported that shy kindergarten children elicited more questions from teachers during a show-and-tell task than their bolder peers. However, while more teacher questions were associated with less talk by shy children, when teachers used a low-control style with shy children (*e.g.*, reducing questions, making comments), children's verbal responses increased significantly (Evans, 1992). As these examples show, classrooms and teachers can provide environmental supports that are beneficial to children's social and academic learning.

Conceptualizing children's outcomes from a gene by environment perspective requires both a genetic (nature) and environmental (nurture) perspective. Theoretical views using a gene by environment perspective are either conceptualized as vulnerability models or susceptibility models. In vulnerability models, such as the diathesis-stress model (Zubin & Spring, 1977), children with aversive temperaments are thought to be at greater risk for negative outcomes in poor or low-quality environments. In this view, a child is born with a predisposition to react a certain way in a given situation, but that predisposition is only expressed when the environment provides the appropriate stressor.

In susceptibility models, such as differential susceptibility (Belsky, 1997), children with more aversive temperaments are at greater risk for negative outcomes in poor or low quality environments and are also more likely to have positive outcomes in good or high quality environments. In both types of models, a child with a difficult temperament would be likely to fare worse than other children in a hostile, insensitive, or negative environment. However, according to differential susceptibility, a child with difficult temperament would be more likely than other children to thrive in a high quality and responsive environment. These prevailing theoretical approaches provide the basis for our view of the role of the classroom environment as it interacts with a child's temperament. We begin with a discussion of culture and temperament.

Cultural Considerations

Culture is defined by Mascolo (2004) as "a dynamic distribution of meanings, practices, and artifacts throughout a linguistic community" (p. 83). Two leading perspectives have been discussed. The first is the *ecological systems model*

(Bronfenbrenner & Morris, 2006), which suggests that an understanding of behaviors, attitudes, and emotional characteristics are relevant to an individual's particular socioecological environments, explained as micro, meso, exo, and chrono-systems respectively. Second is the sociocultural theory (Vygotsky, 1978) that details social interactions as cultural, such that the actions of the child are in turn shaped by a caregiver's cultural knowledge, beliefs and expectations. Cultures have been shaped for generations, and the actions of a child may be viewed from differing standards.

Cultural effects on temperament have been studied widely (Klein & Ballantine, 1991; Ahadi, Rothbart, & Ye, 1993; Gartstein *et al.* 2009; Gartstein *et al.* 2010), with most emphasizing differences between Western and Eastern cultures. Indeed, temperamental qualities described in Western culture as maladaptive may be conceptualized as adaptive in Eastern cultures. The child who is viewed as inhibited in Western society may be viewed as typical in Eastern society; a highly active child may be viewed as typical in Western culture where individual autonomy is valued, but viewed as maladjusted in Eastern culture where collectivist values are stronger. These differences are driven by variation in parenting practices, social values, and environment. Yet, it is still unclear whether differences between cultures are purely the product of environment, or if they stem in part from genetic diversity (Fullard *et al.*, 1989). Critical for the purposes of understanding temperament in the classroom is that a child's display of temperament may have different causes or connotations, depending on cultural background.

Thus, links between temperament and children's behaviors are influenced by the *goodness-of-fit* between a child's temperament and environment, with environmental "fit" related to influences due to genes and context. Reviewed in the sections below are research studies focusing on mental health, academic achievement and social outcomes, with particular focus on classroom and school settings. We conclude with a discussion of interventions or practices that seem to facilitate better outcomes for children.

Temperament and Mental Health

Mental health plays a large role in a child's ability to succeed in the classroom. A child who is suffering from mental illness may have reduced academic and social success. If teachers, counsellors, and educators have a better understanding of this relationship they can give these students the care and attention they need to succeed. Temperament has been shown to be associated with mental health in childhood and throughout adolescence (Degnan, Almas, & Fox, 2010; Oldehinkel, Hartman, Winter, Veentra, & Ormel, 2004).

There are different models regarding the association between temperament and mental health. Some models conceptualize temperament and psychopathology as caused by a different factor or factors, some conceptualize temperament as a precursor to psychopathology, and others see psychopathology as the precursor to temperament. Although there is disagreement about the specifics of the relationship between temperament and psychopathology, there is ample research to support the extent to which temperament and internalizing and externalizing behaviors are related and may reach clinical levels of psychopathology.

Internalizing and Externalizing Behaviors and Disorders

Many of the behaviors exhibited by children and adolescents can be categorized as externalizing or internalizing, and may be adaptive in some situations, such as fear of strangers or worry about a test. However, these behaviors may quickly become maladaptive or reach pathological levels depending on the severity and frequency of the behavior. Many individuals are able to overcome the challenges involved with these internalizing and externalizing behaviors (Oldehinkel *et al.*, 2004), and not all children who exhibit these behaviors reach levels high enough to warrant a clinical diagnosis.

Both psychosocial and genetic research has shown a relationship between various temperaments and different levels of internalizing and externalizing behaviors (Degnan *et al.*, 2010). Some temperament traits, such as high levels of negative affectivity and low levels of effortful control, have been associated with *both* internalizing and externalizing behaviors (Oldehinkel *et al.*, 2004; Rew & Horner, 2003).

Internalizing Behaviors and Disorders

Internalizing behaviors involve at least some level of internal distress, such as nervousness or worry, and can be associated with clinical diagnoses including anxiety and depression, if levels of these behaviors are observed to be excessive. Children with certain temperaments are more at risk for internalizing disorders, such as anxiety and depression, than others. For example, behavioral inhibition is related to a higher likelihood of developing an anxiety disorder such as social anxiety disorder, panic disorder, social phobia, and agoraphobia (Degnan *et al.*, 2010). When behaviorally inhibited children are faced with a new situation, they are likely to cope with avoidance. Although this avoidant behavioral reaction decreases fear and stress, it can also support anxious cognitions and reflexes, and can compound into an anxiety disorder.

Research shows links between the conceptually related traits of fear, shyness, behavioral inhibition, and low surgency, and a tendency toward internalizing behaviors (Oldehinkel *et al.*, 2004; Rew & Horner, 2003). Shy and behaviorally inhibited children may show avoidance or discomfort in the face of social situations or novel stimuli because they are more likely to perceive those situations as difficult or demanding (Crozier & Badawood, 2009). There is also evidence that early temperament predicts internalizing problems in later childhood and beyond.

Kagan, Snidman, Zentner, and Peterson (1999) found that an inhibited child was significantly more likely to develop anxiety by age seven than a non-inhibited child, while Bohlin and Hagekull (2009) found that these effects persisted into adulthood. Caspi and colleagues (2003) found that behavioral inhibition at age 3 predicted less positive emotionality at ages 18 and 26, and Kagan and others (2007) found that highly reactive infants were more likely to develop internalizing problems such as anxiety and/or depression by adolescence and young adulthood. However, shyness may have some protective benefits longitudinally; Caspi and Silva (1995) found that inhibited children tended to score lower on tests of impulsivity, danger seeking, and aggression when they became adolescents.

Externalizing Behaviors and Disorders

Externalizing behaviors involve an outward expression of distress, such as hitting or impulsivity, which, when consistently observed, may result in diagnosis of a disorder such as Attention Deficit Hyperactivity Disorder (ADHD), Conduct Disorder (CD), or other impulse control disorders (Oldehinkel *et al.*, 2004).

The relationship of temperament to ADHD has been studied extensively (see Nigg *et al.*, 2004, for a review), and has many implications for the school environment. Children with ADHD often exhibit social and academic problems due to their limited cognitive and emotional regulatory capacities, which are based in temperament. Because attention, for example, is a temperamental trait, it has been linked to cognitive regulation in children with ADHD (Posner & Rothbart, 2000). However, research suggests that temperamental traits related to emotional regulation may be more salient predictors of ADHD. Melnick and Hinshaw (2000) noted that the effect of low emotional regulation in boys on ADHD symptomology was moderated by parent-child interactions. Bacchini, Affuso, and Trotta (2008) found that inhibition to novelty was highly associated, even more than attention, with children's higher ADHD symptoms.

Research has also shown a relationship between impulsivity and adaptability and an increase in externalizing behaviors. Gottfried and Thomas (1997) found that adaptability scores were predictive of externalizing problems at school entry and into late elementary school. This finding is in keeping with other research linking adaptability to school adjustment (Carey *et al.*, 1977). In another longitudinal study, Caspi and Silva (1995) found that an "Undercontrolled" (more impulsive, more active) group of three year-olds was more likely to score higher on measures of impulsivity and aggression as 18 year olds.

Temperament, Environment, and Mental Health

It is clear that temperament can affect the classroom environment and children's classroom experiences directly and indirectly, in that a child's temperament may make him or her more prone to internalizing or externalizing behaviors. However, temperament alone does not cause behavior problems. There are other factors that can mediate or moderate the relationship between temperament and internalizing and externalizing behaviors and presence of a psychological disorder. As discussed earlier, the goodness-of-fit between temperament and the environment is critical for understanding children's behavior and outcomes (Rew & Horner, 2003).

Research shows that relationships with others can contribute to the association between temperament and internalizing and externalizing behaviors. For example, children who have easy temperament styles tend to have fewer negative interactions with their parents and caregivers. This low amount of negative interaction may protect children from exhibiting externalizing behaviors (Rutter, 1979). Indeed, maternal parenting behavior, perceived parenting styles, mother-child attachment, family relationships, and maternal personality have all been associated with children's internalizing and externalizing behaviors (Degnan *et al.*, 2010). For example, sensitive parenting can help reduce arousal and children's internalizing and externalizing behaviors before they reach clinical levels. A mother's personality style is also related to the child's displays of behavioral inhibition and anxiety (Degnan *et al.*, 2010).

There is much support for the idea that temperament and childhood relationships and experiences contribute to the development of psychopathology (Joyce, McKenzie, Luty, Mulder, Carter, Sullivan, & Cloninger, 2003). Similarly, peer interactions and friendships are associated with various internalizing and externalizing behaviors. Rejected boys may display more aggression, impulsivity, and emotional reactivity (Coie, 2004), but peer rejection can also lead to increased social withdrawal. Some rejected children show increased levels of shyness and social reticence (Hymel, *et al.*, 2011). Close friendships have been shown to mediate the relationship between social isolation and withdrawal and internalizing problems (Joyce *et al.*, 2003).

Happiness and Well-Being

The study of psychopathology has focused on deficits in health and functioning, but positive psychology is an emerging trend away from the deficit model. Even though much of the current positive psychology research looks at happiness in adults, researchers are beginning to investigate well-being and happiness in children. Various studies have shown a relationship between temperament and more positive factors in children, including happiness and resilience. For example, less harm avoidance and novelty seeking are associated with well-being (Cloninger & Zohar, 2011). Holder and Klassen (2010) found that children with high sociability were happier than those with low sociability, and children with low emotionality were happier than those with high emotionality. Previous research has also shown that social interactions are positively associated with happiness in children (Holder & Coleman, 2009). This suggests that temperaments that encourage social interaction would be associated with more happiness in children than temperaments that encourage social withdrawal.

Temperament and Academic Outcomes

Although general intelligence remains one of the main determinants of a child's academic outcomes, child temperamental traits (*e.g.* effortful control, shyness, and activity level) have been consistently identified as important predictors of academic success. Thomas and Chess (1977) found that an easy infant's adaptability and sociability were positively related to intelligence (defined as general cognitive ability), and, conversely, that a negative correlation between temperament and intelligence was observed in infants with lower adaptability, lower attentional focusing, and higher reactivity. Other studies show that this association persisted into childhood and adolescence (Martin & Holbrook, 1985; Matheny, 1989). Specifically, the dimensions of approach/withdrawal and adaptability were found to be salient to IQ level across the school years, but also differentially related at various ages (Guerin *et al.*, 2003; Matheny, 1989, Petrill & Thompson, 1993). Notably, intelligence has been found to be less of a factor in grade attainment as students move closer to and complete post-secondary education (Jensen, 1980).

Beyond intelligence, children's ability to adjust to the classroom environment (*i.e.*, teachability) is important for predicting academic success, and this ability is inherently connected to temperament (Keogh, 2003). *Teachability* often is used to describe a teacher's assessment of a student's potential for academic success, but also is related to social success (Keogh, 1994). According to Keogh (2003) a teachable student is one who is able to inhibit negative responses, is agreeable, and high in attention and task/orientation. A less *teachable* student is therefore one who has more difficulty regulating attention and self-control. Keogh (2003) found that less *teachable* students also were less likely to develop a close relationship with their teachers because the teachers' time is dominated by meeting the children's instructional needs, leaving little opportunity for social interaction and relationship building. A detailed discussion of the temperament characteristics that have been studied and linked to academic achievement follows.

Effortful Control, Persistence, and Conscientiousness

The regulatory traits of effortful control and persistence are two of the most robust predictors of children's and adolescents' academic outcomes, including school readiness, academic grades and standardized test performance, and school adjustment. The strong and significant effect of effortful control on academic achievement and skills can be observed across all ages and grade levels. McClelland *et al.* (2006) found, at the transition to formal school, that children classified as self-regulated (*i.e.*, higher in effortful control) had significantly higher teacher-reported academic skills than those classified as lower in self-regulation. In a study that controlled for intelligence, Blair and Razza (2007) found that low-income pre-schoolers' levels of effortful control strongly predicted standardized achievement scores after their transition to formal school. Martin (1989) found similar results using parent and teacher ratings of self-regulation abilities in early primary school children.

Effortful control is believed to increase across the school years. For example, an adolescent is more capable than a kindergartener of listening to a long lecture, a direct outgrowth of his/her more developed self-regulatory capacities. For older children and adolescents, effortful control has been linked to the personality dimension of conscientiousness, particularly as a predictor of course grades. Duckworth, Quinn, and Tsukayama (2012) found that self-control in middle school students was a stronger predictor of grades than IQ. Although course grades and standardized test scores show a strong correlation, Duckworth and Allred (2012) note that effortful control is particularly related to grade attainment in later grades, perhaps because it underlies the persistence and long-term, focused task orientation that characterizes high-achieving students. Two longitudinal studies involving adolescents showed that the level of effortful control in earlier grades was predictive of effortful control in later grades, even up to graduation from high school (Duncan *et al.*, 2007; Vitaro *et al.*, 2005). Kochanska and colleagues (2000), as well as other researchers, have noted that the already strong effect of effortful control increases with age (Eisenberg, Fabes, Nyman, Bernzweig, & Pinulas, 1994; Valiente *et al.*, 2003).

A related temperament dimension, persistence (the ability to stick with a task, even when distracted or interrupted), is another significant predictor of children's academic achievement. Schoen and Nagle (1994) found that persistence was related to children's reading achievement (over and above intelligence alone) in a sample of kindergarten children. Newman, Noel, Chen, and Matsopoulos (1998) found that persistence was particularly important for predicting reading achievement in children with lower IQ scores and was associated with growth in reading from kindergarten through third grade. Palisin (1986) found that parent-rated persistence when children were 4 years old was positively associated with academic achievement in second grade, and Bramlett and colleagues (Bramlett, Rowell, & Mandenberg, 2000; Bramlett, Scott, & Rowell, 2000) showed links between persistence and early math achievement. Such findings are consistent with those from a middle school sample (Walker, Stieber, & O'Neill, 1990), where persistence seems particularly helpful for navigating the transition to more difficult academic work (Gurerin, Gottfried, Oliver, & Thomas, 1994).

For students in later adolescence and young adulthood, conscientiousness, which is conceptually similar to effortful control and marked by high self-control and low distractibility, predicts grade point average (GPA) in both high school and college (Oliver, Guerin, & Gottfried, 2007; Credé & Kuncel, 2008). In an analysis of college grades, students' levels of conscientiousness were more predictive of GPA than college admissions tests (Credé & Kuncel, 2008). Conscientiousness (along with neuroticism) also has been shown to predict successful graduation from high school (Bowman & Matthews, 1960; Gough, 1964; Hathaway, Reynolds, & Monachesi, 1969). In a meta-analysis, Poropat (2009) found that conscientiousness, significantly more than any other personality dimension, was increasingly related to course grades as students moved from primary school to post-secondary education.

Shyness and Behavioral Inhibition

Shyness and behavioral inhibition have been associated with children's academic outcomes as well, and the mechanism through which this association is hypothesized is reluctance to engage in large-group class activities and interact with teachers and peers (Hughes & Coplan, 2010). These inhibited behaviors can reduce the dose of instruction these children receive by suppressing their active participation in classroom activities and their opportunities to engage in productive interactions with others. Further, reticence to speak up may be misconstrued as a lack of ability, rather than social withdrawal from fear (*e.g.*, Evans, 2010). Either way, shyness and behavioral inhibition appear to be liabilities in the classroom *via* links to lower academic achievement.

Children's language and literacy skills have been most clearly linked to shyness. Crozier and Badawood (2009) found that parent assessments of children's shyness were negatively related to children's receptive vocabulary scores, with high shyness ratings related to lower vocabulary. This finding is consistent with other research linking shyness with lower verbal scores (Crozier & Perkins, 2002; Evans, 1993). In multiple studies, Evans (1993, 1996, 2001) has found that shy children display lower verbal skills than their bolder peers. Children who appear shy *and* inattentive may be particularly at risk for academic difficulties; withdrawn/inattentive fourth grade students performed more poorly than disruptive students on seven achievement tests (Finn, Pannozzo, & Voelkl, 1995). This is particularly alarming given the notion that shy children are less likely to be engaged in class (Hughes & Coplan, 2010), receive teacher attention, or make bids for teacher attention (Rudasill, 2011). Interestingly, verbal skill also has been found to be protective for shy children; in one study, more verbally competent, shy children were better able to maintain good social adjustment than their less verbally competent shy peers (Coplan & Armer, 2005).

Adaptability

Adaptability, or how well and how quickly a child adjusts to shifting circumstances or environments (*e.g.*, new rules, changes in activities), has been extensively studied in research on parenting, but less so in terms of school and classroom settings. Yet schools and classrooms demand that children adapt to new situations, and some evidence shows that children's ability to adapt to these demands is associated with their academic performance (Martin & Holbrook, 1985). Indeed, adaptability was positively associated with first grade children's math and reading grades, as well as standardized test scores for math (but not reading), above and beyond the effects of IQ. Martin and Holbrook theorized that the connection to grades may be due to teachers' perceptions of adaptable students as having more potential, given their ease in adjusting to classroom demands.

Similarly, Martin, Nagle and Paget (1983) found that teachers' perceptions of first grade students' adaptability were positively related to the children's observed self-directed and constructive classroom behavior. Not surprisingly, teacher ratings of children's adaptability (as well as other temperament traits such as persistence) were also positively correlated with reading and math grades. However, although Martin and colleagues (Martin & Holbrook, 1985; Martin *et al.*, 1983) cite adaptability as one of the more general temperament traits that can be easily tied to academic performance, empirical work on the specific role of adaptability in children's academic success has been very limited in the last thirty years.

Activity and Distractibility

Formal schooling requires students to sit quietly for long periods of time, to listen carefully, and to follow teacher directions. Children who can exhibit these behaviors often do better in school, and indeed, research shows that such behaviors are directly related to school performance (Alexander, Entwistle, & Dauber, 1993). For children with high activity levels, the demands of schooling may be more difficult to meet. Activity is related to mental and physical impulsivity (Martin, 1989), and has been found to predict academic scores. Martin (1989) and Martin, Olejnik, and Gaddis (1994) found sizable correlations between reading and math scores in elementary school and activity level. Coplan, Barber, and Lagacé-Séguin (1999) reported that children with a lower activity level (along with lower negative emotionality and greater attention span) tended to show better academic performance on tests of early literacy and numeracy skills.

However, some evidence suggests that activity may be a temperament trait that facilitates *better* academic performance. Rudasill, Gallagher, and White (2010a) found that activity (rated at preschool age) was positively related to reading and math performance in third grade, and postulated that perhaps activity in younger ages is indicative of inquisitiveness and excitement, whereas later activity may be a sign of poor regulation. Higher levels of activity have also been linked to more behavior problems in school; indeed, Bramlett, Scott, and Rowell (1999) found that behavior problems related to lower math skills for a preschool sample. Given that test performance is influenced by activity level, it may not be possible to link activity and academic performance, a point also argued by Palisin (1989). The weight of evidence appears to support the conclusion that activity may be a liability for children when it is expressed in school, given the sedentary nature of most classrooms and the demands placed on children to be quiet and still for long periods of time.

Temperament and Social Success

A discussion of temperament in the classroom must include attention to the important role of social interactions and the ways temperament hinders or promotes the positive development of these interactions. Children's social experiences with peers and teachers are critical for their academic success; indeed, children's social and academic worlds are correlated domains where success in one area is likely to promote success in the other (Ladd, Birch, & Buhs, 1999). Because social experiences are so important for academic success, we can examine them as outcomes in and of themselves. In addition, we can (and should) consider social experiences as mechanisms by which children have more positive or more negative academic outcomes. Both of these conceptualizations will be discussed here. We begin, though, with a look at temperament as it predicts children's social experiences in school.

Relationships with Peers

Potential connections between children's temperament and the quality of their social behaviors and peer interactions have been an area of scholarly inquiry. It is not yet clear, however, whether temperament directly contributes to the quality of social behaviors with peers *via* increasing or decreasing exposure to peer interactions (*e.g.*, the extent to which a child is approach-oriented), or whether some temperamental characteristics are simply more supportive of positive peer relationships (*e.g.*, inhibitory control; Sanson, Hemphill, & Smart, 2004). We know that demanding or difficult temperamental characteristics (*i.e.*, those indicative of high reactivity and low regulation), seem to put children at risk for development of more negative social behaviors and, subsequently, poorer peer relationships (Eisenberg, Fabes, Murphy, Maszk, Smith, & Karbon, 1995; Eisenberg, Guthrie, *et al.*, 1997; Walker, Berthelsen, & Irving, 2001). Similarly, temperament traits linked to more aggressive behavior (*e.g.*, low inhibitory control and higher anger and activity), are associated with poorer relationships with peers and less social competence (Gleason, Gower, Hohmann, & Gleason, 2005; Ladd & Burgess, 1999; Sterry *et al.*, 2010; Walker *et al.*, 2001).

On the other hand, children who are more regulated and less reactive (*e.g.*, high inhibitory control and lower anger and activity) tend to have higher quality peer interactions and display more social competence (Corpaci, 2008; Eisenberg & Fabes, 1992; Gleason *et al.*, 2005; Rubin, Burgess, & Hastings, 2002). Indeed, low levels of negative reactivity (*e.g.*, anger) and high levels of positive reactivity (*e.g.*, anticipation of upcoming events), plus higher regulation (*e.g.*, inhibitory control) work together to optimize children's peer relationship quality in contrast to children with less positive reactivity and regulation (Goldsmith, Aksan, Essex, Smider, & Vandell, 2001). Collectively, evidence suggests that lower negative reactivity and higher regulation promote children's positive interactions with peers and build social skills that facilitate children's capacity to make and keep supportive peer relationships.

Relationships with Teachers

The importance of teacher-student relationship quality has been demonstrated by a number of researchers (*e.g.*, Davis, 2003; Hamre & Pianta, 2001; Hughes & Kwok, 2007). Indeed, the quality of the relationship between teachers and students has been shown to have beneficial effects on the children's attitudes towards school, as well as their academic gains (Baker, 1999; Birch & Ladd, 1997; Hughes, Cavell, & Willson, 2001). Positive teacher-child relationships, marked by mutual trust and respect, can be supportive resources for children and adolescents, promoting positive outcomes (Pianta, 1999; Rudasill, Reio, Stipanovic, & Taylor, 2010b; Hughes & Kwok, 2007; Hughes, Luo, & Kwok, 2008), particularly for children at risk for academic difficulties (Hamre & Pianta, 2001).

Alternatively, negative teacher-child relationships, marked by consistent discord or struggle, have serious implications for children's negative outcomes. Such relationships are predicated on characteristics of both teachers and children, and there is growing evidence showing that children's temperament is associated with the quality of these relationships (Rudasill & Rimm-Kaufman, 2009; Rudasill *et al.*, 2006; Rydell, Bohlin, & Thorell, 2005).

Children with temperament traits that are more difficult for caregivers and teachers to manage (*i.e.*, difficult temperament – low levels of regulation and/or high levels of reactivity) often have more difficulty forming positive relationships with teachers. For example, students with more difficult temperaments are more likely to have conflict with teachers in elementary grades (Rudasill, Niehaus, Buhs, & White, 2013a). There is also evidence indicating that shyness, anger, and effortful control predict children's relationships with teachers (*e.g.* Justice *et al.*, 2008; Rudasill *et al.*, 2006; Rudasill & Rimm-Kaufman, 2009; Rydell *et al.*, 2005), with anger associated with more conflict, effortful control predicting less conflict and more closeness, and shyness predicting both lower conflict and lower closeness.

In addition, Rudasill (2011) and Rudasill and Rimm-Kaufman (2009) found that children's temperament was related to their teacher-child relationships *via* teachers' and children's frequency of initiating interactions. That is, children's shyness was predictive of fewer child-initiated interactions with teachers, which then explained why closeness was lower. On the other hand, children's higher effortful control was predictive of fewer child- and teacher-initiated interactions, as well as less conflict and more closeness.

Classroom, School Supports, and Temperament

There is emerging research showing that classroom and school supports, such as positive student-teacher relationships and high quality classroom environments, can be protective for children with temperament traits that make academic and social success more challenging. There also is growing evidence that characteristics of classrooms and schools (such as student-teacher conflict) can exacerbate children's negative temperament traits, thus cultivating suboptimal outcomes because of poor environmental fit. Positive student-teacher relationships are typically conceptualized as being high in closeness and low in conflict and dependency, and negative relationships are viewed as low in closeness and high in conflict and dependency. Closeness is expressed through teachers' perceptions of mutual warmth, positive regard, and respect between teachers and students. Conflict is indicated by perceptions of stress or hostility in interactions between teachers and students. Dependency is marked by teacher perceptions that the child is excessively needy or clingy (Pianta, 2001).

Student-Teacher Relationships

As mentioned above, there is robust empirical support for the notion that positive student-teacher relationships facilitate children's academic and social success (*e.g.*, Hamre & Pianta, 2001; Hughes & Kwok, 2007). Such relationships can be potential points of intervention in helping students with more aversive (*i.e.*, difficult) temperaments adjust to and navigate the school environment (see Arbeau *et al.*, 2010; Griggs *et al.*, 2009). It also seems that poor teacher-child relationships may present an avenue through which children with more aversive temperaments have negative outcomes (Rudasill, Niehaus, Buhs, & White, 2013a; Rudasill *et al.*, 2010b).

For example, Rudasill and colleagues (2013a) examined student-teacher relationships in early elementary grades as mechanisms by which children with early difficult temperament may have more positive interactions with peers in later grades. Contrary to expectations, they did not find that positive student-teacher relationships were protective. Rather, negative student-teacher relationship quality (*i.e.*, conflict) was a mechanism explaining how children with more difficult temperament also had poorer peer interactions in third grade (*i.e.*, more aggression, more relational aggression, more victimization, and less prosocial interaction).

Similarly, Rudasill and others (2010b) observed that early difficult temperament was predictive of risky behavior in sixth grade, and this association was explained in part by higher conflict with teachers in fourth, fifth, and sixth grades. In a recent study, Rudasill, Pössel, Winkeljohn Black, and Neihaus (2013b) noted that student-teacher conflict in fourth through sixth grades emerged as a mechanism by which children's temperament predicted depressive symptoms, such that more emotional reactivity was associated with more conflict with teachers, and conflict with teachers was a predictor of more depressive symptoms.

There is evidence that children with difficult temperament may be buffered from negative outcomes by high quality teacher-child relationships. For example, Griggs, Gagnon, Huelsman, Kidder-Ashley, and Ballard (2009) found, in a sample of preschool children, that those with difficult temperament had better peer play interactions when they had positive teacher-child relationships. Arbeau, Coplan, and Weeks (2010) discerned that positive teacher-child relationship quality was protective for shy first grade children's likelihood of developing anxious or asocial behavior.

With preschool children, Pluess and Belsky (2009) reported that infants with difficult temperaments, compared to infants with easy temperaments, displayed more problem behaviors in kindergarten when they had been in low quality childcare, but displayed fewer problem behaviors when they had been in high quality childcare. In an extension of this work, Belsky and Pluess (2012) followed difficult and easy infants into high school, and concluded that difficult infants who had been exposed to low quality childcare reported more externalizing behavior than those who had easy temperament as infants. This work points to the promise of positive classroom environments as avenues for ameliorating negative outcomes, particularly for students with temperaments predisposing them to academic, social, or behavioral problems.

Teacher support, or the extent to which students feel connected to and supported by a teacher, has been particularly noteworthy as protective for students at risk for negative outcomes. In a large study of children in third through twelfth grades, Demaray and Malecki (2002) found student reports of teacher support were positively related to parent, teacher, and self-ratings of social skills, self-concept, and adaptive skills, and negatively related to problem behavior, and parent-rated externalizing and internalizing behavior. For lower SES students in middle grades (received free/reduced lunch), teacher support was positively associated with reading, language, and science grades, whereas the associations did not remain for students of higher socio-economic status (SES) (Malecki & Demaray, 2006).

For middle grade students identified as at-risk due to poverty, minority status, and poor achievement on standardized tests, teacher support was related to less negative attitudes towards teachers and school (Demaray & Malecki, 2002). Teachers' emotional support was particularly important in predicting 5th – 8th grade students' social skills and academic competence (Malecki & Demaray, 2003), and was related to lower levels of depressive symptoms in sixth grade (Rudasill *et al.*, 2013b). There is scant work testing students' perceptions of teacher support as protective for students with more aversive temperaments, but research showing that teacher support is protective for students at risk for other reasons, such as poverty, suggests this is likely.

Classroom Quality

Mounting evidence links three broad components of teacher behavior (instructional, organizational, and socio-emotional) to students' academic and psychosocial adjustment. Instructional behavior is used during the delivery of instruction, with the intention of promoting concept or skill development and critical thinking (Croninger & Valli, 2009; Pianta, LaParo, & Hamre, 2008). Organizational behavior refers to structures established by the teacher to facilitate smooth transitions between activities, minimize disruptions, and efficiently use class time (Connor *et al.*, 2009; Pianta *et al.*, 2008). Teachers' socio-emotional behavior is marked by warmth and responsiveness in interactions between students and teachers, and encourages students' feelings of belonging and acceptance in the classroom (Connor *et al.*, 2009; Pianta *et al.*, 2008).

Teaching behavior that is instructionally supportive (*e.g.*, provides opportunities for students to respond, to choose, or to receive positive feedback) promotes academic achievement (Curby, Rudasill, Edwards, & Perez-Edgar, 2011; Hamre & Pianta, 2005). Organizational strategies designed to increase students' time on task and decrease disruptions have been linked to increased student engagement (Rimm-Kaufman *et al.*, 2010) and more productive use of available instructional time across the school year (Cameron, Connor, & Morrison, 2005).

Both instructional and organizational teaching behaviors promote academic achievement which, in turn, has been associated with less negative affect, but unassociated with positive affect (for a review see Soar & Soar, 1987). In addition, there is growing evidence showing that socio-emotional teaching behavior is positively linked to better academic performance (*e.g.*, Hamre & Pianta, 2005; Rudasill, Gallagher, & White, 2010a), a variety of psychosocial variables (*e.g.*, more positive student-teacher relationships; Thijs, Koomen, & van der Leij, 2008), and mental health outcomes such as lower levels of anxiety and depression (Perry, Donohue, & Weinstein, 2007).

Emerging research suggests that high quality classrooms, particularly those that are socio-emotionally or instructionally supportive, are protective for outcomes of students who have high levels of temperament traits that make adjustment to school more difficult. For example, Curby and colleagues (2011) found that emotional and instructional support in first grade were protective when reviewing teacher ratings of academic skills for children with difficult temperament in infancy, and that instructional support was also protective for teacher-child relationship quality in first grade. With the same dataset, Hamre and Pianta (2005) and Rudasill and others (2010a) reported that more emotional support in first and third grades, respectively, was protective for academic outcomes for students with low attention in preschool. Similarly, Gazelle (2006) examined the protective effects of a positive emotional climate in first grade for children with a history of anxious solitude (socially withdrawn or shy behavior). Results indicated that anxious solitary children were less likely to be excluded by peers and more likely to be accepted by peers when in first grade classrooms with a positive emotional climate.

Teacher Temperament

Teacher temperament may contribute to the *goodness-of-fit* between a child and his or her environment. Lerner and Lerner (1994) examined how child temperament and teacher expectations interacted, and called for even more research in this area, which has been echoed by others (Coplan, Hughes, Bosacki, & Rose-Krasnor, 2011; Keogh, 2003). Indeed, there is very little recent research on how teacher temperament or personality contributes to student outcomes. In one of the rare studies of teacher temperament as a predictive variable, Coplan, Hughes, Bosacki and Rose-Krasnor (2011) found that teacher temperament may affect teacher assessment of students' intellectual capabilities. Specifically, shy teachers were more likely to rate shy children as equally intelligent as non-shy children, whereas non-shy teachers were more likely to rate shy children as having lower intelligence than non-shy children.

Some studies in the area of communication research have focused on temperament, or personality, of the instructor and his or her communication behaviors (McCroskey, Valencic, & Richmond, 2004). With a college sample, Osbourne (1985) found that teacher self-reports of temperament had significant correlations with their behaviors towards students, including the tendency to make irrelevant comments, instructional choices, and provide feedback. Students appear to be attuned to, and impacted by, these potentially temperament-based behaviors.

Intervention Approaches: Strategies for Teachers and Parents

The sheer number of publications is evidence that much is known about temperament. As is often the case, however, our understanding of temperament from the theoretical and research perspective is much stronger than our knowledge of how to respond to temperamental differences in children that impact classroom learning. Raver, Jones, Li-Grining and Zhai (2009) noted that "children who are persistently emotionally dysregulated and behaviorally disruptive have been found to receive less instruction from teachers and to have fewer opportunities for learning from peers" (p. 2). Others have argued that children at the other end of the continuum who are highly regulated and emotionally reactive to the environment, such as children who are anxious and restrained, may also not be fully engaged in classroom learning opportunities (Rothbart & Jones, 1998). Thus it is critical that we identify temperament-based and temperament-focused interventions for facilitating children's positive outcomes.

Child Focused Interventions

Enabling children to attend to task demands, inhibit incorrect responses and distractions, and complete tasks more quickly, termed *cognitive control* by Kray and Ferdinand (2013), are all critical skills important for classroom learning. Kay and Ferdinand (2013) identified two intervention approaches that have shown promising results for enhancing cognitive control skills in young children. The first is the use of verbal labels. Kray, Kipp and Karbach (2009) found that children's use of a verbal label helped them to remember task rules of when to respond ("yes") and when not to respond ("no"), and the use of verbal labels enabled them to respond faster and more accurately when task rules changed across trials. Zirkham, Cruess and Diamond (2003) reported that 3 and 4 year old children were able to use verbal labels to help them focus their attention when the dimension needed to sort cards changed from one trial to the next. The results of both studies provide evidence that attentional skills needed for problem solving can be enhanced if children are given specific strategies, such as using verbal labels.

The other strategy for enhancing children's cognitive control is the use of training programs (Kray & Ferdinand, 2013). For example, Dowsett and Livesey (1999) included 3 and 4 year-old children in a study of inhibitory control skills. Children were either exposed to additional practice on an inhibition task (go-no go) with which they had prior experience, or were trained on two different but related tasks: a card sorting task and a stop signal task. Children in both the practices and training conditions improved their inhibitory responses, but the training group outperformed the practice group. The authors concluded that training provided the children with experiences related to "representational flexibility, the ability to maintain information in working memory, the selective control of attention, and proficiency at error correction" (p. 161), are all important skills for cognitive control.

Teacher Focused Interventions

The most frequent approaches to teacher interventions focusing on children's temperament and classroom management involve professional development provided to in-service teachers. Professional development can be provided as one-day workshops or workshops distributed over longer periods of time. However, workshops that include ongoing coaching may be more effective in supporting teachers' implementation of their training in the classroom.

Alkon, Ramler, and MacLennan (2003) described a mental health consultation model designed to create a partnership between the mental health consultant and teachers to increase teacher efficacy in understanding and management of children's social and emotional skills, and teacher's competence related to implementing mental health activities. After a year of consultation services, positive changes were found in measures of teachers' efficacy and competence. Interestingly, comments from focus groups with teachers obtained after the intervention reflected more interest in and empathy for children's difficult behaviors. Teachers had more "overt recognition that (difficult behavior) had meaning, and it taught them something about the life experience of the child" (p. 97).

Raver, Jones, Li-Grining and Zhai (2009) described components of the Chicago School Readiness project focusing on children's emotional and behavioral adjustment. Teachers in Head Start programs were involved in four intervention components: training in strategies for behavior management, weekly mental health consultation to support teachers in implementing classroom strategies, stress reduction workshops designed to reduce teacher burnout, and clinical services provided to children with the most challenging behaviors. Differences between teachers in the treatment group compared to control teachers were found on measures of increased emotional and behavioral supports in classrooms obtained from the Classroom Assessment Scoring System (La Paro, Pianta and Stuhlman, 2004) and teacher ratings of children's behavior reflected fewer problem behaviors in the treatment classrooms. The authors recommended that multi-day professional development training should be followed by on-site, weekly coaching supports.

Temperament-Based Interventions

In general, interventions involving teachers, parents and children as partners in the education process tend to be very successful. An example of such an intervention is *INSIGHTS* into Children's Temperament (*INSIGHTS*), which is designed as a social-emotional skills program for early elementary grades (McClowry & Collins, 2010). *INSIGHTS* has three phases: Phase 1 involves training teachers and parents on how to "recognize, reframe and respond" (p. 612) to temperamental differences of children; Phase 2 trains behavior management strategies; and Phase 3 focuses on strategies to enable children to develop self-regulation. The teachers and parents participate in workshops across 10 weekly sessions, while the children are involved in classroom activities in which trainers use puppets with different temperaments to teach children about problem solving strategies.

These problem solving strategies involve three steps: "Stop: recognize a dilemma; Caution: think and plan; Go try it out." (p. 612). McClowry and Collins (2010) reported results from two studies. The first study involved elementary grade children and found positive results in reducing behavior problems at home and in the classroom, as well as in increasing teacher feelings of efficacy in handling behavior problems. Results on parents' feeling of efficacy were not reported. A second study involved a variation on the *INSIGHTS* in which two groups of parents and teachers were created. Parents and teachers in the "collaborative" group jointly participated in half of the 10 workshops and had a separate session for the other half of the session. Parents and teachers in the "parallel" group were engaged in separate workshops.

Children's behavior problems were found to decrease in both groups, but the greatest reductions were found for the collaborative group. Differences were also reported for children with high maintenance temperaments, or those that are high in reactivity and low in regulation (McCormick *et al.*, 2015). In addition, children in INSIGHTS classrooms had higher math and reading scores, and better critical thinking skills (O'Connor *et al.*, 2014). Together these results offer encouraging information on the use of an intervention for that might be effective for all types of temperament in a classroom, rather than specifically targeting a single temperament.

Resource	http://steinhardt.nyu.edu/insights

In contrast, Cool Little Kids, developed by Rapee and his colleagues (*e.g.*, Rapee, Lyneham, Schniering, Wuthrich, Abbott, Hudson, & Wignall, 2006) targets anxiety in preschool children with inhibited temperaments. Parents are involved in a series of six group therapy sessions targeting parenting skills, the nature and management of anxiety, and "graded" exposures to feared events or situations. The first study (Rapee, Kennedy, Ingram, Edwards & Sweeney, 2005) found that intervention sessions with parents targeting parental overprotectiveness when children were four years old resulted in fewer anxiety disorders assessed when the children were five and seven years old compared to children whose parents were in the control group.

A follow up study (Kennedy, Rapee & Edwards, 2009) reported positive outcomes for both anxious parents and their anxious, inhibited children six months after participation in a version of Cool Little Kids that involved 8 intervention sessions. Rapee and colleagues argued that screening preschool children who are temperamentally inhibited and addressing the needs of those young children with internalizing problems through parenting intervention can be economically effective in reducing anxiety disorders in early childhood.

Resource	http://www.centreforemotionalhealth.com.au/pages/cool-little-kids-program.aspx

CONCLUSIONS

In conclusion, the research suggests several important points regarding temperament in school. First, children's temperament contributes to their behavior in school, particularly the expression of internalizing and externalizing behavior. Second, temperament is clearly implicated in children's academic performance, with the strongest ties from regulatory temperament traits, but significant contributions from some reactive traits too, such as shyness and adaptability. Third, there is ample evidence that children's temperament plays a role in their social relationships, such that more regulation and less reactivity are typically associated with higher quality relationships with peers and teachers.

Emerging research suggests that classroom characteristics may be protective for outcomes of children at risk for difficulties in school due to having more aversive temperaments. Specifically, positive student-teacher relationships and high quality classrooms can buffer students from negative social and academic outcomes, indicating that teachers' behaviors and perceptions of children may be a point of intervention to promote success for children with temperaments that make school more challenging.

There are several promising interventions using focused instruction so that children or teachers or both learn skills that improve the goodness-of-fit between children's temperament and the classroom environment. To start, though, it is critical that teachers and other school personnel understand temperament and its role in children's school success so that they can more readily recognize and meet children's temperament-based needs.

CONFLICT OF INTEREST

The authors confirm that they have no conflict of interest to declare for this publication.

ACKNOWLEDGEMENTS

Declared none.

REFERENCES

Ahadi, S.A., Rothbart, M.K., Ye, R.M. (1993). Children's temperament in the U.S. and China: Similarities and differences. *Eur. J. Pers., 7*, 359-377.
[http://dx.doi.org/10.1002/per.2410070506]

Alexander, K.L., Entwisle, D.R., Dauber, S.L. (1993). First-grade classroom behavior: its short- and long-term consequences for school performance. *Child Dev., 64*(3), 801-814.
[http://dx.doi.org/10.2307/1131219] [PMID: 8339696]

Arbeau, K.A., Coplan, R.J., Weeks, M. (2010). Shyness, teacher-child relationships, and socio-emotional adjustment in grade 1. *Int. J. Behav. Dev., 34*, 259-269.
[http://dx.doi.org/10.1177/0165025409350959]

Bacchini, D., Affuso, G., Trotta, T. (2008). Temperament, ADHD and peer relations among schoolchildren: the mediating role of school bullying. *Aggress. Behav., 34*(5), 447-459.
[http://dx.doi.org/10.1002/ab.20271] [PMID: 18512705]

Bayer, J.K., Rapee, R.M., Hiscock, H., Ukoumunne, O.C., Mihalopoulos, C., Clifford, S., Wake, M. (2011). The Cool Little Kids randomised controlled trial: population-level early prevention for anxiety disorders. *BMC Public Health, 11*, 11.
[http://dx.doi.org/10.1186/1471-2458-11-11] [PMID: 21208451]

Belsky, J. (1997). Variation in susceptibility to environmental influence: An evolutionary argument. *Psychol. Inq., 8*(3), 182-186.
[http://dx.doi.org/10.1207/s15327965pli0803_3]

Belsky, J. (2007). For better and for worse differential susceptibility to environmental influences. *Curr. Dir. Psychol. Sci., 16*(6), 300-304.
[http://dx.doi.org/10.1111/j.1467-8721.2007.00525.x]

Belsky, J., Pluess, M. (2012). Differential susceptibility to long-term effects of quality of child care on externalizing behavior in adolescence. *Int. J. Behav. Dev., 36*, 2-10.
[http://dx.doi.org/10.1177/0165025411406855]

Blair, C., Razza, R.P. (2007). Relating effortful control, executive function, and false belief understanding to emerging math and literacy ability in kindergarten. *Child Dev., 78*(2), 647-663.
[http://dx.doi.org/10.1111/j.1467-8624.2007.01019.x] [PMID: 17381795]

Bohlin, G., Hagekull, B. (2009). Socio-emotional development: from infancy to young adulthood. *Scand. J. Psychol., 50*(6), 592-601.
[http://dx.doi.org/10.1111/j.1467-9450.2009.00787.x] [PMID: 19930258]

Bowman, P.H., Mathews, C.V. (1960). *Motivations of Youth for Leaving School, US Department of Health, Education and Welfare, Office of Education, Cooperative Research Program Project 200.*. Quincy: Quincy Youth Development Project.

Bramlett, R.K., Rowell, R.K., Mandenberg, K. (2000). Predicting first grade achievement from kindergarten screening measures: A comparison of child and family predictors. *Res. Schools, 7*, 1-9.

Bramlett, R.K., Scott, P., Rowell, R.K. (1999). A comparison of temperament and social skills in predicting academic performance in first graders. *Spec. Serv. Schools, 16*(1-2), 147-158.
[http://dx.doi.org/10.1300/J008v16n01_10]

Bronfenbrenner, U., Morris, P.A. (2006). The bioecological model of human development. In: Damon, W., Lerner, R.M., (Eds.), *Theoretical models of human development.* (6th ed., Vol. 1, pp. 793-828). New York:

John Wiley.Handbook of child psychology

Buss, A.H., Plomin, R. (1975). *A temperament theory of personality development.*. New York: Wiley.

Cameron, C.E., Connor, C.M., Morrison, F.J. (2005). Effects of variation in teacher organization on classroom functioning. *J. Sch. Psychol., 43*, 61-85.
[http://dx.doi.org/10.1016/j.jsp.2004.12.002]

Carey, W.B., Fox, M., McDevitt, S.C. (1977). Temperament as a factor in early school adjustment. *Pediatrics, 60*(4 Pt 2), 621-624.
[PMID: 263276]

Caspi, A., Silva, P.A. (1995). Temperamental qualities at age three predict personality traits in young adulthood: longitudinal evidence from a birth cohort. *Child Dev., 66*(2), 486-498.
[http://dx.doi.org/10.2307/1131592] [PMID: 7750379]

Caspi, A., Harrington, H., Milne, B., Amell, J.W., Theodore, R.F., Moffitt, T.E. (2003). Children's behavioral styles at age 3 are linked to their adult personality traits at age 26. *J. Pers., 71*(4), 495-513.
[http://dx.doi.org/10.1111/1467-6494.7104001] [PMID: 12901429]

Cloninger, C.R., Zohar, A.H. (2011). Personality and the perception of health and happiness. *J. Affect. Disord., 128*(1-2), 24-32.
[http://dx.doi.org/10.1016/j.jad.2010.06.012] [PMID: 20580435]

Coie, J. (2004). The impact of negative social experiences on the development of antisocial behavior. In: Kupersmidt, J.B., Dodge, K.A., (Eds.), *Children's peer relations: From development to intervention.*. Washington, DC: American Psychological Association.
[http://dx.doi.org/10.1037/10653-013]

Connor, C.M., Morrison, F.J., Fishman, B.J., Ponitz, C.C., Glasney, S., Underwood, P.S., Piasta, S.B., Crowe, E.C., Schatschneider, C. (2009). The ISI Classroom Observation System: Examining the literacy instruction provided to individual students. *Educ. Res., 38*, 85-99.
[http://dx.doi.org/10.3102/0013189X09332373]

Coplan, R.J., Armer, M. (2005). Talking yourself out of being shy: Shyness, expressive vocabulary, and socioemotional adjustment in preschool. *Merrill-Palmer Q., 51*, 20-41.
[http://dx.doi.org/10.1353/mpq.2005.0004]

Coplan, R.J., Barber, A.M., Lagacé-Séguin, D.G. (1999). The role of child temperament as a predictor of early literacy and numeracy skills in preschoolers. *Early Child. Res. Q., 14*, 537-553.
[http://dx.doi.org/10.1016/S0885-2006(99)00025-3]

Coplan, R.J., Prakash, K. (2003). Spending time with teacher: Characteristics of preschoolers who frequently elicit *versus* initiate interactions with teachers. *Early Child. Res. Q., 18*, 143-158.
[http://dx.doi.org/10.1016/S0885-2006(03)00009-7]

Coplan, R.J., Hughes, K., Rose-Krasnor, L., Bosacki, S. (2011). Is silence golden? Elementary school teachers' strategies and beliefs towards hypothetical shy-quiet and talkative-exuberant children. *Journal of Educational Psychology, 103*(4), 939-951.

Corpaci, F. (2008). The role of child temperament on Head Start preschoolers' social competence in the context of cumulative risk. *J. Appl. Dev. Psychol., 29*, 1-16.
[http://dx.doi.org/10.1016/j.appdev.2007.10.003]

Credé, M., Kuncel, N.R. (2008). Study habits, skills, and attitudes: The third pillar supporting collegiate academic performance. *Perspect. Psychol. Sci., 3*(6), 425-453.
[http://dx.doi.org/10.1111/j.1745-6924.2008.00089.x] [PMID: 26158971]

Croninger, R.G., Valli, L. (2009). "Where is the action?" Challenges to studying the teaching of reading in elementary classrooms. *Educ. Res., 38*, 100-108.
[http://dx.doi.org/10.3102/0013189X09333206]

Crozier, W.R., Badawood, A. (2009). Shyness, vocabulary and children's reticence in Saudi Arabian preschools. *Infant Child Dev., 18*, 255-270.
[http://dx.doi.org/10.1002/icd.623]

Crozier, W. R., Perkins, P. (2002). Shyness as a factor when assessing children. *Educational psychology in practice: Theory, research and practice in educational psychology., 18*, 239-244.

Curby, T.W., Rudasill, K.M., Edwards, T., Perez-Edgar, K. (2011). The role of classroom quality in ameliorating the academic and social risks associated with difficult temperament. *Sch. Psychol. Q., 26*, 175-188.
[http://dx.doi.org/10.1037/a0023042]

Davis, H.A. (2003). Conceptualizing the role and influence of student-teacher relationships on children's social and cognitive development. *Educ. Psychol., 38*, 207-234.
[http://dx.doi.org/10.1207/S15326985EP3804_2]

Demaray, M., Malecki, C. (2002). Critical levels of perceived social support associated with student adjustment. *Sch. Psychol. Q., 17*(3), 213-241.
[http://dx.doi.org/10.1521/scpq.17.3.213.20883]

Degnan, K.A., Almas, A.N., Fox, N.A. (2010). Temperament and the environment in the etiology of childhood anxiety. *J. Child Psychol. Psychiatry, 51*(4), 497-517.
[http://dx.doi.org/10.1111/j.1469-7610.2010.02228.x] [PMID: 20158575]

Dowsett, S.M., Livesey, D.J. (2000). The development of inhibitory control in preschool children: effects of "executive skills" training. *Dev. Psychobiol., 36*(2), 161-174.
[http://dx.doi.org/10.1002/(SICI)1098-2302(200003)36:2<161::AID-DEV7>3.0.CO;2-0] [PMID: 10689286]

Drogosz, L. M., Lévy, P. E. (1996). Another look at the effects of appearance, gender, and job type on performance-based decisions. *Psychology of Women Quarterly, 20*, 437-445.

Duckworth, A.L., Allred, K.M. (2012). Temperament in the classroom. In: Shiner, R.L., Zentner, M., (Eds.),

Handbook of Temperament. (pp. 627-644). New York, NY: Guilford Press.

Duncan, G.J., Dowsett, C.J., Claessens, A., Magnuson, K., Huston, A.C., Klebanov, P., Pagani, L.S., Feinstein, L., Engel, M., Brooks-Gunn, J., Sexton, H., Duckworth, K., Japel, C. (2007). School readiness and later achievement. *Dev. Psychol., 43*(6), 1428-1446.
[http://dx.doi.org/10.1037/0012-1649.43.6.1428] [PMID: 18020822]

Eisenberg, N., Fabes, R.A. (1992). Emotion, regulation, and the development of social competence. In: Clark, M., (Ed.), *Emotion and social behavior.* (Vol. 14, pp. 119-150). Newbury Park, CA: Sage.Review of personality and social psychology

Eisenberg, N., Fabes, R.A., Murphy, B., Maszk, P., Smith, M., Karbon, M. (1995). The role of emotionality and regulation in children's social functioning: a longitudinal study. *Child Dev., 66*(5), 1360-1384.
[http://dx.doi.org/10.2307/1131652] [PMID: 7555221]

Eisenberg, N., Fabes, R.A., Nyman, M., Bernzweig, J., Pinuelas, A. (1994). The relations of emotionality and regulation to children's anger-related reactions. *Child Dev., 65*(1), 109-128.
[http://dx.doi.org/10.2307/1131369] [PMID: 8131642]

Eisenberg, N., Spinrad, T.L. (2004). Emotion-related regulation: sharpening the definition. *Child Dev., 75*(2), 334-339.
[http://dx.doi.org/10.1111/j.1467-8624.2004.00674.x] [PMID: 15056187]

Eisenberg, N., Guthrie, I.K., Fabes, R.A., Reiser, M., Murphy, B.C., Holgren, R., Maszk, P., Losoya, S. (1997). The relations of regulation and emotionality to resiliency and competent social functioning in elementary school children. *Child Dev., 68*(2), 295-311.
[http://dx.doi.org/10.2307/1131851] [PMID: 9180003]

Evans, M.A. (1992). Control and paradox in teacher conversations with shy children. *Can. J. Behav. Sci., 24*, 502-516.
[http://dx.doi.org/10.1037/h0078758]

Evans, M.A. (1993). Communicative competence as a dimension of shyness. In: Rubin, K.H., Asendorpf, J.B., (Eds.), *Social withdrawal, inhibition, and shyness in children.* (pp. 189-212). Hillsdale, NJ: Erlbaum.

Evans, M.A. (1996). Reticent primary grade children and their more talkative peers: Verbal, nonverbal, and self-concept characteristics. *J. Educ. Psychol., 88*, 739-749.
[http://dx.doi.org/10.1037/0022-0663.88.4.739]

Evans, M.A. (2001). Shyness in the classroom and home. In: Crozier, W.R., Alden, L.E., (Eds.), *International handbook of social anxiety: Concepts, research and interventions relating to the self and shyness.* (pp. 159-183). Westport, CT: Wiley.

Evans, M.A. (2010). Language performance, academic performance, and signs of shyness: A comprehensive review. In: Rubin, K.H., Coplan, R.J., (Eds.), *The development of shyness and social withdrawal in childhood and adolescence..* New York: Guilford Press.

Finn, J.D., Pannozzo, G.M., Voelkl, K.E. (1995). Disruptive and inattentive-withdrawn behavior and achievement among fourth graders. *Elem. Sch. J., 95*, 421-434.
[http://dx.doi.org/10.1086/461853]

Fox, N.A., Calkins, S.D. (2003). The development of self-control of emotion: Intrinsic and extrinsic influences. *Motiv. Emot., 27*(1), 7-26.
[http://dx.doi.org/10.1023/A:1023622324898]

Fullard, W., Simeonsson, R., Huntington, G. (1989). Sociocultural factors and temperament. In: Kohnstamm, G.A., Bates, J.E., Rothbart, M.K., (Eds.), *Temperament in childhood.* (pp. 523-536). Chichester: Wiley.

Gartstein, M.A., Slobodskaya, H.R., Putnam, S.P., Kinsht, I.A. (2009). A cross-cultural study of infant temperament: Predicting preschool effortful control in the United States of America and Russia. *Eur. J. Dev. Psychol., 6*(3), 337-364.
[http://dx.doi.org/10.1080/17405620701203846]

Gartstein, M.A., Slobodskaya, H.R., Zylicz, P.O., Gosztyla, D., Nakagawa, A. (2010). A cross-cultural evaluation of temperament: Japan, USA, Poland and Russia. *Int. J. Psychol. Psychol. Ther., 10*(1), 55-75.

Gazelle, H. (2006). Class climate moderates peer relations and emotional adjustment in children with an early history of anxious solitude: a Child X Environment model. *Dev. Psychol., 42*(6), 1179-1192.
[http://dx.doi.org/10.1037/0012-1649.42.6.1179] [PMID: 17087551]

Gleason, T.R., Gower, A.L., Hohmann, L.M., Gleason, T.C. (2005). Temperament and friendship in preschool-aged children. *Int. J. Behav. Dev., 29*(4), 336-344.
[http://dx.doi.org/10.1177/01650250544000116]

Goldsmith, H.H., Aksan, N., Essex, M., Smider, N.A., Vandell, D.L. (2001). *Temperament and socioemotional adjustment to kindergarten: A multi-informant perspective. Temperament in context.* (pp. 103-138). Mahwah, NJ: Erlbaum.

Gough, H.G. (1964). Academic achievement in high school as predicted from the California Psychological Inventory. *J. Educ. Psychol., 55*(3), 174.
[http://dx.doi.org/10.1037/h0046186]

Griggs, M.S., Gagnon, S.G., Huelsman, T.J., Kidder-Ashley, P., Ballard, M. (2009). Student-teacher relationships matter: Moderating influences between temperament and preschool social competence. *Psychol. Sch., 46*, 553-567.
[http://dx.doi.org/10.1002/pits.20397]

Guerin, D.W., Gottfried, A.W., Oliver, P.H., Thomas, C.W. (2003). *Temperament: Infancy through adolescence..* New York: Kluwer Academic/Plenum.
[http://dx.doi.org/10.1007/978-1-4615-0175-6]

Hamre, B.K., Pianta, R.C. (2001). Early teacher-child relationships and the trajectory of children's school outcomes through eighth grade. *Child Dev., 72*(2), 625-638.

[http://dx.doi.org/10.1111/1467-8624.00301] [PMID: 11333089]

Hamre, B.K., Pianta, R.C. (2005). Can instructional and emotional support in the first-grade classroom make a difference for children at risk of school failure? *Child Dev., 76*(5), 949-967.
[http://dx.doi.org/10.1111/j.1467-8624.2005.00889.x] [PMID: 16149994]

Hathaway, S.R., Reynolds, P.C., Monachesi, E.D. (1969). Follow-up of the later careers and lives of 1,000 boys who dropped out of high school. *J. Consult. Clin. Psychol., 33*(3), 370-380.
[http://dx.doi.org/10.1037/h0027613] [PMID: 4389336]

Holder, M.D., Coleman, B. (2009). The contribution of social relationships to children's happiness. *J Happiness Stud., 10*(3), 329-349.
[http://dx.doi.org/10.1007/s10902-007-9083-0]

Holder, M.D., Klassen, A. (2010). Temperament and happiness in children. *J Happiness Stud., 11*, 419-439.
[http://dx.doi.org/10.1007/s10902-009-9149-2]

Hughes, J., Kwok, O.M. (2007). Influence of student-teacher and parent-teacher relationships on lower-achieving readers' engagement and achievement in the primary grades. *J. Educ. Psychol., 99*(1), 39-51.
[http://dx.doi.org/10.1037/0022-0663.99.1.39] [PMID: 18084625]

Hughes, J.N., Luo, W., Kwok, O.M., Loyd, L.K. (2008). Teacher-student support, effortful engagement, and achievement: A 3-year longitudinal study. *J. Educ. Psychol., 100*(1), 1-14.
[http://dx.doi.org/10.1037/0022-0663.100.1.1] [PMID: 19578558]

Hughes, K., Coplan, R.J. (2010). Exploring processes linking shyness and academic achievement in childhood. *Sch. Psychol. Q., 25*(4), 213-222.
[http://dx.doi.org/10.1037/a0022070]

Hymel, S., Closson, L.M., Caravita, C.S., Vaillancourt, T. (2011). Social status among peers: From sociometric attraction to peer acceptance to perceived popularity. In: Smith, P.K., Hart, C.H., (Eds.), *Wiley-Blackwell handbook of childhood social development.* (2nd ed.). New York: Wiley.
[http://dx.doi.org/10.1002/9781444390933.ch20]

Jensen, A.R. (1980). *Bias in mental testing.*. New York: Free Press.

Joyce, P.R., McKenzie, J.M., Luty, S.E., Mulder, R.T., Carter, J.D., Sullivan, P.F., Cloninger, C.R. (2003). Temperament, childhood environment and psychopathology as risk factors for avoidant and borderline personality disorders. *Aust. N. Z. J. Psychiatry, 37*(6), 756-764.
[PMID: 14636393]

Justice, L.M., Cottone, E.A., Mashburn, A., Rimm-Kaufman, S.E. (2008). Relationships between teachers and preschoolers who are at risk: Contribution of children's language skills, temperamentally based attributes, and gender. *Early Educ. Dev., 19*, 600-621.
[http://dx.doi.org/10.1080/10409280802231021]

Kagan, J., Reznick, J.S., Snidman, N., Gibbons, J., Johnson, M.O. (1988). Childhood derivatives of inhibition

and lack of inhibition to the unfamiliar. *Child Dev., 59*(6), 1580-1589.
[http://dx.doi.org/10.2307/1130672] [PMID: 3208569]

Kagan, J., Snidman, N., Zentner, M., Peterson, E. (1999). Infant temperament and anxious symptoms in school age children. *Dev. Psychopathol., 11*(2), 209-224.
[http://dx.doi.org/10.1017/S0954579499002023] [PMID: 16506531]

Kagan, J., Snidman, N., Kahn, V., Towsley, S. (2007). The preservation of two infant temperaments into adolescence. *Monogr. Soc. Res. Child Dev., 72*(2), 1-75.
[PMID: 17661895]

Kennedy, A.E., Rubin, K.H., Hastings, P.D., Maisel, B. (2004). Longitudinal relations between child vagal tone and parenting behavior: 2 to 4 years. *Dev. Psychobiol., 45*(1), 10-21.
[http://dx.doi.org/10.1002/dev.20013] [PMID: 15229872]

Kennedy, S.J., Rapee, R.M., Edwards, S.L. (2009). A selective intervention program for inhibited preschool-aged children of parents with an anxiety disorder: effects on current anxiety disorders and temperament. *J. Am. Acad. Child Adolesc. Psychiatry, 48*(6), 602-609.
[http://dx.doi.org/10.1097/CHI.0b013e31819f6fa9] [PMID: 19454916]

Keogh, B.K. (1994). Temperament and teachers' views of teachability. In: Carey, W.B., McDeveitt, S.C., (Eds.), *Prevention and early intervention: Individual differences as risk factors for the mental health of children.* (pp. 246-254). New York: Brunner/Mazel.

Keogh, B.K. (2003). *Temperament in the classroom: Understanding individual differences.*. Baltimore, MD, US: Paul H Brookes Publishing.

Kirkham, N.Z., Cruess, L., Diamond, A. (2003). Helping children apply their knowledge to their behavior on a dimension-switching task. *Dev. Sci., 6*, 449-476.
[http://dx.doi.org/10.1111/1467-7687.00300]

Klein, H., Ballantine, J. (1991). Children's temperament: Patterns across cultures. *J. Res. Child. Educ., 6*(1), 47-53.
[http://dx.doi.org/10.1080/02568549109594821]

Kochanska, G., Murray, K.T., Harlan, E.T. (2000). Effortful control in early childhood: continuity and change, antecedents, and implications for social development. *Dev. Psychol., 36*(2), 220-232.
[http://dx.doi.org/10.1037/0012-1649.36.2.220] [PMID: 10749079]

Ladd, G.W., Birch, S.H., Buhs, E.S. (1999). Children's social and scholastic lives in kindergarten: related spheres of influence? *Child Dev., 70*(6), 1373-1400.
[http://dx.doi.org/10.1111/1467-8624.00101] [PMID: 10621962]

Ladd, G.W., Burgess, K.B. (1999). Charting the relationship trajectories of aggressive, withdrawn, and aggressive/withdrawn children during early grade school. *Child Dev., 70*(4), 910-929.
[http://dx.doi.org/10.1111/1467-8624.00066] [PMID: 10446726]

Lee, C.L., Bates, J.E. (1985). Mother-child interaction at age two years and perceived difficult temperament. *Child Dev., 56*(5), 1314-1325.
[http://dx.doi.org/10.2307/1130246] [PMID: 4053745]

Lengua, L.J., Kovacs, E.A. (2005). Bidirectional associations between temperament and parenting and the prediction of adjustment problems in middle childhood. *Journal of Applied Developmental Psychology: An International Lifespan Journal, 26*(1), 21-38.
[http://dx.doi.org/10.1016/j.appdev.2004.10.001]

Leve, L.D., Kim, H.K., Pears, K.C. (2005). Childhood temperament and family environment as predictors of internalizing and externalizing trajectories from ages 5 to 17. *J. Abnorm. Child Psychol., 33*(5), 505-520.
[http://dx.doi.org/10.1007/s10802-005-6734-7] [PMID: 16195947]

Malecki, C., Demaray, M.K. (2003). Carrying a weapon to school and perceptions of social support in an urban middle school. *J. Emot. Behav. Disord., 11*, 169-178.
[http://dx.doi.org/10.1177/10634266030110030401]

Malecki, C.K., Demaray, M.K. (2003). What Type of Support Do They Need? Investigating Student Adjustment as Related to Emotional, Informational, Appraisal, and Instrumental Support. *Sch. Psychol. Q., 18*(3), 231-252.
[http://dx.doi.org/10.1521/scpq.18.3.231.22576]

Malecki, C.K., Demaray, M.K. (2006). Social support as a buffer in the relationship between socioeconomic status and academic performance. *Sch. Psychol. Q., 21*(4), 375-395.
[http://dx.doi.org/10.1037/h0084129]

Martin, R.P. (1989). Activity level, distractibility, and persistence: Critical characteristics in early schooling. In: Kohnstamm, G.A., Bates, J.E., Rothbart, M.K., (Eds.), *Temperament in childhood.* (pp. 451-461). Oxford, England: Wiley.

Martin, R.P. (1994). Child temperament and common problems in schooling: Hypotheses about causal connections. *J. Sch. Psychol., 32*(2), 119-134.
[http://dx.doi.org/10.1016/0022-4405(94)90006-X]

Martin, R.P., Holbrook, J. (1985). Relationship of temperament characteristics to the academic achievement of first-grade children. *J. Psychoed. Assess., 3*, 131-140.
[http://dx.doi.org/10.1177/073428298500300204]

Martin, R.P., Nagle, R., Paget, K. (1983). Relationships between temperament and classroom behavior, teacher attitudes, and academic achievement. *J. Psychoed. Assess., 1*, 377-386.
[http://dx.doi.org/10.1177/073428298300100407]

Martin, R.P., Olejnik, S., Gaddis, I. (1994). Modelling effects of temperament and scholastic ability on academic achievement. In: Carey, W., McDevitt, S., (Eds.), *Prevention and Early intervention: Individual differences as risk factors for mental health of children.* (pp. 59-68). New York: Bruner/Mazel.

Matheny, A.P., Jr (1989). Children's behavioral inhibition over age and across situations: genetic similarity for a trait during change. *J. Pers., 57*(2), 215-235. [http://dx.doi.org/10.1111/j.1467-6494.1989.tb00481.x] [PMID: 2769555]

McClelland, M.M., Acock, A.C., Morrison, F.J. (2006). The impact of kindergarten learning-related skills on academic trajectories at the end of elementary school. *Early Child. Res. Q., 21*, 471-490. [http://dx.doi.org/10.1016/j.ecresq.2006.09.003]

McClowry, S.G., Collins, A. (2012). Temperament-based intervention: Reconceptualised from a response to intervention framework. In: Shiner, R., Zentner, M., (Eds.), *Handbook of childhood temperament.* (pp. 607-627). New York: Guilford Press.

McCormick, M.P., O'Connor, E.E., Cappella, E., McClowry, S.G. (2015). Examining differential effects of INSIGHTS children with high maintenance temperaments. *Early Childhood Research Quarterly., 30*, 128-139.

Merivelde, I., De Pauw, S.S. (2012). Models of child temperament. In: Shiner, R., Zentner, M., (Eds.), *Handbook of childhood temperament.* (pp. 21-40). New York: Guilford Press.

Newman, J., Noel, A., Chen, R., Matsopoulos, A.S. (1998). Temperament, selected moderating variables, and early reading achievement. *J. Sch. Psychol., 36*, 215-232. [http://dx.doi.org/10.1016/S0022-4405(98)00006-5]

Nigg, J.T., Goldsmith, H.H., Sachek, J. (2004). Temperament and attention deficit hyperactivity disorder: the development of a multiple pathway model. *J. Clin. Child Adolesc. Psychol., 33*(1), 42-53. [http://dx.doi.org/10.1207/S15374424JCCP3301_5] [PMID: 15028540]

O'Connor, E.E., Cappella, E., McCormick, M.P., McClowry, S.G. (2014). An examination of the efficacy of INSIGHTS in enhancing the academic and behavioral development of children in early grades. *Journal of Educational Psychology., 106*, 1156-1169.

Oliver, P.H., Guerin, D.W., Gottfried, A.W. (2007). Temperamental task orientation: Relation to high school and college educational accomplishments. *Learn. Individ. Differ., 17*, 220-230. [http://dx.doi.org/10.1016/j.lindif.2007.05.004]

Palisin, H. (1986). Preschool temperament and performance on achievement tests. *Dev. Psychol., 22*(6), 766-770. [http://dx.doi.org/10.1037/0012-1649.22.6.766]

Perry, K.E., Donohue, K.M., Weinstein, R.S. (2007). Teaching practices and the promotion of achievement and adjustment in first grade. *J. Sch. Psychol., 45*, 269-292. [http://dx.doi.org/10.1016/j.jsp.2007.02.005]

Petrill, S.A., Thompson, L.A. (1993). The phenotypic and genetic relationships among measures of cognitive ability, temperament, and scholastic achievement. *Behav. Genet., 23*(6), 511-518. [http://dx.doi.org/10.1007/BF01068141] [PMID: 8129692]

Pianta, R.C. (2001). *Student-Teacher Relationship Scale.*. Odessa, FL: Psychological Assessment Resources, Inc..

Pianta, R.C., LaParo, K.M., Hamre, B.K. (2008). *Classroom assessment scoring system.*. Baltimore, MD: Brookes.

Pluess, M., Belsky, J. (2009). Differential susceptibility to rearing experience: the case of childcare. *J. Child Psychol. Psychiatry, 50*(4), 396-404.
[http://dx.doi.org/10.1111/j.1469-7610.2008.01992.x] [PMID: 19175816]

Posner, M.I., Rothbart, M.K. (2000). Developing mechanisms of self-regulation. *Dev. Psychopathol., 12*(3), 427-441.
[http://dx.doi.org/10.1017/S0954579400003096] [PMID: 11014746]

Rapee, R.M., Kennedy, S., Ingram, M., Edwards, S., Sweeney, L. (2005). Prevention and early intervention of anxiety disorders in inhibited preschool children. *J. Consult. Clin. Psychol., 73*(3), 488-497.
[http://dx.doi.org/10.1037/0022-006X.73.3.488] [PMID: 15982146]

Raver, C. C., Jones, S., Li-Grining, C., Zhai, F. (2009). Reducing young children's risk of behavioral difficulty in Head Start: Benefits of a classroom-based approach. *National Head Start Association (NHSA) Dialog: A Research-to-Practice Journal for the Early Intervention Field., 12*, 1-7.

Resnick, J.S., Kagan, J., Snidman, N., Gersten, M., Baak, K., Rosenberg, A. (1986). Inhibited and uninhibited children: A follow-up study. *Child Dev., 57*, 660-680.
[http://dx.doi.org/10.1111/j.1467-8624.1986.tb00235.x]

Rew, L., Horner, S.D. (2003). Youth Resilience Framework for reducing health-risk behaviors in adolescents. *J. Pediatr. Nurs., 18*(6), 379-388.
[http://dx.doi.org/10.1016/S0882-5963(03)00162-3] [PMID: 15058534]

Rimm-Kaufman, S.E., Kagan, J. (2005). Infant predictors of kindergarten behavior: The contribution of inhibited and uninhibited temperament types. *Behav. Disord., 30*, 329-345.

Rothbart, M.K., Ahadi, S.A., Evans, D.E. (2000). Temperament and personality: origins and outcomes. *J. Pers. Soc. Psychol., 78*(1), 122-135.
[http://dx.doi.org/10.1037/0022-3514.78.1.122] [PMID: 10653510]

Rothbart, M.K., Bates, J.E. (1998). Temperament. In: Eisenberg, N., (Ed.), *Social, emotional, and personality development.* (5th ed., Vol. Vol. 3, pp. 105-176). New York: Wiley.

Rothbart, M., Bates, J. (2006). Temperament. In: Eisenberg, N., Damon, W., Richard , L.M., (Eds.), *Handbook of child psychology: Social, emotional, and personality development.* (6th ed., Vol. Vol. 3, pp. 99-166). New York: John Wiley & Sons Inc..

Rothbart, M.K., Jones, L.B. (1998). Temperament, self-regulation, and education. *School Psych. Rev., 27*, 479-491.

Rothbart, M.K., Posner, M.I. (2005). Genes and experience in the development of executive attention and effortful control. In: Jenson, L.A., Larson, R., (Eds.), *New horizons in developmental theory and research.*. San Francisco: Jossey-Bass.
[http://dx.doi.org/10.1002/cd.142]

Rubin, K.H., Burgess, K.B., Hastings, P.D. (2002). Stability and social-behavioral consequences of toddlers' inhibited temperament and parenting behaviors. *Child Dev., 73*(2), 483-495.
[http://dx.doi.org/10.1111/1467-8624.00419] [PMID: 11949904]

Rudasill, K.M. (2011a). Child temperament, teacher-child interactions, and teacher-child relationships: A longitudinal investigation from first to third grade. *Early Child. Res. Q., 26*, 147-156.
[http://dx.doi.org/10.1016/j.ecresq.2010.07.002]

Rudasill, K.M., Gallagher, K.C., White, J.M. (2010). Temperamental attention and activity, classroom emotional support, and academic achievement in third grade. *J. Sch. Psychol., 48*(2), 113-134. a
[http://dx.doi.org/10.1016/j.jsp.2009.11.002] [PMID: 20159222]

Rudasill, K.M., Niehaus, K., Buhs, E., White, J.M. (2013a). Temperament in early childhood and peer interactions in third grade: the role of teacher-child relationships in early elementary grades. *J. Sch. Psychol., 51*(6), 701-716.
[http://dx.doi.org/10.1016/j.jsp.2013.08.002] [PMID: 24295144]

Rudasill, K.M., Pössel, P., Winkeljohn-Black, S., Niehaus, K. (2013b). Teacher support as a mediator of concurrent and longitudinal associations between temperament and depressive symptoms. *Early Child Dev. Care, 184*(6) b
[http://dx.doi.org/10.1080/03004430.2013.821610]

Rudasill, K.M., Reio, T.G., Jr, Stipanovic, N., Taylor, J.E. (2010a). A longitudinal study of student-teacher relationship quality, difficult temperament, and risky behavior from childhood to early adolescence. *J. Sch. Psychol., 48*(5), 389-412.
[http://dx.doi.org/10.1016/j.jsp.2010.05.001] [PMID: 20728689]

Rudasill, K.M., Rimm-Kaufman, S.E. (2009). Teacher-child relationship quality: The roles of child temperament and teacher child interactions. *Early Child. Res. Q., 24*(2), 107-120.
[http://dx.doi.org/10.1016/j.ecresq.2008.12.003]

Rudasill, K.M., Rimm-Kaufman, S.E., Justice, L.M., Pence, K. (2006). Temperament and language skills as predictors of teacher-child relationships in preschool. *Early Educ. Dev., 17*, 271-291.
[http://dx.doi.org/10.1207/s15566935eed1702_4]

Rutter, M. (1979). Maternal deprivation, 1972-1978: new findings, new concepts, new approaches. *Child Dev., 50*(2), 283-305.
[http://dx.doi.org/10.2307/1129404] [PMID: 114367]

Rydell, A.M., Bohlin, G., Thorell, L.B. (2005). Representations of attachment to parents and shyness as predictors of children's relationships with teachers and peer competence in preschool. *Attach. Hum. Dev.,*

7(2), 187-204.
[http://dx.doi.org/10.1080/14616730500134282] [PMID: 16096193]

Sanson, A., Hemphill, S.A., Smart, D. (2004). Connections between temperament and social development: A review. *Soc. Dev., 13*(1), 142-170.
[http://dx.doi.org/10.1046/j.1467-9507.2004.00261.x]

Saudino, K.J., Wang, M. (2012). Quantitative and molecular genetic studies of temperament. In: Zentner, M., Shiner, R.L., (Eds.), *Handbook of Temperament.*. New York: Guilford.

Schoen, M.J., Nagle, R.J. (1994). Prediction of school readiness from kindergarten temperament scores. *Journal of School Readiness, 32*(2), 135-147.

Soar, R.S., Soar, R.M. (1987). Classroom climate. In: Dunkin, M.J., (Ed.), *The international encyclopedia of teaching and teacher education.* (pp. 336-342). Oxford: Pergamon Press.

Sterry, T.W., Reiter-Purtill, J., Gartstein, M.A., Gerhardt, C.A., Vannatta, K., Noll, R.B. (2010). Temperament and peer acceptance: The mediating role of social behavior. *Merrill-Palmer Q., 56*(2), 189-219.
[http://dx.doi.org/10.1353/mpq.0.0047]

Thijs, J.T., Koomen, H.M., van der Leij, A. (2008). Teacher-child relationships and pedagogical practices: Considering the teacher's perspective. *School Psych. Rev., 37*(2), 244-260.

Thomas, A., Chess, S. (1977). *Temperament and development.*. New York: Brunner/Mazel.

Thomas, A., Chess, S., Birch, H.G. (1970). The origin of personality. *Sci. Am., 223*(2), 102-109.
[http://dx.doi.org/10.1038/scientificamerican0870-102] [PMID: 5447967]

Valiente, C., Eisenberg, N., Smith, C.L., Reiser, M., Fabes, R.A., Losoya, S., Guthrie, I.K., Murphy, B.C. (2003). The relations of effortful control and reactive control to children's externalizing problems: a longitudinal assessment. *J. Pers., 71*(6), 1171-1196.
[http://dx.doi.org/10.1111/1467-6494.7106011] [PMID: 14633062]

Vitaro, F., Brendgen, M., Larose, S., Tremblay, R.E. (2005). Kindergarten disruptive behaviors, protective factors, and educational achievement by early adulthood. *J. Educ. Psychol., 97*(4), 617-629.
[http://dx.doi.org/10.1037/0022-0663.97.4.617]

Vygotsky, L.S. (1978). *Mind in Society.*. Cambridge, MA: Harvard University Press.

Walker, S., Berthelsen, D., Irving, K. (2001). Temperament and acceptance in early childhood: Sex and social status differences. *Child Study J., 31*, 177-192.

Walker, H.M., Stieber, S., O'Neill, R.E. (1990). Middle school behavioral profiles of antisocial and at-risk control boys: Descriptive and predictive outcomes. *Exceptionality, 1*, 61-77.
[http://dx.doi.org/10.1080/09362839009524742]

Zubin, J., Spring, B. (1977). Vulnerability--a new view of schizophrenia. *J. Abnorm. Psychol., 86*(2), 103-126.
[http://dx.doi.org/10.1037/0021-843X.86.2.103] [PMID: 858828]

CHAPTER 4

Adolescent Pregnancy: Rejecting Preference *via* 'Profiles in Courage' in Policy and Practice

Kimberly M. Wickersham, **Raymond J. Waller***, **Suzanne Tew-Washburn** and **Sherrionda H. Crawford**

Troy University, Troy, AL 36082, United States

Abstract: Ideally, best practice methods are built upon an edifice of informed policy guided by the low star of serving student best interests. Unfortunately, such a stalwart foundation is non-existent for many psychosocial and educational initiatives. In fact, it is lamentably common for policy to be constructed on a sand dune comprised of presumption, special interests, or intuition. Unfortunately, innumerable examples exist to warn us that human behavior is frequently counterintuitive, increasing the risk of policy decisions guided by presumption or face validity. While abstinence-only efforts to reduce adolescent pregnancy and associated adverse outcomes sometimes occurring as a result of high risk sexual behavior might have initially been defended as plausible, the evidence is compelling that such efforts are ineffective compared with other methods. Pregnancy and risk reduction policy and practice supported by empirical inquiry are discussed, and this issue is presented as an example actually and conceptually representative of divergence of public policy from the body of scientific knowledge.

Keywords: Abstinence, Contraceptives, Peer education, Sexual activity, Sexually transmitted infections.

INTRODUCTION

Prior to the invention and wide accessibility of the automobile, a would-be traveler desiring either greater convenience or alacrity than was offered by their

* **Corresponding author Raymond J. Waller:** Troy University, Troy, AL 36082, United States; Tel: (334) 983-6556 Ext. 1438; Email: rjwaller@troy.edu.

own feet often resorted to transport by horse. When this traveler did not own a horse, she might charter the use of a horse by a stable owner, the historical equivalent of a contemporary would-be traveler renting an automobile. A stable owner of distal repute was Thomas Hobson

(Webber & Feinsilber, 1990) of Cambridge, England. A potential customer of Hobson's might survey the equestrian options available for hire and specify their preference for the animal they desired, but their stated preference did not impact the outcome. Hobson, in apparent contradiction of the idea that the customer is always right, had a rigorous practice of personally choosing the horse he leased so that he could rotate the use of his animals, thereby avoiding the overuse of his best animals. This arcane business practice gained so much attention that it became a narrative and literary term that continues to be used today; thus, audiences hearing the term *Hobson's choice* know that, for all practical purposes, the conveyed meaning is that one has no choice at all (The Phrase Finder, 2015).

Perhaps the contemporaneous practice equivalent of Hobson's choice involves those domains of psychosocial and educational practice in which the scientific knowledge base is at variance with public policy and programming. When public funding supports one primary method or program, administrators have the option of providing any programs deemed appropriate-and 'appropriate' options tend to align themselves with the legislated funding stream-or tend to cease operation. Historically there are innumerable illustrations of these occurrences in the US. An excellent example includes pregnancy prevention, legislation and incentives based on abstinence-only approaches to reducing teen pregnancy. This chapter will therefore discuss teen pregnancy rates *vis-à-vis* contradictions between policy and practice and the role that preference of the body politic or of special interest groups therein can play in influencing implementation of effective practices.

Description of Teen Sexual Behaviors and Pregnancy in the United States

The national Youth Risk Behavior Survey (YRBS) is a tool that the Centers for Disease Control and Prevention (CDC) uses to monitor health risk behaviors of students in grades 9-12. Among recent findings from this survey, 46.8% of high school students in the US reported that they have had sexual intercourse (CDC,

2014), although this reflects a decrease from the 1991 rate of 54.1%.

Perhaps a more important question to ask adolescents is *whether they are* currently sexually active. The indicators on the YRBS fail to capture this information, asking instead whether the student has had sexual intercourse in the past three months. Although the rate of current sexual activity reported by high school students is currently lower than much of the history for which records were kept, "a significant decrease among black students, where the proportion who are sexually active declined from 59% in 1991 to 42% in 2013" (Child Trends, 2014, p. 2). Traditionally, it has been thought that males had higher rates of sexually activity; however, recent findings indicate that 12th grade females report having a higher rate of sexual activity (50.7%) than any other group (Child Trends, 2014).

Risks

Unprotected sexual activity among adolescents can lead to myriad consequences, from unplanned pregnancies to the contracting of sexually transmitted infections (STIs). Protection during first sexual contact has decreased, but unprotected teen sex is still far too prevalent (see Table **1**).

According to the Alan Guttmacher Institute (AGI, 2014), almost half of those diagnosed annually with STIs are under the age of 24. More alarmingly, the Office of Adolescent Health (2014) has released the statement that "four in 10 sexually active teen girls have had an STD that can cause infertility and even death" (para 1).

Due to findings such as these, the CDC also collects data on condom usage. Although data is collected on other methods of birth control, only condom usage is directly associated with the reduction of STIs (see Table **2**). The CDC found that slightly more than half (59.1%) of the adolescents surveyed in YRBS 2013 stated that either the respondent or their partner used a condom during last sexual intercourse. This reflects a significant increase in condom usage since 1991 (46.2%), but unfortunately indicates a *drop* in condom usage since 2003 (63.0%) (see Table **2**).

Table 1. Note: Reprint permissions given. Guttmacher Institute, American teens' sexual and reproductive health, Fact Sheet, New York: Guttmacher Institute, 2014, http://www.guttmacher.org/pubs/FB-ATSRH.html, November 17, 2014.

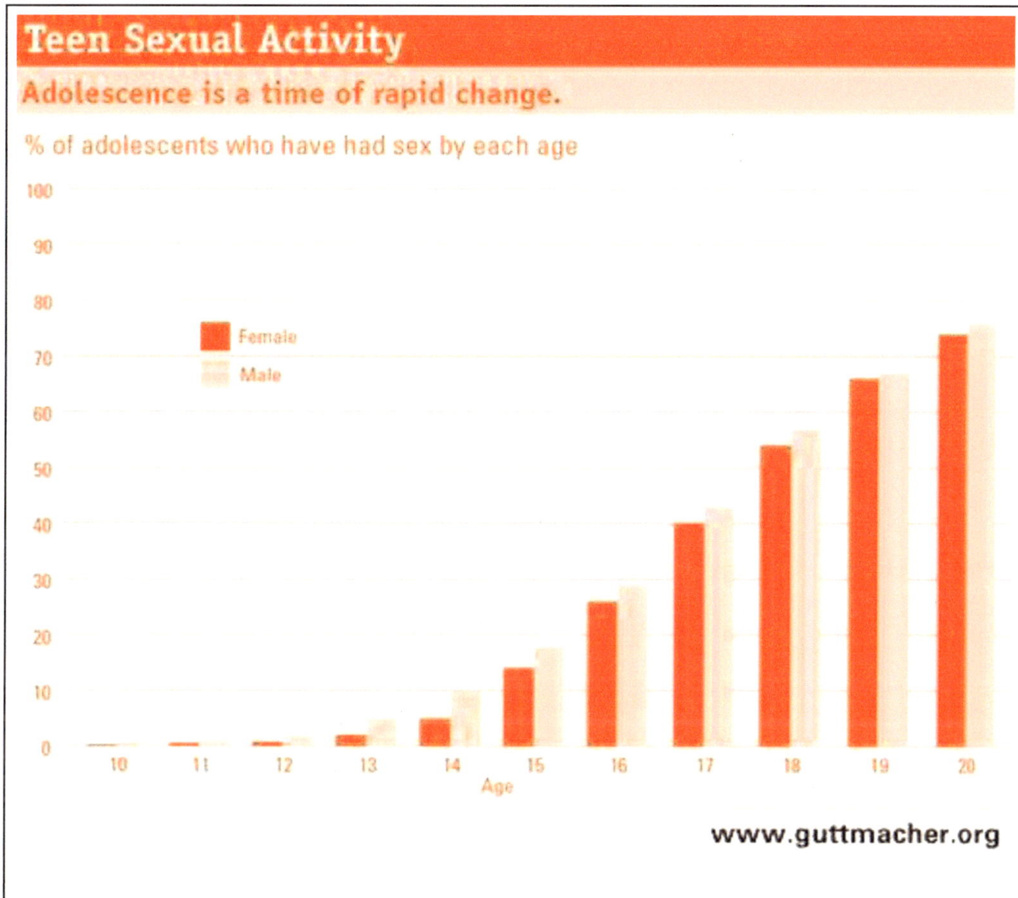

Despite the use of birth control, Finer and Philbin (2013) reported that, in the US, annually there are:

- **16,000 pregnancies in adolescents who are under the age of 15,**
- **252,000 pregnancies among female adolescents aged 15 to 17, and**
- **an additional 425,410 pregnancies among females ages 18-19 (The National Campaign, 2014b).**

Though high, this is an improvement from the unprecedented report issued by

AGI in 1999, which, at that time, estimated that one million female adolescents became pregnant each year.

The National Campaign (2014b) reported that US birth rates fell 57% from 1991 to 2013 in adolescent females aged 15-19 years. As we are concerned with looking at school-age students, it should be pointed out that in 2013, 72% of teen births occurred among those 18-19 years of age (The National Campaign, 2014a). Also of importance is that, of the adolescents that were pregnant in 2013, 60% of these young women carried their pregnancies to birth (The National Campaign, 2014b).

Of course, for every pregnant female, there is a good likelihood that there is a participatory male. Scott, Steward-Streng, Manlove, and Moore (2012) analyzed data from the National Longitudinal Survey of Youth (1997) and estimated that 9% of adolescent males were fathers and that 39% of the young men who were fathers-to-be were 18 years old at the time of their first child's birth.

Table 2. Note: Reprint permissions given. Guttmacher Institute, American teens' sexual and reproductive health, Fact Sheet, New York: Guttmacher Institute, 2014, http://www.guttmacher.org/pubs/FB-ATSRH.html, November 17, 2014.

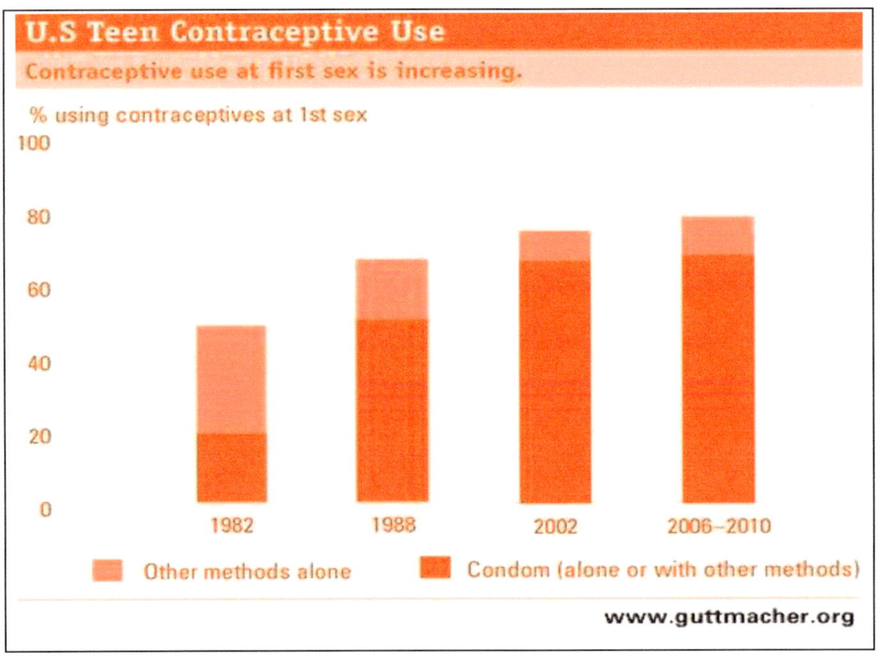

Deficits in the Body of Evidence

A school demographic that has not been included extensively in the research is adolescents with special needs, noted Jones, Domenico and Valente (2006), who pointed out that "all teenagers, including those with disabilities, have the potential to become parents" (p. 24). To begin the process off addressing this gap in the knowledge base these researchers completed a nation-wide study of 2,818 Family and Consumer Science (FACS) teachers. They reported that:

> Forty-eight percent of the teachers responded that they had no pregnant or parenting students with disabilities at the time they completed the survey. Twenty-six percent of teachers reported having 1 or 2 students with disabilities who were currently pregnant or parenting. Eleven percent of the teachers reported having 3 to 4 students with disabilities who were pregnant or parenting. Ten percent of the teachers had 5 to 9 students while 5% reported 10 or more pregnant or parenting students with disabilities. Additionally, 14% of teachers reported they taught students with disabilities who were parenting more than one child (p. 28).

The study further reported that 62% of the student participants were classified as having a learning disability and almost another third (30%) had a mental disability. They went on to state that the majority of the programs that address adolescent sexuality do not address the learning needs of this student population.

Variables Influencing Teen Pregnancy

There are a number of risks associated with early pregnancy. The National Campaign (1999) conducted focus groups with teens, parents, and other community leaders, finding that "teen pregnancy is inextricably intertwined with other issues teens face, such as drug use, violence, sexually transmitted diseases, and early onset of sexual experimentation" (p. 2). Determining directional causality remains elusive. The Planned Parenthood Federation of America (1999) contended that to "truly reduce the incidence of teen pregnancy, we must address many other contributing factors, including poverty, low expectations for educational achievement, decaying social institution, and hopelessness" (p. 4).

A frequently presumed risk of various high risk behaviors among adolescents is that they perceive themselves as being invulnerable or immune to negative outcomes. This bias is refuted by Reyna and Farley (2006), who went on to identify empirical complications to reducing the prevalence of risk behaviors, including:

- **adolescents have yet to achieve full neurological development,**
- **certain risk behaviors, including early sexual activity, have an evolutionary advantage, and**
- **negative consequences of some high risk behaviors occur so distal to one another that contingency learning does not occur.**

Research has documented that teen pregnancy is also associated with socio-economic status, level of education obtained, ethnic background, substance use, and intrapersonal factors (Dryfoos, 1990, 1998; Luker, 1996; McWhirter, McWhirter, McWhirter, & McWhirter, 1998). Specifically, the rate of teen pregnancy is higher among those:

- **of low socioeconomic status,**
- **of African American ethnic background,**
- **who report higher levels of alcohol use and cigarette use,**
- **who have lower levels of self-esteem, and**
- **who do not have fully developed decision-making skills.**

Complicating the potential risk is that age of onset has a similar effect to numerous psychosocial phenomena-earlier onset is generally related to more complicated outcomes. A female who becomes sexually active at a younger age is less likely to use contraceptives and more likely to have multiple partners (Dryfoos, 1990, 1998; Luker, 1996; McWhirter *et al.*, 1998).

Further Consequential Associations

School dropout and/or failure are intertwined with poverty and teen pregnancy (AGI, 1998; Dryfoos, 1990, 1998; Luker, 1996). Does the teen believe she has limited opportunities due to socioeconomic status, which leads her to engage in high risk behaviors such as unprotected sexual activity, which result in an unplanned pregnancy, which leads her to dropping out of school, and thereby limiting her job earning capacity? Alternatively, does the school failure come first? On the other hand, is the pregnancy the catalyst? We cannot say with clarity.

Cause or Effect?

Causality between adolescent pregnancy and the variables previously discussed continues to be debated. For example, Luker (1996) advanced the argument that pregnancy does not make teenage mothers poor, but that poor teenagers often become mothers. She reasoned that affluent teenagers appear more likely to have access to birth control and/or abortions. In addition, the more affluent teens-both male and female-have higher aspirations than do his or her *despondent*, *poorer* counterparts. Accordingly, if one does not have future goals, there are no identifiable reasons to delay having a child. Obviously, significant assumptions underlay such hypotheses. Knopf and Gordon (1997) concurred that there are correlations, but asserted that the measurements used to identify these behaviors are often problematic. Brown and Eisenburg (1995) summarized well:

> It is not always clear what the precise relationship is between these factors and the risk of unintended pregnancy. Nonetheless, taken together, they help to form the environment in which individual decisions about contraception and sexual activity occur. Consideration of them must be part of any serious inquiry into the reasons that lie behind high rates of unintended pregnancy in the United States (pp. 183-184).

Societal Costs of Adolescent Pregnancy in the United States

These questions are not merely academic. In 1989, at the apex of adolescent pregnancy rates, the average cost of public assistance for a teenage mother and her child was $9,200 per year (Rodriquez & Moore, 1995). This was in contrast to the average cost of family planning at the time, which was $64.00. More recently, The National Campaign (2013) estimated that adolescent childbearing costs $9.4 billion annually. Although $9.4 billion is an astronomical figure, The National Campaign contrasts this number with the $12 billion saved in 2010 due to the drastic drop in teen births since 1991. However, with a decreased chance of obtaining a high school diploma and an increased rate of poverty for the adolescent and her child, the real costs of adolescent pregnancy are certainly dramatically higher than many estimates represent, especially when factors such as the health burdens that can be imposed from unprotected sexual activity are included in the cost.

Opinion-Based Policy

During the last 30 years, the topic of adolescent pregnancy has been the subject of much attention from political, educational, and religious arenas. Adolescent pregnancy, along with its related problems, programs, and issues cannot be adequately addressed until there is first a consensus regarding the presence and definition of an actual problem or preferred course of action.

What determines national priority for the numerous issues revolving around adolescent pregnancy, such as the types of and availability of sex education, abortion, contraception, funding for prevention programs, and costs of births or housing? In the US, key factors- especially funding-are determined by legislators elected to represent their constituents' interests. In the domain of public discourse, adolescent sexuality inspires intense emotions for many in the voting (and nonvoting) public. As a result, "Adolescent health is often injected into the core political/cultural debates regarding justice and the range and role of government in such areas as abortion, sexuality, family values, poverty and social opportunity" (Knopf & Gordon, 1997 p. 173).

Face Validity Often Fails to Inform

While the barney over abstinence-only approaches as the interventions of choice for reducing teen pregnancy and associated consequences involves propositions with intuitive appeal for many people, presentiment often fails to inform in the psychosocial domain. A widely known example of human conduct being counterintuitive to assumptions was investigated by a former minister and, at the point of inquiry, doctoral student in sociology. He decided it would be useful to the public to apply methods of scientific inquiry to explain the phenomenon of interstate rest stops being a focal point for men to pursue anonymous sex acts with other men and to describe the participants. Law enforcement at the time was using these restrooms as a means to easily catch and prosecute said participants, and appeared to do so as a result of bias against the homosexual participants.

The doctoral student conducted his research as a participant observer. After some time and effort, he discovered that, indeed, rest stops were a meeting point for some men to meet and engage in the aforementioned sex acts. *Intuitively*, it *could* be assumed that these men were homosexual or bisexual. The doctoral student began to collect car license plate numbers, tracking these men to their homes and, after a judicious time period during which he hoped that memory of his presence in the rest stop would fade, doing interviews to learn more about the men. Counter to what intuition might suggest, he discovered that the majority of these men, in fact, were in heterosexual married relationships. *Intuitively*, these married men pursuing anonymous sex might be unhappy in their relationships. However, from all appearances, the majority of the participants were paragons of family unity and satisfaction.

He eventually published his dissertation findings (Humphreys, 1975). His book is still widely discussed in academic settings, perhaps more so related to deviations from contemporary standards of ethical research practices than the findings. It provides an exemplary case of plausible suppositions regarding human behavior that are antithetical to reality. Thus, even seemingly logical presumptions are completely insufficient as a standard for informing practice and policy, and scientific fields endorse the philosophy of evidence-based practice; support of rigorous, empirical inquiry is the foundation of informed endeavors.

Plausibility of Advocating Abstinence

Abstinence-only protagonists did not arise devoid of any semblance of defensible logic. Among the most common contentions of advocates endorsing abstinence is the concern that comprehensive approaches to reducing adolescent pregnancies, including, for example, providing widespread access to birth control (particularly condoms), would *encourage* teens to engage in high risk behavior. Though a coherent claim in the absence of additional knowledge, research has consistently found this argument to be largely unfounded (*e.g.* Harper *et al.*, 2005).

Another endorsement for abstinence rather than comprehensive sex education comes from some faith-based organizations that preclude extra-marital sexual activity on the hermeneutical grounds that such comportment violates acceptable canons of conduct (Malone & Rodriquez, 2011). These assenting organizations exert momentous influence to policy priorities, including school-based practices, in many areas (*e.g.* Anderson, 2012). Unfortunately, scientific inquiry has demonstrated that insistence on abstinence rather than comprehensive education is tantamount to sanctioning *ideal* at the expense of *outcome*. It also provides yet another counterintuitive finding tinged, this one perhaps tinged with a modicum of irony. Whereas abstinence programs do not reduce the occurrences of adolescent sexual activity, comprehensive sex education programs do (Kantor, 2008).

Years ago, Allen-Mears and Shapiro (1989) prognosticated that the first major campaign facing practitioners was that "sex educators needed to confront the public's assumption that sex education would make people promiscuous and would encourage them to experiment with sexual behaviors that would not otherwise have occurred to them" (p. 145). Wise were these words. Abstinence-only has often been the program of choice for sex education in the schools. Boonstra's (2014) research indicated that, even now, 19 states continue to prefer abstinence-only instruction in their schools.

Howard and McCabe (1992) partially articulated the folly: "Providing abstinence information to youth who have decided to have or *are already* having sexual intercourse without also giving them information they need to protect themselves is unconscionable" (p. 88; emphasis added). Christopher (1995) concurred with those concerns when he summarized his review of abstinence programs, stating, "Probably the best conclusion that can be reached at this time is that there is little compelling evidence that purely abstinence programs are effective in changing coital or contraceptive behaviors that would impact on teenage pregnancy" (p. 386). Twenty years later, this finding has held true.

History of Legislation Related to Adolescent Pregnancy in the United States

Although it was addressed at the state level and by community groups, adolescent pregnancy prevention did not appear to be a national statutory priority until the proverbial political wheel began turning in the 1970s. President Jimmy Carter adopted the issue as a legislative focus, reporting success in reducing teen pregnancy rates in his final State of the Union Address (Carter, 1981). His initiatives culminated in the *Adolescent Family Act*, though for close to two decades there were no definitive guidelines for program implementation or research.

The Adolescent Family Life (AFL) Program was enacted as Title XX of the Public Health Service Act in 1981 and is administered by the Department of Health and Human Services (HHS). The *AFL Program* demonstration projects provided "comprehensive health, education, and social services (including life and career planning, job training, safe housing, decision-making and social skills)," either directly or through partnerships with other community agencies (Solomon-Fears, 2012, p.14).

The Personal Responsibility and Work Opportunity Reconciliation Act of 1996 (PL 104-193) was enacted October 1, 1996, supplanting Aid to Families with Dependent Children (AFDC) with *Temporary Assistance for Needy Families* (TANF). Legislation specifically targeting adolescent parents was incorporated due to excessive use of AFDC monies by this population. This new law mandated states to develop programs preventing and reducing the number of out-of-wedlock pregnancies. It also greatly expanded abstinence-only spending, but bypassed allocation *via* the public health departments in favor of faith and community-based initiatives (Kantor, 2008). This means of allocation no doubt delayed advancement and development of comprehensive sex education initiatives. TANF also provided monetary incentives annually to those states that showed significant decreases in adolescent *illegitimate* births (Office of the Assistant Secretary for Planning and Evaluation, 1997), and established explicit standards and monies dedicated to research, which could be quantitative or qualitative in nature. For the first time, not only was replication of a program important for ongoing funding of these grants, but stringent evaluation was required. States were encouraged to obtain the most from their TANF block grant dollars in a competitive effort to obtain bonus incentives.

Another addition of PL 104-193 not seen in previous legislation was the objective for at least 25% of communities to have teen pregnancy prevention programs (Office Of The Assistant Secretary For Planning And Evaluation, 1997).

However, much to the chagrin of many program planners and researchers, the flexibility of Title XX-Social Services Block Grant funds facilitated directing monies into abstinence-only education.

The Title V Abstinence Education Program, authorized under the 1996 Welfare Reform Law, provided a mandatory formula grant based on a state's number of low-income children. The *Patient Protection and Affordable Care Act* (PPACA; enacted March 23, 2010) reauthorized the program. Programs such as *Promoting Health Among Teens, Abstinence Only Intervention, Adult Identity Mentoring (Project AIM)*, and *Making a Difference* have frequently been used as model abstinence programs. Between 1996 and 2009, such legislative acts directed $1.5 billion into abstinence-only programs (Malone & Rodriquez, 2011).

The Tide Begins to Turn

Historically, the government has funded educational interventions that have favored abstinence-only-until marriage teenage pregnancy prevention programs. Ironically, these programs were funded for decades, despite the lack of empirical support of effectiveness (Trenholm, Devaney, Fortson, Quay, Wheeler, & Clark, 2007). Since these programs were based on the principle of abstinence-only-until-marriage, access to information on contraceptives was limited. However, over the last decade, numerous federal and state programs with a more comprehensive focus on sex education have been developed and implemented to address teen pregnancy.

As a part of the President's Teen Pregnancy Initiative (TPPI), the CDC and the Federal Office of the Assistant Secretary for Health (OASH) has been charged with the responsibility of identifying and funding evidence-based program models to help facilitate the reduction of teenage pregnancy (The National Campaign, 2006). A result of the aforementioned collaboration was funding for the Teen Pregnancy Prevention and Personal Responsibility Education Program (PREP).

PREP is a component requirement of the *Patient Protection and Affordable Care Act* (PPACA) and provides funding enabling states to establish educational initiatives on abstinence and extends the outcomes to include contraception use for prevention of pregnancy and sexually transmitted diseases. "PREP" Programs are required to identify and perpetuate operative evidence-based programs or constituents of those programs, which emphasize delaying sexual activity and increasing condom use. It further requires that medically accurate information be provided on both abstinence and contraceptive use. Additionally, programs must include education regarding the following topics:

- **healthy relationships,**
- **adolescent development,**
- **financial literacy,**
- **parent-child communication,**
- **education and employment skills, and**
- **healthy life skills (Zief, Shapiro, and Strong, 2013).**

Teen Outreach Program (TOP) is a widely used program funded under PREP. *TOP* is authorized by the FY 2010 *Consolidated Appropriations Act* and provides competitive funding to both public and private businesses for replicating successful programs and services that reduce teen pregnancy. TOP has been successfully implemented in both the school and community; and it can be adapted to middle school and high school settings and can be used with diverse populations.

The program utilizes a multifaceted approach, combining community service learning, mentor support and support, and curriculum-based programming. The goal of the program is reduction in risk behaviors associated with teen pregnancy and school dropout. Research evaluations of TOP report reduced rates of risk-related problems such as pregnancy, school suspension, class failure, and/or school dropout (Advocates for Youth, 2012). Additional programs that have been funded *via* PREP include *Making Proud Choices, Be Proud! Be Responsible!, Reducing the Risk, Making a Difference*, *¡Cuidate!* Additional evidence-based programs funded by PREP can be reviewed at:

Resource	http://www.hhs.gov/ash/oah/prevention/research/programs/index.html

Summary of the Current Findings

Research conducted by The National Campaign (2011) summarized broad components of effective interventions as those that:

- **help teens delay sexual activity,**
- **increases contraceptive use, and/or**
- **prevents teen pregnancies.**

They identified a variety of effective programs and concluded:

> Reducing teen pregnancy requires a combination of community programs *and* broader efforts to influence social norms, values, and popular culture by parents, family, faith communities, and the media. It also requires ensuring that sexually active teens have access to effective contraception (p. 2).

School Based Interventions: What Really Works?

As the debate and controversy continues regarding the best way-or whether to-implement sex education in our schools, the fact remains that the United States continues to have the highest teen birth rate among any industrialized nation (CDC, 2013). Many educational professionals (*e.g.* school counselors, school nurses, teachers, school social workers, school psychologists, administrators, health care professionals, mental health professionals) are still trying to determine what types of programs reduce the high risk sexual behavior of teens and adolescents. More specifically, which programs show success in regards to effectively facilitating a delay in sexual initiation, improving contraceptive use between sexually teens engaging in sexual behavior, and/or reducing the rates of teen pregnancy? Fortunately, though much remains to be learned, much is known, and the energy expended on the abstinence debate can be directed elsewhere.

The current weight of evidence supports the use of a combination of abstinence-only and comprehensive sex education, which have been the most successful in accelerating the reduction of adolescent pregnancy *via* the increase of condom usage and delay in initiating sexual intercourse in adolescent females, who are most at risk (Kirby, 2007). Succinctly, findings indicate that students who receive comprehensive sex education rather than abstinence-only interventions are less likely to report teen pregnancy (Kohler, Manhart & Lafferty, 2008).

More specifically, Kohler and others (2008) compared the sexual health risks of adolescents receiving various sex education programs and determined that, for adolescents receiving a multifaceted sex education program, the risk of teen pregnancy was lowered by 50%, while abstinence-only programs did not show any significant impact in a reduction in teen pregnancy. A range of supportive strategies have been implemented to facilitate the declining incidence of pregnancy in adolescent females, to include:

- **school based sex education programs,**
- **peer counseling programs,**
- **increased access to contraceptive, as well as**
- **web-based programs for both parents and students.**

Additional Considerations for School-Based Implementation

As just mentioned, some studies have found adolescents to be more receptive to programs delivered by their peers. For example, in terms of communicating accurate knowledge and promoting condom use, it has been suggested that peer educators may be more effective as instructors than adults. It also has been implied that youth may be more comfortable with educators who are similar in age and may therefore be more likely to believe and follow what these peer tutors teach, as compared to adults. Peer education (or peer mentoring), has often been practiced within the school and community arenas as an agent of behavioral change and knowledge attainment. Other health behavior programs, such as smoking cessation and eating correctly, employ peer education with success. Klein and colleagues (1994) noted that peers were utilized to address health education for college students as early as 1957. Peter Finn (as cited in Sawyer *et al.*, 1997) conveyed,

> Peer education takes place constantly among youngsters and adults *regardless* of instructional efforts to promote the use of more 'reliable' sources of information and advice. It is essential that we seek, through

> formal training, to put the inevitable peer education that will take place to positive use, rather than leave it to the vagaries of chance (p. 211).

One program that employs peer education is *Postponing Sexual Involvement* (PSI). PSI was developed in 1983 as part of a hospital-based outreach program. It is based on the social influence model (or peer model). PSI has been described as a program that teaches junior high and high school student's strategies to resist peer pressures that might lead them into early sexual activity (Moore, *et al.*, 1995). This is an abstinence-based model, which asserts self-restraint is the best choice until marriage; however, if one chooses not to remain abstinent, one should know how to obtain and use contraception appropriately. Eighth graders are instructed by peer educators who teach them decision-making skills and encourage classmates to have a good attitude toward abstinence.

The Teen Prevention Education Program (Teen PEP) is intended to decrease the incidence of pregnancy and sexually transmitted diseases among high school students by providing sex education programs led by peers. Research indicates that well-trained teen PEP peer educators are able to facilitate

- **a reduction in pregnancy,**
- **an increase in the use of birth control, and**
- **the development of communication skills regarding discussing concerns and setting boundaries with current or potential sexual partners (CDC, 2014).**

Finally, *Postponing Sexual Involvement* focuses on helping students develop the skills they need to handle peer pressure and delay sexual involvement until they reach their late teens. Ten classes, taught by high school juniors and seniors, target eighth grade students and assist them to identify not only the pressures they feel to engage in sexual behavior, but also their motivations for doing so. Although in the strictest sense *Postponing Sexual Involvement* might be labeled as an abstinence program, it also includes a series of classes on human sexuality and birth control.

Curriculum-Based Programs

Curriculum-Based Programs may include a combination of educational components regarding abstinence and contraceptive use. These programs are frequently programs of choice within schools. *Self-Center (School-linked health center)* is one such example. This program is considered comprehensive in that it provides education, counseling and reproductive services. The intervention approach is interdisciplinary in that it includes a team of social workers and nurses who provide services within the school environment. The social workers and nurses provide reproductive and extended counseling services, as well as providing referrals for teens requiring medical care (Advocates for Youth, 2012). Evaluations of *Self-Center* indicates participants:

- **delay onset of sexual contact,**
- **reduce incidence of unprotected sex,**
- **increase use of reproductive health care, and**
- **reduce pregnancy in both high school and younger female participants (Advocates for Youth, 2012; The National Campaign, 2006).**

Safer Choices, an educational program designed to increase "protective behaviors" (Coyle *et al.*, 2001, p.82) and prevent pregnancy among teens, combines a twenty-lesson curriculum with school-wide activities and parent education to reinforce concomitant classroom learning. Coyle and colleagues (2001) evaluated the long-term effectiveness of *Safer Choices* over a 2 ½ year period with nearly 4,000 high school freshmen. Results indicated that the program had a strong effect on increasing the consistent use of condoms and therefore, preventing teenage pregnancy.

Reducing the Risk consists of fifteen classes taught by high school teachers with specialty training in the curriculum. The goals of the sessions are preventing unprotected intercourse by remaining abstinent or by using contraceptives. *Reducing the Risk* is intended for high school sophomores.

Teen Talk's curriculum can be used effectively in the schools or in the community to raise teenagers' awareness about the consequences of unprotected sexual relations and the possibility of pregnancy occurring in their lives. Surprisingly, according to a summary of research on stayteen.org (2014), almost half of all teenagers, both sexually abstinent and active, reported never thinking about becoming pregnant or causing a partner to become pregnant. The curriculum's approach involves lectures, small-group discussions, and role-playing to encourage clear, personal expression intended to promote either delay sexual experience or consistently using contraceptives. The curriculum can be covered in a two-day workshop by a health agency and/or school personnel.

Building School-Community Linkages

There are numerous, compelling reasons for the school community to build strong partnerships within the larger community. The shared public health implications for both may provide a communal opportunity to build these relationships. *The School/Community Program* represents a comprehensive approach to pregnancy prevention that enlists the participation of parents and the community as well as public school system teachers, staff, and administrators. Children in all grades receive sex education integrated into the other courses they take. A school clinic staffed by a nurse provides counseling and contraceptives at no cost to the students.

Service Learning Programs typically focus on nonsexual factors that affect the behavior of adolescents and are another venue through which school-community partnership can be fostered. Participants in service learning usually volunteer to participate in community service programs such as:

- **tutoring,**
- **working in a nursing home,**
- **mentoring younger students, or**
- **helping individuals in poverty**

in exchange for class time or credit.

The programs often encourage participants to reflect on their experiences as well as receive education credit (Advocates for Youth, 2012). Interestingly, there is some evidence that these programs increase behaviors linked to prevention of pregnancy and sexually transmitted diseases (Kirby, 2007). *Reach for Health Community Youth Service* is an example of a service learning program, designed to help students acquire the knowledge and attitudes-and ultimately the obligatory in healthy choice-making and risk avoidance (Advocates for Youth, 2012).

Program evaluation indicates that *Reach for Health Community Youth Service* participants shows:

- **delayed sexual contact,**
- **reduced high-risk sexual behavior,**
- **higher condom and healthcare use, as well as**
- **decreased rates of teen pregnancy (Advocates for Youth, 2012; O'Donnell, Stueve, O'Donnell, Duran, San Doval, Wilson, Haber, Perry, & Pleck, 2002).**

Finally, *John Snow, Inc.* (JSI) concentrates on identifying best practices in pregnancy prevention and equitable reproductive health services for at-risk youth. In terms of program planning, they recommend the following:

- **Engage and recruit a diverse group of community partners, including those not typically engaged in the target community, to collaborate in teen pregnancy prevention efforts.**
- **Identify and implement best practices that address the social determinants of teen pregnancy among diverse youth.**
- **Ensure that prevention efforts are inclusive of both male and female youth.**
- **Ensure that clinical providers provide culturally competent and adolescent-centered clinical reproductive health services, assess appropriately for social determinants, and link youth to needed social services.**
- **Identify and educate a diverse group of community stakeholders on strategies that have an impact on teen pregnancy prevention and related social determinants (retrieved from John Snow website).**

Resource	http://www.cdc.gov/teenpregnancy/preventteenpreg.htm

CONCLUSION

A discussion of evidenced based pregnancy prevention programs is complicated by the emotional investment sometimes incited by divergent views. Broadly speaking, in order to reduce rates of teen pregnancy, programs must either increase teenage contraceptive use, reduce teens' sexual activity, or both. (Bennett & Assefi, 2003). When initiating a new pregnancy prevention program, there are some important factors to consider. The most optimistic findings indicate that abstinence-only education has had limited success; most findings report no positive outcome. Comprehensive sex education programs, especially those including training on the importance and use of contraceptives, significantly influence students' knowledge and use of birth control. Moreover, consistent findings (*e.g.* Bennett & Assefi, 2003; Frost & Forrest, 1995) indicate "Multi-component programs with a clear message" (Coyle, *et al.*, 2001, p. 92) are the ones that reduce sexual risk behaviors and delay sexual initiation.

Bennett and Assefi (2005), offered additional descriptors of effective teen pregnancy prevention programs as being ones that:

- **convince teens that not having sex or that using contraception consistently and carefully is the right thing to do;**
- **last a sufficient length of time (*i.e.*, more than a few weeks);**
- **are operated by leaders who believe in their programs and who are adequately trained;**
- **actively engage participants and personalize the program information;**
- **address peer pressure issues;**
- **teach communication skills; and**
- **reflect the age, sexual experience, and culture of young persons in the programs (p.78).**

Pregnancy prevention programs that are developed collaboratively with teens, parents, school personnel, community members, and program experts have more clearly understood goals and are particularly successful in addressing values and coping skills (Solomon-Fears, 2013). Community attitudes toward teenage sexuality may affect the availability and success of pregnancy prevention programs, arguing in favor of active community involvement.

Future Research

After reviewing information regarding adolescent unplanned pregnancy prevention, certain omissions in the knowledge base were conspicuous. The lack of information regarding students with special needs is indefensible. There were also few prevention programs that singularly focused on males. Neither of these populations had an abundance of data or evidence based programs exposed to the scrutiny of evaluation. In addition, it would be of great advantage to know more regarding programs that work to encourage parenting teens to remain in school or pursue other avenues of education and job training, assisting them in their future endeavors. Obviously, schools could serve instrumental functions in serving teens that have children as well as in reducing teen pregnancy.

Final Word

Prior to election to the office of President of the United States, Senator John F. Kennedy wrote a book, *Profiles in Courage* (1955), in which he penned biographical sketches of previous US Senators who had acted in opposition to their constituents' preferences in favor of doing what they judged was right. In each case, these senators knowingly assented to popular scorn, loss of political support, and party marginalization in order to acquit himself with integrity. The book became a best seller for which Senator Kennedy was awarded a Pulitzer Prize.

We extend the exemplars described by Kennedy to educators in areas in which school policy is predicated on special interests or popular preference in clear divergence with the knowledge base and client best interests. The hazards associated with high risk adolescent sexual behaviors (and numerous other areas of practice uninformed by substantive evidence) are too potentially consequential to your students to abide. That encouragement notwithstanding, integrity inspired by the objects of Kennedy's descriptive prose compels us to concede that your commitment to students in opposition to concession to popular demand is more likely to impact you in ways resembling the written about than the writer. It is unlikely that you can optimally serve your students and maximize self-protection.

Increased access to, and education regarding contraception has contributed to unprecedented success in decreasing pregnancy and birthrates among teens. Adolescence is a time of knowledge attainment and attitude formation. Many health behaviors in later life are developed and maintained due to the knowledge and behavioral competences acquired at school. Adolescents look to their peers, the media, parents, and educators to procure the knowledge that is acquired, retained, and used to make decisions regarding present and future behaviors. School serves as a logical focal point for service delivery of programming designed to reduce risk exposure. Educators should ensure that those programs and curricula adopted and sanctioned within their walls are programs that will meet the needs of students. Schools provide a natural forum for the implementation of the effective strategies discussed above, but educators must be open to discarding ineffective intervention approaches such as those based exclusively on abstinence to reduce adolescent pregnancy. We extend the call to action to overcome popular zeitgeist in pursuit of client best interests in the numerous areas in which preference or intuition supersedes evidence in policy and practice.

CONFLICT OF INTEREST

The authors confirm that they have no conflict of interest to declare for this publication.

ACKNOWLEDGEMENTS

Declared none.

REFERENCES

Advocates for Youth. (2012). *Science & success: Programs that work to prevent teen pregnancy, hiv and sexually transmitted infections*. Retrieved from: http://www.advocatesforyouth.org/storage/advfy/documents/sciencesuccess.pdf/

The Alan Guttmacher Institute. (1998). *Teenage pregnancy and the welfare reform debate*. New York: Author.

The Alan Guttmacher Institute. (1999). *Teen sex and pregnancy: Facts in brief.* Retrieved from: http://www.agi-usa.org/pubs/fb_teen_sex.html/

Allen-Mears, P., Shapiro, C.H. (1989). *Adolescent sexuality: New challenges for social work.* New York: The Haworth Press.

Anderson, N. (n.d). Commentary: Abstinence-only approach out of date. *Mississippi Business Journal.* MasterFile. Retrieved Dec. 9, 2015

Bennett, S.E., Assefi, N.P. (2005). School-based teenage pregnancy prevention programs: a systematic review of randomized controlled trials. *J. Adolesc. Health, 36*(1), 72-81. [http://dx.doi.org/10.1016/j.jadohealth.2003.11.097] [PMID: 15661604]

Brown, S., Eisenburg, L. (1995). *The best intentions: Unintended pregnancy and the well-being of children and families.* Washington, DC: National Academy Press.

Carter, J. (1981). *State of the Union Address.* Retrieved from: http://www.jimmycarterlibrary.gov/documents/speeches/su81jec.phtml

Centers for Disease Control and Prevention. (2013). *Reducing Teen Pregnancy in the United States.* Retrieved from: http://www.cdc.gov/cdcgrandrounds/archives/2013/march2013.htm/

Centers for Disease Control and Prevention. (2014). *Teen pregnancy prevention 2010–2015: Integrating services, programs, and strategies through communitywide initiatives: national organizations.* Retrieved from: http://www.cdc.gov/teenpregnancy/preventteenpreg.htm/

Child Trends. (2014). Sexually active teens: Indicators on children and youth. *Child Trends Data Bank.* Retrieved from: http://www.childtrends.org/?indicators=sexually-active-teens/

Christopher, F.S. (1995). Adolescent pregnancy prevention. *Fam. Relat, 44*, 384. [http://dx.doi.org/10.2307/584994]

Coyle, K., Basen-Engquist, K., Kirby, D., Parcel, G., Banspach, S., Collins, J., Baumler, E., Carvajal, S., Harrist, R. (2001). Safer choices: reducing teen pregnancy, HIV, and STDs. *Public Health Rep, 116* (Suppl. 1), 82-93. [http://dx.doi.org/10.1093/phr/116.S1.82] [PMID: 11889277]

Franklin, C., Corcoran, J. (2000). Preventing adolescent pregnancy: a review of programs and practices. *Soc Work, 45*(1), 40-52. [http://dx.doi.org/10.1093/sw/45.1.40] [PMID: 10634085]

Dryfoos, J.G. (1990). Prevalence of adolescent pregnancy. *Adolescents at risk: Prevalence and prevention* (pp. 61-78). New York: Oxford University Press.

Dryfoos, J.G. (1998). *Safe passage: Making it through adolescence in a risky society.* New York: Oxford University Press.

Finer, L.B., Philbin, J.M. (2013). Sexual initiation, contraceptive use, and pregnancy among young adolescents. *Pediatrics, 131*(5), 886-891. [http://dx.doi.org/10.1542/peds.2012-3495] [PMID: 23545373]

Frost, J.J., Forrest, J.D. (1995). Understanding the impact of effective teenage pregnancy prevention programs. *Fam. Plann. Perspect, 27*(5), 188-195.

[http://dx.doi.org/10.2307/2136274] [PMID: 9104605]

Guttmacher Institute. (2014). American teens' sexual and reproductive health. *Fact Sheet.* New York: Guttmacher Institute. Retrieved from: http://www.guttmacher.org/pubs/FB-ATSRH.html/

Harper, C.C., Cheong, M., Rocca, C.H., Darney, P.D., Raine, T.R. (2005). The effect of increased access to emergency contraception among young adolescents. *Obstet. Gynecol, 106*(3), 483-491. [http://dx.doi.org/10.1097/01.AOG.0000174000.37962.a1] [PMID: 16135577]

Howard, M., McCabe, J. B. (1992). An information and skills approach for younger teens: Postponing sexual involvement program. In: Miller, B., Card, J., Paikoff, R., Peterson, J., (Eds.), *Preventing adolescent pregnancy* (pp. 83-109). Newbury Park, CA: Sage.

Humphreys, L. (1975). *Tearoom trade: Impersonal sex in in personal places* (2nd ed.). New Jersey: Aldine Transaction.

Jones, K. H., Domenico, D. M., Valente, J. S. (2006, Fall/Winter). Incidence of pregnant and parenting teens with disabilities within FACS programs. *Journal of Family and Consumer Sciences Education, 24*(2), 24-35. Retrieved from: http://www.natefacs.org/Pages/v24no2/v24no2Jones.pdf

Kennedy, J.F. (1955). *Profiles in courage: Decisive moments in the lives of celebrated Americans.* New York: Harper Collins.

Kirby, D. (2007). *Emerging answers 2007: New research findings on programs to reduce teen pregnancy and sexually transmitted diseases-full report.* Washington, DC: The National Campaign to Prevent Teen and Unplanned Pregnancy. Retrieved from: http://thenationalcampaign.org/resource/ emerging-answer--2007—full-report/

Klein, N. A., Sondag, A., Drolet, J. C. (1994). Understanding volunteer peer health educators' motivations: Applying social learning theory *College Health, 43*, 126-130.

Kohler, P.K., Manhart, L.E., Lafferty, W.E. (2008). Abstinence-only and comprehensive sex education and the initiation of sexual activity and teen pregnancy. *J. Adolesc. Health, 42*(4), 344-351. [http://dx.doi.org/10.1016/j.jadohealth.2007.08.026] [PMID: 18346659]

Knopf, D., Gordon, T.E. (1997). Adolescent health. In: Kotch, J.B., (Ed.), *Maternal* (pp. 173-224). Gaithersburg, MD: Aspen.

Luker, K. (1996). *Dubious conceptions: The politics of teenage pregnancy.* Cambridge, MA: Harvard University Press.

Malone, P., Rodriquez, M. (2011). Comprehensive sex education *vs.* abstinence-only-until-marriage programs. *Human Rights, 38*(2), 5-22.

McWhirter, J. J., McWhirter, B. T., McWhirter, A. M., McWhirter, E. H. (2013). *At-risk youth: A comprehensive response for counselors, teachers, psychologists, and human services professionals* (2nd ed..). Albany, NY: Brooks/Cole Publishing.

Moore, K. A., Sugland, B. W. (1996). *Next steps and best bets: Approaches to preventing adolescent childbearing.* Washington, DC: Child Trends, Inc. (Child Trends Publication No. 96-02)

National Campaign to Prevent Teen and Unplanned Pregnancy. (2014, August). *Fast facts: Teen childbearing in the United States, 2013 birth data.* Retrieved from: The National Campaign http://TheNationalCampaign.org/

National Campaign to Prevent Teen and Unplanned Pregnancy. (2014, August). *Fast facts: Teen pregnancy in the United States.* Retrieved from: The National Campaign http://TheNationalCampaign.org/

National Campaign to Prevent Teen and Unplanned Pregnancy. (2013, December). *Counting it up: The public costs of teen childbearing.* Retrieved from: The National Campaign http://TheNationalCampaign.org/

National Campaign to Prevent Teen Pregnancy. (2011, December). *A summary of effective interventions.* Retrieved from: The National Campaign http://TheNationalCampaign.org/

National Campaign to Prevent Teen Pregnancy. (2006). *Putting what works to work: Curriculum-based programs that prevent teen pregnancy* . Retrieved from: https://thenationalcampaign.org/sites/default/files/resource-primary-download/WhatWorks.pdf

National Campaign to Prevent Teen Pregnancy. (1999). *What about the teens? Research on what teens say about teen pregnancy: A focus group report.* Washington, DC: National Campaign to Prevent Teen Pregnancy.

O'Donnell, L., Stueve, A., O'Donnell, C., Duran, R., San Doval, A., Wilson, R. F. (2002). Long-term reductions in sexual initiation and sexual activity among urban middle schoolers in reach for health service learning program. *Journal of Adolescent Health, 31*, 93-100.

Office of the Assistant Secretary for Planning and Evaluation. (1997). *Comparison of prior law and the Personal Responsibility and Work Opportunity Act of 1996 (P.L. 104-193). (DHHS).* . Retrieved from: http://aspe.os.dhhs.gov/hsp/isp/reform.htm/

Planned Parenthood Federation of America, Inc.. (1999). *Adolescent sexuality.* Retrieved from: http://www.plannedparenthood.org/library/sexuality.html/

Reyna, V.F., Farley, F. (2006). Risk and rationality in adolescent decision making: Implications for theory, practice, and public policy. *Psychol. Sci. Public Interest, 7*(1), 1-44.
[PMID: 26158695]

Rodriquez, C., Moore, N. B. (1995). Perceptions of pregnant/parenting teens: Reframing issues for an integrated approach to pregnancy problems. *Adolescence, 30*, 685-707.

Scott, M. E., Steward-Streng, N. R., Manlove, J., Moore, K. A. (2012). The characteristics and circumstances of teen fathers: At the birth of their first child and beyond. *Child Trends.* Retrieved from: http://www.childtrends.org/wp-content/uploads/2013/03/Child_Trends-2012_06_01_RB_TeenFathers.pdf/

SIECUS. (2007). No More Money. *Spending on Abstinence-only-until-Marriage Programs (1982-2007).*

Retrieved from: http://www.nonewmoney.org/historyChart.html/ accessed 4/9/2007

Solomon-Fears, C. (2013). Teenage pregnancy prevention statistics and programs. *Congressional Research Service, (7-5700).* Retrieved from: www.crs.gov RS20301.

stayteen.org. (2014). Retrieved from: http://stayteen.org/teen-pregnancy/

The Phrase Finder. (2015). *Hobson's choice.* Retrieved from: http://phrases.org.uk/

Trenholm, C. (2007). *Impacts of Four Title V, Section 510, Abstinence Education Programs: Final Report, submitted to the U.S. Dept. of Health & Human Services, Office of the Assistant Secretary for Planning & Evaluation.* Princeton, NJ: Mathematica Policy Research.

U.S. Department of Health and Human Services, Office of Adolescent Health. (2014). *Sexually transmitted diseases: Did you know?.* Retrieved from: http://www.hhs.gov/ash/oah/adolescent-health-topics/ reproductive-health/stds.html/

U.S. Department of Health and Human Services, Centers for Disease Control and Prevention. (2014). Youth risk behavior surveillance—United States *Morbidity and Mortality Weekly Report, 64*(4), 1-128.

Webber, E., Feinsilber, M. (1990). *Grand allusions: A lively guide to those expressions, terms, & references you ought to know but might not.* Washington, DC: Faragut Publishing.

Zief, S., Shapiro, R., Strong, D. (2013). *The personal responsibility education program (PREP): Launching a nationwide adolescent pregnancy prevention effort, OPRE Report # 2013-37, Washington, DC: Office of Planning, Research and Evaluation, Administration for Children and Families, U.S. Department of Health and Human Services.* Retrieved from: http://www.acf.hhs.gov/programs/opre/index.html/

CHAPTER 5

Creating Safer Environments for Lesbian, Gay, Bisexual, and Transgender (LGBT) Youth and Families: Opportunities for School Mental Health Promotion

Carly A. Scarton and **Elizabeth A. Mellin**[*]

College of Community and Public Affairs, Binghamton University, Binghamton, New York, USA

Abstract: As schools reflect the sociopolitical climate of the country, educators and school mental health professionals are increasingly attending to the school climate for lesbian, gay, bisexual, a nd transgender (LGBT) youth as well as children raised in LGBT-headed households. This chapter provides school mental health professionals and educators with a summary of LGBT issues common in school settings as well as concomitant impacts on the mental health of LGBT students and families. Lastly, this chapter offers pragmatic thoughts for creating safer school environments that promote mental health for all students.

Keywords: Bisexual, Coming out, Discrimination, Diversity, Gay, Harassment, Lesbian, Sexual identity, Sexual orientation, Stigma, Transgender.

INTRODUCTION

Schools, which are responsible for creating safe environments for all students to learn and grow, often mirror the sociopolitical climate of our country. Debates about same-sex marriage and second parent adoption as well as news stories of suicides related to anti-gay bullying permeate both the households in which children live as well as the schools they attend. Our national dialogue about the

[*] **Corresponding author Elizabeth A. Mellin:** College of Community and Public Affairs Binghamton University PO Box 6000 Binghamton, New York 13902-6000 USA; Tel: 607-777-9243; Fax: 607-777-2406; Email: emellin@binghamton.edu

Raymond J. Waller (Ed.)

civil rights of lesbian, gay, bisexual, and transgender (LGBT) persons is also occurring in schools where there is increasing reflection on, and attention to, the school climate for LGBT youth and families.

The positioning of schools within these sociopolitical debates urges school mental health professionals and educators to consider the role they play in creating safer school environments for all students and their families. Many same-sex parents and sexual minority youth encounter an unwelcome school climate and face difficulties in their school communities (Kosciw & Diaz, 2008). Findings from the 2011 National School Climate Survey indicated that many LGBT students are targets of physical and verbal harassment and discrimination throughout the school day (Kosciw *et al.*, 2012).

As the political and social debates ensue, they will pervade classrooms and affect children with a LGBT parent. In fact, recent studies have suggested that the school related experiences of LGBT parents are often similar to the experiences of LGBT students; a negative school climate also affects LGBT parents and their children (Kosciw & Diaz, 2008; Kozik-Rosabal, 2000; Lamme & Lamme, 2002). There is an obvious relationship between school contextual factors such as school climate and psychosocial health of students and families. A negative school climate has been linked to:

- **LGBT youth suicide (Morrison & L'Heureux, 2001),**
- **escalation of depression, increased absenteeism (Kosciw *et al.*, 2012), and**
- **additional undesirable educational outcomes (Mayberry, 2006).**

All school mental health professionals and educators are ethically obligated to meet the needs of all students, sexual orientation notwithstanding. Many professional ethical standards clearly articulate the role of school counselors, psychologists, and social workers in addressing the health outcomes of LGBT youth by assisting in the creation of a respectful climate free of discrimination (ACA, 2005; ASCA, 2007; Tomaszewski, 2002; NASP, 2011).

School mental health professionals should likewise be advocates for all students. Their multiple roles allow them to communicate with students, parents, administrators, teachers, and staff and, in turn, offer support, help develop an inclusive climate, prevent bullying and victimization, affect change at the institutional level, and promote acceptance of diversity. The purpose of this chapter is to provide information about the mental health needs and related opportunities for school mental health promotion of LGBT youth and children in LGBT-headed households in school settings. We will begin with an overview of what is known about the school experiences of LGBT youth in both elementary and secondary schools, and about children from LGBT-headed households. Opportunities and suggestions for mental health promotion strategies that best support LGBT youth and families are also offered.

LGBT Issues in School Settings

LGBT youth and families are vulnerable populations that may encounter many obstacles because of their sexual orientation or gender expression. A surge of recent studies (Kosciw *et al.*, 2012; Kosciw & Diaz, 2008; D'Augelli, Grossman, & Starks, 2006; Bontempo & D'Augelli, 2002) have indicated that many LGBT youth encounter hostile school environments in which students in a sexual minority or children having same-sex parents too often encounter stigma, verbal harassment, and violence. These experiences with victimization are associated with poorer mental health outcomes compared to their heterosexual counterparts (Balsam & Hughes, 2013).

Despite the increase in attention to LGBT issues in secondary schools, particularly concerning bullying, investigations of LGBT youth and families in elementary schools are scarce (Cianciotto & Cahill, 2012). The primary barrier to researching LGBT issues in elementary schools is access; teachers, parents, and guardians have concerns about whether or not young children should be learning about LGBT issues in school-particularly in the early grades, primarily because most adults continue to equate LGBT with sexual behavior rather than relationships. There are also often conflicting opinions and varying perspectives on whether it is the school's responsibility to address such issues (Boyd, 1999).

Regardless of one's view, schools should be held accountable for promoting acceptance of all types of individuals and families, and preventing prejudice and discrimination (Boyd, 1999). One way to do this is to teach children about the diversity of all people in a safe and respectful learning environment. A call for research devoted to the experiences of LGBT youth and families at the elementary level is certainly needed now in order to promote optimal development and better mental health across the lifespan.

School mental health professionals and educators in both elementary and secondary school settings, however, need to be aware of the stressors that occur in school environments and contribute to and cause negative health outcomes. A deep understanding of the unique experiences of LGBT youth and youth from LGBT-headed households can ignite ideas for school mental health promotion opportunities. In the paragraphs below, we highlight common LGBT related issues faced by elementary and secondary school students and families.

Coming Out

Adolescence often involves many transformative challenges, including the exploration of sexuality (Rosario *et al.*, 2008), and some researchers report that youth come out around age 16 (*e.g.* Shilo & Savaya, 2011). It is an emerging probability that those who identify with a sexual attraction pattern that differs from the cultural norm or that those who have a gender expression that differs from their biological sex, became *aware* of the stigma associated with being a sexual minority at a much younger age than peers. This may serve as an explanatory hypothesis of why there would be such disparity with sexual identity and sexual orientation and the divulgence of any manifestation of sexuality that differs from the cultural majority. People who identify as transgender later in life report being aware of their difference significantly prior to the middle teen years (Pazos, 1999). As was the previously stated case for lesbian and gay youth, the body of literature examining the lives of transgender youth is very small, particularly concerning experiences in elementary schools.

For reasons discussed earlier, the body of evidence guiding practice with LGBT children is insufficient. There is evidence that mental health promotion in schools, if LGBT are to benefit, must be implemented in elementary schools. One longitudinal study reported that ¾ of LGBT individuals reported feeling atypical as children, with the difference, on average, perceived by the age of 8 (D'Augelli, Grossman, & Starks, 2006). Savin-Williams and Diamond (2000) had similarly related that the age for initial same-sex attractions is between 8-9 years of age for both girls and boys. Harrison (2003) likewise reported findings that the process of sexual identity begins earlier than high school, at around 10 years of age. This has specific and significant implications for school mental health professionals and educators. Children around this age are learning how to navigate the often-turbulent waters of one of the most divisive divergences from the cultural majority in many parts of the world. Youth who are LGBT would almost certainly benefit from the support of school professionals in mental health promotion initiatives.

Resource	http://www.aacap.org/AACAP/Families_and_Youth/Facts_for_Families/Facts_for_Families_Pages/Gay_Lesbian_and_Bisexual_Adolescents_63.aspx

Results from the 2011 National School Climate Survey show that a large number of students (14% of those who responded to the question) felt limited by school policies that imposed gender-specific dress codes, limiting students' gender roles, gender expression, and gender identity (Kosciw & Diaz, 2008). LGBT students often experience a disunion between their gender identity and body that is exacerbated by school rules, such as who is an acceptable guest at a school dance. Many transgender students have reported that school rules often made them present themselves as someone they were not. Transgender students also felt restricted in their gender identity in policies regarding locker rooms, restrooms, and in formal recognition of class documents. Students believed they were in danger when they were only allowed to use the restrooms or locker rooms of their legal sex. Additionally, transgender students in this study felt discriminated against by school forms that were limited to binary gender options, or by the school's refusal to address them by their preferred pronoun or names (Kosciw *et al.*, 2012).

Transgender individuals are often expected to adopt a gender identity, while those who have same-sex experiences are also expected to label themselves and declare an identity. As one can imagine, the process of deciding when to disclose can be very stressful for lesbian, gay, and bisexual youth. Once they do decide to come out, these adolescents may then experience rejection from family members and peers. This fear of rejection may cause many LGBT youth to be reluctant to tell their parents or other family members about their sexual orientation. The coming out process will look different for each unique individual. However, various patterns describe what the coming out process may be like for most youth.

Outdated models delineating the coming out process described it as a progression:

- **beginning with same-sex attraction,**
- **moving towards same-sex behavior, and**
- **concluding with the formation of a stable sexual identity (Cass, 1979).**

Many of these studies included samples of gay adult men who reflected on their coming out years (Eliason, Dibble, DeJoseph, & Chin, 2009). More recent studies, and those with a more diverse representation from the LGBT community, have shed light on the fact that the sexual identity-or one's personal identity as heterosexual, gay, or bisexual (Psychology Dictionary, 2015)-process is much more complicated and fluid than the single direction trajectory that older models suggested (Eliason & Schope, 2007). D'Augelli (1994), for example, proposes a model in which processes of lesbian, gay, and bisexual identity development operate more independently and not necessarily in stages. This framework suggests that identity development is not necessarily congruent over time.

The process of coming out to peers can be a difficult road to navigate for many youth. Adolescents who consider disclosing their sexual orientation to peers may fear that they will become rejected, harassed, or socially isolated by their peers in school. Teens come out in school environments where teachers and administrators cannot assure their safety against peer abuse in the form of verbal and physical attacks and where LGBT issues are not represented in the school curriculum (Holmes & Cahill, 2004). In some schools, teachers and administrators may even overtly or covertly engage in anti-gay harassment and discrimination. Along with peer-to-peer relationships, anti-gay discrimination and violence is an epidemic in our elementary, middle, and high schools (Cianciotto & Cahill, 2003).

Anti-LGBT Harassment

No matter what the coming out process looks like, this period in an LGBT person's life may include confusion, questioning, and stigma. Those who identify as LGBT or are perceived by peers to be LGBT may become victims of harassment and abuse. Russell and others (2010) defined harassment as relational and physical aggression, name-calling, antigay language, and verbal teasing. This type of abuse can have detrimental effects on the mental health of LGBT students and children in LGBT-headed households. Devastating outcomes include elevations in:

- **suicidal thinking and behavior,**
- **depressive symptoms, and**
- **substance abuse (Birkett *et al.*, 2009; Bontempo & D'Augelli, 2002).**

Harassment that students may experience is not restricted to verbal abuse. The physical and, at times, brutal, violence that we hear so much about at the secondary school level also happens in elementary schools. Children who do not conform to stereotypical gender roles may become targets of discrimination. Unfortunately, this type of behavior often goes undocumented and dismissed as typical childhood antics. These antigay behaviors are much more than antics. Harris Interactive, Inc. and the Gay, Lesbian, and Straight Education Network (GLSEN) conducted a survey of 1,065 elementary grades students (grades 3-6) and 1,099 elementary teachers (Kindergarten - 6th grade). Elementary students and teachers who participated in the survey were asked about how often they hear biased remarks at school. Their findings suggested that homophobic slurs such as "lesbo" or "fag" are used by children and meant to be hurtful. It is clear that children are learning, from a very young age, that these words have negative overtones. It is unlikely that students are the only individuals hearing, or even using, such words.

Elementary school teachers reported that students frequently used the word "gay" to imply that something is bad or 'less than' (GLSEN & Harris Interactive, 2012). It is not uncommon to hear the word "gay" from elementary school to high school as the word of choice to indicate that something is undesirably different (Kosciw *et al.*, 2012), an interesting phenomenon. For example, a child asked his father if he knew what "faggot" meant. When the child's father asked him why he wanted to know, the child replied that another student had called him this name during recess (Reis, 1999).

Children begin using homophobic slurs early. It is evident that elementary students know about LGBT issues; they are already talking about them, yet the important adults in their lives are often avoiding the conversation. Another problematic layer is added when LGBT-specific language is used with the intent to be hurtful, and without even knowing what these words mean. Elementary students may gather a false understanding that to be gay is to be bad. If these false beliefs are not challenged at the elementary level, misinformed youth may then go on to high school and continue the cycle of discrimination, as studies have shown.

In their 2011 National School Climate Survey, the Gay, Lesbian, and Straight Education Network (GLSEN) found that nonconformity with norms of sexual orientation of the cultural majority were the identified motives reported for being threatened or harassed at school. Results from this survey of students indicated that 4 in 10 students felt unsafe due to their gender expression while 6 in 10 LGBT students reported safety concerns due to their sexual orientation (Kosciw *et al.*, 2012). Specific reasons these students felt unsafe included both verbal and physical attacks.

Such concerns can scarcely be dismissed as paranoia, considering a greater than 80% occurrence of this student group reported being verbally harassed due to nonconformity with sexual orientation of the majority; moreover, 1 in 5 students were physically assaulted due to their gender, gender expression, or sexual orientation. Students with higher levels of victimization motivated by these biases had more depression and suffered from a lower self-esteem than those who with lower levels of such abuse (Kosciw *et al.*, 2012). These feelings of jeopardy are the impetus for extremely high levels of school avoidance (Kosciw *et al.*, 2012). Higher incidence of psychosocial symptoms may become causal influences of the use of drugs, alcohol, or unsafe behavior (IOM, 2011). Suicide is also a very serious concern among all students, especially LGBT youth.

Bias Coming Home

Children growing up in LGBT-headed households may also feel like they are unable to tell their peers about their own family composition. Youth realize that disclosing this information may similarly lead to feelings of discrimination and experiences of harassment. Little is known about the school experiences of children who have same-sex parents. Kosciw and Diaz (2008) studied the experiences of children with LGBT parents and asked students questions about their exposure to biased language, harassment, bullying, and their safety and comfort at school. About 24% of students in their study had experienced a negative event at school specifically because they had LGBT parents (Kosciw & Diaz, 2008).

Kosciw and Diaz also found that 51% of their participants reported feeling unsafe in school, and 23% of this group of students stated that they felt unsafe because of reasons related to their family structure (*i.e.*, same-sex parents). Unfortunately and unconscionably, mistreatment not only came from students, but also from adult members within the school community. Some individuals in this study were harassed during school due to their perceived sexual orientation, meaning they were presumed to be lesbian or gay simply because they had a lesbian, gay, or bisexual (LGB) parent. They found that students from LGBT families might experience forms of harassment not experienced by other students, such as verbal harassment (Kosciw & Diaz, 2008), who reported that 72% of student participants heard the expressions, "that's so gay" or "you're so gay" and 65% heard negative remarks such as "dyke" and "faggot". This same study included a smaller number of students (17%) who reported hearing homophobic comments made about their families and having an LGBT parent (Kosciw & Diaz, 2008). This type of verbal communication reflects the quality of the school environment. A school environment in which LGBT-specific families are discussed openly and positively may not encounter such intolerance.

Inclusive Curriculum

Previous research suggests that there are very few schools that incorporate an LGBT inclusive curriculum and/or include policies prohibiting discrimination laws on these grounds (Kosciw *et al.*, 2012). The exclusion of LGBT people from the school curriculum is bias in its most basic form (McGarry, 2013). This neglect of support for LGBT youth within our educational system perpetuates the bias and discrimination against sexual minorities. Such bias is, unfortunately, often far more overt in nature than mere lack of inclusion or support. Evidence of this is provided by national news reports such as came from a Mississippi high school that forsook their prom rather than grant attendance to a lesbian couple (Weston, 2010). Another example involves the Georgia high school that removed a student from his position as President of Student Council for proposing the idea of having a gay-friendly prom rather than an exclusive one (Caulfield, 2012).

The large majority of students who are LGBT do not have an inclusive curriculum at their school. Including information about the history and events concerning LGBT people may actually help reduce the prejudice of LGBT individuals. Research by GLSEN continuously shows that an inclusive curriculum is related to an improvement of peer support for LGBT students (Kosciw & Diaz, 2012). LGBT families are also excluded here, which can be confusing for students who have different family constellations than what the school presents as the norm.

For some children growing up in LGBT-headed households, schools are their first experience with messages reinforcing the traditional family structure of mother and father (Fedewa & Clark, 2009). The reality is that parents may be single or part of a couple, gay, straight, adoptive, step, remarried, or foster (Jeltova, 2005). LGBT parents of children in K-12 schools may feel pressured to keep their family characteristics a secret. Casper, Schultz and Wickens (1992) found that children bring their family experiences to school *via* discussions, play, and general comments that demonstrate their thoughts about what and who constitutes a family.

The Connection to Mental Health

There are many variables that shape mental health, many of which are discussed throughout this text. Innate factors may create vulnerabilities or predispositions to certain mental conditions, while the environment may also influence an individual's mental wellbeing (Cochran & Mays, 2013). These environmental factors include a variety of influences that intersect including:

- **developmental experiences,**
- **social advantages or disadvantages, and**
- **actual or anticipated discrimination.**

Among these, sexual orientation stands out as a particularly pertinent individual characteristic that may contribute to the risk one has for developing physiological or psychological mental concerns (Cochran & Mays). Research on youth in asexual minority has also suggested that there are significant mental health disparities between LGBT youth and heterosexual youth (D'Augelli, 2006; Ryan, Huebner, Diaz, & Sanchez, 2009). Mental health distress, victimization, substance abuse, and suicidal ideation are just some of the risk factors that occur because of stigma from members of society (Hershberger & D'Augelli, 1999).

Growing up often involves many transformative challenges, including the exploration of sexuality. For the youth who are LGBT, this can be an even more demanding time as they are faced with:

- **social prejudices,**
- **victimization,**
- **discrimination,**
- **bullying, and**
- **injustice in their schools (D'Augelli, Pilkington, & Hershberger, 2002; Kosciw *et al.*, 2012).**

Depression

Youth who have same-sex attractions or a gender expression that differs from the norm may be at an increased risk for anxiety or depression. D'Augelli and Hershberger (1993) studied LGB youth under the age of 21 in various communities and found that 41% of males and 28% of females reported feeling depressed. Another study of 1,032 high school students in 18 different schools found that LGBT youth reported higher levels of depressive symptoms than heterosexual and nontransgender youth (Almeida *et al.*, 2009). In this same study,

33.7% of youth who identified with a sexual minority status reported perceived discrimination. Birkett and colleagues (2009) found that middle school students who were questioning their sexual orientation status reported higher levels of depressive symptoms than those who were not questioning their sexual orientation. This same study also highlights the role that schools play in supporting LGBT and questioning students.

Children who attended schools with a positive climate and who did not experience homophobic bullying reported the lowest levels of depression and suicidality (Birkett *et al.*, 2009). It is this discrimination and stigma that often leads to depression, which can then lead to suicidal ideation among our LGBT youth. Schools are responsible for meeting the needs of all students. These needs include avoiding direct detriment to mental health, thus, school mental health professionals and educators who work in schools can help to enrich the lives of LGBT students and promote a more accepting society. When homophobic teasing, harassment, and discrimination occurs, the quality of life of LGBT youth is compromised. These negative conditions put LGBT students at an increased risk not only for suicide and depression, but also for substance abuse.

Substance Abuse

Numerous studies have indicated that youth in a sexual minority report more substance abuse and initiating usage at younger ages than heterosexual youth (Corliss *et al.*, 2010; Marshall *et al.*, 2009). The trajectory for increased substance abuse begins in adolescence (Marshall *et al.*, 2009). A meta-analysis of 18 studies suggested that youth in a sexual minority are 2-5 times more likely than their heterosexual counterparts to abuse substances (Marshall *et al.*, 2008). Findings from a study by Marshal and others (2009) suggested that LGBT youth who were using substances early on in life will likely continue on this path, extending their substance abuse well into adulthood though suggested that prevention efforts may help reduce mental health problems among LGB youth, including reducing the risk for substance abuse.

Reis and Saewyc (1999) actually found an association between youth who were bullied due to their sexual orientation and an increased risk for substance abuse.

School supports that thwart bullying behaviors, especially those targeted at LGBT youth, can help curb this risk and instead, decrease the stress that may lead to engagement in substance abuse. Moreover, these school interventions may help promote a greater sense of well-being and acceptance in other areas of students' lives as well.

Suicide

Most researchers will concur that being LGBT is not the direct cause of having a mental illness; rather, mental health problems including suicidality are a result of the stress associated with having such a stigmatized identity, fear of disapproval and rejection, victimization, or negotiating things like coming out to friends and family members (Kitts, 2005). Regardless of the reason, we know that suicide is not the answer to such stress. However, those who identify as LGBT may be at an increased risk, and schools are in a key position to support these students.

While it is difficult to say for sure that more LGBT youth than heterosexual youth commit suicide, there have been many studies done that suggest LGBT youth are more likely to attempt suicide (Kitts, 2005; Russell, 2003). Kitts (2005) proposes that lesbian, gay, and bisexual youth are 20-40% more likely to attempt suicide than their heterosexual counterparts. Russell and Joyner (2001) studied the link between adolescent sexual orientation and suicidal thoughts and behaviors using data from the National Longitudinal Study of Adolescent Health. Their sample data represented more than 6,000 adolescent girls and 5,000 adolescent boys. Based on findings from this study, they purport that youth in a sexual minority were more likely to attempt suicide (Russell & Joyner, 2001).

Interventions for School Mental Health Professionals and Educators

School mental health professionals and educators working with lesbian, gay, bisexual, and transgender youth and children growing up in LGBT-headed households need to be aware of the stressors that occur in school environments and the causes of these negative health outcomes. Avenues through which a professional can help do not need to be limited to the school setting. This section will highlight specific areas in which action steps can be taken. These steps are important for schools to provide safe and welcoming environments, as well as important for the professionals who work with LGBT youth.

Jan Goodman, an elementary school principal, eloquently describes a model school environment:

> In a model school, issues of sexual orientation are blended into the curriculum. Gay, lesbian, bisexual, and transgender community members feel safe to be open about their sexuality; gay-parented families are welcomed from the day they enter the school. There are positive images of LGBT people in the school's curriculum and program. Classrooms and hallways are free of put downs because staff members consistently intervene, regardless of their personal beliefs about homosexuality. An anti-slur policy is in place that includes, among many other categories, homophobic comments. Parents and guardians are informed when their child insults another, and the student is expected to make amends. Students feel safe because they know that adults will listen to them and protect them (Goodman, 2005, p. 116).

Schools are one of the institutions that nearly all LGBT youth must attend. Thus, school mental health professionals are in a position to advocate for LGBT students when they experience prejudice, discrimination, and abuse and are instrumental in the prevention of these illegal and destructive acts. They can be essential in establishing this very type of school environment that so readily welcomes diversity. They have connections to not only the children themselves, but too many key stakeholders within the various systems that influence schools.

Specific strategies can be implemented from a systems approach, at the individual, institutional, and larger societal level. Urie Bronfenbrenner's (1979) Ecological Systems Theory provides a relevant conceptualization framework, because it directs attention to the interrelations between and within various settings in an individual's life and illustrates the impact of the interaction between gender and sexual identity and environment on mental health. Bronfenbrenner (1979) defined four concepts (microsystem, mesosystem, macrosystem, and mesosystem) and later added a fifth (chronosystem) that are central to a child's development.

There is much overlap between and within each system as they continuously influence one another over time (Bronfenbrenner, 1979). Bronfenbrenner (1979) described his model as, "a set of nested structures, each inside the next, like a set of Russian dolls" (Bronfenbrenner, 1979, p. 22). This model acknowledges that children do not develop solely on their own, but instead, in relation to their educational setting, family life, peer groups, and society. Bronfenbrenner's ecological systems theory helps to explain the influence that interactions between teachers, parents, peers, and broader systems can have on the development of children.

Utilizing a systems approach enables school mental health professionals and educators to focus on empowering all systems and individuals, thus establishing effective collaboration between heterosexual and LGBT members of the community to create lasting change. Fig. (**1**) provides a visual framework for school intervention.

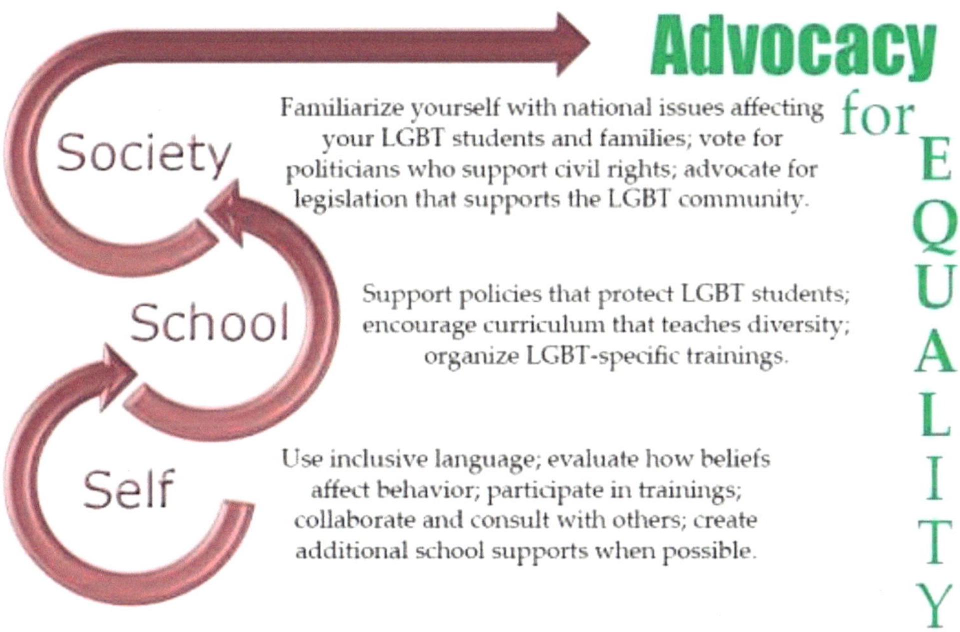

The lists below suggest practical interventions for school mental health professionals and educators working in both elementary and secondary school settings.

SELF

- **Be mindful of using inclusive language.**
- **Evaluate your own systems of belief that affect your behavior.**
- **Participate in training opportunities that will advance your knowledge in this area.**
- **Talk to LGBT individuals and others to find out what issues directly affect your school.**
- **Create a group or additional system of support for LGBT students and children of LGBT-headed households.**

SCHOOL

- **Support school policies and procedures that protect LGBT students from discrimination, bullying, and other forms of victimization.**
- **Challenge the traditional definition of family that is often taught in schools and encourage a curriculum that includes various family forms, including children of same-sex partners.**
- **Organize or advocate for staff training that addresses LGBT competency and diversity.**

SOCIETY

- **Familiarize yourself with national issues affecting those who are LGBT.**
- **Vote for politicians who support civil rights for all people, regardless of sexual orientation, gender, and gender expression.**
- **Write to your policy makers and advocate for legislation that supports the LGBT community.**

CONCLUSION

Promoting change that is in the best interests of LGBT students and families requires working across all three of these levels and collaborating with heterosexual allies and members of the LGBT community. What follows are culturally appropriate action steps, in no particular order, that can be taken by school mental health professionals and educators to create safer environments and promote mental health in schools. These action steps may also be relevant to other adults who are part of the school community such as administrators, support personnel (*e.g.*, bus drivers, cafeteria staff), community partners who deliver services in schools, and parent volunteers.

1. Help to Create a Safe and Welcoming Space for Students

It is important for school personnel to understand the negative health outcomes that occur because of homophobia, bullying, discrimination, and other types of victimization. These behaviors often create an unsafe and unwelcome school climate for LGBT youth. Consider the effects of the overall school climate. Are they positive or negative? The effects of a negative environment may include depression, suicide, stress, and other health issues. LGBT students need to feel protected. This protection may take the form of support groups, guidance counseling, or establishing positive role models within the school (Mayberry, 2006). Shilo and Savaya (2011) suggest that counselors working with LGB youth should focus on interventions that increase support and acceptance from family, friends, and others in the social environment.

The Gay, Lesbian, and Straight Education Network (GLSEN) suggested that school professionals designate safe spaces in the school (GLSEN, 2011). GLSEN (2011) defines a safe space as an environment that is supportive and welcoming of students who identify as LGBT. GLSEN provides safe space stickers that can be placed in offices or classrooms; these stickers let students know that the area or individual is safe and supportive. You may also consider initiating conversations with administrators or speaking with the school board about the value in having an inclusive and welcoming school (Human Rights Campaign Foundation, 2012).

2. Know Your Resources

In order to develop a plan of action, one must first consider the level of existing support among administration, teachers, and parents/guardians. Familiarize yourself with the demands your school may be facing and know the local school, district, and state policies (Human Rights Campaign Foundation, 2012). This may prove helpful before conducting staff training on LGBT issues, as it is important for trainers to identify the needs at the school (Fisher & Kennedy, 2012). An expert from an outside organization can come in to educate staff on best practices for working with LGBT youth and families. There may be someone within the school who is competent and qualified for such a task (Fisher & Kennedy, 2012).

Consider what level of support exists among the parent/guardian community, the administration, and the teachers (Human Rights Campaign Foundation, 2012). Familiarize yourself with your school's policies and procedures. Does your school have anti-discrimination laws in place to protect LGBT youth, same-sex parents, and children of same-sex parents? Are the laws inclusive of sexual orientation and gender identity? Resources that encourage education and awareness may lead to a reduction of anti-LGBT behaviors, which may then lead to a safer school environment for all students (Greytak *et al.*, 2013). Advocate for policy change if necessary.

Resource	https://www.hrc.org/

3. Recognize the Need for LGBT-inclusive Curriculum and Language

Promote LGBT content to be infused into the curriculum. This can be achieved by displaying materials that support LGBT individuals in visible places throughout the school and within the curriculum. For example, include quotes of famous LGBT people in history on a bulletin board. Support the diversity of family constellations by supporting various family structures to be included in the school curriculum (Fisher and Kennedy, 2012). Include stories, documents, flyers, assignments, and other written materials that reflect the diversity of families that your school serves.

Be prepared for pushback from those who may not be ready for an inclusive curriculum. If individuals question this inclusion, the Human Rights Campaign Foundation (2012) suggests that you let them know it is simply about *family*. When LGBT-specific topics are off limits, it only creates the illusion that different necessarily means bad. For example, use neutral pronouns when referring to people; this will help LGBT students feel more comfortable (GLSEN, 2011).

4. Understand the Effects of Social Stigma that many LGBT Youth and Families Face

This stigma is what perpetuates the discrimination and lack of validation those members of the LGBT community often experience. Stigma leads to stress, which may then cause mental and physical health problems such as anxiety, depression, substance abuse, even asthma and cancers (Meyer, Levahot & Frost, 2015). Stigma influences the way individuals interact with and treat LGBT individuals. This is particularly detrimental in a school system, where students spend so much of their time. Please do not ignore anti-LGBT comments or behavior. Students who are LGBT are too often victims of acts of school violence and harassment, and nearly 40% of students who reported assaults of harassment to a school staff member state that school staff did nothing (Kosciw *et al.*, 2012). It can be challenging learning how to respond to anti-LGBT behavior; however, not doing so sends a message that it is okay to discriminate or harass others (GLSEN, 2011; Human Rights Campaign Foundation, 2012). Practice ways that you feel comfortable addressing homophobic slurs or behavior.

5. Encourage LGBT-specific Professional Development Trainings at Your School

School mental health professionals can facilitate training sessions for staff, educators, students, and parents to educate about homophobia, heterosexism, and discrimination. Being aware of issues does not always equate into taking action.

Resource	http://www.hrc.org/youth

Educators and other school personnel need to have opportunities to learn the appropriate skills and knowledge to work effectively with the LGBT population

(D'Augelli, Grossman, & Starks, 2006; Fisher & Kennedy, 2012). There are a multitude of trainings that can improve awareness and help others be sensitive to LGBT issues. Goals of these professional development trainings include teaching staff how to intervene when someone is being mistreated, implement strategies in classrooms, and reviewing terminology and facts specific to LGBT issues (Fisher & Kennedy, 2012).

Many of these trainings are customizable to specific schools. A study by the Gay, Lesbian, Straight, and Education Network (GLSEN) found that same-sex parents who said their child's school offered trainings on LGBT issues for school staff were less likely than other parents to report that their child had been harassed or bullied (Kosciw & Diaz, 2008). If you are in a position to do so, offer to provide the training for the rest of the staff. Above all else, do not contribute to this discriminatory behavior.

CONFLICT OF INTEREST

The authors confirm that they have no conflict of interest to declare for this publication.

ACKNOWLEDGEMENTS

Declared none.

REFERENCES

Almeida, J., Johnson, R.M., Corliss, H.L., Molnar, B.E., Azrael, D. (2009). Emotional distress among LGBT youth: the influence of perceived discrimination based on sexual orientation. *J. Youth Adolesc., 38*(7), 1001-1014.
[http://dx.doi.org/10.1007/s10964-009-9397-9] [PMID: 19636742]

American Counseling Association. (2005). *ACA Code of Ethics.*. Alexandria, VA: ACA.

American School Counselor Association. (2007). *Ethical Guidelines for Professional School Counselors.*. Alexandra, VA: ASCA.

Balsam, K., Hughes, T. (2013). Sexual Orientation, Victimization, and Hate Crimes. In: Patterson, C.J., D'Augelli, A.R., (Eds.), *Handbook of psychology and sexual orientation.* (pp. 204-222). New York: Oxford University Press.

Birkett, M., Espelage, D.L., Koenig, B. (2009). LGB and questioning students in schools: the moderating

effects of homophobic bullying and school climate on negative outcomes. *J. Youth Adolesc., 38*(7), 989-1000.
[http://dx.doi.org/10.1007/s10964-008-9389-1] [PMID: 19636741]

Bontempo, D.E., D'Augelli, A.R. (2002). Effects of at-school victimization and sexual orientation on lesbian, gay, or bisexual youths' health risk behavior. *J. Adolesc. Health, 30*(5), 364-374.
[http://dx.doi.org/10.1016/S1054-139X(01)00415-3] [PMID: 11996785]

Boyd, B.F. (1999). Should gay and lesbian issues be discussed in elementary school? *Child. Educ., 76*(1), 40.
[http://dx.doi.org/10.1080/00094056.1999.10522069]

Bronfenbrenner, U. (1979). *The ecology of human development: Experiments by nature and design.*. Cambridge, MA: Harvard University Press.

Casper, V., Schultz, S., Wickens, E. (1992). Breaking the silences: Lesbian and gay parents and the schools. *Teach. Coll. Rec., 94*, 109-137.

Cass, V.C. (1979). Homosexual identity formation: a theoretical model. *J. Homosex., 4*(3), 219-235.
[http://dx.doi.org/10.1300/J082v04n03_01] [PMID: 264126]

Caulfield, P. (2012). *High school student sues high school over gay prom king, queen proposal.* New York Daily News.
http://www.nydailynews.com/news/national/georgia-high-school-student-sues-high-school-gay-prom-king-queen-proposal-article-1.1050609

Cianciotto, J., Cahill, S. (2003). *Education policy: Issues affecting lesbian, gay, bisexual, and transgender youth.*. New York: The National Gay and Lesbian Task Force Policy Institute.

Cochran, S.D., Mays, V.M. (2013). Sexual Orientation and Mental Health. In: Patterson, C.J., D'Augelli, A.R., (Eds.), *Handbook of psychology and sexual orientation.* (pp. 204-222). New York: Oxford University Press.

Corliss, H.L., Rosario, M., Wypij, D., Wylie, S.A., Frazier, A.L., Austin, S.B. (2010). Sexual orientation and drug use in a longitudinal cohort study of U.S. adolescents. *Addict. Behav., 35*(5), 517-521.
[http://dx.doi.org/10.1016/j.addbeh.2009.12.019] [PMID: 20061091]

Daley, A., Solomon, S., Newman, P.A., Mishna, F. (2007). Traversing the margins: Intersectionalities in the bullying of lesbian, gay, bisexual and transgender youth. *J. Gay Lesbian Soc. Serv., 19*(4), 9-29.

D'Augelli, A.R. (1994). Identity development and sexual orientation: Toward a model of lesbian, gay, and bisexual Development. In: Trickett, E.J., Watts, R.J., Birman, D., (Eds.), *Human Diversity: Perspectives on People in Context.*. San Francisco: Jossey-Bass.

D'Augelli, A.R. (2006). Developmental and contextual factors and mental health among lesbian, gay, and bisexual youths. In: Omoto, A.M., Kurtzman, H.S., (Eds.), *Sexual orientation and mental health.* (pp. 37-53). Washington, DC: American Psychological Association.
[http://dx.doi.org/10.1037/11261-002]

D'Augelli, A.R., Grossman, A.H., Starks, M.T. (2006). Childhood gender atypicality, victimization, and PTSD among lesbian, gay, and bisexual youth. *J. Interpers. Violence, 21*(11), 1462-1482.
[http://dx.doi.org/10.1177/0886260506293482] [PMID: 17057162]

D'Augelli, A.R., Hershberger, S.L. (1993). Lesbian, gay, and bisexual youth in community settings: personal challenges and mental health problems. *Am. J. Community Psychol., 21*(4), 421-448.
[http://dx.doi.org/10.1007/BF00942151] [PMID: 8192119]

D'Augelli, A.R., Pilkington, N.W., Hershberger, S.L. (2002). Incidence and mental health impact of sexual orientation victimization of lesbian, gay, and bisexual youths in high school. *Sch. Psychol. Q., 17*(2), 148-167.
[http://dx.doi.org/10.1521/scpq.17.2.148.20854]

Eliason, M.J., Dibble, S.D., DeJoseph, J., Chinn, P. (2009). *LGBTQ cultures: What health professionals need to know about sexual and gender diversity.*. Philadelphia: Lippincott.

Eliason, M.J., Schope, R. (2007). Shifting sands or solid foundation: Lesbian, gay, bisexual, and transgender identity formation. In: Meyer, I.H., Northridge, M., (Eds.), *The health of sexual minorities.* (pp. 3-26). New York: Springer Science.
[http://dx.doi.org/10.1007/978-0-387-31334-4_1]

Fedewa, A.L., Clark, T.W. (2009). Parent practices and home-school partnerships: A differential effect for children with same-sex coupled parents? *J. GLBT Fam. Stud., 5*, 312-339.
[http://dx.doi.org/10.1080/15504280903263736]

Fisher, E.S., Kennedy, K.S. (2012). *Responsive school practices to support lesbian, gay, bisexual, transgender, and questioning students and families.* Retrieved from: http://www.eblib.com

Gay, Lesbian Straight Education Network (GLSEN). (2011). *The safe space kit: Guide to being an ally.*. New York: GLSEN.

Goodman, J.M. (2005). Homophobia prevention and intervention in elementary schools: A principal's responsibility. *J. Gay Lesbian Issues Educ., 3*(1), 111-116.
[http://dx.doi.org/10.1300/J367v03n01_12]

Greytak, E.A., Joseph, G., Madelyn, J.B. (2013). Putting the "T" in resource: The benefits of LGBT-related school resources for transgender youth. *J. LGBT Youth, 10*, 45-63.
[http://dx.doi.org/10.1080/19361653.2012.718522]

Harrison, T.W. (2003). Adolescent homosexuality and concerns regarding disclosure. *J. Sch. Health, 73*(3), 107-112.
[http://dx.doi.org/10.1111/j.1746-1561.2003.tb03584.x] [PMID: 12677729]

Hershberger, S.L., D'Augelli, A.R. (1999). Issues in counseling lesbian, gay, and bisexual adolescents. In: Perez, R.P., DeBord, K.A., Bieschke, K.J., (Eds.), *Handbook of counseling and psychotherapy with lesbian, gay, and bisexual clients.* (pp. 225-247). Washington, DC: American Psychology Association.

Holmes, S., Cahill, S. (2004). School experiences of gay, lesbian, bisexual and transgender youth. *J. Gay Lesbian Issues Educ., 3*, 54-66.

Human Rights Campaign Foundation. (2012). Welcoming schools: A project of the human rights campaign foundation. *Welcomingschools.org*. Retrieved October 1st, 2013, from: http://www.welcomingschools.org

IOM (Institute of Medicine). (2011). *The health of lesbian, gay, bisexual, and transgender people: Building a foundation for better understanding.*. Washington, DC: The National Academies Press.

Jeltova, I., Fish, M.C. (2005). Creating school environments responsive to gay, lesbian, bisexual, and transgender families: Traditional and systemic approaches for consultation. *J. Educ. Psychol. Consult., 16*(1), 17-33.
[http://dx.doi.org/10.1207/s1532768xjepc161&2_2]

Kitts, R.L. (2005). Gay adolescents and suicide: understanding the association. *Adolescence, 40*(159), 621-628.
[PMID: 16268137]

Kosciw, J.G., Diaz, E.M. (2008). *Involved, Invisible, Ignored: The Experiences of Lesbian, Gay, Bisexual and Transgender Parents and Their Children in Our Nation's K–12 Schools.*. New York: GLSEN.

Kosciw, J.G., Greytak, E.A., Bartkiewicz, M.J., Boesen, M.J., Palmer, N.A. (2012). *The 2011 National School Climate Survey: The experiences of lesbian, gay, bisexual and transgender youth in our nation's schools.*. New York: GLSEN.

Kozik-Rosabal, G. (2000). "Well, we haven't noticed anything bad going on," said the principal. Parents speak about their gay families and schools. *Educ. Urban Soc., 32*, 368-389.
[http://dx.doi.org/10.1177/0013124500323006]

Lamme, L.L., Lamme, L.A. (2002). Welcoming children from gay and lesbian families into our schools. *Educ. Leadersh., 59*, 65-72.

Meyer, I.H., Lehavot, K., Frost, D.M. (2015). Minority stress and the health of sexual minority individuals. *J. Behav. Med., 38*(1), 1-8.

Marshal, M.P., Friedman, M.S., Stall, R., King, K.M., Miles, J., Gold, M.A., Bukstein, O.G., Morse, J.Q. (2008). Sexual orientation and adolescent substance use: a meta-analysis and methodological review. *Addiction, 103*(4), 546-556.
[http://dx.doi.org/10.1111/j.1360-0443.2008.02149.x] [PMID: 18339100]

Marshal, M.P., Friedman, M.S., Stall, R., Thompson, A.L. (2009). Individual trajectories of substance use in lesbian, gay and bisexual youth and heterosexual youth. *Addiction, 104*(6), 974-981.
[http://dx.doi.org/10.1111/j.1360-0443.2009.02531.x] [PMID: 19344440]

Mayberry, M. (2006). School reform efforts for lesbian, gay, bisexual, and transgendered students. *Clearing House, 79*(6), 262-264.

[http://dx.doi.org/10.3200/TCHS.79.6.262-264]

McGarry, R. (2013). Build a curriculum that includes everyone: Ensuring that schools are more accepting of LGBT students and issues requires more than passing mentions of diversity in sex education classes. *Phi Delta Kappan, 94*(5), 27.
[http://dx.doi.org/10.1177/003172171309400506]

Morrison, L.L., L'Heureux, J. (2001). Suicide and gay/lesbian/bisexual youth: implications for clinicians. *J. Adolesc., 24*(1), 39-49.
[http://dx.doi.org/10.1006/jado.2000.0361] [PMID: 11259069]

National Association of School Psychologists. (2011). *Lesbian, gay, bisexual, transgender, and questioning (LGBTQ) youth (Position Statement).* Bethesda, MD.

Pazos, S. (1999). Practice with female-to-male transgendered youth. In: Mallon, G., (Ed.), (pp. 65-82). NY, Harrington: Park Press.

Dictionary, P. (n.d.). Retrieved from: http://psychologydictionary.org/sexual-identity/

Reis, B. (1999). *They don't even know me! Understanding anti-gay harassment and violence in schools..* Seattle, WA: Safe Schools Coalition.

Reis, E., Saewyc, E. (1999). *83,000 Youth: Select Findings of Eight Population-based Studies as They Pertain to Anti-gay Harassment and the Safety and Well-being of Sexual Minority Students..* Seattle, WA: Safe Schools Coalition of Washington.

Rosario, M., Schrimshaw, E.W., Hunter, J. (2008). Predicting different patterns of sexual identity development over time among lesbian, gay, and bisexual youths: a cluster analytic approach. *Am. J. Community Psychol., 42*(3-4), 266-282.
[http://dx.doi.org/10.1007/s10464-008-9207-7] [PMID: 18972204]

Russell, S.T., Joyner, K. (2001). Adolescent sexual orientation and suicide risk: evidence from a national study. *Am. J. Public Health, 91*(8), 1276-1281.
[http://dx.doi.org/10.2105/AJPH.91.8.1276] [PMID: 11499118]

Russell, S.T. (2003). Sexual minority youth and suicide risk. *Am. Behav. Sci., 46*, 1241-1257.
[http://dx.doi.org/10.1177/0002764202250667]

Russell, S.T., Kosciw, J.G., Horn, S.S., Saewyc, E. (2010). Safe schools policy for LGBTQ Students. *Soc. Policy Rep., 24*(4), 3-17. [Washington DC: Society for Research in Child Development.].

Ryan, C., Huebner, D., Diaz, R.M., Sanchez, J. (2009). Family rejection as a predictor of negative health outcomes in white and Latino lesbian, gay, and bisexual young adults. *Pediatrics, 123*(1), 346-352.
[http://dx.doi.org/10.1542/peds.2007-3524] [PMID: 19117902]

Savin-Williams, R.C., Diamond, L.M. (2000). Sexual identity trajectories among sexual-minority youths: gender comparisons. *Arch. Sex. Behav., 29*(6), 607-627.

[http://dx.doi.org/10.1023/A:1002058505138] [PMID: 11100265]

Shilo, G., Savaya, R. (2011). Effects of Family and Friend Support on LGB Youths' Mental Health and Sexual Orientation Milestones. *Fam. Relat., 60*(3), 318.
[http://dx.doi.org/10.1111/j.1741-3729.2011.00648.x]

Tomaszewski, E.P. (2002). *Equity: practice update for the National Association of Social Workers.* Retrieved from: http://www.naswdc.org/diversity/Equity0803.pdf

Weston, J.H. (2010). School prom cancelled after ACLU insists on cross dressing and gay dates. *Catholic Exchange.* . Retrieved from: http://catholicexchange.com/school-prom-canceled- after-aclu-insists-on-c-oss-dressing-and-gay-dates

CHAPTER 6

Student Athletics: Opportunity, Challenge, and the Byzantine Construct 'Body Image'

John J. Miller*

Troy University, Troy, AL 36082, United States

Abstract: Student interscholastic sport involvement is often presumed to be a protective factor for participating athletes, and this is no doubt the case for some. This protection derives from influences such as extra privileges, adoration, popularity, and beliefs about future prospects. However, student athletic participation can be a significant risk for others. Risk occurs as a result of significant pressures for low body weight, ideal physique, and coaching methods used. These pressures are different based on gender, and even based on sport of preference. This chapter describes student athletes as a potentially vulnerable population and discusses the risks that can be experienced using the example of increased incidence of eating disorders.

Keywords: Anabolic steroid, Binge, Body image, Body weight, Coach*, Eating disorder, Performance enhancing drugs, Purge, Student athlete.

INTRODUCTION

Christy Henrich, a former gymnast of near-Olympic caliber, died at the age of 22 due to complications of an eating disorder (Pace, 1994). According to her mother, "… 99 percent of what has happened to Christy is because of the sport" (Pace, 1994, para. 9). While sports and sports figures are lauded by society, various exigencies on the athlete may exist that are far from the popular presumption of glamor. Often these stressors include factors such as an exaggeration on winning, poor coach/parent–athlete relationships, and pressure for young people to succeed

* **Corresponding author John J. Miller:** Troy University, Troy, AL 36082, United States; Tel/Fax: 334-80--6468/334-670-3743; Email: johnm@troy.edu.

Raymond J. Waller (Ed.)

(Holt, Hoar, & Fraser, 2005). In the case of Christy Henrich, an offhanded comment by a judge at a meet was taken to mean she was overweight (Wilstein, 1994). This comment led Henrich to compare herself to the thin Soviet and Romanian gymnasts. As a result, Henrich believed these gymnasts were, in fact, getting better scores due to their size and condition (Wilstein, 1994). Although Henrich sought reassurance from her coach regarding her perceived physical condition of being overweight, it was never given (Wilstein, 1994).

While the Henrich scenario is extreme, body image issues involving the female athlete population occur regularly (Bissell, 2004; Bissell & Zhou, 2004; Mendelson, Mendelson, & White, 2001). Previous investigations have indicated an increased likelihood of eating disorders in athletes participating in sports that accentuate leanness or a low body weight (Byrne & McLean, 2001; Smolak, Murnen, & Ruble, 2000). Since by their very nature, athletes often evaluate themselves in juxtaposition to others, they may tend to compare themselves to others in actual or perceived competitive positions, as evidenced in Christy Henrich's situation (Pace, 1994). For example, Henrich did not ask for reassurance that she was good enough, but rather if she was thin enough, in comparison to the other elite athletes.

The lack of acknowledgement regarding the gravity of eating disorders in athletes – frequently idealized as the healthiest of individuals - has created a health cataclysm for the affected individuals and the people closest to them (Klump, Bulik, Kaye, Treasure, & Tyson, 2008) with potentially life threatening results (Myers, 2006). Yet, some states such as Illinois and New Jersey have been sluggish in recognizing eating disorders as "serious mental illnesses" (SMIs), "biologically based mental illnesses" (BBMIs), or, in the case of children, "serious emotional disturbances" (SEDs) (Klump *et al.*, 2008 p. 97). Such lack of recognition may be due to the perception that individuals afflicted with eating disorders can recover from them independently or volitionally (Crips, Gelder, Rix, Meltzer, & Rowlands, 2000).

The athletic environment offers a distinctive confluence of stressors increasing the potential manifestation of eating pathology. Athletes at elite levels are often under pressure to perform well for a variety of reasons such as living up to parental, coaching, and spectator expectations. Athletes may be influenced by numerous psychosocial stressors associated with pathological eating including explicit "weight restrictions either by sport or coach, judging criteria that emphasizes thin and stereotypically attractive body builds, performance demands that encourage very low percentage body fat, coaches applying pressure to lose weight and peer pressure" (Zeigler, 2011, para. 8).

Coaches have been found to play an important role in shaping an athlete's experiences in sports. Specifically, the method of providing feedback preferred by coaches may be a primary source of stress and anxiety in sporting experiences (Smith, Zane, & Smoll, 1983; Ntoumanis & Biddle, 1999). When coaches are consistently and negatively critical about performance or emphasize winning to the point of giving most of their attention to only the "best" on the team, student athletes may develop questions about their physical competencies and performances (Brustad, Babke, & Smith, 2001).

Distinct Experience Necessitates Targeted Inquiry

Brownell, Rodin, and Wilmore (1992) identified some personality characteristics related to eating problems that could be descriptive of student athletes:

- **competitiveness,**
- **performance anxiety,**
- **obsessive uneasiness with body image, and**
- **meticulousness.**

Athlete leanness is often perceived as improving functioning during competition against heavier opponents who are presumed to be slower and less formidable rivals (Brownell *et al.*, 1992). The moniker 'lean sports' is often applied to those activities that presume a competitive advantage due to the more slender contestant. Lean sports have been discussed by numerous scholars and include examples such as running, swimming, gymnastics, dancing, and diving (Otis *et al.*, 1997; Smolak, Murnen, & Ruble, 2000). Internalization and pursuit of the thin ideal, endemic to participation in these activities, is a significant risk factor for the onset of problematic eating behaviors (Stice & Shaw, 2002).

Significantly higher levels "of participation of women in collegiate sports has brought an improved awareness of the unique physiological and behavioral responses of women to athletic activity" (Reinking & Alexander, 2005, p. 47). As awareness of participation increased, the need for knowledge of participants similarly grew. Research long ago informed practitioners that early involvement in certain athletic pursuits correlated with increases in eating pathologies (Davis, Kennedy, Ravelski, & Dionne, 1994; Epling & Pierce, 1996; Sundgot-Borgen, 1994), supporting the ongoing need and suggesting the urgency of building a body of professional knowledge rather than erroneously generalizing from other study groups. Female athletes similarly constitute a unique group and should be examined as such empirically; only by this can the impact of dynamics such as training, eating pattern, extreme diets, limitation of nutrition intake, and psychosocial variables distinguishing athletes from non-athletes, gender differences effects, and other variables be investigated and used to inform educators and sports professionals (Sundgot-Borgen, 1993).

Eating Disorders in Female Athletes

Participation in school athletics serves to enhance psychosocial resilience for some and is a risk factor for others *vis a vis* mediational influences known, suspected, and undoubtedly yet to be identified. Among the most established causal links between student athletic participation and psychosocial risk is the development of eating pathology. The example of eating disorder risk and student athletic participation is offered and may be illustrative of how such risk may become manifest. The contributory risks of developing pathological eating behaviors in female athletes are multifaceted and include the broad developmental domains so critically associated with higher functioning and quality of life: social, psychological, and physiologic factors (Putukin, 1998; Otis, Drinkwater, Johnson, Loucks, & Wilmore, 1997).

Additional risk factors that may be associated with disordered eating behaviors in female athletes include social pressures to be attractive and slim (Otis *et al.*, 1997; Putukian, 2001). According to Bissell (2004), collegiate females are considered to be a vulnerable population in relation to the development of eating disorders caused by body image disturbances. This is notable, as it is documented that this population is considered to be prone to pressures from a variety of sources (Gorham, 2012). In fact, college athletes may be at an especially conspicuous risk, considering the physical and emotional demands placed upon them and their body to remain fit (Davis & Cowles, 1989; Rao & Overman, 1986; Zeigler, 2011).

Johnson, Powers, and Dick (1999) reported that the occurrence of eating disorders amongst university female athletes is dreadfully high in sequence of findings that became more alarming quickly; that more than 1% female sportspersons DSM criteria for bulimia, and none for anorexia nervosa, 13% clearly demonstrated pathological strategies for weight maintenance or weight loss (Johnson, Powers, & Dick, 1999). These results supported the Sundgot-Borgen (1993) investigation, which had reported that 18% of elite female Norwegian athletes exhibited behavioral indices of eating disorders. Other investigations have indicated parallel rates of disordered eating among female athletes (Davis & Cowles, 1989; Evers, 1987, Sundgot-Borgen, 1993).

Previous research has shown an increased likelihood of weight and diet apprehension in female athletes (Rouveix, Rhea, 1999; Reinking & Alexander, 2005). Furthermore, other studies have revealed that female athletes who were involved in lean sports had an elevated risk for developing eating disorders when compared to athletes who were involved in sports that did not require leanness for perform well (DePalma, Koszewski, Case, Barile, Depalma, & Oliaro, 1993; Thiel, Gottfried, & Hesse, 1993). Sundgot-Borgen and Torstveit (2004) related that athletes participating in a lean sport such as gymnastics developed higher incidence of eating disorders than athletes involved in nonlean sports.

Engel and colleagues (2003) concluded that a potential risk of developing an eating disorder correlated with the sport the athlete chose to enter. By choosing the sport, the athlete also accepted adherence to the diet and weight control practices that are accepted in that sport. For example, competitive sports that require speed (track sprinters) or are popularly considered aesthetically striking (divers or gymnasts) may be enticing to some potential athletes, yet could have specific, increased risks for eating disorders as a direct result of participation (Williams *et al.*, 2003; Pernick *et al.*, 2006; Reinking & Alexander, 2005). However, in sports that are less dependent on physical allure, the athlete may still be encouraged or expected to reach and sustain a weight that correlates with a low percentage of body fat.

In female athletes, other influences that may foster disordered eating-and appeared contributory in the case of Christy Henrich, including:

- **untenable expectations of athletic flawlessness, and**
- **belief that there is an inverse causal relationship between smaller body mass and increased athletic prowess (Sanborn, Horea, Siemers, & Dieringer, 2000).**

A key method that athletes employ to improve their performance often includes a change of their eating patterns (Smolak, Murnen, & Ruble, 2000; Sundgot-Borgen & Torsveit, 2004), an subject that poses increasing risk as performance achievements have increased over time as some cultural influences have encouraged lower standards of preferred body weight.

For example, Ryan (1995) indicated that a winning female gymnastics team in 1972 averaged 5 feet 3 inches in height and weighed 106 pounds. Twenty years later, the average height and weight averages of the winning teams were down to 4 feet 9 inches and 83 pounds, respectively. It has been argued that, in addition to exemplary athletic performance, success in sports such as gymnastics or diving requires a particular aesthetic visage, sometimes practically a prepubescent appearance. This results in immense stress for athletes from throughout the structure of a sport (Sundgot-Borgen, 1994). This stress for unattainable physical perfection clearly can be enormously influential when interacting synergistically with the simultaneous pressure for athletic perfection (Smolak, Murnen, & Ruble, 2000).

Eating Disorders in Male Athletes

Female athletes are not alone in experiencing the need to be models of physical faultlessness as a *sine qua non* of academic stardom. Men characteristically feel similarly compelled to the lean muscular physique that lies beyond the range of attainability (Murray & Baghurst, 2013).

> In some sports (*e.g.*, wrestling), athletes must make specific weight limits or they cannot compete, whereas in others (*e.g.*, cross-country), a low body weight is thought to offer a performance advantage. Still, in others (*e.g.*, diving), the aesthetics of the athlete's body strongly influences the outcome of his performance. Thus, in addition to the general pressures that are present for all men, athletes may experience direct and indirect pressures from coaches, teammates, and judges to alter their weight, strength, body size, and appearance in hopes of improving their performances (Petrie, Greenleaf, Reel, & Carter, 2008 p. 268).

As you no doubt noted, the general patterns of perception and occurrence of unrealistic physical perfection bears stark similarities for both male and female athletes. On which group the most intensity for physical perfection is experienced is a question whose answer does not inform the current discuss, so it will be deferred to a different opportunity for discussion.

A circumstance that no doubt impacts female athletes but is probably consequential and applicable to higher numbers of males is the exacerbated danger imposed by dramatically divergent physical ideals that must be sought with expedience of athletes involved in multiple sports. A comparison they may provide immediate clarity for many readers is to consider the secondary student who, almost immediately upon completion of football, begins the wrestling season and the appositional physical expectations espoused as being associated with success (Galli, Reel, Petrie, Chatterton, & Baghurst, 2013).

Beyond the dangerous practices of bingeing and purging, male wrestlers may adhere to dangerous calorie and fluid restriction or overindulge in the use of laxatives and diuretics in an effort to make their weight class limit prior to a match. One report that shares significant commonalities of many other athlete accounts is the above student, feeling intense, multi-directional feeling beleaguered to attempt rapid, dramatic weight loss and determining laxative abuse his best option for success made his plan to purchase purgatives *via* the internet. Unwisely choosing to make the internet purchase during school hours, the student found the plan interrupted by being caught by the coach imposing the expectations, who neither intervened nor interrupted, opting instead to leave the vicinity (Baum, 2006). Explicit and tacit approval of high risk practices that may convey consequences of the severest order while actively preventing public awareness have clearly disengaged from professional and ethical expectations of promoting long-term health and wellbeing of the individual athlete in favor of an agenda of pure self-interest.

Less evidence is available related to eating disorders of male athletes than female athletes, potentially resulting from flawed assumptions that these diagnoses are primarily or exclusively manifest in females. For example, a study involving high school wrestlers revealed that 1.7% manifested the clinical profile for bulimia nervosa (Cooper, 2003) which, the reader may recall, is a higher rate of prevalence than was reported in investigations of female athletes. Wrestlers, incentivized to compete at the lowest weight attainable though often incorrectly assuming these pathological eating practices will not impact their strength, are engaged in absurdity. Their strength is lessened by disordered eating behaviors (Cooper, 2003). So that the point is communicated with the gravity of the risks, there have been deaths that have occurred to male athletes as a result of body image and dangerous eating behaviors. These practices occurring among developing youth is terrifying (Baum, 2006).

Comparison of Athlete Eating Disorders by Sex

A study of male and female intercollegiate athletes by Burckes-Miller and Black (1988) revealed that 3% had anorexia nervosa and 21.5% had bulimia nervosa. In contrast, Johnson, Powers, and Dick (1999) revealed the absence of bulimia nervosa in male athletes and slightly more than 1% of the female athletes were so diagnosed, there were higher rates identified of pathological eating. While males binged at a higher rate than females (13% *vs.* 11%, respectively), females engaged in purging at more twice the rates of male counterparts (5.52% *vs* 2.04%, respectively).

The results of the study failed to establish a causal relationship between student sports and eating pathology (Johnson *et al.*, 1999). A complication faced by researchers is that there may be a developing culture of intentional mis-representation in some places.

Differences in prevalence of eating disorders between males and females, when reported, have been hypothesized to result from numerous influences. Reports of lower self-esteem in female athletes is one such explanatory hypothesis. Male athletes can maintain a considerably lower level of body fat (around 1%) with low levels of physiological harm (Johnson *et al.*, 1999). Conversely, in order to avoid amenorrhea, females' body fat must stay at about 17%, and efforts to decrease body fat levels beyond the point at which it poses increasing medical peril. This difference in effort required to pursue societal expectations could incorrectly be considered a weakness of character rather than the science of calorie metabolism, thereby negatively impacting the self-esteem of female athletes.

The Effect of Increasingly Untenable Ideals…

As a matter of history and experience, a compelling case both empirical and anecdotal could support the contention that societal pressures to attain cultural ideals of physical appearance have been significantly more demanding and inflexible than those same pressures on males. Though no argument could be made that gender equality has been achieved in this area (or in many other areas), the gap in inequity has narrowed-not in a reduction in focus on women, but in increasing evidence of the growing magnitude and effect of ideal male body image being a more significant factor in masculinity (Soban, 2006). Over the past twenty years, the social values and cultural ideals of men's bodies have changed, with body image gaining eminence in defining masculinity.

Historically, societal definitions of the male ideal placed much more emphasis on accomplishments. Men report being acutely aware of the pressure to achieve the physical male ideal and that the pressure to meet the physical expectations are increasing (Cafri *et al.*, 2005), responses similar to those provided by contemporary women. It is interesting that this phenomenon has occurred at a point in human history in which the need to engage in intense physical labor has decreased concurrently with increased access to food for increasing numbers of members of the global community.

This places human evolution in direct contradiction with human expectation, resulting in increasingly counterproductive means by which people strive to meet physical ideals. One path of evidence of this conclusion is the prevalence and incidence of eating disorders such as anorexia and bulimia nervosa, the presence of which have been a significant and growing concern for nearly 100 years (*e.g.* Gammelmark *et al.*, 2015). During much of that time period, eating disorders in males were statistically nearly irrelevant, but a clear, significant increase in eating disorders has been clearly documented in recent years (*e.g.* International Association of Eating Disorders Professional, 2014). There are additional counterproductive strategies by which people attempt to meet societal body image expectations as well.

Body Image and Performance-Enhancing Drugs

Various additional psychological–behavioral risk factors may escalate the potential use of performance-enhancing drugs (PEDs), including eating and weight concerns (Irving, Wall, Neumark-Sztainer, & Story, 2002) and body image disturbance (Hildebrandt, Alfano, & Langenbucher, 2010), though other expectations imposed on many athletic participants such as the "alpha male" or "alpha female" personas likely contribute to the risk of using PEDs as well (Irving 2002).

Because of the desire to achieve success and an idealized appearance, athletes have looked for avenues to gain an advantage or edge for many years. One way that has been available for athletes to create an advantage has been through the use of performance enhancing drugs such as anabolic steroids (Eichner, 1997; Silver, 2001). To achieve such goals, athletes may incorporate supplements and performance-enhancing drugs into their training, with the belief in school athletes that PEDs are a necessity in successful performance widely documented (*e.g.* Dickerson, 2005).

It is important to note that male athletes are not the only population that may use PEDs. In the 1990s, three different national surveys of US adolescents documented a two to four fold increase in the frequency of anabolic steroid use among adolescent girls (Yesalis, Barsukiewicz, Kopstein, & Barke, 1997). According to Elliot, Goldberg, Moe, DeFrancesco, Durham and Hix-Small, (2004) disordered eating habits and drugs that enhance appearances are common among 50% of young female high school athletes. Public awareness concerning increasing female anabolic steroid use was further advanced in 2004 when the Centers for Disease Control and Prevention (CDC) indicated that more than 7% of high school freshmen girls revealed that they were currently using or had previously engaged in anabolic steroid use.

The 7% reported by CDC surpassed reports of some young male subgroups (Berning, Adams, & Stamford, 2004). While these reports point toward the risk of steroid use by high school students, they may identify the proverbial "tip of the iceberg" for steroid use in interscholastic sports. Moreover, it is alarming that significantly few high school students perceive steroids use as being harmful (Johnston, O'Malley, Bachman, & Schulenberg, 2003), often idealizing steroid use rather than vilifying them.

Performance enhancing drugs, broadly conceived, are those substances taken for specific purposes of modifying appearance and/or escalation of physical performance. *Anabolic steroids* (also referred to as anabolic androgenic steroids) are artificial forms of male sex hormones that boost metabolism, increase protein synthesis, and promote growth of skeletal muscle (Mazzeo & Ascion, 2009; Miller, 2000; National Institute on Drug Abuse [NIDA], 2004). Obscuring the recognition of PED use is the range of body image superlatives that are accepted within certain sports. Venerated swimmers or gymnasts will pursue a body image much different than that pursued by a powerlifter or shot putter. Such divergence in athletic iconography is a familiar phenomenon among men and women (Hildebrandt, Alfano, & Langenbucher, 2010).

Nutritional Supplements

Historically, athletes have used nutritional supplements to augment their abilities early in the athletic endeavors. As the athlete continues and achieves success in their sport, nutritional supplements may act as a gateway other PED's (Irving *et al.*, 2002). Hildebrandt, Harty, and Langenbucher (2012) agree that increasingly potent substances with increasing completion and pressure to gain a competitive advantage. As a result, vulnerable athletes, such as those in interscholastic or intercollegiate athletics, find these temptations particularly compelling. As young athletes attain success, they may succumb to the inflated promises of PEDs

(Hildebrandt, Harty, & Langenbucher, 2012).

Estimated Number of High School Athletes Ingesting Performance-Enhancing Drugs

Whether a professional athlete uses steroids is not a large societal issue *per se* (Latiner, 2006). After all, older, professional athletes should be better informed, possess a greater capacity to understand the potential health risks related to steroid use, and might attempt mitigation of those risks through access to the best medical treatment available (Latiner, 2006).

Miller and Wendt (2007) suggested that high school athletic directors suspected athletes in other secondary athletic programs of being "on" steroids. Moreover, in addition to "other's athletes" taking steroids, one-third of the athletic directors believed that some their "own athletes" had taken steroids. The prominence that is given to high achieving athletes without imposition of any sanctions for dangerous behavior, legal or otherwise, sends the message that performance-enhancing drugs such as steroids are accepted, if not essential, to athletic success. This perception was very evident as a young athlete confessed to his father just prior to committing suicide that was linked to steroid use:

> I'm on steroids, what do you think? Who do you think I am? I'm a baseball player, baseball players take steroids. How do you think Bonds hits all his home runs? How do you think all these guys do all this stuff? You think they do it from just working out normal? (Fainaru-Wada, 2004, p. A1).

It has been estimated that 1 to 3 million athletes in the United States has taken steroids (Silver, 2001). Blue Cross/Blue Shield (2003) indicated more than 1 million adolescents between the ages of 12-17 had taken performance-enhancing supplements and drugs. A more significant finding of this study was the revelation that *all* youths surveyed knew someone using performance-enhancing substances such as steroids.

An investigation by the American College of Sports Medicine (ACSM) (2004) stated that more than one out of every ten students in the United States would have used steroids by 2010. The CDC (2004) has indicated that illegal steroid use between ninth through twelfth grade students has more than doubled in the last decade from 2.7% in 1991 to 6.1% in 2003. A subsequent study by the CDC providing an alarming example of steroid use. Among high schoolers, with 11.2% of Louisiana males in and 5.7% of Tennessee girls acknowledging steroid use (Office of the National Drug Control Policy, 2005).

Though it may be of academic, policy, or barroom debate how much societal vigor should be allocated to regulatory oversight of steroid use in professional athletics, neither plausible debate nor leeway to tolerate deliberation of sanctioning steroid use in interscholastic sports similarly abides. School athletes lack sufficient developmental capacity, maturity, autonomy, and perspicacity to make such a decision.

Despite physical stature, student athletes are a vulnerable population, largely compelled by decisions beyond their empowerment to make and in the service of whose interests is not always certain. The medical risks for PED use are as variable and substantial as those associated with pathological eating, with variability resulting from substances used and doses taken. A particularly dangerous effect is cardiac damage, the risk of which is synergistic when the following are combined: strenuous weight training, stimulants, and anabolic steroids (Langenbucher, Hildebrandt, & Carr, 2008).

Despite the fact that steroids can be used in a positive way for individuals who, for example, have undergone surgery or for some medical conditions, they can cause irreparable physical and psychological harm in otherwise healthy individuals. Among the most serious physical damages that can occur due to anabolic steroid use include:

- **the enlargement of breast tissue in men,**
- **shrunken breasts in women,**
- **hypertension or heart disease due to the over-retention of fluid in the body, and**
- **liver damage (Adler, 2004; Heckman, 2003; Taylor, 2002; U.S. Department of Health & Human Services, 2003).**

Additionally, the results of a study of 16,000 private and public school students indicated that steroid users were considerably were more likely to engage in:

- **other use,**
- **fighting,**
- **suicide,**
- **high risk sexual behavior,**
- **risky driving, and**
- **dangerous weight control practices (Miller, Barnes, Sabo, Melnick, & Farrell, 2002).**

Research has also indicated that use of anabolic steroids may increase the likelihood of mental illness conditions (Malone, Dimeff, Lombardo, & Sample, 1995). Among the best-known psychological harm that may be incurred through steroid use is an increased aggression of the individual resulting in a state popularly referred to as steroid rage or 'roid rage'. 'Roid rage' describes a steroid-induced spontaneous, highly aggressive, out-of-control behavior (Lubell, 1989). This is one of the most dangerous, unpredictable psychosocial phenomena associated with steroids because it may put innocent people in danger. Kuipers (1998) indicated that while aggressiveness may be needed or advantageous for athletic training, it impairs functional capacity outside of the athletic realm with few meaningful exceptions.

"Roid rage" can impose risk by increasing the users' likelihood of atypical behaviors that they would normally not do and which could culminate in physical harm as well as in criminal charges. An individual with "roid rage" will display such behavioral reactions as over-confidence, violence or paranoia (Fish, Goldberg & Spratt, 2004; Franks, 2004). However, even opponents of steroid use admit that "roid" rage occurs in less than one percent among steroid users (Yesalis & Cowart, 1998).

Other mood disruptions occur with more regularity. An investigation by Pope and Katz (1988) indicated that 22 percent of 41 steroid abusers were manic or depressive while using or withdrawing from steroids use. Moreover, steroid use has also been attributed to experiencing"

- **euphoria or enthusiasm,**
- **irritability,**
- **hyperactivity, paranoia, and**
- **insomnia (Freinhar & Alvarez, 1985; Wilson, Prange, & Lara, 1974).**

Finally, a study by Kashkin and Kleber (1989) contended that using steroids could be so addictive that they could thoroughly control and ultimately devastate the user's life.

CONCLUSION

Generally, eating disorders have been linked to some of the most consequential medical and psychosocial outcomes among mental illness conditions (Klump *et al.*, 2008). Student athletics are frequently assumed to convey significant benefits to participants, and in some circumstances, this assumption is accurate. However, student athletic participation can also be a risk factor associated with numerous undesirable psychosocial outcomes. An example of such an outcome is the increased risk of student athletes to develop eating disorders. These disorders can convey substantial cost and harm to the athlete, their social and familial networks, and to society at large (Klum *et al.*, 2008). Athletes afflicted with eating disorders can experience substantial decreases in athletic performance, numerous health consequences, and can cause death.

The sociocultural pressures on young athletes to pursue ideal physical appearance that are culturally imposed are often physiologically atypical, practically unachievable, and – representing the most momentous irony – contrary to good health practices. Compounding the pressure for "leanness" similar stressors to be the best in their selected sport (Elliott *et al.*, 2004). Such burdensome expectancies can result in the development of disordered eating behaviors as well as the use of performance enhancement drugs such as diet pills, diuretics, laxatives, amphetamines, and anabolic steroids (Elliott *et al.*, 2004). Young athletes are being put too often under increasing scrutiny. Certain sports that accentuate appearances (diving or gymnastics) or weight loss (wrestling) may lend themselves to the particularly increased likelihood of developing eating problems.

Participation in school athletics is often assumed to be a protective factor for contestants, with 'jocks' receiving preferential treatment and esteem. This is undoubtedly true in some cases. It is less often understood that student athletics can also serve as a factor of significant risk to the health, mental and physical, of students. This is particularly poignant when recalling that participation in athletics-especially school athletics-is first and foremost intended to be an activity of health promotion.

The purpose of this chapter was to highlight the potentiality of such risk using the example of body image disorders, though the risk can manifest in myriad other ways. Of distinction is the clear, causative role in such risk directly linked with teachers (or coaches) and the techniques they employed. This example is hoped to provide compelling caution with the realization that school and school programs can, if pursued outcomes stray from student best interests and systematic promotion of health-including mental health-have life–altering consequences that are diametrically opposed to the outcomes most professional educators profess to hold as the focal point of desired outcomes.

CONFLICT OF INTEREST

The author confirms that author have no conflict of interest to declare for this publication.

ACKNOWLEDGEMENTS

Declared none.

REFERENCES

Baum, A. (2006). Eating disorders in the male athlete. *Sports Med, 36*(1), 1-6.
[http://dx.doi.org/10.2165/00007256-200636010-00001] [PMID: 16445307]

Berning, J.M., Adams, K.J., Stamford, B.A. (2004). Anabolic steroid usage in athletics: facts, fiction, and public relations. *J. Strength Cond. Res, 18*(4), 908-917.
[PMID: 15574100]

Bissell, K. (2004). Sports model/sports mind: The relationship between entertainment and sports media exposure, sports participation, and body image distortion in Division I female athletes. *Mass Commun. Soc, 4*, 453-473.

[http://dx.doi.org/10.1207/s15327825mcs0704_5]

Bissell, K., Zhou, P. (2004). Must-see TV or ESPN: Entertainment and sports media exposure and body-image distortion in college women. *J. Commun, 54*, 5-21.
[http://dx.doi.org/10.1111/j.1460-2466.2004.tb02610.x]

Black, D.R., Burckes-Miller, M.E. (1988). Male and female college athletes: use of anorexia nervosa and bulimia nervosa weight loss methods. *Res. Q. Exerc. Sport, 59*(3), 252-256.
[http://dx.doi.org/10.1080/02701367.1988.10605513]

Brustad, R.J., Babkes, M.L., Smith, A.L. (2001). Youth in sport: Psychological considerations. In: Singer, R.N., Hausenblaus, H.A., Janelle, C.M., (Eds.), *Handbook of Sport Psychology* (2nd ed., pp. 604-635). New York: John Wiley.

Byrne, S., McLean, N. (2001). Eating disorders in athletes: a review of the literature. *J. Sci. Med. Sport, 4*(2), 145-159.
[http://dx.doi.org/10.1016/S1440-2440(01)80025-6] [PMID: 11548914]

Cooper, M. (2003). *The psychology of bulimia nervosa: A cognitive perspective.* Oxford: Oxford University Press.
[http://dx.doi.org/10.1093/med:psych/9780192632654.001.0001]

Davis, C., Cowles, M. (1989). A comparison of weight and diet concerns and personality factors among female athletes and non-athletes. *J. Psychosom. Res, 33*(5), 527-536.
[http://dx.doi.org/10.1016/0022-3999(89)90060-3] [PMID: 2795525]

DePalma, M.T., Koszewski, W.M., Case, J.G., Barile, R.J., DePalma, B.F., Oliaro, S.M. (1993). Weight control practices of lightweight football players. *Med. Sci. Sports Exerc, 25*(6), 694-701.
[http://dx.doi.org/10.1249/00005768-199306000-00008] [PMID: 8321106]

Elliot, D.L., Goldberg, L., Moe, E.L., Defrancesco, C.A., Durham, M.B., Hix-Small, H. (2004). Preventing substance use and disordered eating: initial outcomes of the ATHENA (athletes targeting healthy exercise and nutrition alternatives) program. *Arch. Pediatr. Adolesc. Med, 158*(11), 1043-1049.
[http://dx.doi.org/10.1001/archpedi.158.11.1043] [PMID: 15520341]

Engel, S.G., Johnson, C., Powers, P.S., Crosby, R.D., Wonderlich, S.A., Wittrock, D.A., Mitchell, J.E. (2003). Predictors of disordered eating in a sample of elite Division I college athletes. *Eat. Behav, 4*(4), 333-343.
[http://dx.doi.org/10.1016/S1471-0153(03)00031-X] [PMID: 15000960]

Galli, N., Reel, J.J., Petrie, T.A., Chatterton, J.M., Baghurst, T. (2013). Assessing the Validity of the Weight Pressures in Sport Scale for Male Athletes. *Psychol. Men Masc.*
[http://dx.doi.org/10.1037/a0031762]

Gammelmark, C., Jensen, S.O., Plessen, K.J., Skadhede, S., Larsen, J.T., Munk-Jørgensen, P. (2015). Incidence of eating disorders in Danish psychiatric secondary healthcare 1970-2008. *Aust. N. Z. J. Psychiatry, 49*(8), 724-730.

[http://dx.doi.org/10.1177/0004867414567758] [PMID: 25648144]

Gorham, E. (2012). *Eating disorders: College athletes at increased risk.* Retrieved from: http://www.momsteam.com/nutrition/eating-disorders-college-athletes-at-increased-risk

Hildebrandt, T., Alfano, L., Langenbucher, J.W. (2010). Body image disturbance in 1000 male appearance and performance enhancing drug users. *J. Psychiatr. Res, 44*(13), 841-846. [http://dx.doi.org/10.1016/j.jpsychires.2010.01.001] [PMID: 20110092]

Hildebrandt, T., Harty, S., Langenbucher, J.W. (2012). Fitness supplements as a gateway substance for anabolic-androgenic steroid use. *Psychol. Addict. Behav, 26*(4), 955-962. [http://dx.doi.org/10.1037/a0027877] [PMID: 22486333]

Holt, N.L., Hoar, S.D., Fraser, S. (2005). A revitalized conceptual approach to understanding social support in sport. In: Hanton, S., Mallalieu, S.D., (Eds.), *Literature reviews in sport psychology* (pp. 199-225). Hauppauge, NY: Nova Science.

(2014). An upswing in eating disorders is noted in Great Britain. *Eating Disorders Review, 25*(2), 1.

Irving, L.M., Wall, M., Neumark-Sztainer, D., Story, M. (2002). Steroid use among adolescents: findings from Project EAT. *J. Adolesc. Health, 30*(4), 243-252. [http://dx.doi.org/10.1016/S1054-139X(01)00414-1] [PMID: 11927236]

Johnson, C., Powers, P.S., Dick, R. (1999). Athletes and eating disorders: the National Collegiate Athletic Association study. *Int. J. Eat. Disord, 26*(2), 179-188. [http://dx.doi.org/10.1002/(SICI)1098-108X(199909)26:2<179::AID-EAT7>3.0.CO;2-Z] [PMID: 10422607]

Langenbucher, J., Hildebrandt, T., Carr, S.J. (2008). Medical consequences of anabolic steroids. *Handbook of the Medical Consequences of Alcohol and Drug Abuse,* 385-421.

Longman, J. (2003). An athlete's dangerous experiment: Using steroids enhanced his physique, but he died trying to stop. *New York Times,* C15-16.

Mendelson, B.K., Mendelson, M.J., White, D.R. (2001). Body-esteem scale for adolescents and adults. *J. Pers. Assess, 76*(1), 90-106. [http://dx.doi.org/10.1207/S15327752JPA7601_6] [PMID: 11206302]

Murray, S.B., Baghurst, T. (2013). Revisiting the diagnostic criteria for muscle dysmorphia. *Strength Condit. J, 35*(1), 69-74. [http://dx.doi.org/10.1519/SSC.0b013e3182723f24]

Myers, L.L. (2006). Anorexia nervosa, bulimia nervosa, and obesity. In: Waller, R.J., (Ed.), *Fostering child and adolescent mental health in the classroom.* Thousand Oaks, CA: Sage. [http://dx.doi.org/10.4135/9781452232355.n9]

Ntoumanis, N., Biddle, S.J. (1999). A review of motivational climate in physical activity. *J. Sports Sci, 17*(8), 643-665.

[http://dx.doi.org/10.1080/026404199365678] [PMID: 10487465]

Otis, C.L., Drinkwater, B., Johnson, M., Loucks, A., Wilmore, J. (1997). American College of Sports Medicine position stand. The female athlete triad. *Med. Sci. Sports Exerc, 29*(5), i-ix.
[http://dx.doi.org/10.1097/00005768-199705000-00037] [PMID: 9140913]

Pace, E. (1994). *Christy Henrich, 22, Gymnast who suffered from anorexia. The New York Times.* Retrieved from: http://www.nytimes.com/1994/07/28/obituaries/christy-henrich-22-gymnast-who-suffered-from-anorexia.html

Petrie, T.A., Greenleaf, C., Reel, J., Carter, J. (2008). Prevalence of eating disorders and disordered eating behaviors among male collegiate athletes. *Psychol. Men Masc, 9*(4), 267-277.
[http://dx.doi.org/10.1037/a0013178]

Putukian, M. (1998). The female athlete triad. *Clin. Sports Med, 17*(4), 675-696.
[http://dx.doi.org/10.1016/S0278-5919(05)70111-3] [PMID: 9922894]

Putukian, M. (2001). The female athlete triad. *Curr. Opin. Orthop, 12*, 132-141.
[http://dx.doi.org/10.1097/00001433-200104000-00010]

Rao, V.V., Overman, S.J. (1986). Psychological well-being and body image: A comparison of black women athletes and nonathletes. *J. Sport Behav, 9*(2), 79-91.

Reinking, M.F., Alexander, L.E. (2005). Prevalence of disordered-eating behaviors in undergraduate female collegiate athletes and nonathletes. *J. Athl. Train, 40*(1), 47-51.
[PMID: 15902324]

Rhea, D.J. (1999). Eating disorder behaviors of ethnically diverse urban female adolescent athletes and non-athletes. *J. Adolesc, 22*(3), 379-388.
[http://dx.doi.org/10.1006/jado.1999.0229] [PMID: 10462428]

Rouveix, M., Bouget, M., Pannafieux, C., Champely, S., Filaire, E. (2007). Eating attitudes, body esteem, perfectionism and anxiety of judo athletes and nonathletes. *Int. J. Sports Med, 28*(4), 340-345.
[http://dx.doi.org/10.1055/s-2006-924334] [PMID: 17024652]

Sanborn, C.F., Horea, M., Siemers, B.J., Dieringer, K.I. (2000). Disordered eating and the female athlete triad. *Clin. Sports Med, 19*(2), 199-213.
[http://dx.doi.org/10.1016/S0278-5919(05)70199-X] [PMID: 10740755]

Smith, R.E., Zane, N.W., Smoll, F.L., Coppel, D.B. (1983). Behavioral assessment in youth sports: coaching behaviors and children's attitudes. *Med. Sci. Sports Exerc, 15*(3), 208-214.
[http://dx.doi.org/10.1249/00005768-198315030-00005] [PMID: 6621307]

Smolak, L., Murnen, S.K., Ruble, A.E. (2000). Female athletes and eating problems: a meta-analysis. *Int. J. Eat. Disord, 27*(4), 371-380.
[http://dx.doi.org/10.1002/(SICI)1098-108X(200005)27:4<371::AID-EAT1>3.0.CO;2-Y] [PMID: 10744843]

Sundgot-Borgen, J. (1993). Prevalence of eating disorders in elite female athletes. *Int. J. Sport Nutr, 3*(1),

29-40.
[PMID: 8499936]

Sundgot-Borgen, J. (1999). Eating disorders among male and female elite athletes. *Br. J. Sports Med, 33*(6), 434.
[http://dx.doi.org/10.1136/bjsm.33.6.434] [PMID: 10597857]

Sundgot-Borgen, J., Larsen, S. (1993). Nutrient intake of female elite athletes suffering from eating disorders. *Int. J. Sport Nutr, 3*(4), 431-442.
[PMID: 8305916]

Sundgot-Borgen, J. (1994). Risk and trigger factors for the development of eating disorders in female elite athletes. *Med. Sci. Sports. Exerc., 26*, 414-419.

Sundgot-Borgen, J., Torstveit, M.K (2004). Prevalence of eating disorders in elite athletes is higher than in the general population. *Clin J Sport Med, 14*(1), 25-32.

Sykora, C., Grilo, C.M., Wilfley, D.E., Brownell, K.D. (1993). Eating, weight, and dieting disturbances in male and female lightweight and heavyweight rowers. *Int. J. Eat. Disord, 14*(2), 203-211.
[http://dx.doi.org/10.1002/1098-108X(199309)14:2<203::AID-EAT2260140210>3.0.CO;2-V] [PMID: 8401553]

Thiel, A., Gottfried, H., Hesse, F.W. (1993). Subclinical eating disorders in male athletes. A study of the low weight category in rowers and wrestlers. *Acta Psychiatr. Scand, 88*(4), 259-265.
[http://dx.doi.org/10.1111/j.1600-0447.1993.tb03454.x] [PMID: 8256643]

Torstveit, M.K., Sundgot-Borgen, J. (2005). The female athlete triad: are elite athletes at increased risk? *Med. Sci. Sports Exerc, 37*(2), 184-193.
[http://dx.doi.org/10.1249/01.MSS.0000152677.60545.3A] [PMID: 15692312]

Wilmore, J.H. (1991). Eating and weight disorders in the female athlete. *Int. J. Sport Nutr, 1*(2), 104-117.
[PMID: 1844989]

Wilstein, S. (1994). *Beasts' of anorexia nervosa, bulimia ravaged gymnast's body: Health: Christy Henrich was 22 and weighed less than 60 pounds when she died. Her family hopes her story will save others. L.A. Times.* Retrieved from: http://articles.latimes.com/keyword/christy-henrich

Yang, C.F., Gray, P., Pope, H.G., Jr (2005). Male body image in Taiwan *versus* the West: Yanggang Zhiqi meets the Adonis complex. *Am. J. Psychiatry, 162*(2), 263-269.
[http://dx.doi.org/10.1176/appi.ajp.162.2.263] [PMID: 15677589]

Yeager, K.K., Agostini, R., Nattiv, A., Drinkwater, B. (1993). The female athlete triad: disordered eating, amenorrhea, osteoporosis. *Med. Sci. Sports Exerc, 25*(7), 775-777.
[http://dx.doi.org/10.1249/00005768-199307000-00003] [PMID: 8350697]

Yesalis, C.E., Barsukiewicz, C.K., Kopstein, A.N., Bahrke, M.S. (1997). Trends in anabolic-androgenic steroid use among adolescents. *Arch. Pediatr. Adolesc. Med, 151*(12), 1197-1206.

[http://dx.doi.org/10.1001/archpedi.1997.02170490023005] [PMID: 9412594]

Yesalis, C., Cowart, V. (1998). The Steroids Game. Champaign, IL: Human Kinetics Publishers.

CHAPTER 7

Students Coping with Chronic Physical Conditions

Laura L. Myers[1,*] and **Allison M. Wiman**[2]

[1] *Florida A&M University, Tallahassee, FL 32307, United States*

[2] *Florida TaxWatch, Tallahassee, FL 32301, United States*

Abstract: Students with chronic physical conditions may experience substantial risk of undesirable outcomes in school. The experience of physical challenges may synergistically affect mental health and school performance. School personnel and families may experience additional stress meeting the needs of students for whom the expertise or resources necessary for care provision is insufficient. Information, support, and effective programming can result in a more desirable outcome for everyone. While often considered synonymous with disability, these are distinct issues.

Keywords: Absenteeism, Chronic illness, Chronic mental condition, Chronic physical condition, Family functioning, Side effects, Suicide, Symptoms.

INTRODUCTION

The number of children and adolescents in the United States living with chronic physical conditions has increased dramatically in the past four decades (Perrin, Bloom, & Gortmaker, 2007). Such conditions can have significant, disparate effects. Though there can be effects on student participation in school, children with chronic physical conditions, like other youth, have the need and the right to be educated:

> Up to 98% of children suffering from a chronic illness, which may have been considered fatal in the past, now reach early adulthood. It is estimated that as many as 30% of school-aged children are affected by a chronic ill-

* **Corresponding author Laura L. Myers:** Florida A&M University, Tallahassee, FL 32307, United States; Tel: 850-412-7552; Fax: 850-599-3215; Email: laura.myers@famu.edu.

Raymond J. Waller (Ed.)

> ness. For this population of children, the prevalence of educational and psychological problems is nearly double in comparison with the general population. (Martinez & Ercikan, 2009, p. 391).

Bethell, Read, Blumberg, and Newacheck (2008) estimate the number of children and youth with one or more chronic health conditions range from 12.8% to 19.3%. In a large-scale survey in Minnesota, Barnes, Eisenberg, and Resnick (2010) found that 9.5% of children and youth had a chronic physical health condition, 6.6% had a chronic mental health condition, and 3.0% had co-occurring chronic mental and physical conditions.

Children and adolescents from minority ethnic groups are disproportionately represented among youth with chronic illnesses, and the prognosis of their illnesses are complicated by factors such as poverty and access to quality health care (Perrin *et al.*, 2007; Zylke & DeAngelis, 2007). In a study of 4,746 ethnically diverse middle and high school students, Erickson, Patterson, Wall, and Neumark-Sztainer (2005) found that adolescents who were African American, Native American, or from a mixed-other race grouping were significantly more likely than Caucasian adolescents to report having a chronic health condition. They also found that adolescents from a low socioeconomic status (SES) were significantly more likely to have chronic health conditions than youth from a high socioeconomic level.

Newacheck, Stein, Bauman, and Hung (2003) also reported a higher prevalence of health disabilities among African American children compared to Caucasian children, but that the differences were entirely attributable to higher poverty rates among the African American children. It has also been reported that minority and low-SES youth with chronic health conditions are less likely to utilize health services and mental health services (Newacheck, Hung, & Wright, 2002), leading to poorer physical and mental health prognoses.

Occurrence of Affected Youth is Rising

The prevalence of children with medical conditions is increasing. This increase is related to an increase in the incidence rates (particularly with such conditions as asthma and obesity) as well as duration, caused principally by advancements in medical care. For example, Steck-Silvestri *et al.* (2013) state, "advances in neonatal care have resulted in increased survival rates of extremely low birth weight or very preterm infants" (p. 300). Extremely low birth weight infants are more likely to have:

- **cerebral palsy,**
- **asthma,**
- **low IQ and adaptive functioning, and**
- **motor impairments (Taylor, Drotar, Schluchter, & Hack, 2006),**

and the increased survival rates of extremely low birth weight infants can explain, in part, the increased prevalence of children with these chronic health conditions. Another chronic health condition, congenital heart disease, has seen a one-year survival rate increase from 20% in the 1940s to over 85% today (Warnes *et al.*, 2001). Erickson *et al.* (2005) stated:

> Due to advances in medicine improving the morbidity and mortality of children with chronic health conditions, many of them are surviving through adolescence and into adulthood. Working with these youth to manage their chronic illnesses or disabilities is an increasingly important issue confronting health care providers. Pediatricians and other health care professionals need to be informed and able to assess the psychosocial distress experienced by these adolescents, which very often compounds the management of their chronic health conditions. (p. 181).

Children and adolescents who live with chronic illnesses bear not only the physical corollaries of their illness, but also experience psychological, behavioral, and educational consequences. Erickson *et al.* (2005) suggested that the normal challenges of adolescence combined with the additional stress of living with and managing a chronic health condition contribute to higher levels of both internalizing (*e.g.*, depression, anxiety, self-esteem) and externalizing (*e.g.*, tobacco use, illicit drug use, sexual activity) behavior problems.

Similarly, other researchers found externalizing behavior problems, such as delinquent and aggressive behaviors, and internalizing problems, such as somatic complaints, anxiety, depression, and social withdrawal, among this population

(Pinquart & Shen, 2010a). These problems can be triggered by a perceived lack of control over:

- **the illness and its symptoms (*e.g.*, epilepsy, sickle cell disease),**
- **the presence of frightening symptoms (*e.g.*, asthma, epilepsy),**
- **restriction of activities (*e.g.*, due to hospitalization, physical disabilities),**
- **peer rejection (*e.g.*, in case of visible abnormalities, such as obesity or cleft lip), and**
- **side effects of treatment (*e.g.*, radiation and chemotherapy of cancer patients).**

Symptoms of the physical condition or its treatment may exacerbate the psychological and behavioral effects of the condition. For example, the presence of physical symptoms, such as fatigue and pain, may interfere with regular school attendance and social functioning, causing frustration, peer rejection, and lowered self-concept (Sandstrom & Schanberg, 2004; Suris, Michaud, & Viner, 2004). If left untreated, these consequences can have significant negative impacts on quality of life (Chavira, Stein, Bailey, & Stein, 2004). Research suggests that children with chronic illnesses are at a higher risk for developing anxiety disorders (Chavira *et al.*, 2004; Freilinger *et al.*, 2006), and depressive disorders and suicide (Barnes *et al.*, 2010).

Taras and Potts-Datema (2005a; 2005b; 2005c) found that children with a variety of chronic medical conditions, including diabetes, sickle cell anemia, epilepsy, obesity, and certain subpopulations of children with asthma, perform worse on achievement tests and may be at a higher risk for developing learning disabilities than their healthy peers. Symptoms of atopic dermatitis can lead to unstable emotional and behavioral status, such as frustration, depression, anxiety, restlessness and difficulty concentrating, which in turn, can lead to difficulties in family and academic functioning (Dennis, Rostill, Reed, & Gill, 2006).

Martinez and Ercikan (2009) stated, "Despite increased health management and medical advancements prolonging the lives of chronically ill children, the educational and psychological effects of child chronic illnesses continue to be pervasive" (p. 397). It must be recognized that "chronic illness" encompasses a physiologically diverse set of diseases with varying degrees of impact on children and their families. Thus, to provide a general summary, we have focused on meta-analyses and systematic reviews in the area of psychological, behavioral, and educational effects on children and adolescents who are suffering from a chronic illness. These reviews generally consider pediatric chronic conditions in aggregate.

Definitions

Van der Lee, Mokkink, Grootenhuis, Heymans, and Offringa (2007) contended that there is no uniform definition of the concept of chronic physical conditions in children, leading to diverse estimates of prevalence. Even the selection of what term to use (*i.e.*, chronic physical condition, chronic disease, chronic health condition, chronic illness) affects inclusion criteria, prevalence, incidence, prognosis, and other issues related to research methodology.

For the purposes of this paper, the term chronic physical condition has been selected to identify the large array of long-term physical conditions experienced by children and adolescents. Williams (1997) defined a chronic physical condition as a "medically diagnosed ailment with a duration of 6 months or longer which shows little change or slow progression" (p. 312). Barlow and Ellard (2006) pointed out that chronic physical condition should not be confused with disability. They define disability as "a restriction or lack of ability to perform an activity in the manner or within the range considered normal for a human being" (p. 19). Chronic physical conditions include physical disabilities, but also include conditions that do not necessarily involve any restriction to physical activity, such as cleft lip or palate. Other conditions, such as cancer or migraine headache, may restrict physical activity at some times, but at other times, the child may live without physical restrictions or limitations.

Based on the research reviewed, chronic physical conditions include, but are not limited to, arthritis, asthma, atopic dermatitis, cancer, cerebral palsy, chronic fatigue syndrome, cleft lip and palate, cystic fibrosis, diabetes, epilepsy and other seizure disorders, fetal alcohol spectrum, hearing impairment, heart disease, hemophilia, HIV infection/AIDS, inflammatory bowel disease, kidney/liver disease, Lyme disease, migraine/tension-type headache, multiple sclerosis, muscular dystrophy, obesity, severe allergies, sickle cell anemia, spina bifida, traumatic brain injury, and visual impairment.

Psychological Problems

Research has shown that anxiety, depression, and emotional-behavioral problems are more common in children and adolescents with special care needs than in those without these needs (Canty-Mitchell, Austin, Jaffee, Qi, & Swigonski, 2004). Barnes *et al.* (2010) conducted a large study (n= 136,549) of Minnesota students who ranged in age from 10 to 19 years. Using a standard mental health assessment tool, this group found that children and adolescents with no chronic health conditions had "high" (mean score 18.5) overall emotional well-being, youth with chronic physical health conditions alone had a mean score of 17.2, youth with chronic mental health conditions alone had a mean score of 13.1, and youth with both physical and mental health conditions had "low" overall emotional well-being (mean score of 12.4).

Other research (Aarons *et al.*, 2008; Chavira, Garland, Daley, & Hough, 2008; Freilinger *et al.*, 2006) highlighted the link between chronic physical problems and chronic mental health problems, particularly anxiety, depressive, oppositional defiant, and conduct disorders. Steck-Sylvestri *et al.* (2013) found various neuropsychiatric characteristics associated with certain chronic medical conditions in children and youth. Some examples include:

- **cerebral palsy is often associated with psychosocial and socioemotional impairments and attention deficit hyperactivity disorder (ADHD),**
- **traumatic brain injury is associated with socioemotional and social competence deficits, obsessive-compulsive disorder (OCD), conduct disorder (CD), and depressive and anxiety disorders,**
- **HIV/AIDS is associated with ADHD, CD, anxiety and depressive symptoms, and socioemotional and behavioral deficits,**
- **fetal alcohol spectrum is associated with poor social skills, ADHD, early-onset bipolar disorder, depressive and anxiety disorders, oppositional defiant disorder (ODD), and CD, and**

- **epilepsy is associated with ADHD, social skills deficits, and depressive and anxiety disorders.**

Internalizing Behaviors

Pinquart and Shen (2010b) conducted a meta-analysis to determine the level of depressive symptoms in children and adolescents with chronic physical illness. They concluded that youth with chronic physical illnesses have higher levels of depressive symptoms than their healthy peers. Depressive symptoms were highest among children and adolescents with chronic fatigue syndrome, cleft lip and palate, epilepsy, and diseases characterized by chronic pain, such as fibromyalgia and migraine headaches. They also found that the depressive symptoms were greatest in youth experiencing two or more of the following factors:

- **visibility and social consequences of their disease,**
- **restrictions of positive activities,**
- **brain dysfunction,**
- **side effects of treatment, and**
- **pain as a symptom of the illness.**

Interestingly, they found that youth with arthritis, cancer, cystic fibrosis, diabetes, HIV infection, and sickle cell disease did not show higher levels of depressive symptoms than children without chronic health problems. This was due, in part, to the fact that many of the youth with these illnesses reported that they were currently experiencing few or even no symptoms of their disease.

Pinquart and Shen (2010b) found it interesting that some youth with life-threatening diseases, such as cancer, did not show more depressive symptoms than their healthy peers. Jorngarden, Mattsson, and von Essen (2007) found that adolescents with cancer did show increased level of depressive symptoms 6 months after being diagnosed, but actually showed lower levels of depressive symptoms than healthy adolescents 18 months later. It is possible that early successes in treatment will lead to positive attitudes toward life and increased hopefulness toward the future.

Erickson *et al.* (2005) found that adolescents with chronic health conditions were

1½ times more likely to consider suicide, and over 3½ times more likely to report suicide attempts in the past year. These youth were also more likely to report depressive symptoms and lowered self-esteem compared to their healthy peers. Erickson *et al.* (2005) suggested that these findings were not surprising given:

> the ongoing stress of living with a chronic health condition and the potential for recurrent episodes of pain; limited social interactions with peers; emotional reactions to the illness and treatments involved; worries about the future; experiencing social stigma; and/or having to deal with the reactions of family members, friends, teachers, and others (p. 188).

In a study of 136,549 children and youth, Barnes *et al.* (2010) found that youth with co-occurring chronic physical and mental conditions had significantly higher odds of self-harm (odds ratio [OR]: 2.5), suicidal ideation (OR: 2.5), and suicide attempts (OR: 3.5) than their healthy peers. Youth with chronic physical conditions alone were at a slightly elevated risk for all 3 outcomes (OR: 1.2). These results suggest that "suicide and self-harm may be more prevalent than previously thought in children with chronic health conditions" (p. 893). They concluded:

> Whereas most youth with chronic conditions enjoy normal levels of emotional well-being and do not have suicidal thoughts or self-injurious behaviors, there may be a developmental trajectory among certain children with chronic conditions, not yet fully elucidated, that contributes to excess emotional distress and suicide risk (Barnes *et al.*, 2010, p. 893).

Borowsky, Ireland, and Resnick (2001) found adolescents' overall health status to be a risk factor for suicidality. Blum, Kelly, and Ireland (2001) reported that adolescents with mobility impairments were nearly three times more likely to report suicide attempts than other adolescents.

Additional Psychosocial Outcomes

Martinez and Ercikan (2009) stated, "It remains important that this mental health concern is addressed in its early stages given the pathogenesis of anxiety disorders in the general population" (p. 399). They further state that educators in particular "need to learn to be more sensitive to anxiety symptomatology, and not misjudge these symptoms with other effects of the illness (*e.g.*, side effects of medication), so that children can be referred to a mental health professional as soon as possible" (p. 399).

Pinquart (2012) conducted a meta-analysis of 621 research studies that compared the levels of self-esteem of children with chronic physical illness with healthy peers. He states, "Knowing whether children with a chronic physical illness have lower levels of self-esteem has implications for interventions aimed at improving psychological functioning of these children" (p. 153). Lowered self-esteem may be caused by peer rejection (Sandstrom & Schanberg, 2004) or fewer successful experiences due to decreased physical, social, and/or academic functioning (Pinquart & Teubert, 2012).

Because earlier meta-analyses looking at self-esteem among this population had shown inconsistent results, Pinquart (2012) compared the self-esteem levels of children across a large number of diseases. He found only a small difference in self-esteem between children with and without chronic illness, indicating that many children with chronic illnesses protect their self-esteem. When looking at specific chronic diseases, the largest decrease in self-esteem was associated with chronic fatigue syndrome and chronic headaches. In addition, diseases with a visible physical effect, such as cerebral palsy, obesity, and spina bifida, were associated with reduced self-esteem. Other variables related to lower self-esteem were adolescents rather than children, females, children from developing countries, and observer rather than child reports.

Externalizing Problems

Research has shown that chronic physical health conditions are a risk factor for behavior problems in children and adolescents (Barlow & Ellard, 2006; Pinquart & Shen, 2010a). Pinquart and Shen (2010a) found elevated levels of externalizing behavior problems, specifically aggressive and delinquent behaviors, in children and adolescents with chronic physical illnesses. The illnesses with the highest occurrence of externalizing problems were those associated with impaired brain functions, including epilepsy, migraine/tension-type headache, and hearing impairments.

Brain abnormalities in children with epilepsy and migraine headaches have been shown to affect behavioral inhibition (Schmitz *et al.*, 2008), and the side effects of medications (*e.g.*, corticosteroids) used to treat children with kidney and liver disease may cause an increase in behavioral problems (Soliday, Grey, & Lande, 1999). Interestingly, though chronic fatigue syndrome is associated with higher levels of depression and lowered self-esteem, it did not show elevated levels of externalizing behavior problems, possibly because fatigue may inhibit such external behaviors (Pinquart & Shen, 2010a).

Erickson *et al.* (2005) found that adolescents with chronic health conditions were more likely to report use of tobacco, marijuana, and other illicit drugs that their healthy peers. Other researchers (Blum *et al.*, 2001; Choquet, DuPasquier Fediaevsky, & Menfredi, 1997) also found that adolescents with chronic health conditions participate in high-risk behaviors, such as tobacco use, alcohol use, and sexual behavior, at higher rates than peers. Erickson *et al.* (2005) did point out, however, that some older studies (*e.g.*, Alderman, Lauby, & Coupey, 1995; Hobbs, Perrin, & Ireys, 1985; Orr, Weller, Satterwhite, & Perrin, 1984) reported lower rates of alcohol use, tobacco use, marijuana use, unprotected sexual activity, and drunk driving among adolescents with chronic illnesses.

The authors of these earlier studies speculated that the presence of chronic health conditions might lead to increased involvement with parents and health care professionals, providing a protective barrier against negative outcomes for these youth. As more recent research is finding increased behavior problems among these adolescents, further research is necessary to determine if there is indeed a change in outcomes with this population, or if methodological differences of the studies can account for the differences in outcome.

Social and Academic Functioning

Social functioning describes an individual's overall functioning in a social situation, including making friends and the ability to participate in conversations. Academic functioning involves performance in academic subjects, particularly reading, writing, and mathematical tasks, but also refers to behaviors that contribute to academic success, such as study skills, attention skills, and completion of tasks. Social and academic functioning are closely related, particularly in the school setting. Children must be physically present in the classroom and able to perform tasks in order to grow both socially and academically. Pinquart and Teubert (2012) provided five potential explanations for reduced social and academic functioning in children with chronic conditions:

- **Some chronic conditions result in physical restrictions (*e.g.*, cerebral palsy, spina bifida, paraplegia), reduced motivation and persistence (*e.g.*, chronic fatigue syndrome), and reduced school attendance (*e.g.*, long or repeated stays in hospital for cancer treatment);**
- **Many conditions directly affect the central nervous system (*e.g.*, spina bifida or epilepsy), which may result in cognitive impairment in intelligence, memory, attention, or problem solving;**
- **Side effects of therapy may impair academic and social functioning (*e.g.*, cranial irradiation, chemotherapy, medications);**
- **Parent or teacher perceptions of physical vulnerability may cause adults to place limitations on the child, and peer rejection and/or bullying may limit opportunities for social growth; and**
- **Behavior problems associated with chronic illness may affect social and academic functioning (p. 377).**

Martinez, Carter, and Legano (2011) conducted a meta-analysis to determine the impact of chronic illness on social functioning. Their analysis, which encompassed 57 studies with 90 unique outcomes, found that children with a chronic illness had poorer social competence than children without chronic illness. The authors concluded, "Although the effect size was smaller than expected, overall results supported typical study hypotheses that children with chronic illness would show deficits in social competence" (p. 885). Additionally, they found that the effects varied according to diagnosis. Children with obesity and neurological disorders had the poorest social competence of all groups, while children with blood disorders had moderate levels of poor social competence. Finally, children with asthma and diabetes did not exhibit social competence scores that differed from their peers.

As mentioned above, absenteeism is a factor in the academic and social functioning of many children with chronic physical conditions. Numerous studies have found that a chronic condition results in more days absent, which adversely affect academic and social performance for some children (Taras & Potts-Datema, 2005a). For example, children with sickle cell who experience frequent painful crises and have related school absences, also experience decreased academic and school performance. Other meta-analyses found lower academic functioning in children with leukemia (Campbell *et al.*, 2007), lower social functioning in children with chronic illness (Martinez *et al.*, 2011), as well as lower levels of academic and social functioning in children with cerebral palsy (Shields, Murdoch, Loy, Dodd, & Taylor, 2006) and spina bifida (Shields, Taylor, & Dodd, 2008).

Finally, in a meta-analysis of 954 studies, Piquart and Teubert (2012) determined that children and adolescents with chronic physical illness had lower levels of both academic and social functioning, with a moderate effect on academic functioning and a small effect on social functioning. They found that effects on academic functioning were large in children with cerebral palsy, spina bifida, and sickle cell disease. In addition, they found stronger effects on all functioning in studies with larger percentages of the sample from ethnic minorities or from developing and threshold countries.

Family Functioning

Cousino and Hazen (2013) conducted a systematic review of parenting stress among caregivers of children with asthma, cancer, cystic fibrosis, diabetes, epilepsy, juvenile rheumatoid arthritis, and/or sickle cell disease. They stated:

> Parents must face the devastating news of their child's diagnosis, the associated medical risks, and in some instances, their child's potential for a shortened life expectancy. Although some families may demonstrate resiliency in the face of such stressors, the demanding treatment regimens and shifts in roles, responsibilities, and resources may negatively affect family functioning (p. 809).

Their review led to the following conclusions:

- **caregivers of children with chronic illness experience greater general parenting stress than caregivers of healthy children,**
- **caregivers of children with chronic illness are also likely to experience illness-related parenting stress, such as frequent clinic appointments or demanding treatment regimens,**
- **greater parental responsibility for treatment management and/or less child self-care behaviors was related to increased parental stress,**
- **both general and illness-related parenting stress were unrelated to illness duration or severity, and**
- **more frequent and/or intense child pain episodes were related to increased parenting stress.**

In addition to factors that influence parenting stress, Cousino and Hazen (2013) also found that increased parenting stress is associated with negative psychological adjustment to the illness by caregivers and the children, and may contribute to poorer health-related outcomes in the children. Therefore, they concluded that, in an effort to promote both psychological and health outcomes in children with chronic illness, parenting stress should be considered a possible modifiable intervention target.

Barlow and Ellard (2006) looked at the available meta-analyses and systematic reviews of the effects on the parents and siblings of children afflicted with chronic physical conditions. They found a consensus across studies that:

> Emotional distress (*e.g.* anxiety, depression) is greater among parents of newly diagnosed children with cancer or children who are in treatment when compared with normative data. Moreover, emotional distress remains heightened one year after diagnosis but appears to decrease over time (pp. 27-28).

Although parents continue to experience loneliness, uncertainty, symptoms of post-traumatic stress, fear of relapse, and worry about their children's futures, Barlow and Ellard (2006) also noted positive attributes among these parents, such as the development of good support systems, new values and attitudes, re-evaluation of personal goals, increased closeness with the family, and stronger marital relationships.

Brown *et al.* (2007) looked specifically at the impact of single parenting on the psychosocial functioning of children with chronic illness, as well as the impact of the presence of the chronic illness on the caregiver functioning. Since parents are generally responsible for the child's illness management, it is clear that parents experience a myriad of stressors, including financial stress, separations due to hospitalizations, loss of work caused by child absences from school and medical appointments, and general uncertainty with regard to the child's future.

In their review of the literature, Brown *et al.* (2007) found a dearth of studies that examined the association between single parenting and childhood chronic physical conditions. When examining studies not specific to single parent households, they found that research suggests a "reciprocal relationship between chronic illness and parental adaptation, whereby the child's illness impacts the parents' functioning and parental functioning also influences child adaptation" (p. 410). Since 35% of children in the US live in single-parent homes, and 37% of children who live in single-parent homes live in poverty (National Kids Count, 2012), it is clear that single-parenting of children with chronic illnesses may be an area that requires our attention and intervention. Brown *et al.* (2007) concluded:

> As more children are being raised in single-parent homes, the burdens and functioning of these families who are raising ill children clearly need the focused attention of our children's hospitals and health care system (p. 415).

Grootenhuis and Last (1997) looked at protective factors among the parents of children with chronic health conditions. They concluded that having a strong social support had a protective effect on the parents' psychosocial well-being. Other protective factors included parents who had open and frequent communication about the child's disease, and who had the ability to maintain hope and remain optimistic. Dennis *et al.* (2006) found that parental psychological health and a supportive family environment might be protective factors against developing internalizing behavioral problems (depression, anxiety, low self-esteem, and social withdrawal) for children with atopic dermatitis.

Sharpe and Rossiter (2002) conducted a meta-analysis of studies that focused on the psychosocial functioning of siblings of children with a chronic illness. They found a small, negative effect on these children compared with comparison or control groups. Specifically, psychological functioning, social functioning, and cognitive development were lower for siblings compared with controls, with larger negative effects associated with internalizing behaviors (*e.g.*, anxiety and depression) than externalizing behaviors (*e.g.*, behavior problems or aggression).

Interestingly, while severity of illness did not seem to have an effect on the siblings' psychosocial functioning, illnesses that more drastically affected day-to-day functioning of the family (*e.g.*, bowel disease, cancer) were associated with greater negative effects on the siblings. While having a sibling with a chronic condition may result in negative outcomes for siblings, some positive characteristics may result. Houtzager, Grootenhuis, and Last (1999) found that these siblings were more caring, mature, supportive, responsible, and independent than were control or comparison groups.

Practical Application of Intervention Research

Children with chronic illnesses or disabilities are normal children in abnormal situations. The primary purpose of intervention research with children with chronic illnesses is "to increase our understanding of the effects of chronic illnesses, and thereby increase the health-related quality of life in children with chronic illnesses" (Martinez & Ercikan, 2009, p. 399). While many children and their families adapt well to chronic illnesses, Engelke, Guttu, Warren, and Swanson (2008) pointed out:

> Frequent hospitalizations, fatigue, anxiety, pain, and other symptoms can put children at risk for academic problems and health complications, particularly when they are first diagnosed. School-based interventions play an important role in ensuring that students with chronic illness have the same educational opportunities as other students (pp. 205-206).

Patterson and Geber (1991) suggested that many mental health issues in children with chronic illness might be prevented or minimized by focusing on the development of competencies that facilitate adaptation and inclusion. The authors suggested the following competencies are protective:

- **encouraging normal life experiences,**
- **increasing coping skills,**
- **increasing use of social support,**
- **coordinate delivery of care, and**
- **empowerment.**

The building of these competencies starts in the home, but schools have the obligation to work to increase these competencies and provide the support chronically ill children need to navigate through their school experience.

Encouraging Normal Life Experiences

Attending school is perhaps the most normal and normative of childhood experiences. Proper education of staff enables teachers to provide appropriately for the education and socialization of children with chronic illness and ultimately facilitates inclusion (American Diabetes Association [ADA], 2002). Teachers are a front-line resource for children with chronic conditions and they are often the first to respond to the academic, social, and psychological needs of children in their care (Huffman, Fontaine & Price, 2003). While teachers are responsible to help meet the needs of a child with a medical condition, they may feel ill equipped to fulfill this role (Clay, Cortina, Harper, Cocco, & Drotar, 2004).

Studies have shown that the majority of school personnel have an inadequate understanding of the ramifications of chronic childhood illness (ADA, 2002; Lindsey, Jarrett & Hillman, 1987; Wysocki, Meinhold, Cox & Clarke, 1990). Gomes and Smith (2007) conducted a survey of 60 newly hired teachers in a medium-sized California school district. Results indicated that 71% of teachers had one student in their classroom with a chronic condition; however, only 35% of the teachers surveyed felt they were adequately educated on chronic health conditions. Likewise, Nabors, Little, Akins-Little and Lobst (2008) found that the majority of teachers, even special education teachers, are not confident in their ability to meet the social and academic needs of children with chronic medical conditions. The fact that academic and social successes often make a critical difference in these children's lives highlights a critical issue in the education of children with chronic physical conditions (Thompson & Gustafson, 1996; Walsh

& Murphy, 2003).

Child-specific training for all teachers that work directly with children with chronic health needs should be mandatory. School psychologists and school nurses can assist in training teachers and staff to ensure a working understanding of the medical technicalities of a health issue, as well as any social, academic, and mental health ramifications. Schools should develop a resource library that contains information on the management of chronic conditions.

Nabors, Lehmkuhl, Christos, and Andreone (2003) conducted a survey of 105 type 1 diabetic children aged 5 to14. Survey results indicate that while children felt supported at school, additional flexibility and individual care plans may improve their ability to manage their diabetes at school. Detailed care plans that address the health, academic, and social needs of children with chronic conditions should be developed using input from the child, the child's parents, physicians, and nurses.

Increasing Coping Skills, Resilience, and Social Support

Coping is the process of restoring balance (equilibrium) between excessive demands and inadequate resources. Charron-Prochownik (2002) presents a chronic illness stress/coping paradigm that outlines the interplay between individual characteristics, social network characteristics, stress, and quality of life (see Fig. **1**). Schools must work to increase the chronically ill child's individual and social coping resources. One way to achieve this goal is to increase resilience and reduce stress. Luthar, Cicchetti, and Becker (2000) define resilience as "the ability to withstand and rebound from disruptive life challenges, becoming strengthened and more resourceful. Not simply general strengths, resilience involves dynamic processes that foster positive adaptation in the context of significant adversity" (p. 543).

For example, despite the many vulnerabilities associated with atopic dermatitis, Im and Kim (2011) pointed out that there are children who do not have psychological problems accompanying this condition. These authors suggested that we look beyond the individuals' weaknesses and vulnerabilities in facing this challenging situation, and focus on defining the strengths and resilience of these individuals. They believed that "the concept of resilience can be applied to explain the level of positive adjustment of these vulnerable children in spite of their challenges" (p. 81). Kim and Yoo (2010) reported that factors such as:

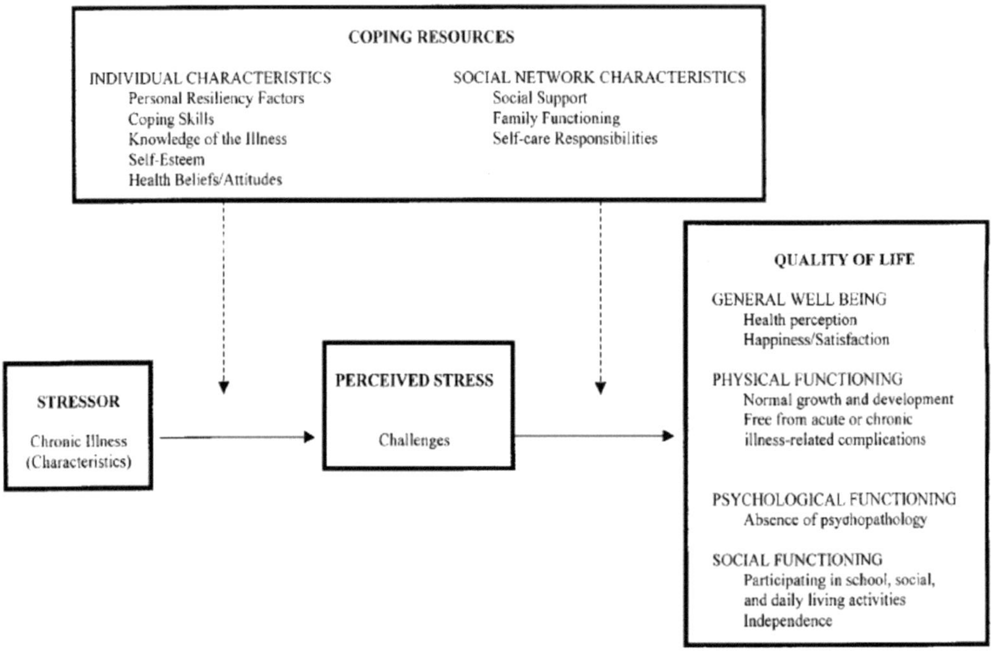

Fig. (1). Chronic Illness stress/coping paradigm.

- **positive self-concept,**
- **confidence,**
- **interpersonal intimacy,**
- **resourcefulness, and**
- **independence**

affect the resilience of children. They further suggested that resilience could lead to positive adaptations and good physical and psychosocial outcomes. Teachers and staff can help reinforce these factors by providing a supportive, caring environment while fostering independence.

If resilience can act as a protective factor against psychological and behavioral problems in children with chronic physical conditions, the next logical step is the development of interventions that can strengthen the resilience in these children.

With this goal in mind, Kim and Yoo (2010) developed an instrument to measure resilience in children with chronic illness. It includes 32 questions, and is composed of three sub-scales:

- **Intrapersonal – child's feelings about self;**
- **Coping – ability to cope with adverse situations; and**
- **Interpersonal – ability to develop positive relationships with others.**

Using this instrument to measure resilience, Im and Kim (2011) found that responsive and supportive parenting by both mother and father, positive relationships with friends, and positive relationships with teachers were associated with greater resilience in children. In addition, longer duration and greater severity of the illness were associated with lowered resilience. They concluded:

> Although school-aged children still need positive support from parents, the significant role of positive peer relationships in affecting resilience explains a future direction for nursing care plans...The careful nursing intervention to build a positive relationship with parents, friends, and teachers would be helpful to enhance the resilience of school-aged children having atopic dermatitis (p. 86).

They added, since resilience seems to be lower in children with conditions of longer duration and greater severity, these children should comprise the initial target group for treatment so their resilience can be strengthened and the negative impact of their condition reduced.

Perrin, MacLean, Gortmarker, and Asher (1992) found that a stress management intervention was successful in reducing the level of behavior problems of children with asthma. A prevention program aimed at providing information about the child's illness, enhancing social competence, and reframing stressors increased the self-esteem of adolescents with chronic illnesses (Last, Stam, Onland-van Nieuwenhuizen, & Grootenhuis, 2007). Knight, Scheinberg, and Harvey (2013) conducted a systematic review of interventions with pediatric chronic fatigue syndrome, and found strong evidence in support of cognitive-behavioral therapy. Likewise, Kraaij and Garnefski (2012) studied coping and depressive symptoms in adolescents with chronic medical conditions, and found cognitive coping strategies had the strongest influence on depressive symptoms.

School personnel must not lose sight of the fact that a child's chronic illness influences all members of the family. A meta-analysis conducted by Cousino and Hazen (2013) concluded that caregivers of children with chronic illness reported significantly greater parenting stress than caregivers of healthy children ($d = .40$; $p = \leq .0001$). Furthermore, this increase in stress had a negative impact on both the psychological and health outcomes of children.

Barlow and Ellard (2006) noted the absence of intervention studies designed to alleviate emotional distress and provide support for the parents of children suffering from chronic health conditions. They suggested, "the implementation of interventions addressing the psychosocial well-being of the whole family unit from the time of diagnosis onwards would be an ideal to work towards" (p. 30). Interventions, such as web-based support services and self-management classes, in which parents of children with chronic conditions teach classes to other parents, have been developed and could help address problems experienced by many families with children suffering from chronic physical illness. One group of researchers (Monaghan, Hilliard, Cogen, & Streisand, 2009) developed a 5-session, phone-based intervention to support parents of young children diagnosed with diabetes, and found that participating in the intervention reduced the illness-related parenting stress.

A growing body of research on resilience supports the idea that family resources can significantly influence positive adaptation to a major health problem. To increase family resilience, teachers and staff can affirm child and family competencies and support the flexible use of medical and psychosocial resources (Rolland & Walsh, 2006). Likewise, it is important for the school nurse, psychologist, and social worker to be aware of support resources within the community.

Coordinated Delivery of Care through Case Management and Problem Solving

Case management is foundational to meeting the educational and medical needs of chronically ill children in school. Case management has been shown to contribute to positive academic and health-related outcomes. Engelke *et al.* (2008) defined "case management" as follows:

> Case management is a process by which the school nurse identifies children who are not achieving their optimal level of health or academic success because they have a chronic illness that is limiting their potential. Case management is based on a thorough assessment by the school nurse and involves activities that not only help the child deal with problems but also prevent and reduce their occurrence. Case management includes nursing care directed toward the child and coordination and communication with parents, teachers, and other care providers. The interventions are goal oriented, based on the specific needs of the child, and evaluated based on their impact (p. 206).

Engelke *et al.* (2008) examined the health, academic functioning, and quality of life of a group of 114 children with chronic physical conditions who received school-based case management from school nurses. The authors found the most common interventions included:

- **teaching and counseling (35%),**
- **direct care (22%),**
- **working with teachers (19%),**
- **working with families (15%), and**
- **making referrals (9%).**

By the end of the school year, the children improved on measures of quality of life, and gained skills and knowledge to improve the proficiencies involved in better management of their illnesses. They reported significant academic improvement in students who were failing in the previous school year. Participation in classroom activities as well as extracurricular activities also increased for many of the children.

This study also emphasizes that family involvement and parent perception of the illness can greatly influence the child's outcome. In about one third of the cases, the major barrier to a positive outcome for the child was parents who were not able to or were unwilling to support their child in trying to reach optimal health. Another barrier is that school nurses often have very large caseloads, covering multiple schools and sometimes even multiple school districts. Research data that show positive outcomes in working with children with chronic illness should be used to support "the expansion of school nursing services in an era of competition for limited resources" (Engelke *et al.*, 2008, p. 214).

Two studies (Crickmore, Jones, Engelke, & Mott, 2002; Taras, Wright, Brennan, Campana, & Lofgren, 2004) found that case management helped students with asthma reduce the severity of the illness, as well as reducing the number of hospitalizations and emergency room visits. Grier and Bradley-Klug (2011) suggested a problem-solving framework for working with children affected by health issues within a school setting. The goal of the process "is to aid in the often complex assessment of strengths and weaknesses of children with health issues and to help design and evaluate effective interventions for these children" (p. 88).

The framework involves the selection of key collaborators, usually the child's teacher, social worker, parents, psychologist, and nurse. The intervention team works together to identify and analyze problems, develop and implement solutions, and evaluate treatments. The analysis step includes a record review, classroom observation, individual assessment of the child, interviews with parents and teachers, and consultation with outside experts, as needed. Intervention is developed and implemented based on the data collected. It is important to note that interventions should extend to the entire family unit if analysis suggests that family dynamics can be improved to support the child. Follow-up and evaluation should be scheduled at regular intervals to continue to monitor academic, behavioral, and social progress and performance.

Empowerment

Empowerment is the process of giving children a sense of control over their lives. Patterson and Geber (1991) stated:

> Rather than the helper doing everything for the person being helped, thus maintaining dependency, a process is begun whereby the help-seeker discovers and builds on his or her own strengths, leading to a greater sense

> of mastery and control over his or her life...The goal is interdependence between self, family, informal support, and formal service providers (p. 158).

Efforts toward empowerment should focus on personal strengths and the learning needs of the child, and should promote child-driven decision-making and participation (Aujoulat, d'Hoore, & Deccache, 2007; Funnell *et al.*, 1991). One pathway toward empowerment is the development of self-efficacy, which is the belief that one can effectively perform necessary skills. The development of self-efficacy is critical to self-management of chronic conditions and contributes in a positive way to a child's normal development in the face of a chronic condition (Mickley, Burkhart, & Sigler, 2013). The goal of self-management of a chronic illness is to enable medical management, carrying out normal roles and activities, and managing the emotional impact of a chronic condition (Lorig & Holman, 2003).

Kirk *et al.* (2013) conducted a systematic review of the effectiveness of self-care support initiatives for children and young people with long-term health conditions. The authors concluded that there is strong evidence of the effectiveness of interventions that target children and young people, but found that well-designed trials of interventions are lacking. Interestingly, this group found no evidence that interventions that focus solely on parents are effective.

Kelo, Martikainen, and Eriksson (2011) conducted an integrative review of empirical studies of self-care in school-aged children with type 1 diabetes with the purpose of lending insight to the development of empowering patient education. The authors state that self-care is a combination of knowledge and skills, and that the goals of self-care are normality, coping and independence. Factors related to self-care involve the nature of the illness and care, characteristics of the child (*e.g.* attitude, motivation, gender, age), support from parents, school environments, peers, and the healthcare team. They conclude the challenge is to find balance between care requirements and a child's stage of development and maturity level. Adults must "adopt an empowering manner of education; recognize and assess a child's readiness to learn diabetes care and be responsible for it" (Kelo *et al.*, 2011, p. 2016). It is essential that teachers, administrators, and school nurses foster self-care by allowing a child to perform tasks that are safely within a child's capability.

CONCLUSIONS

Researchers have called for teachers and others in the school setting to help children and adolescents with chronic physical health conditions who may be suffering with comorbid emotional and behavioral problems. Barnes *et al.* (2010) challenged, "Educational strategies might begin at the practitioner, caregiver, and teacher levels to increase awareness of the risk for suicide in some children with chronic conditions" (p. 894). They further suggested that practitioners in contact with this population should "inquire – sensitively but frequently – about the emotional well-being and suicidality in their young patients with chronic conditions while fostering resiliency and hope" (p. 894). Martinez and Ercikan (2009) contended that the current research looking at children and adolescents with chronic illness points to the "need for co-ordinated services between the home, hospital and school settings so that services and programmes focus on the ecology of the child who is ill" (p. 391).

Teachers and other educational staff play a significant role in addressing social and academic functioning needs of children with chronic illness. Pinquart and Teubert (2012) stated:

> School functioning can be promoted by homebound instruction during times of absence from school, tutors for bridging the gaps associated with absence, and special education interventions if the chronic illness is associated with cognitive or sensory deficits. In addition, intervention programs to improve social skills can be very helpful for children with a chronic pediatric condition. These programs are usually delivered in small groups and teach social skills with role play, such as building contact with peers or dealing with teasing (p. 387).

Researchers (Pinquart & Shen, 2010a; 2010b; Pinquart & Teubert, 2012) suggested that, while the association between chronic physical illness and other problems-such as mental health issues and academic and social functioning-may indicate that chronic illness is a risk factor for these problems, researchers and practitioners must consider that mental health symptoms and poor academic and social functioning may also affect the duration and severity of chronic illness. For example, if a child is depressed, she may be less likely to seek medical help and may fail to comply with medical interventions, such as appointments, therapy, and medication. If a child has poor social functioning, he may be less likely to engage in sports and other physical activities with his peers, which could in turn compound the problems associated with his physical condition.

Pinquart and Shen (2010a) stated, "Since many chronic diseases cannot be cured, a main goal is to reduce the consequences of the diseases on the lives of children and adolescents" (p. 1003). They further called for the need for multidisciplinary teams to establish a "collaborative treatment approach" (p. 1015) in order to develop psychosocial interventions to prevent and treat the problems these children and adolescents are experiencing that are related to their physical conditions. Steck-Silvestri *et al.* (2013) pointed out, "neuropsychological assessments are imperative for detecting individual strengths and weaknesses and for guiding targeted interventions," and added that there is "considerable cognitive, neuropsychological, academic, and behavioral variability" (p. 314) among these illnesses. They called for additional research to identify and develop neuropsychological measures, interpretation strategies, and individualized interventions that can target individual children with specific medical conditions. Engelke *et al.* (2008) concluded:

> School personnel, particularly school nurses, must partner with parents and health care providers to help children to manage their illness and participate fully in academic and extracurricular activities. They can do this by implementing strategies that reduce disruption to the school day, ensuring the school environment is safe, and providing case management when indicated (p. 206).

Final Word

In summary, chronic physical challenges carry substantive risk to multiple health domains. The scope of impact can be systemic. These outcomes should neither be expected nor tolerated. This chapter, it is hoped, offered clear, practical opportunities for intervention that schools might implement, providing many students an alternate ending to a story not decided by the presence of challenge.

CONFLICT OF INTEREST

The authors confirm that authors has no conflict of interest to declare for this publication.

ACKNOWLEDGEMENTS

Declared none.

REFERENCES

Aarons, G.A., Monn, A.R., Leslie, L.K., Garland, A.F., Lugo, L., Hough, R.L., Brown, S.A. (2007). Association between mental and physical health problems in high-risk adolescents: a longitudinal study. *J. Adolesc. Health, 43*(3), 260-267.
[http://dx.doi.org/10.1016/j.jadohealth.2008.01.013] [PMID: 18710681]

Alderman, E.M., Lauby, J.L., Coupey, S.M. (1995). Problem behaviors in inner-city adolescents with chronic illness. *J. Dev. Behav. Pediatr., 16*(5), 339-344.
[http://dx.doi.org/10.1097/00004703-199510000-00005] [PMID: 8557834]

American Diabetes Association. (2002). Care of children with diabetes in the school and day care setting. *Diabetes Care, 25*, S122-S126.
[http://dx.doi.org/10.2337/diacare.25.2007.S122]

Aujoulat, I., d'Hoore, W., Deccache, A. (2007). Patient empowerment in theory and practice: polysemy or cacophony? *Patient Educ. Couns., 66*(1), 13-20.
[http://dx.doi.org/10.1016/j.pec.2006.09.008] [PMID: 17084059]

Barlow, J.H., Ellard, D.R. (2006). The psychosocial well-being of children with chronic disease, their parents and siblings: an overview of the research evidence base. *Child Care Health Dev., 32*(1), 19-31.
[http://dx.doi.org/10.1111/j.1365-2214.2006.00591.x] [PMID: 16398788]

Barnes, A.J., Eisenberg, M.E., Resnick, M.D. (2010). Suicide and self-injury among children and youth with chronic health conditions. *Pediatrics, 125*(5), 889-895.
[http://dx.doi.org/10.1542/peds.2009-1814] [PMID: 20385631]

Bethell, C.D., Read, D., Blumberg, S.J., Newacheck, P.W. (2008). What is the rate of children with special health care needs: Towards an understanding of variations in prevalence and methods across three national surveys. *Matern. Child Health J., 12*, 1-14.
[http://dx.doi.org/10.1007/s10995-007-0220-5] [PMID: 17566855]

Blum, R.W., Kelly, A., Ireland, M. (2001). Health-risk behaviors and protective factors among adolescents with mobility impairments and learning and emotional disabilities. *J. Adolesc. Health, 28*(6), 481-490.

[http://dx.doi.org/10.1016/S1054-139X(01)00201-4] [PMID: 11377992]

Borowsky, I.W., Ireland, M., Resnick, M.D. (2001). Adolescent suicide attempts: risks and protectors. *Pediatrics, 107*(3), 485-493.
[http://dx.doi.org/10.1542/peds.107.3.485] [PMID: 11230587]

Brown, R.T., Wiener, L., Kupst, M.J., Brennan, T., Behrman, R., Compas, B.E., David Elkin, T., Fairclough, D.L., Friebert, S., Katz, E., Kazak, A.E., Madan-Swain, A., Mansfield, N., Mullins, L.L., Noll, R., Patenaude, A.F., Phipps, S., Sahler, O.J., Sourkes, B., Zeltzer, L. (2007). Single parents of children with chronic illness: an understudied phenomenon. *J. Pediatr. Psychol., 33*(4), 408-421.
[http://dx.doi.org/10.1093/jpepsy/jsm079] [PMID: 17906331]

Campbell, L.K., Scaduto, M., Sharp, W., Dufton, L., Van Slyke, D., Whitlock, J.A., Compas, B. (2007). A meta-analysis of the neurocognitive sequelae of treatment for childhood acute lymphocytic leukemia. *Pediatr. Blood Cancer, 49*(1), 65-73.
[http://dx.doi.org/10.1002/pbc.20860] [PMID: 16628558]

Canty-Mitchell, J., Austin, J.K., Jaffee, K., Qi, R.A., Swigonski, N. (2004). Behavioral and mental health problems in low-income children with special health care needs. *Arch. Psychiatr. Nurs., 18*(3), 79-87.
[http://dx.doi.org/10.1016/j.apnu.2004.03.003] [PMID: 15199535]

Charron-Prochownik, D. (2002). Special needs of the chronically ill child during middle childhood: application of a stress-coping paradigm. *J. Pediatr. Nurs., 17*(6), 407-413.
[http://dx.doi.org/10.1053/jpdn.2002.129792] [PMID: 12518281]

Chavira, D.A., Garland, A.F., Daley, S., Hough, R. (2008). The impact of medical comorbidity on mental health and functional health outcomes among children with anxiety disorders. *J. Dev. Behav. Pediatr., 29*(5), 394-402.
[http://dx.doi.org/10.1097/DBP.0b013e3181836a5b] [PMID: 18714205]

Chavira, D.A., Stein, M.B., Bailey, K., Stein, M.T. (2004). Child anxiety in primary care: prevalent but untreated. *Depress. Anxiety, 20*(4), 155-164.
[http://dx.doi.org/10.1002/da.20039] [PMID: 15643639]

Choquet, M., Du Pasquier Fediaevsky, L., Manfredi, R. (1997). Sexual behavior among adolescents reporting chronic conditions: a French national survey. *J. Adolesc. Health, 20*(1), 62-67.
[http://dx.doi.org/10.1016/S1054-139X(96)00091-2] [PMID: 9007661]

Clay, D.L., Cortina, S., Harper, D.C., Cocco, K.M., Drotar, D. (2004). Schoolteachers' experiences with childhood chronic illness. *Child. Health Care, 33*, 227-239.
[http://dx.doi.org/10.1207/s15326888chc3303_5]

Cousino, M.K., Hazen, R.A. (2013). Parenting stress among caregivers of children with chronic illness: a systematic review. *J. Pediatr. Psychol., 38*(8), 809-828.
[http://dx.doi.org/10.1093/jpepsy/jst049] [PMID: 23843630]

Crickmore, K., Jones, A., Engelke, M., Mott, J. (2002). Pediatric asthma case management. *Health Forum J.,*

45(6), 24-30.
[PMID: 12506792]

Dennis, H., Rostill, H., Reed, J., Gill, S. (2006). Factors promoting psychological adjustment to childhood atopic eczema. *J. Child Health Care, 10*(2), 126-139.
[http://dx.doi.org/10.1177/1367493506062552] [PMID: 16707541]

Engelke, M.K., Guttu, M., Warren, M.B., Swanson, M. (2008). School nurse case management for children with chronic illness: health, academic, and quality of life outcomes. *J. Sch. Nurs., 24*(4), 205-214.
[http://dx.doi.org/10.1177/1059840508319929] [PMID: 18757353]

Erickson, J.D., Patterson, J.M., Wall, M., Neumark-Sztainer, D. (2005). Risk behaviors and emotional well-being in youth with chronic health conditions. *Child. Health Care, 34*(3), 181-192.
[http://dx.doi.org/10.1207/s15326888chc3403_2]

Freilinger, M., Reisel, B., Reiter, E., Zelenko, M., Hauser, E., Seidl, R. (2006). Behavioral and emotional problems in children with epilepsy. *J. Child Neurol., 21*(11), 939-945.
[http://dx.doi.org/10.1177/08830738060210110501] [PMID: 17092458]

Funnell, M.M., Anderson, R.M., Arnold, M.S., Barr, P.A., Donnelly, M., Johnson, P.D., Taylor-Moon, D., White, N.H. (1991). Empowerment: an idea whose time has come in diabetes education. *Diabetes Educ., 17*(1), 37-41.
[http://dx.doi.org/10.1177/014572179101700108] [PMID: 1986902]

Gomes, P., Smith, M. (2007). Responding to school health crises: Students with chronic health conditions may need monitoring on a daily basis and assistance with health emergencies. *Leadership, 36*, 28.

Grier, E.C., Bradley-Klug, K.L. (2011). A biopsychoeducational model of consultation for students with pediatric health disorders. *J. Educ. Psychol. Consult., 21*, 88-105.
[http://dx.doi.org/10.1080/10474412.2011.571522]

Grootenhuis, M.A., Last, B.F. (1997). Adjustment and coping by parents of children with cancer: a review of the literature. *Support. Care Cancer, 5*(6), 466-484.
[http://dx.doi.org/10.1007/s005200050116] [PMID: 9406361]

Hobbs, N., Perrin, J.M., Ireys, H.T. (1985). *Chronically ill children and their families.*. London: Jossey-Bass.

Houtzager, B.A., Grootenhuis, M.A., Last, B.F. (1999). Adjustment of siblings to childhood cancer: a literature review. *Support. Care Cancer, 7*(5), 302-320.
[http://dx.doi.org/10.1007/s005200050268] [PMID: 10483815]

Huffman, D.M., Fontaine, K.L., Price, B.K. (2003). *Health problems in the classroom 6 – 12: An A–Z reference guide for educators.*. Thousand Oaks, CA: Corwin.

Im, Y.J., Kim, D.H. (2011). Factors associated with the resilience of school-aged children with atopic dermatitis. *J. Clin. Nurs., 21*(1-2), 80-88.
[http://dx.doi.org/10.1111/j.1365-2702.2011.03750.x] [PMID: 21762420]

Jörngården, A., Mattsson, E., von Essen, L. (2007). Health-related quality of life, anxiety and depression among adolescents and young adults with cancer: a prospective longitudinal study. *Eur. J. Cancer, 43*(13), 1952-1958.
[http://dx.doi.org/10.1016/j.ejca.2007.05.031] [PMID: 17624761]

Kelo, M., Martikainen, M., Eriksson, E. (2011). Self-care of school-age children with diabetes: an integrative review. *J. Adv. Nurs., 67*(10), 2096-2108.
[http://dx.doi.org/10.1111/j.1365-2648.2011.05682.x] [PMID: 21635284]

Kim, D.H., Yoo, I.Y. (2010). [Development of a questionnaire to measure resilience in children with chronic diseases]. *J. Korean Acad. Nurs., 40*(2), 236-246.
[http://dx.doi.org/10.4040/jkan.2010.40.2.236] [PMID: 20453570]

Kirk, S., Beatty, S., Callery, P., Gellatly, J., Milnes, L., Pryjmachuk, S. (2013). The effectiveness of self-care support interventions for children and young people with long-term conditions: a systematic review. *Child Care Health Dev., 39*(3), 305-324.
[http://dx.doi.org/10.1111/j.1365-2214.2012.01395.x] [PMID: 22676438]

Knight, S.J., Scheinberg, A., Harvey, A.R. (2013). Interventions in pediatric chronic fatigue syndrome/myalgic encephalomyelitis: a systematic review. *J. Adolesc. Health, 53*(2), 154-165.
[http://dx.doi.org/10.1016/j.jadohealth.2013.03.009] [PMID: 23643337]

Kraaij, V., Garnefski, N. (2012). Coping and depressive symptoms in adolescents with a chronic medical condition: a search for intervention targets. *J. Adolesc., 35*(6), 1593-1600.
[http://dx.doi.org/10.1016/j.adolescence.2012.06.007] [PMID: 22771158]

Last, B.F., Stam, H., Onland-van Nieuwenhuizen, A.M., Grootenhuis, M.A. (2007). Positive effects of a psycho-educational group intervention for children with a chronic disease: first results. *Patient Educ. Couns., 65*(1), 101-112.
[http://dx.doi.org/10.1016/j.pec.2006.06.017] [PMID: 16870387]

Lindsay, R., Jarrett, L., Hillam, K. (1987). Elementary schoolteachers' understanding of diabetes. *Diabetes Educ., 13*(3), 312-314.
[http://dx.doi.org/10.1177/014572178701300315] [PMID: 3665719]

Lorig, K.R., Holman, H. (2003). Self-management education: history, definition, outcomes, and mechanisms. *Ann. Behav. Med., 26*(1), 1-7.
[http://dx.doi.org/10.1207/S15324796ABM2601_01] [PMID: 12867348]

Luthar, S.S., Cicchetti, D., Becker, B. (2000). The construct of resilience: a critical evaluation and guidelines for future work. *Child Dev., 71*(3), 543-562.
[http://dx.doi.org/10.1111/1467-8624.00164] [PMID: 10953923]

Martinez, W., Carter, J.S., Legano, L.J. (2011). Social competence in children with chronic illness: a meta-analytic review. *J. Pediatr. Psychol., 36*(8), 878-890.

[http://dx.doi.org/10.1093/jpepsy/jsr035] [PMID: 21745809]

Martinez, Y.J., Ercikan, K. (2009). Chronic illnesses in Canadian children: what is the effect of illness on academic achievement, and anxiety and emotional disorders? *Child Care Health Dev., 35*(3), 391-401. [http://dx.doi.org/10.1111/j.1365-2214.2008.00916.x] [PMID: 19397602]

Mickley, K.L., Burkhart, P.V., Sigler, A.N. (2013). Promoting normal development and self-efficacy in school-age children managing chronic conditions. *Nurs. Clin. North Am., 48*(2), 319-328. [http://dx.doi.org/10.1016/j.cnur.2013.01.009] [PMID: 23659816]

Monaghan, M.C., Hilliard, M.E., Cogen, F.R., Streisand, R. (2009). Nighttime caregiving behaviors among parents of young children with Type 1 diabetes: associations with illness characteristics and parent functioning. *Fam. Syst. Health, 27*(1), 28-38. [http://dx.doi.org/10.1037/a0014770] [PMID: 19630443]

Nabors, L.A., Little, S.G., Akin-Little, A., Lobst, E.A. (2008). Teacher knowledge of and confidence in meeting the needs of children with chronic medical conditions: Pediatric psychology's contribution to education. *Psychol. Sch., 45*, 217-226. [http://dx.doi.org/10.1002/pits.20292]

Nabors, L., Lehmkuhl, H., Christos, N., Andreone, T.L. (2003). Children with diabetes: perceptions of supports for self-management at school. *J. Sch. Health, 73*(6), 216-221. [http://dx.doi.org/10.1111/j.1746-1561.2003.tb06563.x] [PMID: 12899102]

National Kids Count. (2012). Retrieved November 5, 2013 from: http://datacenter.kidscount.org/data/tables/106-children-in-single-parent-families?loc=1&loct=2#ranking/2/any/true/868/any/430

Newacheck, P.W., Hung, Y.Y., Wright, K.K. (2002). Racial and ethnic disparities in access to care for children with special health care needs. *Ambul. Pediatr., 2*(4), 247-254. [http://dx.doi.org/10.1367/1539-4409(2002)002<0247:RAEDIA>2.0.CO;2] [PMID: 12135397]

Newacheck, P.W., Stein, R.E., Bauman, L., Hung, Y.Y. Research Consortium on Children With Chronic Conditions. (2003). Disparities in the prevalence of disability between black and white children. *Arch. Pediatr. Adolesc. Med., 157*(3), 244-248. [http://dx.doi.org/10.1001/archpedi.157.3.244] [PMID: 12622673]

Orr, D.P., Weller, S.C., Satterwhite, B., Perrin, I.B. (1984). Psychosocial implications of chronic illness in adolescence. *J. Pediatr., 104*(1), 152-157. [http://dx.doi.org/10.1016/S0022-3476(84)80616-2] [PMID: 6690661]

Patterson, J.M., Geber, G. (1991). Preventing mental health problems in children with chronic illness or disability. *Child. Health Care, 20*(3), 150-161. [http://dx.doi.org/10.1207/s15326888chc2003_4] [PMID: 10170810]

Perrin, J.M., Bloom, S.R., Gortmaker, S.L. (2007). The increase of childhood chronic conditions in the United States. *JAMA, 297*(24), 2755-2759.

[http://dx.doi.org/10.1001/jama.297.24.2755] [PMID: 17595277]

Perrin, J.M., MacLean, W.E., Jr, Gortmaker, S.L., Asher, K.N. (1992). Improving the psychological status of children with asthma: a randomized controlled trial. *J. Dev. Behav. Pediatr., 13*(4), 241-247. [http://dx.doi.org/10.1097/00004703-199208000-00001] [PMID: 1506461]

Pinquart, M. (2012). Self-esteem of children and adolescents with chronic illness: a meta-analysis. *Child Care Health Dev., 39*(2), 153-161. [http://dx.doi.org/10.1111/j.1365-2214.2012.01397.x] [PMID: 22712715]

Pinquart, M., Shen, Y. (2010a). Behavior problems in children and adolescents with chronic physical illness: a meta-analysis. *J. Pediatr. Psychol., 36*(9), 1003-1016. a [http://dx.doi.org/10.1093/jpepsy/jsr042] [PMID: 21810623]

Pinquart, M., Shen, Y. (2010b). Depressive symptoms in children and adolescents with chronic physical illness: an updated meta-analysis. *J. Pediatr. Psychol., 36*(4), 375-384. b [http://dx.doi.org/10.1093/jpepsy/jsq104] [PMID: 21088072]

Pinquart, M., Teubert, D. (2012). Academic, physical, and social functioning of children and adolescents with chronic physical illness: a meta-analysis. *J. Pediatr. Psychol., 37*(4), 376-389. [http://dx.doi.org/10.1093/jpepsy/jsr106] [PMID: 22173882]

Rolland, J.S., Walsh, F. (2006). Facilitating family resilience with childhood illness and disability. *Curr. Opin. Pediatr., 18*(5), 527-538. [http://dx.doi.org/10.1097/01.mop.0000245354.83454.68] [PMID: 16969168]

Sandstrom, M.J., Schanberg, L.E. (2004). Peer rejection, social behavior, and psychological adjustment in children with juvenile rheumatic disease. *J. Pediatr. Psychol., 29*(1), 29-34. [http://dx.doi.org/10.1093/jpepsy/jsh004] [PMID: 14747363]

Schmitz, N., Arkink, E.B., Mulder, M., Rubia, K., Admiraal-Behloul, F., Schoonman, G.G., Kruit, M.C., Ferrari, M.D., van Buchem, M.A. (2008). Frontal lobe structure and executive function in migraine patients. *Neurosci. Lett., 440*(2), 92-96. [http://dx.doi.org/10.1016/j.neulet.2008.05.033] [PMID: 18556120]

Sharpe, D., Rossiter, L. (2002). Siblings of children with a chronic illness: a meta-analysis. *J. Pediatr. Psychol., 27*(8), 699-710. [http://dx.doi.org/10.1093/jpepsy/27.8.699] [PMID: 12403860]

Shields, N., Murdoch, A., Loy, Y., Dodd, K.J., Taylor, N.F. (2006). A systematic review of the self-concept of children with cerebral palsy compared with children without disability. *Dev. Med. Child Neurol., 48*(2), 151-157. [http://dx.doi.org/10.1017/S0012162206000326] [PMID: 16417673]

Shields, N., Taylor, N.F., Dodd, K.J. (2008). Self-concept in children with spina bifida compared with typically developing children. *Dev. Med. Child Neurol., 50*(10), 733-743.

[http://dx.doi.org/10.1111/j.1469-8749.2008.03096.x] [PMID: 18834386]

Soliday, E., Grey, S., Lande, M.B. (1999). Behavioral effects of corticosteroids in steroid-sensitive nephrotic syndrome. *Pediatrics, 104*(4), e51.
[http://dx.doi.org/10.1542/peds.104.4.e51] [PMID: 10506276]

Steck-Silvestri, E.L., Phelps, L., MacAllister, W.S., Ensign, J., Crevier-Quintin, E., Hale, J.B. (2013). Chronic pediatric medical conditions and comorbid psychopathology. In: Reddy, L.A., Weissman, A.S., Hale, J.B., (Eds.), *Neuropsychological assessment and intervention for youth: An evidence-based approach to emotional and behavioral disorders.* (pp. 299-323). Washington, DC: American Psychological Association.
[http://dx.doi.org/10.1037/14091-013]

Suris, J.C., Michaud, P.A., Viner, R. (2004). The adolescent with a chronic condition. Part I: developmental issues. *Arch. Dis. Child., 89*(10), 938-942.
[http://dx.doi.org/10.1136/adc.2003.045369] [PMID: 15383438]

Taras, H., Potts-Datema, W. (2005a). Chronic health conditions and student performance at school. *J. Sch. Health, 75*(7), 255-266. a
[http://dx.doi.org/10.1111/j.1746-1561.2005.00034.x] [PMID: 16102088]

Taras, H., Potts-Datema, W. (2005b). Obesity and student performance at school. *J. Sch. Health, 75*(8), 291-295. b
[http://dx.doi.org/10.1111/j.1746-1561.2005.00040.x] [PMID: 16179079]

Taras, H., Potts-Datema, W. (2005c). Childhood asthma and student performance at school. *J. Sch. Health, 75*(8), 296-312. c
[http://dx.doi.org/10.1111/j.1746-1561.2005.tb07347.x] [PMID: 16179080]

Taras, H., Wright, S., Brennan, J., Campana, J., Lofgren, R. (2004). Impact of school nurse case management on students with asthma. *J. Sch. Health, 74*(6), 213-219.
[http://dx.doi.org/10.1111/j.1746-1561.2004.tb07935.x] [PMID: 15468525]

Taylor, H.G., Drotar, D., Schluchter, M., Hack, M. (2006). Consequences and risks of <1000-g birth weight for neuropsychological skills, achievement, and adaptive functioning. *J. Dev. Behav. Pediatr., 27*(6), 459-469.
[http://dx.doi.org/10.1097/00004703-200612000-00002] [PMID: 17164618]

Thompson, R.J., Gustafson, K.E. (1996). *Adaptation to chronic childhood illness..* Washington, DC: American Psychological Association.
[http://dx.doi.org/10.1037/10188-000]

van der Lee, J.H., Mokkink, L.B., Grootenhuis, M.A., Heymans, H.S., Offringa, M. (2007). Definitions and measurement of chronic health conditions in childhood: a systematic review. *JAMA, 297*(24), 2741-2751.
[http://dx.doi.org/10.1001/jama.297.24.2741] [PMID: 17595275]

Walsh, M.E., Murphy, J.A. (2003). Children, health, and learning: A guide to the issues. In: Lerner , R.M., (Ed.), *Contemporary youth issues* (pp. 1-86). Westport, CT: Praeger.

Warnes, C.A., Liberthson, R., Danielson, G.K., Dore, A., Harris, L., Hoffman, J.I., Somerville, J., Williams, R.G., Webb, G.D. (2001). Task force 1: the changing profile of congenital heart disease in adult life. *J. Am. Coll. Cardiol., 37*(5), 1170-1175.
[http://dx.doi.org/10.1016/S0735-1097(01)01272-4] [PMID: 11300418]

Williams, P.D. (1997). Siblings and pediatric chronic illness: a review of the literature. *Int. J. Nurs. Stud., 34*(4), 312-323.
[http://dx.doi.org/10.1016/S0020-7489(97)00019-9] [PMID: 9306166]

Wysocki, T., Meinhold, P., Cox, D.J., Clarke, W.L. (1990). Survey of diabetes professionals regarding developmental changes in diabetes self-care. *Diabetes Care, 13*(1), 65-68.
[http://dx.doi.org/10.2337/diacare.13.1.65] [PMID: 2298112]

Zylke, J.W., DeAngelis, C.D. (2007). Pediatric chronic diseases--stealing childhood. *JAMA, 297*(24), 2765-2766.
[http://dx.doi.org/10.1001/jama.297.24.2765] [PMID: 17595280]

CHAPTER 8

A Review of Sexual Exploitation Risk Factors for Our Children and Ways to Create Positive Classroom and Community Environments

Denise M. Green[1,*], **Sarah E. Twill**[2] and **Rebecca Fensler**[2]

[1] *Troy University, Troy, AL 36082, United States*

[2] *Wright State University, Dayton, OH 45435, United States*

Abstract: All families experience some degree of discord. When that discord becomes severe and synergistically mediated by environmental challenges such as low performance and disconnectedness at school, students may experience behavioral and psychosocial risks associated too commonly with highly undesirable outcomes. Among the most dangerous example is that students can become targets of recruiters of prostitution by human traffickers, who are often amazingly adept at exploiting the physiological and psychosocial needs of children and adolescents for nurturance and attachment in numerous ways. Predators can immerse disaffected youth into networks so convoluted that recovery is difficult, if not impossible. Engagement with the juvenile justice system is another undesirable outcome for those youth who disaffiliate from peers, family, and the school community, whether by choice, manipulation, or both. Considering the severity of the potential consequences, it is incumbent upon schools to play an assertive role in promoting resilience, connectedness, and engagement in school community membership and fostering school success.

Keywords: Abuse, Drug mule, Dysfunctional family, Human trafficking, Neglect, Organ harvesting, Prostitution, Sexual exploitation.

INTRODUCTION

Human trafficking, sexual exploitation, and prostitution of youth are a 150 billion

* **Corresponding author Denise M. Green:** Troy University, Troy, AL 36082, United States; Tel: 334-670-5767; Email: dmgreen@troy.edu.

Raymond J. Waller (Ed.)

dollar industry in the world today (UNICEF: USA, n.d.). In most cases, the recruiter of children is familiar to the victim – often an intimate or close family member. It is estimated there are 85 million child victims involved in commercial sexual exploitation, hazardous physical labor, and organ harvesting (World Vision, 2015). The major issue fueling the ability of traffickers to operate worldwide is the lack of birth certificates documenting live births (World Vision, 2014). Without this documentation, children are unaccounted for and unrecognized by governments. The *Girls Count Act* is currently pending in the United States Senate and would require registration of all children in order for a nation to receive US Foreign or Domestic Aid.

The gateway to human trafficking of youth appears to depend on a constellation of several risk factors, with the research highlighting several main areas of importance. A previous study done by the authors identified risk factors such as:

- **challenging family systems,**
- **childhood maltreatment,**
- **mental health issues,**
- **poor social skills, and**
- **substandard school performance**

as contributing to becoming the victim of human trafficking, sexual exploitation, and prostitution (Twill, Green, & Traylor, 2010).

This chapter is divided into two sections. In the first section, a brief review of the literature of risk factors will be delineated. Afterward, a discussion concerning the juvenile justice issues related to sexual exploitation will be highlighted. The purpose of the first section is to provide a frame for discussing the complex issues that contribute to human trafficking, sexual exploitation, and juvenile prostitution.

Understanding the life experiences of those at-risk youth gives the reader a better appreciation of the challenges and the necessity to re-think the social construction of the classroom and community as preventative environments. Further, being grounded in this literature will allow readers to assess implications for practice and explore ways to manage the classroom and school experience to optimize positive influences that can help palliate negative life experiences. The second section will provide suggestions for the creation of positive classroom and school community environments for the purpose of mitigating these risk factors.

Sexual Exploitation Risk Factors for Youth

Twill *et al.* (2010) outlined several categories of risk factors influencing the propensity of juveniles to fall victim to human trafficking, sexual exploitation, and prostitution. The risk factors of negative family systems, childhood abuse and neglect, mental illness, poor social skills, insufficient school performance, and juvenile delinquency seem to be predominant on the list of critical life events favoring the risk of involvement in human trafficking. A review of additional literature corroborates these categories with additional foci on substance abuse and sexually transmitted disease infection complicating the lives of victims (Hudson & Nandy, 2012; Jani & Anstadt, 2013; Murphy, 2010; Surratt, Kurtz, Chen, & Mooss, 2012; Wilson & Widom, 2010).

Negative Family Systems

Negative, unstable, and dysfunctional families systems comprise an assemblage of factors forcing youth to the streets (Tyler, Hoyt, & Whitbeck, 2000). In a study conducted almost twenty years ago, Brannigan and Van Brunschot (1997) reported that juveniles who were prostituted, compared to other students of the same age, were "more likely to characterize parental home life more negatively, to report higher levels of physical abuse, sexual abuse, non-traditional family structures, parental drug and alcohol abuse… [and] higher levels of running away behavior" (p. 350). This study highlights what has now become common knowledge – lack of a solid foundation with nurturing care at a basic level is detrimental to a child's development and growth.

The common belief that human trafficking, sexual exploitation, and prostitution only befell those of lower socioeconomic backgrounds (Estes & Weiner, 2005) is not accurate. Exploiters prey on unsupervised youth in suburban areas, offering friendship, money, and other popular commodities (*e.g.*, cell phones, clothes, and high-end accessories) to lure children away from home and family. Milloy's (2002) study of youth living on the street revealed 75% originated from working and middle class families with the majority being white. Milloy (2002) and Widom and Kuhns (1996) found that parental neglect was a significant risk factor irrespective of socioeconomic status. A more recent qualitative study done by Jani *et al.* (2013) cited lack of family support as the most reported issue in young girls agreeing to trafficking work.

Once the connection to family is broken, the trafficking network quickly ensconces the child in a maze of underground linkages designed to put this human commodity on the market to illegal ends. Most exploiters are part of the family constellation; these are known individuals hanging around families and communities looking for victims (End Trafficking Info Sheet, UNICEF: USA). They are observant and opportunistic - waiting for the moment of strife and vulnerability to be evident to make their promises and exert efforts to lure a child. Quite simply, the system of human trafficking, sexual exploitation, and prostitution is an opportunistic, market-driven business operating on the fact that negative family systems can pull a child away from home.

Childhood Abuse and Neglect

The authors previously found a relationship between a history of abuse and neglect and the early entry into delinquent behavior, which leads to further marginalization and the risks of exposure to human trafficking (Twill *et al.*, 2010). Wilson and colleagues (2010) looked at the enmeshment of problem behaviors with abuse and neglect resulting in prostitution. They found that childhood physical abuse, sexual abuse, and neglect were all predictors for delinquency and prostitution. Wilson and Widom (2008) also found there was a connection between childhood maltreatment and earlier initiation of sexual activity. That is, those with a history of abuse may lack coping skills and emotional defense mechanisms, making them more likely to be re-victimized (Tyler, *et al.*, 2000). Additionally, in order to meet basic essentials such as food or shelter, runaways were often compelled to engage in 'survival sex' (Brannigan & Van Brunschot, 1997).

Mental Illness

Juveniles who were sexually exploited appeared to suffer from multiple mental health issues, including posttraumatic stress disorder (Twill *et al.*, 2010). Posttraumatic stress disorder (PTSD) is an illness caused by exposure to a traumatic event and the accompanying negative psychological and physiological response to thoughts and events associated with the trauma (American Psychiatric Association, 2013).

In addition to PTSD, mental health issues such as anxiety and depression are also common in those who experience trauma. Of particular concern in this group are the approximately 26,000 youth aging out of foster care annually in the United States (National Alliance to End Homelessness, 2009). As reported in a study done by Hudson and Nandy (2012), former youth in foster care showed higher levels of homelessness, depression, alcohol and other drug use, more frequently engaged in survival sex, and had higher sexually transmitted disease infection rates, placing them at greater risk than other homeless youth.

Poor Social Skills

Children in dysfunctional families learn to cope with a toxic environment - often learning how to maneuver around a parent with poor self-control, unclear boundaries, and substance abuse (Green, 2010). These maladaptive survival skills are often not, however, appropriate in the outside world. Because these maladaptive survival skills are necessary to live at home, it is very easy for a child to become trapped in poor and destructive social exchanges. As the child is further marginalized, delinquent and aggressive behaviors can develop (Green, 2010). These problem behaviors in turn, set the stage for further abuse and neglect. This cycle, in each stage of progression, compounds risk of behavior problems, substance abuse, and early sexual activity (Lloyd, 2005). These behaviors are further exploited by the trafficker saying things like "Your parent does not understand you. I do." In the case of female prostitutes, Lloyd (2005) reports these victims engage in frequent short-term relationships with older males that were highly manipulative and very risky in attempts to find a caring relationship and social support.

Inadequate School Performance

The families of children at risk have patterns of dysfunctional behavior that become cyclic. Often imbedded in these patterns are multiple moves, poor employment histories and low educational attainment for parents (Green, 2005). These parental issues have direct and negative influences on children. Children with unstable home lives, whether because of homelessness, placement in the foster care system, or other issues, are at risk of school failure.

The National Coalition for Homelessness (NAEH, 2009) finds minors account for 39% of the homeless population. This places the estimate at 800,000 homeless students yearly. These children are four times more liable to renounce school, nine times more likely to be retained, and three times more likely to require special education services (National Alliance to End Homelessness, 2009). Finally, NAEH reports there is limited school funding to address the needs of homeless children.

Similarly, youth in foster care are at risk of school failure that may result in additional risk for exploitation. While in care, 65% of foster youth move schools seven or more times (Pecora *et al.*, 2006). These school disruptions result in:

- **more absenteeism (Zorc, O'Reilly, Matone, Long, Watts, & Rubin, 2013),**
- **repeating grades (Pecora, *et al.*, 2006),**
- **increased need for special education services (Scherr, 2007),**
- **being more harshly disciplined than their peers (Courtney, Terao, & Bost, 2004; Scherr, 2007), and**
- **not completing high school (Pecora, *et al.*, 2006).**

Resource	http://www.endhomelessness.org

Juvenile Delinquency and Sexual Exploitation

To begin this section, the authors present the stance the current legal system has not adjusted to address the massive and sophisticated black market business of sexual exploitation and human trafficking. A juvenile is regulated by the state laws of consent, and as Mir (2013) succinctly argues, unable to give consent to sexual acts, further pointing to the obvious: the juvenile is arrested for a crime in which they are a victim of statutory rape. Juveniles (and the adults) caught in this black hole are victims and should be treated as such. The time has passed for the Hollywood version of romanticizing the glamorous call girl and labeling her prostitution a 'choice'. Of equal abhorrence is the lack of attention given to the male juvenile trafficked for a drug mule, foot soldier, sexual exploitation, or organ harvesting.

As established throughout this chapter, the process by which a juvenile engages in delinquent acts seems to have a strong correlation to the abuse and neglect of that juvenile as a child. While there is not a clear delineation between physical abuse, sexual abuse, and neglect - all seem to impose burden increasing the risk of any exploitation. Roe-Sepowitz (2012, p. 574) found "that childhood emotional abuse leads to the psychological effects that result in the adolescent victims not having adequate coping strategies."

The younger the age of entry into the juvenile justice system, the more additional risk factors increase the likelihood of negative outcomes such as continued victimization, STD infection – especially AIDS and HIV, and substance abuse keep these juveniles on the street (Hudson *et al.*, 2012; Reid & Piquero, 2014; Wilson *et al.*, 2010). In addition, "The role of substance dependency in CSE [commercial sexual exploitation]/prostitution initiation and persistence during adolescence and young adulthood has been a recurrent theme of researchers for several decades" (Reid *et al.*, 2014, p. 248).

Finally, research supports that the stability of the primary care taker is clearly of importance. Issues of mental health, substance abuse, education attainment, and employment efficacy in the primary care taker often have a serious developmental impact on the child (Twill *et al.*, 2010).

While the juvenile delinquent is seen as being out of control, her behavior may be the result of childhood of neglect, physical or sexual abuse, and emotional deprivation. It is the system charged with taking care of the child that needs help. The authors propose the better practice method of care and treatment is a System of Care (SOC) imbedded in the community. A System of Care involves collaborative engagement of the parent(s) and the child, as well as the agencies involved in their lives including child protective services, juvenile justice, mental health, and the school system (Stroul, & Friedman, 1986). A case manager is assigned to organize the care of this child and break down the 'silos of communication' resulting frequently within and between bureaucratic systems (Green & Twill, 2012). This type of community model is designed to treat the family system in the least restrictive environment in a cost effective manner utilizing the primary safety net for the child (Stroul, & Friedman, 1986). This is a purpose for which schools are incomparably situated.

Creating Positive School Climate

The first step in creating a positive school climate is to have well trained staff that is able to identify and assist at-risk youth, including those youth who have been sexually exploited. In this section, school interventions involving teachers, classrooms, peers, parents, after school programing, and community efforts used to promote well-being and reduce delinquency are reviewed. In some cases, the literature reviewed is specific to sexually exploited youth (Hinkelman & Bruno, 2008). In others, the literature is focused either on universal interventions that promote the well-being of all children (Nichols, Birnbaum, Bryant, and Botvin, 2009; Vo, Sutherland, & Conroy, 2012) or those most at risk for delinquency or out of home placements (Solovery & Grove, 2013; Twill, MacLachlan, & Noxel, in press).

Hinkelman and Bruno (2008) reviewed ways that schools can improve the identification and reporting of child sexual abuse. In addition to reviewing the signs and symptoms of abuse, the authors suggested that schools work to develop a systematic approach to responding to child abuse. A systematic response includes:

1. working with child protective services, law enforcement, and legal professions to understand mandated reporting responsibility;
2. developing a school response team to support others in making reports of abuse;

3. promoting training for all school personnel, and;
4. implementing school-wide prevention efforts to promote a safe environment for students to report problems.

One such prevention program was described by Baker, Gleason, Naai, Mitchell, and Trecker (2012). This prevention effort used the train-the-trainer model as it empowered school staff to be better educated about child sexual abuse and created school capacity to respond to future incidences of abuse. Staff participated in 6-18 hours of training on the curriculum, *My Bod, My Boundaries* (MBMB). MBMB curriculum is designed for 3rd-5th grades, and focuses on helping students differentiate between appropriate and inappropriate touch, and how to get help if they are abused. Students who participated in the MBMB curriculum had a better understanding of inappropriate touch than their peers who did not participate. In addition, students who participated in MBMB knew what to do if they were abused (*i.e.*, tell someone, and keep telling until you are believed) compared to peers who did not participate.

Another way schools can address at-risk behaviors and school climate, modifying the environment rather than formal programming, is restructuring lunchtime. Nichols, Birnbaum, Bryant, and Botvin (2009) examined how middle school students spend their lunch (*e.g.*, in school, out of school, or do not eat), and whether this was related to ten delinquent behaviors (*e.g.*, fighting, stealing, property damage), and the use of cigarettes, alcohol, and marijuana. Students were surveyed in the 6th grade and again in the 8th about lunch habits and at-risk behaviors. The authors found that students who ate lunch outside of school instead of within a more structured and supervised setting, were more likely to engage in problem behaviors. As a way to buffer students from risk factors, schools may want to contemplate ways to increase prosocial lunchtime. Strategies such as:

- **having a closed campus,**
- **increasing adult supervision,**
- **providing desirable lunch menus,**
- **offering activities during lunch such as clubs or recreational sports, and**
- **promoting a welcoming atmosphere**

may be ways to engage students and prevent delinquency.

Finally, Li, and colleagues (2011) examined whether engagement with school helps protect students from delinquency. Using multi-wave longitudinal data, the researchers asked 5th-11th graders about their behavioral school engagement (*e.g.*, how frequently they went to school without homework completed), emotional school engagement (*e.g.*, "teachers in this school care about me"), delinquency (*e.g.*, "during the last 12 months, how many times have you hit or beat up someone?"), and use of substances (*i.e.*, cigarettes, alcohol, and marijuana).

Findings that behavioral and emotional engagement with school delayed and protected students from engaging in at-risk behaviors are consistent with the wide variety of outcomes positively associated with engagement. Efforts to promote attachment to school should be examined as an investment in delinquency prevention. For example, encouraging positive teacher-student relationships, promoting prosocial and anti-bullying peer relationships, hosting family fun/dinner nights at the school, offering prevention programming related to at-risk behaviors, and finding ways for students with diverse interests (*i.e.*, not just sports and the arts) to participate in school activities are all ways schools can create opportunities for student engagement.

Change in the Classroom is About Relationships

Positive relationships with teachers lead to better school adjustment and positive outcomes for children (Vo, Sutherland, & Conroy, 2012). However, many children with behavior problems do not develop these positive relationships with their teachers. Chronic early behavior problems in children can lead to emotional and behavioral disorders that have a negative impact on academic performance. School-based prevention and intervention programs that target nonpreferred or disruptive behaviors in children that lead to delinquency have shown positive results (Eddy, Reid, & Fetrow, 2000).

Vo *et al.*, (2012) describe the *Best in Class* intervention model. This model was created to address the needs of children who exhibit chronic behavior problems and are at-risk for emotional and behavioral disorders. "Best in Class" provides teachers with strategies that can be used to promote positive teacher-student interactions, increase learning and engagement, and decrease problem behaviors. Through this model, teachers are trained and coached in the use of evidence-based practices that promote a prosocial classroom. These practices include:

- **developing rules, routines, and expectations,**
- **giving behavior-specific praise, and**
- **using pre-correction and active supervision to remind students of behavioral expectations.**

Teachers are also coached in instructional pacing, providing opportunities for children to respond, and giving feedback. Initial investigation of the "Best in Class" intervention indicates that it is a promising model for improving teacher-student relationships, decreasing problem behaviors, and increasing social skills.

Anti-social behavior can lead to an increased risk of rejection by prosocial peers, leading to association with deviant peers and a greater likelihood of delinquency (Reid, Eddy, Fetrow, & Stoolmiller, 1999). "Linking the Interests of Families and Teachers" (LIFT) is another school and classroom-based intervention that can be used to reduce conduct problems and anti-social behavior. LIFT includes three main components: classroom-based social skills training, playground-based behavioral modification, and group-delivered parent training (Eddy *et al.*, 1999).

The classroom component involves role-playing social and problem-solving skills, and helps students practice new skills in small and large groups. A point-based system is used to reward students for prosocial behavior. LIFT also uses the playground environment as a way to reward individuals and class groups for displaying positive behaviors. Finally, parent training is included as part of the LIFT program; caregivers participate in lectures, discussions, and role-play activities. Caregivers are coached on home-practice activities so that they can continue to reinforce positive behaviors during non-school hours. LIFT has been shown to decrease aggressive behaviors in children. Over time, LIFT participants have been found to have fewer delinquent behaviors in adolescence.

Resource	https://www.crimesolutions.gov/ProgramDetails.aspx?ID

An evidence-based intervention known as the "Good Behavior Game" is a classroom-based behavior management strategy designed to reduce disruptive classroom behavior (Barrish, Saunders, & Wolf, 1969). In the "Good Behavior Game," children and teachers work together to establish classroom rules and behavior expectations. The teacher divides the students into teams who work together to monitor their own and their classmates' behavior. A non-competitive game, teams win when they meet behavioral expectations (Poduska & Kurki, 2014). The "Good Behavior Game" has been shown effective in reducing problem behavior and increasing time on task (Flower, McKenna, Bunuan, Muething & Vega, 2014).

Pivotal to interventions like "Best in Class," LIFT, and the "Good Behavior Game" is the recognition of the important role that teachers and schools play in the social and emotional development of children. These universal interventions not only improve the behaviors of youth at risk but benefit all students in the class. Schools can increase positive outcomes for youth by implementing interventions and strategies that clearly communicate behavioral expectations and how to meet them, emphasize teacher-student partnerships, reward students for positive behavior, and integrate school-home communication.

Promoting Positive Peer Relationships

Positive school experiences lead to better outcomes for all children, but are particularly important for those who have experienced the trauma of abuse. Childhood sexual abuse increases the likelihood that a person will experience a mental health disorder, such as PTSD (Kendall-Tackett, Williams, & Finkelhor, 1993). Further, children with a history of maltreatment often exhibit behavior problems such as aggression, delinquency, and social withdrawal (Mathews, Fawcett, & Sheldon, 2009). Aggressive and disruptive behavior can have negative implications for academic achievement (Reinke, Splett, Robeson, & Offutt, 2009).

Behavior problems can lead to decreases of classroom instructional time. A student may lose instruction time if he or she is pulled out of class for disruptive or problem behavior or whenever a teacher takes time away from instruction to correct problem behavior.

Children who are resilient are often those who receive good social support both from within and outside of the family (Marriott, Hamiltion-Giachritsis, & Harrop, 2013). Strong relationships with peers help mediate some of the problems maltreated children may experience (Mathews, Fawcett, & Sheldon, 2009). Children who have a friend they can confide in are better able to resolve emotional pain (Marriott, *et al.*, 2013). Quality relationships are important for coping and may mitigate the effects of maltreatment (Adams & Bukowski, 2007).

Children who display defiant and aggressive behavior early in life are at risk for rejection by prosocial peers, and are more likely to become criminal offenders as juveniles. Children who are skilled at social problem solving typically have better relationships with peers than children who do not (Fraser, Nash, Galinsky, & Darwin, 2000). Making Choices is a school-based intervention designed to help children in elementary and early middle school improve social problem-solving skills, build friendships, work effectively in groups, and react positively to new social situations. It can be facilitated in the classroom as a primary prevention program or in small groups targeting at-risk children.

Using a pre to post-test design, Smokowski, Fraser, Day, Galinsky, and Bacallao (2004) found the Making Choices curriculum improved peer relationships and prosocial behavior for at-risk children. Children who received the Making Choices intervention scored higher in social contact, peer acceptance, cognitive concentration, and exhibited fewer aggressive behaviors than children who were not in the Making Choices group.

Children with a history of maltreatment may benefit from peer mentors who exhibit positive behaviors. Schools can help promote positive peer relationships for children with a history of maltreatment by creating opportunities for peer mentorship and social skills training. Mathews *et al.*, (2009) studied the effects of a "Peer Engagement Program" on the behavior of children aged 7-14 with a history of maltreatment who participated in an after school program. The program combined three elements: peer mentoring, social skills training, and positive reinforcement.

Children who exhibited prosocial behavior were trained to act as mentors to other children by modeling positive behaviors. Social skills training addressed topics such as interpersonal communication, problem solving, stress management, and self-control. Children received positive reinforcement in the form of tokens that could be exchanged for rewards. The "Peer Engagement Program" was found to increase engagement in social interactions, decrease internalizing and externalizing behaviors, and increase social skills competence.

Interventions that help children and youth build social networks may mediate the negative impact of childhood maltreatment. School-based interventions are particularly effective in improving outcomes for at-risk children who may not otherwise receive treatment. Schools can facilitate the development of positive peer relationships for at-risk youth by implementing interventions that develop social skills and promote prosocial behavior.

Working with Parents

Preventing and reducing problem behavior has important implications for both childhood mental health and educational achievement. Schools are important environments for reinforcing appropriate social behavior (Reinke *et al.*, 2009). Because factors related to both school and family life contribute to behavior problems, integrating family and school-based interventions is potent in mediating the risks associated with disruptive behaviors.

Evidence-based practices that integrate school and home-based interventions can be effective for mediating problem behavior. The "Family Check-Up" (FCU) is a brief family intervention that can be implemented with families in a school setting (Dishion & Kavanagh, 2003). Using motivational interviewing, the three-session FCU involves an initial contact, assessment, and a feedback session. During the feedback session, the family is provided with a menu of intervention and support options. Parents may be more motivated to implement changes when provided with options. Information obtained through the FCU can be used to provide supportive services like parenting skills training or to link the family with needed resources (Stormshak, Connell, Veronneau, Myers, Dishion, Kavanagh, & Caruthers, 2011).

Broad Benefits

Schools can play a vital role in strengthening families and decreasing emotional and behavioral issues in children. "Families and Schools Together" (FAST) is a school-based intervention that targets at-risk children and families. Its goal is to help youth succeed academically and socially by reducing behaviors that lead to delinquency, violence, addiction, and school failure (McDonald & Frey, 1999). Further, FAST aims to strengthen the parent-child relationship, improve family functioning, and help at-risk families increase social connectedness and school involvement (Kratochwill, McDonald, Levin, Scalia, & Coover, 2009). The FAST program is a multi-family support group that targets vulnerable families, such as those experiencing stress and isolation as a result of poverty, domestic violence, and child abuse.

FAST is implemented by a team of parents, school personnel, and social service professionals. The program, which initially involves weekly sessions, includes a meal, parent discussion groups, parent-led family games, and skill-building activities. Studies on the success of the FAST program have shown its effectiveness in improving family functioning, reducing family stress, enhancing family-school relationships, and increasing prosocial behavior (Ackley & Cullen, 2010; Crozier, Rokutani, Russett, Godwin, & Banks, 2010).

Promoting After School Programming

Providing at-risk youth structured activities during traditionally unstructured and unsupervised times such as after school, weekends, and summers are endorsed by popular beliefs and public policies to buffer youth from poor outcomes. However, the findings are mixed about the success of these programs. While some produce positive results in the areas of strengthening academic skills (Gardner, Roth & Grooks-Gunn, 2008) and improving overall well-being (Fredricks & Eccles, 2008), others produce mixed findings, especially for middle and high school students.

Greenberg (2013) studied 7,694 school-aged students to determine immigrant children's participation in after school programming compared to non-Hispanic Whites' participation. Children with a foreign-born mother who spoke a language other than English at home, were less likely to participate in after school activities. Likewise, mothers with lower educational attainment and lower income were less likely to enroll their children in programs. Children with higher academic performance were also more likely to be enrolled than their less academically successful peers. When immigrant mothers did enroll their children in an activity, it was most apt to be a sport activity.

One way to address this inequality may be to offer after school programming with no financial burden. Schools should be mindful of transportation issues when offering after school programming to low-income families. In addition, in districts with a large immigration population, schools should consider sending home information to parents about after school programming in the native language that clearly explains the benefits of participation.

There is considerable debate about participation in sports and its impact on reducing delinquency, and a subsequent chapter clarifies why this may be the case. Some findings indicate sports participation reduced delinquency (Pate, Strost, Levin, & Dowda, 2000), while others find it either did not (Luthar, Shoum, & Brown, 2006) or may have influenced increases in delinquency (Burton & Marshal, 2005). Gardner *et al.*, (2009) compared three groups: youth who participated in sports, youth who participated only in nonathletic activities, and youth who did not participate in any organized activity.

The researchers found that boys who participated in organized sports were more at risk of non-violent delinquency than their peers who participated in some other organized activities; however, sports participants were no more likely to engage in nonviolent delinquency than their male peers who did not participate in any activity. More unstructured time and prior externalizing behavioral issues mediated the relationship between sports and delinquency. That is, participating in sports may increase social status, and thus offers to participate in unstructured socialization opportunities (*e.g.*, invites to hang out or party) that result in nonviolent delinquency (*e.g.*, underage drinking, loitering).

Participating in sports gives students an opportunity to meet new friends, including those with deviant behaviors. However, youth with prior externalizing behaviors may be more captivated by deviant peers than others. These same findings did not hold for girls; no relationship between participation in sports and delinquency was established for girls. Based on the findings of these researchers, schools may want to offer additional training for coaches to be aware of potential nonviolent delinquency, and provide orientation for parents of athletes to educate them about unstructured socialization time.

Summer presents another time that youth are likely to have unstructured and unsupervised time. Like participation in sports, participation in summer programming offers mixed and complex findings about delinquency prevention. Naccarato, Brophy, and LaClair (2013) studied a summer program designed to engage youth in prosocial activities including employment, education and recreation programs, and community service.

They found that participation in programming was extremely low; of the youth that participated, they were most engaged with work related activities. Participation declined after week three of the program for most activities; however, youth participation in work related activities remained steady over the ten weeks of the summer program. On average, youth who did participate spent 20 hours per week engaged in programming. The number of hours engaged in activities decreased the prospect of re-arrest or revocation for youth with previous juvenile justice involvement by about 2%.

While common sense intimates that providing opportunities for after school and summer programming helps keep students out of trouble by affording worthy activities to engage in, research suggests this is not always true. Schools and communities wishing to provide these opportunities, especially to middle and high school students, should spend time reviewing the literature, and considering their population and outcome goals before investing in this perceived panacea.

Partnering with the Community

It is impossible for schools to meet all of the needs of students; trying to do so reduces focus on their critical mission of educating students, and asks schoolteachers and administrators to practice outside of their training and expertise. Children and families with complex medical and mental health problems, those with involvement in the child welfare system or juvenile court, and families needing intensive support all require schools to collaborate with other agencies to provide for children and their families.

The system of care model discussed earlier was developed by Stroul and Freidman (1986) to serve youth with severe emotional disturbances (SED) who were served by two or more child serving agencies (*e.g.*, schools, mental health, child welfare) in order to coordinate case management between agencies, support the least restrictive environment, and encourage collaboration. Wraparound services help prevent suspensions, reduce absences, and lower rates of assaults and days in detention (Carney & Buttell, 2003; Green *et al.*, 2012).

Lee, Teater, Hsu, Greene, Fraser, Solovery, and Grove (2013) examined how youth at risk of out-of-home placement fared when services were provided using the Integrated Family and Systems Treatment (I-FAST) model. The authors suggested that when a case manager helps a family collaborate with schools, parental competence increases, which then positively predicted the child's level of functioning. Further, school-family collaboration helped reduce a child's negative behaviors, and increased their level of functioning.

Promoting Engagement by Meeting Need

Another way schools can assist children and families is by helping them access basic medical care. Strolin-Goltzman (2010) studied school-based health centers (SBHC). SBHC provide basic health services such as sports physicals, treatment of minor illnesses, education on reproduction and nutrition, limited dental care, and immunizations to students. She found that schools with SBHC were perceived more favorably on ratings of academic expectations, communication, and school engagement than schools without SBHC. Having a SBHC is especially helpful to traditionally underserved low-income and/or immigrant populations.

Sisselman, Strolin-Goltzman, Auerback, and Sharon (2012) examined innovative services offered by SBHCs. They described expanded collaborations (*e.g.*, SBHC partnering with a community hospital to provide smoking cessation programming or working with the Health Department to better track asthma patients), and expanded programming (*e.g.*, healthy lifestyle programs that focused on hand washing or healthy eating, and peer education programs that used teens to discuss anger management or body image with their classmates) which allowed for additional offerings to promote the wellbeing of the student body.

Twill *et al.*, (in press) reviewed one child welfare agency's attempt to fulfill the mandates of the *Adoption and Safe Families Act* (1997) and the *Fostering Connections to Success and Increasing Adoptions Act* (2008) by strengthening the child welfare system's attention to foster children's educational needs. Traditionally, youth in foster care do not academically perform as well as their peers not in foster care (Pecora, *et al.*, 2010). In this program, education specialists who were employed by the child welfare agency were assigned to work with youth in foster care, their foster families, and their schools to improve educational outcomes (Twill, *et al.*, in press).

In the first academic year that services were provided, 203 youth were served; 14 third graders preparing for a state mandated testing, 89 middle school students, and nearly 100 students who needed short-term educational case management. Preliminary qualitative data suggests that connections with schools were strengthened; for example, one teacher said, "The education specialist was vital in IEP meetings as a bridge between foster parents, the school personnel, mental health therapists, and the guardian ad litem. She was the only face-to-face observer who came into the classroom."

Partnering with other experts in the community allows schools to focus on their mission of educating students, while at the same time facilitating additional resources needed by students and their families. Working together with mental health agencies, health centers, and foster care caseworkers helps students receive the additional care they need to be academically successful. In addition, working with the other agencies gives all providers a chance to coordinate care for the betterment of students. Increasing community connections provide linkages and create a network of supports that can assuage marginalization, ostracism, and associated risks that increase the likelihood of recruitment and exploitation by predators.

Case Example

The following is a case example of a child at risk of negative life outcomes because of his exposure to inappropriate sexual content, and possible abuse, as well as other risk factors (*e.g.*, low-income, single parent, witnessing of domestic violence). The school was able to offer both universal programming such as the "Good Behavior Game" and after school programming, as well as targeted intervention like individual and family counseling, and specific community referrals.

Jason and Mad River Elementary School

Jason is an eight-year-old boy in the second grade at an urban public elementary school. He attends Mad River Elementary School. The majority of students are on free-reduced lunch, and the school qualifies for Title I funding. The school is classified by the state as a "School of Excellence" based on high test scores. Jason's teacher, Miss Patel, has been teaching for six years, while his principal, Mr. McIlvenna, has over 25 years of experiences, and was recently named the Principal of the Year by the school district.

Jason completes most of his homework and in-class assignments. His grades are average. Jason enjoys reading, but struggles in math. Outside of school, he enjoys riding his bike and watching television. Jason lives with his mother, Kim, and his younger sister, who is four. Kim works full-time as a waitress, often covering additional evening shifts to earn extra income. She receives some child support from Jason's father, but he has never been present in Jason's life.

Until four months ago, Kim's boyfriend, Dave, also lived in the family's rented apartment. Dave was both emotionally and physically abusive toward Kim, and Jason witnessed this abuse. In addition, after Dave moved out of the house, Jason told his mom, "I'm glad he is gone… He would make me watch naked people movies." Kim freaked out and asked Jason lots of questions – "Did you touch him? Did he touch you? Did he make you touch your sister?" Kim is embarrassed by this situation, and does not contact law enforcement, children's protective services, or a child advocacy center. Kim told Jason, "This is a private family thing. We don't talk about this to other people."

Recently, Kim received a report from Jason's school that he has been showing aggressive behavior toward some of the other children in the classroom and at recess. Miss Patel reports that a few classmates called Jason "a meanie," and that he has had trouble staying on-task. Last week, on the playground, Jason was seen pushing and yelling at a girl in his class during a group game. Miss Patel and the school counselor, Mr. Rekers, contacted Kim and arranged to meet about his behavior problems. During this meeting, Kim told them that Jason will sometimes yell at her when she tries to tell him punish him or enforce rules, such as television hours. She admitted that she sometimes has problems knowing how to deal with his behaviors. Kim said, "We have a lot going on at home. My boyfriend moved out because of some bad stuff going on." Kim did not disclose the family domestic violence or concerns about sexual abuse.

Miss Patel and Mr. Rekers told Kim that the school had recently implemented a program called the "Good Behavior Game" that would provide consequences for bad behavior on the playground and in the classroom while emphasizing and rewarding desired behavior. They explained that teams of students would work together to earn points and could select prizes for good behavior. Miss Patel shared with Kim that she was hopeful that this program might help improve Jason's behavior in the classroom and on the playground. Mr. Rekers also recommended that Jason participate in an after-school mentoring and tutoring program. In this setting, he could receive help with his math homework and be exposed to positive prosocial peers. Kim was willing to enroll Jason in the program because she knows he struggles with math. Also, she often works evening shifts and this would allow her to save some money in childcare expenses.

Mr. Rekers also offered to meet with the family for a "family check-up." Kim was not interested in this, citing reasons such as "I just don't have time because of work," and "We are really doing fine at home. Jason is just having a little trouble at school." Kim did agree to allow Mr. Rekers to meet with Jason during the school day. Mr. Rekers periodically called to check in with Kim. She accepted referrals for community services (*e.g.*, a free health clinic, a local church that was giving students winter boots), but continued to refuse to participate in the "family check-up." Kim always consented to have Jason participate in universal programs that occurred at the school such as a free dental clinic, and accepting hygiene items collected by a service organization. After several months, Miss. Patel and Mr. Rekers reported that Jason has had fewer incidences of aggressive behavior and, consequently, has been able to make new friends. They believe "The Good Behavior" game may have provided Jason with incentives to practice and master good behavior. Miss Patel also told Kim that his time on-task has improved, and that Jason seems to struggle less with math.

Jason's Outcomes

Without support from Jason's teacher and school counselor, Jason's aggressive and disruptive behavior may have led to decreased instruction time or efficiency resulting in poor academic achievement. Jason's aggression may also have made it difficult for Jason to be accepted by prosocial peers. This lack of positive social support would make Jason at-risk for social withdrawal, poor coping skills, delinquency, and possibly exploitation.

Jason's mom, Kim, like many other overwhelmed parents, did not partake in all offered programing, specifically the family counseling. Further, Kim and Jason did not discuss the family's issues with domestic violence, inappropriate sexual exposure, and potential abuse. This example illustrates the common situation in which school personnel notice behavioral issues, intervene assertively, and potentially contravene recruitment and exploitation. Also, the school offered universal programming that benefited not only Jason, but all children. It is likely that some of the child who participated in the universal programming were at-risk but unidentified, and benefitted from partaking. Universal programs also increase resilience and engagement for students currently unencumbered by consequential risk factors.

CONCLUSION

Youth who have a history of sexual exploitation and end up in the family court system are at risk of many catastrophic life insults including poor school performance, dropping out of school, delinquency, and life instability (Pecora, *et al.*, 2010). However, schools and communities can implement programs that help buffer youth from future at-risk behavior, potentially mitigating negative life outcomes. Because schools can offer youth a safe haven from the trouble in their home life, and because children spend much of their time interacting with the education system, schools and school communities are well situated to become one of several safety nets needed to prevent the human trafficking, sexual exploitation, and prostitution of children and youth.

CONFLICT OF INTEREST

The authors confirm that they have no conflict of interest to declare for this publication.

ACKNOWLEDGEMENTS

Declared none.

REFERENCES

Ackley, M.K., Cullen, P.M. (2010). Strengthening families through community collaboration: Implementing the Families and Schools Together (FAST) program. *Child. Schools, 32*(3), 183-186. [http://dx.doi.org/10.1093/cs/32.3.183]

Adams, R.E., Bukowski, W.M. (2007). Relationships with mothers and peers moderate the association between childhood sexual abuse and anxiety disorders. *Child Abuse Negl., 31*(6), 645-656. [http://dx.doi.org/10.1016/j.chiabu.2006.12.011] [PMID: 17590437]

Adoption and Safe Families Act of 1997. (1997). *Pub. L. No. 105-89.* Retrieved from: http://www.gpo.gov/fdsys/pkg/PLAW-105publ89/html/PLAW-105publ89.htm

American Psychiatric Association. (2013). *Diagnostic and statistical manual of mental disorders.* (5th ed.). Arlington, VA: American Psychiatric Association.

Baker, C.K., Gleason, K., Naai, R., Mitchell, J., Trecker, C. (2012). Increasing knowledge of sexual abuse: A study with elementary school children in Hawaii. *Res. Soc. Work Pract., 23*(2), 167-178. [http://dx.doi.org/10.1177/1049731512468796]

Barrish, H.H., Saunders, M., Wolf, M.M. (1969). Good behavior game: effects of individual contingencies for group consequences on disruptive behavior in a classroom. *J. Appl. Behav. Anal., 2*(2), 119-124. [http://dx.doi.org/10.1901/jaba.1969.2-119] [PMID: 16795208]

Brannigan, A., Van Brunschot, E.G. (1997). Youthful prostitution and child sexual trauma. *Int. J. Law Psychiatry, 20*(3), 337-354. [http://dx.doi.org/10.1016/S0160-2527(97)00016-2] [PMID: 9347396]

Burton, J.M., Marshall, L.A. (2005). Protective factors for youth considered at risk of criminal behaviour:

does participation in extracurricular activities help? *Crim. Behav. Ment. Health, 15*(1), 46-64. [http://dx.doi.org/10.1002/cbm.36] [PMID: 16470498]

Carney, M.M., Buttell, F. (2003). Reducing juvenile recidivism: Evaluating the wraparound services model. *Res. Soc. Work Pract., 13*, 551-568. [http://dx.doi.org/10.1177/1049731503253364]

Courtney, M.E., Terao, S., Bost, N. (2004). *Midwest evaluation of the adult functioning of former foster youth: Conditions of youth preparing to leave state care.* Retrieved from: http://www.chapinhall.org/sites/default/files/ChapinHallDocument_8.pdf

Crozier, M., Rokutani, L., Russett, J.L., Godwin, E., Banks, G.E. (2010). A multisite program evaluation of Families and Schools Together (FAST): Continued evidence of a successful multifamily community-based intervention program. *Sch. Community J., 20*(1), 187-207.

Dishion, T.J., Kavanagh, K. (2003). *Intervening in adolescent problem behavior: A family-centered approach.*. New York: Guilford Press.

Eddy, J.M., Reid, J.B., Fetrow, R.A. (2000). An elementary school-based prevention program targeting modifiable antecedents of youth delinquency and violence: Linking the interests of families and teachers (LIFT). *J. Emot. Behav. Disord., 8*(3), 165-176. [http://dx.doi.org/10.1177/106342660000800304]

Estes, R.J., Weiner, N.A. (2005). The commercial sexual exploitation of children in the United States. In: Cooper, S.W., Estes, R.J., Giardino, A.P., Kellogg, N.D., Vieth, V.I., (Eds.), *Medical, legal, and social science aspects of child sexual exploitation: A comprehensive review of pornography, prostitution, and internet crimes* (Vol. Vol. 1). St Louis, Missouri: G. W. Medical Publishing, Inc.

Finkelhor, D., Ormrod, R. (2004). *Prostitution of juveniles: Patterns from NIBRS. Juvenile Justice Bulletin.*. Washington, D.C.: U.S. Department of Justice- Office of Juvenile Justice and Delinquency Prevention Programs.

Flower, A., McKenna, J.W., Bunuan, R.L., Muething, C.S., Vega, R., Jr (2014). Effects of the Good Behavior Game on challenging behaviors in school settings. *Rev. Educ. Res., 84*(4), 546-571. [http://dx.doi.org/10.3102/0034654314536781]

Fostering Connections to Success and Increasing Adoptions Act of 2008. (2008). *Pub. L. No. 110-351.* Retrieved from: http://www.gpo.gov/fdsys/pkg/BILLS-110hr6893enr/html/BILLS-110hr6893enr.htm

Fraser, M.W., Nash, J.K., Galinsky, M.J., Darwin, K.M. (2000). *Social problem-solving skills for children.*. Washington, DC: NASW Press.

Fredricks, J.A., Eccles, J.S. (2010). Breadth of extracurricular participation and adolescent adjustment among African-American and European-American youth. *J. Res. Adolesc., 20*(2), 307-333. [http://dx.doi.org/10.1111/j.1532-7795.2009.00627.x] [PMID: 22837637]

Gardner, M., Roth, J., Brooks-Gunn, J. (2009). Sports participation and juvenile delinquency: the role of the

peer context among adolescent boys and girls with varied histories of problem behavior. *Dev. Psychol., 45*(2), 341-353.
[http://dx.doi.org/10.1037/a0014063] [PMID: 19271823]

Green, D. (2010). The Paradox of self-determination for marginalized individuals. *Social Work & Society, 8*(1) (urn:nbn:de:0009-11-27214)

Green, D.M. (2008). History, discussion and review of a best practices model for service delivery for the homeless. *Soc. Work Ment. Health, 3*(4), 1-16.
[http://dx.doi.org/10.1300/J200v03n04_01] [PMID: 20209071]

Green, D.M., Twill, S.E. (2012). System of care for children with severe emotional disturbance: A framework of mental health promotion based on students most in need. In: Waller, R.J., (Ed.), *Mental health promotion in schools: Foundations.* (pp. 216-256). Oak Park, IL: Bentham Science.

Greenberg, J.P. (2013). Determinants of after-school programming for school-age immigrant children. *Child. Schools, 35*(2), 101-111.
[http://dx.doi.org/10.1093/cs/cdt002]

Hinkelman, L., Bruno, M. (2008). Identification and reporting of child sexual abuse: The role of elementary school professionals. *Elem. Sch. J., 108*(5), 376-391.
[http://dx.doi.org/10.1086/589468]

Hudson, A.L., Nandy, K. (2012). Comparisons of substance abuse, high-risk sexual behavior and depressive symptoms among homeless youth with and without a history of foster care placement. *Contemp. Nurse, 42*(2), 178-186.
[http://dx.doi.org/10.5172/conu.2012.42.2.178] [PMID: 23181370]

Jani, N., Anstadt, S. (2013). Contributing factors in trafficking from South Asia. *J. Hum. Behav. Soc. Environ., 23*(3), 298-311.
[http://dx.doi.org/10.1080/10911359.2013.739010]

Kendall-Tackett, K.A., Williams, L.M., Finkelhor, D. (1993). Impact of sexual abuse on children: a review and synthesis of recent empirical studies. *Psychol. Bull., 113*(1), 164-180.
[http://dx.doi.org/10.1037/0033-2909.113.1.164] [PMID: 8426874]

Kratochwill, T.R., McDonald, L., Levin, J.R., Scalia, P.A., Coover, G. (2009). Families and Schools Together: an experimental study of multi-family support groups for children at risk. *J. Sch. Psychol., 47*(4), 245-265.
[http://dx.doi.org/10.1016/j.jsp.2009.03.001] [PMID: 19480887]

Lee, M.Y., Teater, B., Hsu, K.S., Greene, G.J., Fraser, J.S., Solovey, A.D., Grove, D. (2013). Systems collaboration with schools and treatment of severely emotionally disturbed children or adolescents. *Child. Schools, 35*(3), 155-168.
[http://dx.doi.org/10.1093/cs/cdt013]

Li, Y., Zhang, W., Liu, J., Arbeit, M.R., Schwartz, S.J., Bowers, E.P., Lerner, R.M. (2011). The role of school

engagement in preventing adolescent delinquency and substance use: a survival analysis. *J. Adolesc., 34*(6), 1181-1192.
[http://dx.doi.org/10.1016/j.adolescence.2011.07.003] [PMID: 22118510]

Luthar, S.S., Shoum, K.A., Brown, P.J. (2006). Extracurricular involvement among affluent youth: a scapegoat for "ubiquitous achievement pressures"? *Dev. Psychol., 42*(3), 583-597.
[http://dx.doi.org/10.1037/0012-1649.42.3.583] [PMID: 16756447]

Marriott, C., Hamilton-Giachritsis, C., Harrop, C. (2013). Factors promoting resilience following childhood sexual abuse: A structured, narrative review of the literature. *Child Abuse Rev., 23*(1), 17-34.
[http://dx.doi.org/10.1002/car.2258]

Mathews, T.L., Fawcett, S.B., Sheldon, J.B. (2009). Effects of a peer engagement program on socially withdrawn children with a history of maltreatment. *Child Fam. Behav. Ther., 31*(4), 270-291.
[http://dx.doi.org/10.1080/07317100903333160]

McDonald, L., Frey, H.H. (1999). *Families and schools together: Building relationships.*. Washington, DC: U.S. Dept. of Justice, Office of Justice Programs, Office of Juvenile Justice and Delinquency Prevention.

Milloy, M. (2002). Girls, interrupted. *Essence (Downsview), 33*(5), 429-436.

Mir, T. (2013). Trick or Treat: Why minors engaged in prostitution should be treated as victims, not criminals. *Fam. Court Rev., 51*(1), 163-177.
[http://dx.doi.org/10.1111/fcre.12016]

Murphy, L.S. (2010). Understanding the social and economic contexts surrounding women engaged in street-level prostitution. *Issues Ment. Health Nurs., 31*(12), 775-784.
[http://dx.doi.org/10.3109/01612840.2010.524345] [PMID: 21142598]

Naccarato, T., Brophy, M., LaClair, K. (2013). Summer engagement for at-risk youth: Preliminary outcomes from the New York state workforce development study. *Child Adolesc. Social Work J., 30*(6), 519-533.
[http://dx.doi.org/10.1007/s10560-013-0302-8]

National Alliance to End Homelessness. (2009). *National foster care coalition housing policy platform.* Retrieved from: http://www.endhomelessness.org/content/general/detail/2512

Nichols, T.R., Birnbaum, A.S., Bryant, K., Botvin, G.J. (2009). Lunchtime practices and problem behaviors among multiethnic urban youth. *Health Educ. Behav., 36*(3), 570-582.
[http://dx.doi.org/10.1177/1090198107313472] [PMID: 18319362]

Pate, R.R., Trost, S.G., Levin, S., Dowda, M. (2000). Sports participation and health-related behaviors among US youth. *Arch. Pediatr. Adolesc. Med., 154*(9), 904-911.
[http://dx.doi.org/10.1001/archpedi.154.9.904] [PMID: 10980794]

Pecora, P.J., Kessler, R.C., Williams, J., Downs, A.C., English, D., White, J., O'Brien, K. (2010). *What works in foster care? Key components of success from the northwestern foster care alumni study.*. New York: Oxford University Press.

Pecora, P.J., Williams, J., Kessler, R.C., Hiripi, E., O'Brien, K., Emerson, J., Torres, D. (2006). Assessing the educational achievements of adults who were formerly placed in family foster care. *Child Fam. Soc. Work, 11*(3), 220-231.
[http://dx.doi.org/10.1111/j.1365-2206.2006.00429.x]

Poduska, J.M., Kurki, A. (2014). Guided by theory, informed by practice: Training and support for the Good Behavior Game, a classroom-based behavior management strategy. *J. Emot. Behav. Disord., 22*(2), 83-94.
[http://dx.doi.org/10.1177/1063426614522692] [PMID: 26236144]

Reid, J.B., Eddy, J.M., Fetrow, R.A., Stoolmiller, M. (1999). Description and immediate impacts of a preventive intervention for conduct problems. *Am. J. Community Psychol., 27*(4), 483-517.
[http://dx.doi.org/10.1023/A:1022181111368] [PMID: 10573832]

Reid, J.A., Piquero, A.R. (2014). On the relationships between commercial sexual exploitation/prostitution, substance dependency, and delinquency in youthful offenders. *Child Maltreat., 19*(3-4), 247-260.
[http://dx.doi.org/10.1177/1077559514539752] [PMID: 24920248]

Reinke, W.M., Splett, J.D., Robeson, E.N., Offutt, C.A. (2009). Combining school and family interventions for the prevention and early intervention of disruptive behavior problems in children: A public health approach. *Psychol. Sch., 46*(1), 33-43.
[http://dx.doi.org/10.1002/pits.20352]

Roe-Sepowitz, D.E. (2012). Juvenile entry into prostitution: the role of emotional abuse. *Violence Against Women, 18*(5), 562-579.
[http://dx.doi.org/10.1177/1077801212453140] [PMID: 22790558]

Scherr, T.G. (2007). Educational experiences of children in foster care: Meta-analyses of special education, retention and discipline rates. *Sch. Psychol., 28*(4), 419-436.
[http://dx.doi.org/10.1177/0143034307084133]

Sisselman, A., Strolin-Goltzman, J., Auerbach, C., Sharon, L. (2012). Innovative services offered by school-based health centers in New York City. *Child. Schools, 34*(4), 213-221.
[http://dx.doi.org/10.1093/cs/cds010]

Smokowski, P.R., Fraser, M.W., Day, S.H., Galinsky, M.J., Bacallao, M.L. (2004). Schoolbased skills training to prevent aggressive behavior and peer rejection in childhood: Evaluating the Making Choice program. *J. Prim. Prev., 25*(2), 233-251.
[http://dx.doi.org/10.1023/B:JOPP.0000042392.57611.05]

Stormshak, E. A., Connell, A. M., Veronneau, M., Myers, M. W., Dishion, T. J., Kavanagh, K., Caruthers, A. S. (2011). An ecological approach to promoting early adolescent mental health and social adaptation: Family-centered intervention in public middle schools *Child Development, 82*(1), 209-225.
[http://dx.doi.org/10.1111/j.1467-8624.2010.01551.x]

Strolin-Goltzman, J. (2010). The relationship between school-based health centers and the learning environment. *J. Sch. Health, 80*(3), 153-159.

[http://dx.doi.org/10.1111/j.1746-1561.2009.00480.x] [PMID: 20236418]

Stroul, B.A., Friedman, R.M. (1986). The system of care concept and philosophy. In: Stroul, B.A., (Ed.), *Children's mental health: Creating systems of care in a changing society.* (pp. 3-39). Baltimore: Paul H. Brooks Publishing Co..

Surratt, H.L., Kurtz, S.P., Chen, M., Mooss, A. (2012). HIV risk among female sex workers in Miami: the impact of violent victimization and untreated mental illness. *AIDS Care, 24*(5), 553-561. [http://dx.doi.org/10.1080/09540121.2011.630342] [PMID: 22085330]

Twill, S.E., MacLachlan, H., Noxsel, J. Meeting the education needs of students in foster care: One agency's process of creating an education unit. In: Lawrence, S.K., Anderson, B., Stepteau-Watson, D., (Eds.), *Let Me Say Something: Voices from Inside the Child Welfare System..* Lampeter, Wales: Edwin Mellen.

Twill, S.E., Green, D., Traylor, A. (2010). A Descriptive Study on Sexually Exploited Children in Residential Treatment. *Child Youth Care Forum, 39*(3), 187-199. [http://dx.doi.org/10.1007/s10566-010-9098-2]

Tyler, K.A., Hoyt, D.R., Whitbeck, L.B. (2000). The effects of early sexual abuse on later sexual victimization among female homeless and runaway adolescents. *J. Interpers. Violence, 15*(3), 235-250. [http://dx.doi.org/10.1177/088626000015003001]

UNICEF: United States Fund . (n.d.). *End trafficking.* Retrieved from: http://www.nydailynews.com/news/national/georgia-high-school-student-sues-high-school-gay-prom-king-queen-proposal-article-1.1050609

Vo, A.K., Sutherland, K.S., Conroy, M.A. (2012). Best in class: A Classroom-based model for ameliorating problem behavior in early childhood settings. *Psychol. Sch., 49*(5), 402-415. [http://dx.doi.org/10.1002/pits.21609]

Widom, C.S., Kuhns, J.B. (1996). Childhood victimization and subsequent risk for promiscuity, prostitution, and teenage pregnancy: a prospective study. *Am. J. Public Health, 86*(11), 1607-1612. [http://dx.doi.org/10.2105/AJPH.86.11.1607] [PMID: 8916528]

Wilson, H.W., Widom, C.S. (2010). The role of youth problem behaviors in the path from child abuse and neglect to prostitution: A prospective examination. *J. Res. Adolesc., 20*(1), 210-236. [http://dx.doi.org/10.1111/j.1532-7795.2009.00624.x] [PMID: 20186260]

World Vision. (2015). *Child protection: Our impact on child trafficking.* Retrieved from: http://www.worldvision.org/our-impact/child-protection

World Vision. (2014). *Birth registration bill much closer to becoming law.* Retrieved from: http://www.worldvision.org/news-stories-videos/girls-count-act-senate

Zorc, C.S., O'Reilly, A.L., Matone, M., Long, J., Watts, C.L., Rubin, D. (2013). The relationship of placement experience to school absenteeism and changing schools in young, school-aged children in foster care. *Child. Youth Serv. Rev., 35*(5), 826-833.

CHAPTER 9

Adopted Children in Schools: A Guide for Educators

M. Elizabeth Vonk* and **Katherine N. King**

University of Georgia, Athens, GA 30602, United States

Abstract: Similar to a previous discussion on student athletic participation, adoption is often postulated to be an overwhelmingly protective event. Even more so than in that example, the assumption is, in the following example, likely true. Children who have been adopted do well in many domains of life. Even so, adoption can convey risk to children depending on several factors that are discussed below such as the type of adoption process a child experiences, providing many opportunities for schools to be involved in mental health promotion. Moreover, school practices can convey risk to adopted children, depending on the approach and sensitivity used in presentation. This chapter also, therefore, provides specific examples of how common school exercises that may convey risk can, often with little resource investment, encourage adopted children and facilitate their participation as members of the school community.

Keywords: Adoption, Child welfare, Deprivation, Developmental cognizance, Domestic adoption, Foster care, International adoption, Open adoption.

INTRODUCTION

Adoption is the process by which a child and non-biologically related adult(s) are legally joined in a parent-child relationship. The relationship is permanent and affords the adoptive parent with all responsibilities and rights of a biological parent. In the United States (US), it is estimated that 1.8 million, or approximately 2.5 percent of all children, joined their families through adoption (Vandivere,

* **Corresponding author M. Elizabeth Vonk:** University of Georgia, Athens, GA 30602, United States; Tel:(678) 985-6793; Email: bvonk@uga.edu.

Raymond J. Waller (Ed.)

Malm, & Radel, 2009). However, the numbers of lives that intersect with adoption are much greater when you include birth parents, siblings, adoptive parents, close friends, and so forth. Even if a teacher does not have an adopted child in class, it is quite possible that the class includes a child with a relative or friend of someone who was adopted.

While the purpose of this chapter is to draw attention to the unique needs of adopted children in schools, it is important first to consider the overall well-being among adopted children. Results of a large-scale, representative study of adopted children in the United States indicated that the majority of adopted children are faring well in most areas of their lives (Vandivere, Malm, & Radel, 2009). For example, most adopted children are in excellent physical, emotional, and social health. Compared to non-adopted counterparts, they are more likely to have health insurance, have a parent read to them on a daily basis, and be involved in extra-curricular activities. Importantly, nearly 90% of adoptive parents agreed they would "definitely make the same decision to adopt their child, knowing everything then that they now know about their child" (Vandivere, Malm, & Radel, 2009, p. 5).

Evidently, the majority of adopted children are doing well. However, adopted compared to non-adopted children have a higher number of important, risk congruent outcome measures, including:

- **special health care needs;**
- **developmental and language delays;**
- **mental health difficulties such as attention deficit hyperactivity disorder (ADHD), anxiety, and depression; and**
- **lower levels of educational success, as measured by reading and math scores (Vandivere, Malm, & Radel, 2009; Smith & Riley, 2006; and Harwood, Feng, & Yu, 2013).**

While these outcomes are elevated for only a minority of adopted children, they pose significant challenges for the affected children and their parents.

Of course, adoption in and of itself does not cause problems or school related difficulties. On the contrary, adopted children often fare much better than do their non-adopted peers on school outcome measures (van IJzendoorn, Juffer, & Poelhuis, 2005). Adopted children, however, face some unique challenges and vulnerabilities in school, some of which are due to pre-adoption privations and others to the nature of adoption as a diverse family formation.

Educators occupy an influential position in all children's lives. Children spend a tremendous amount of time each day in school, and learn not just academics, but also about themselves, their peers, and the world. As important role models for children, teachers often serve as facilitators of the development of self- esteem and self- efficacy. It is in the school setting that adopted children generally first realize that their family "stories" are different from their peers. They begin to hear "important messages regarding adoption that help to shape their identity as adopted persons" (Smith & Riley, 2006, p. 2). Teachers are uniquely situated to impart messages about adoption that are positive and normalizing. Consequently, it is imperative for educators to understand the multiple aspects of adoption. This will, in turn, allow educators to better address and serve adopted children's needs in mental health promotion rather than alienating their family experience.

Multiple Routes to Adoption

The purpose of this chapter is to describe educational, psychosocial, and diversity related issues relevant to the needs of adopted children in schools. We will begin with a brief overview of three types of adoption in the US. In each type, the child follows a different path to his or her permanent home. This will be followed by a discussion of potential areas of concern for adopted children in schools. Next, we will describe guiding principles for responsive and inclusive schools for children who join their families through adoption. We will conclude with a discussion of resources for teachers who would like to know more about adopted children in schools.

Types of Adoption

Because regulations guiding adoption can vary so dramatically by nation, basic descriptive information is provided for the United States for example purposes. Children are adopted through three primary methods in the United States. First, more than one-third are domestic, private adoptions (Vandivere, Malm, & Radel, 2009). That is, the children are adopted through facilitation of private attorneys, physicians, or for-profit or non-profit adoption agencies that specialize in placing infants with adoptive parents. In such adoptions, the birth parents make a decision to place a child for adoption, and the agency, physician, or attorney assists with matching a prospective adoptive parent with the child. In some cases, these adoptions are open, that is, the biological parents continue to have an agreed upon type and amount of contact with the adopted child and family.

Slightly more than one-third of additional adopted children are placed through the public foster care systems in each state (Vandivere, Malm, & Radel, 2009). Such children come to need adoptive parents when their biological parents' rights have been terminated, generally following abuse or neglect of the child. These children are unable to be reunified with their birth parents due to history and threat of harm. In addition, they have commonly experienced multiple changes in care-givers and child welfare workers during the time they are in the care of the state.

Finally, somewhat less than the final one-third of adoptions in the United States are international (Vandivere, Malm, & Radel, 2009). That is, the children are born in and adopted from other countries. The majority of children adopted from other countries have experienced some length of time in institutionalized settings. The level of care children receive in such settings varies enormously but for many is woefully inadequate. The majority of these children are adopted by parents of a race or ethnicity different from their own (Vandivere, Malm, & Radel, 2009; Smith & Riley, 2006). Thus, these adoptions pose the potential to be an abrupt and sometimes traumatizing change for a child who is propelled into a different life with new parents, language, food, and culture.

Potential Areas of Concern for Adopted Children

There are several potential areas of concern within the school setting for children who have joined their families through adoption. Considering the wide variability of adopted children's pre- and post-adoption experiences and subsequent functioning, it should not be assumed that problems always exist. This is a common misapprehension about adopted children. On the contrary, it should be remembered the majority of adopted children have good outcomes in schools and at home (Smith & Riley, 2006). Several areas of vulnerability have been identified, however, incorporating educational and psychosocial variables. In addition, adoption is a diversity issue for children in schools.

Educational and Academic Concerns

Existing studies indicate that adopted compared to non-adopted children:

- **have lower math and reading scores,**
- **are referred to special education services at a greater rate, and**
- **more frequently experience behavioral problems that interfere with learning (Raleigh & Kao, 2013; Smith & Riley, 2006; Harwood, Feng, & Yu, 2013).**

In addition, adoptive compared to biological parents report lower rates of children's overall adjustment at school and higher rates of unmet educational needs (Howard, Smith, & Ryan, 2004). Studies have examined educational outcomes of adopted children from each of the three adoption methods described above. The findings provide a picture suggestive of diverging needs of support that vary depending on the method of adoption a child experienced.

For children who were adopted internationally, educational outcomes appear to be affected by pre-adoption institutionalization that often includes physical and relational deprivation (Harwood, *et al.*, 2013). In addition, internationally adopted children experience an abrupt change in language development, most frequently during the critical years of one to four years old (Meacham, 2006). While a nurturing adoptive home helps to improve the effects of these early experiences, a significant minority of internationally adopted children appear to remain vulnerable to school performance difficulties.

This is true especially for children who are adopted at older ages, and who have experienced longer institutionalization and deprivation (Harwood *et al*, 2013). Children who were adopted from Eastern European countries appear to be at greatest risk, showing high rates of speech, language, and cognitive impairment (Beverly, McGuinness, & Blanton, 2008). In contrast, children who were adopted from China have shown similar rates as non-adopted children for language and behavioral problems, perhaps pointing to differences in orphanage or prenatal conditions (Tan & Yang, 2005; Tan & Marfo, 2006).

Almost all children adopted from the child welfare system have experienced serious abuse and neglect followed by foster-care, sometimes involving a series of abrupt changes in placement prior to adoption. In addition, many of these children experienced prenatal substance exposure (Harwood, *et al.*, 2013). Such disruption in children's lives greatly interferes with their school performance before, during, and after foster-care placement. Educational needs, even when identified, often go unmet prior to adoption due to changes in placement, foster-care worker turnover, and lack of coordination with foster parents (Smith & Riley, 2006). Even following adoption, however, parents of these children have reported a high rate of unmet educational needs (Howard *et al.*, 2004).

Children adopted privately are generally placed with their adoptive parents within days or weeks of birth, thus limiting pre-adoptive privation. When compared to children from the foster-care system, this group shows fewer behavioral problems but may still have elevated risk for school-related problems when compared with non-adopted children (Harwood, *et al*, 2013; Smith & Riley, 2006). Much of the research that has been done with domestically adopted children has not distinguished between private and public welfare adoptions; thus, more information is needed to assess the educational needs of children who were adopted privately as infants.

Psychosocial Concerns

Similar to educational vulnerabilities, psychosocial concerns are often correlated to the specific pre-adoption adversities experienced by children. A recent study examining utilization of mental health services for adopted children revealed higher use among boys than girls, as well as by children adopted through the child welfare system. Mental health services were used about equally by internationally and private domestically adopted children (Tan & Marn, 2013).

Some internationally adopted children who have had histories of institutionalized care experience:

- **attachment related difficulties,**
- **problems with emotional regulation,**
- **negative emotions ranging from sadness to worry, and**
- **attentional deficits (Henry & Pollack, 2009).**

Many internationally adopted children have the added dimension of being of a different race than their parents, which may increase stress related to identity and peer relationships.

Children adopted domestically from the foster-care system are vulnerable to psychosocial problems primarily due to their histories of abuse, neglect, and disruptions in care. In addition, some children are in foster-care due to their parents' severe psychiatric or substance use disorders, in which case a genetic predisposition to mental illness may be present. Genetic susceptibilities are associated with many behavioral and mental illness conditions, including:

- **externalizing behaviors such as aggression;**
- **internalizing disorders such as depression and anxiety;**
- **attention deficits and hyperactivity; and**
- **attachment and relational difficulties (Henry & Pollack, 2009).**

The stability of an adoptive home helps to mitigate behavioral issues; however, children adopted from the foster-care system often continue to require mental health assistance at a greater rate than others (Smith & Riley, 2006).

Developmental Cognizance of Adoption

Common to all children who were adopted are issues related to loss, grief, identity, intimacy and mastery/control. Adoption is created through the loss of a child's birth family. This early and significant loss may make subsequent bereavements more profound, create worry about abandonment, and increase rejection sensitivity. With no sense of control over important decisions made for them, some children respond with an importunate desire to control their environments to ward off conceivable losses. While these are normal developmental issues for adopted children, they may at times become overwhelming and distract from academics or interfere with peer relationships. As educators, it is important to know that the adopted child grapples with and gains new understanding of these complex core issues at each developmental stage (Vonk, 2006).

During infancy, from birth to one year old, children are unaware of differences between adopted and non-adopted children. During this first year, all babies need consistent care and nurturance in order to establish a secure attachment that later can become the foundation of trust and intimacy. For children adopted as infants, this involves adjustment to a transition from the biological to the adoptive parents (Brodzinsky, Schechter, & Henig, 1992; Melina, L., 1989; Vonk, 2006) Children in neglectful, abusive, or institutionalized settings are often denied consistent, dependable care, and are vulnerable to attachment deficits.

Toddlers and preschoolers, from one to five years old, experience enormous growth in their motor, cognitive, emotional and relational abilities. They begin to develop a sense of who they are, become aware of themselves as separate from their parents, and begin to notice physical differences among people. Children of this age are naturally curious, and may ask many questions, some of which are related to birth, reproduction, and their own "story" that explains where they came from.

Recounting the details of their adoptions regularly becomes a favorite story that children of this age want to hear from their parents. Although often able to retell their own adoption story, preschoolers think concretely and are not yet able to understand the concepts underlying adoption. This can result in confusion for some children who may think that all children are adopted, or that some children are born while others are adopted. These issues aside, preschoolers are typically very accepting of adoption because they do not yet view their families as being different from others (Brodzinsky, Schechter, & Henig, 1992; Melina, L., 1989; Vonk, 2006).

During middle childhood, from six to eleven years old, cognitive development and exposure to peers facilitates adopted children better understanding the concept of adoption. They generally begin to realize that in order to have adoptive parents; they must also have had biological parents who made a decision to place them for adoption. They may wonder why their biological mother did not keep them. They begin to grieve the loss of their biological families, sometimes worrying about themselves and other times worrying about the sadness they imagine in the biological family members. They may wonder if they were placed for adoption because something about them is wrong or bad. In addition, children of this age begin to understand that they are "different" from most peers due to adoption.

Ambivalence can occur, with a child sometimes wishing they looked more like their adoptive parents, and sometimes fantasizing about life with their biological families. During this period, adopted children are more likely to begin to receive and must learn to handle questions from peers about adoption, their biological parents, and differences in appearance between their adoptive parents and themselves (Brodzinsky, Schechter, & Henig, 1992; Melina, L., 1989; Vonk, 2006).

Adolescence, from twelve to nineteen years old, brings further cognitive, physical, and emotional maturation, all of which contribute to adopted children's deeper understanding of adoption and its meaning in their own lives. As they work toward identity development and independence, adopted adolescents may experience a wide array of feelings from grief, anger and confusion to love, joy and gratitude toward both the adoptive and biological parents. Adoption associated losses continue to be grieved during adolescence and may be heightened by identity issues and questions about belonging. In addition, the ability to think abstractly allows adopted adolescents to contemplate alternative perspectives. For some, this allows for greater understanding of the complexity of their birth mothers' decision to make an adoption plan (Brodzinsky, Schechter, & Henig, 1992; Melina, L., 1989; Vonk, 2006).

Questions related to identity development, an important task of adolescence, also are complex for adopted children. For those who were adopted transracially, racial identity may be challenging. Fantasies about the biological family can continue well into adolescence as they try to understand who they are in relation to both their adoptive and biological families. For example, adopted adolescents may wonder about their biological potential in terms of their appearance, talents, and values. Some may begin to think about searching for their biological family in an attempt to better understand who they are. In short, the adopted adolescent's emerging identity must include both the fact and the personal meaning of their adoption (Brodzinsky, Schechter, & Henig, 1992; Melina, L., 1989; Vonk, 2006).

Diversity Concerns

Adopted children are by definition "different" from many of their peers due to the way in which they joined their families. This sense of difference may be greater for children who do not look like or are not of the same race as their parents. As such, families formed through adoption may be viewed within the conceptual framework of 'diversity' in similar ways that gender, disability, race, and ethnicity have been recognized as such. Stated in the Evan B. Donaldson policy perspective on adoption in schools (Smith & Riley, 2006), adoption needs to be considered a diversity issue "because children should not be less understood or more stigmatized simply because of the type of family they happen to be in" (p. 3). From this perspective, children who join their families by adoption should be included in every way in the classroom. Such inclusion creates an environment that allows children to perform to the best of their abilities with a minimum of energy being diverted to deal with feelings of confusion or questions about belonging.

Feelings of Classroom Exclusion

There are several ways in which adopted children may feel excluded in the school setting (Henry & Pollack, 2009; Smith & Riley, 2006; Barratt, 2012.) First, adopted children and families may not be epitomized in schools and classrooms (this is true also for children who live in a variety of non-traditionally defined family forms). Adopted children, particularly those who do not physically resemble a parent, may not be able to find a display, story, class discussion, or activity in which someone like them or their family is positively represented.

The first author worked with a family who reported the only reading about adoption assigned to their daughter during elementary school was one about "orphan trains". While the story was historically accurate, the teacher provided no information about current adoption practice, leading to children to asking their daughter if her parents picked her out from a train platform. Assignments that are not inclusive are particularly oppressive for adopted children. For example, assignments that require family trees in a traditional format, baby pictures, and charting of genetic traits can be difficult, if not impossible for adopted children to complete.

Another way in which adopted children may feel excluded includes exposure to a variety of myths and negative stereotypes about adoption. While there are many myths, some of the more common ones tend to diminish the legitimacy or worth of adoptive and birth parents. These include such beliefs as "adoptive parents are not as bonded to or do not love their children as much as biological parents"; and "birth parents don't care about or love their children (or they would not have made an adoption plan)".

Stereotypes can be communicated subtly through negative adoption language, such as when a teacher talks about "real" *versus* adoptive parents. However, they are also communicated manifestly, often in the form of intrusive or insensitive questions from peers. For example, a classmate may ask an adopted child why her "real" mother gave her away, or a classmate may tell an adopted teen they "feel sorry for her" because she was adopted. Other questions serve to accentuate difference, such as when a child adopted from China is asked to explain to the class what China is like; or when a child adopted from Ethiopia is asked if he can speak English.

In sum, adopted children have unique needs, some of which are related to pre-adoptive adversities and others to the child's developing understanding of what it means to be adopted. Still other needs are related to adoption as a diversity issue. Most educators receive little to no training specific to adopted children in formal education settings, leaving most with similar knowledge and attitudes about adoption as are held in the general public (Taymans, *et al.*, 2008).

Unfortunately, unless educators have had personal experience with adoption, they are likely to hold beliefs about adoption that are based on what they have seen and heard in the media, including myths and negative stereotypes (Smith & Riley, 2006). Without information and understanding of adoption, educators are not equipped to address the needs of adopted children. With basic knowledge about adoption, however, educators can help create inclusive and responsive school environments that serve adopted children well.

Responsive and Inclusive Schools for Adopted Children

A wealth of information is available to assist educators with adoption related issues in schools. To organize this information, we will borrow from the Center for Adoption Support and Education (CASE) who promote five guiding principles for creating adoption-sensitive schools. The principles:

- **acceptance,**
- **accuracy,**
- **assignments,**
- **assistance, and**
- **advocacy,**

are described briefly in the Evan B. Donaldson policy perspective (2006), and in greater depth in CASE publications.

Resource	http://adoptionsupport.org/

Acceptance

The first principle is to provide personal and social <u>acceptance</u> of adoption as a legitimate and normal means of family formation (Smith & Riley, 2006). As with other forms of family diversity, children who were adopted need to hear that adoption is one of many acceptable ways to become family. Teachers can impart such acceptance at the classroom level when responding to specific questions or comments from students. One way in which acceptance can be communicated is through the use of positive adoption language. Several commonly used terms related to adoption cast doubt about the normalcy or legitimacy of adoption. For example, when the mother of a child who was adopted is asked whether she still wants to have her "own" child, it casts doubt on the authenticity of her current maternal relationship. In the following table, consider the difference in meaning of positive *versus* negative language choices. In each case, a simple change in word choice can convey either denigration or acceptance of adoption or someone in the adoption triad.

Table 1. Positive adoption language.

Positive	Negative	Explanation
Birth or biological parent	Real or natural parent	Imaginary and unnatural parents do not exist.
Make an adoption plan	Give up, put up, or give away	Choosing to place a child for adoption is a difficult decision that is made with thought and care.
Make a decision to parent	Keep	This implies that parents who place children for adoption are discarding them.
Parent	Adoptive parent	We do not routinely call parents of birth children "Biological" parents; there is no need to indicate a child's path into a family.
Child from (country)	Foreign child	Foreign implies a person does not belong.
Child *was* adopted	Child *is* adopted or Adoptee	Adoption is a process, not the sum of a person's identity or a condition.

Accuracy

The next CASE guiding principle, accuracy, refers to teachers having the knowledge necessary to convey correct information about adoption in ways that are understandable to their students (Smith & Riley, 2006). Part of this involves having accurate information to convey, such as topics discussed earlier - understanding the types of adoption, how children understand adoption through the developmental stages, and what vulnerabilities children who were adopted might have. Other useful information about adoption includes its history and famous people who were adopted.

A Brief History of Adoption

Adoption has existed as far back as recorded history. When children were left without parents to care for them, friends or relatives stepped in. While adoption was informal in many cases, legal adoption has been described as early as in the Babylonian civilization. Many teachers and children, familiar with Judeo-

Christian teachings, know the story of Moses, who was adopted as an infant into a family of a different ethnicity than that of his birth.

In the US, legal adoption can be traced to the mid 1850's with the passage of a law in Massachusetts that was focused on the needs of orphaned children rather than adult interests. It was also in the 1850s when the famous "orphan trains" moved immigrant children from the northeast US to the Midwest where they were temporarily or permanently placed with families, often with the intention of exploiting the children as farm hands (Herman, n.d.).

In the first half of the 1900s, the idea of protecting and caring for children through adoption began to firmly take hold. Various child welfare organizations and laws came into play with the goal of protecting children, leading, for example, to procedures to investigate prospective adoptive parents for their suitability to parent. Other legislation has addressed protection of the rights of groups of children, such as Native Americans.

Adoption practices continue to evolve as societal views change, and as new information becomes available about best practices for adopted persons and their families. For example, it was considered best to keep adoption secret in the mid to late 1900s, so birth and adoption records were closed and made unavailable to all members of the adoption triad, even as the adopted persons moved into adulthood. Current practice encourages various levels of open adoption so that adopted persons, as well as birth and adoptive parents, have access to information about one another. Recently, adults who were adopted have led a movement toward legalizing their right to have access to original birth certificates, which in many states are permanently changed to exclude birth parent information when a child is adopted. Such changes in adoption practice can be expected to continue.

Famous People Who Were Adopted

There are famous people in all walks of life who were adopted into their families. This kind of information can be helpful toward normalizing adoption in the classroom. The following table includes just a few, but teachers can easily update their list using any internet search engine.

Table 2. Famous people who were adopted.

Name	Area of Fame
Dave Thomas	Wendy's restaurant founder
Steve Jobs	Apple computers co-founder
Nelson Mandela	Human rights activist and Nobel Peace Prize winner
Melissa Gilbert	Actress best known in *Little House on the Prairie*
Faith Hill	Country music super-star
"Snookie" Polizzi	Reality TV celebrity

Timing

Aside from knowledge, the accuracy principle involves timing. Teachers must find appropriate moments to incorporate adoption education. One of the most obvious places to include information about adoption is when teaching units on diversity and multicultural families. CASE recommends other areas in which adoption can be mentioned in matter-of-fact ways, such as in lessons about genetics or inherited characteristics, the history of immigration in the US, and when assigned literature includes characters, who were adopted (Smith & Riley, 2006). Special lessons can also be incorporated. For example, the first author was invited to her daughters' classrooms each year during elementary school to talk about the Lunar New Year celebration. Inevitably, questions about adoption were addressed during those lessons.

Assignments

The guiding principle of assignments requires sensitivity to practical or emotional difficulties for adopted children inherent to some commonly used school assignments (Smith & Riley, 2006; Henry & Pollack 2009). In many cases, it is not possible for the child to complete the assignments due to lack of information; and they underscore difference. In most cases, the assignments can be broadened in ways that will include all of the children in the class. The following table lists a few of the more problematical assignments, an explanation of the dilemma, and suggestions for alternatives. Resources for finding more assignment ideas will be presented below.

Table 3. Assignments, dilemmas, and alternatives.

Assignment	Dilemma	Alternatives
Autobiographies	Some adopted children lack information, or the information is personal and sensitive.	Rather than write about their entire lives, ask children to write about themselves at a younger age; a special event; the previous year; or a 2-year period of their own choosing.
Baby Pictures	Children adopted at older ages may not have any baby pictures.	Ask for pictures of child at any earlier age; observe change in baby to adult animals; ask for drawings of children as a baby. Remember the guessing game may not be fun for a child who is racially different from classmates as theirs will be obvious.
Family Trees	Confusion about incorporating birth and adoptive family members; underscores difference from classmates.	Family "circles" – birth and adoptive families on either side of child in the middle. Genogram – family diagramming tool that allows for complex information to be depicted using various symbols. Whatever the format, children should be given a choice about how much to share with peers.
Inherited Traits	Some adopted children do not have any information about their birth families.	Study inherited traits/genetics using Mendel's work with pea plants; have adolescents predict traits of a pretend baby with one or two different classmates; avoid tracing traits into previous generations.

Assistance

The guiding principle of assistance refers to teachers helping children learn about appropriate boundaries and adoption-sensitive language (Smith & Riley, 2006). Assistance can be provided when children are asked personal questions about their own adoption stories that might be intrusive or hurtful. Adopted children are sometimes confused by questions about their "real" parents and siblings. For some children, such questions are abrupt reminders of painful or unresolved questions of their own.

Teachers can intervene by providing general information about adoption that takes the focus off an individual child. For example, when a child is asked why her real mother didn't keep her, a teacher might intervene and explain that children who were adopted do indeed live with their real parents. Depending on the age of the children, further explanation about birthparents' decisions to place children for adoption might be included. By providing general information about adoption at such a time, teachers not only take the focus away from personal or sensitive information, they normalize adoption and model responses for the child who may need help knowing how to respond to intrusive, personal questions.

Advocacy

The last CASE principle, advocacy, refers to the need for educators to see that the needs of adopted children are addressed adequately in schools (Smith & Riley, 2006). Educators do this for all children, and in the case of those who were adopted, it is a matter of being sensitive to what those needs are. First, schools need to add adoption, foster-care, and other types of non-traditional family formations into anti-harassment and bullying policies.

As with gender and race, bullying focused on family formation should never be tolerated and should have the same disciplinary consequences (Smith & Riley, 2006). Next, educational plans, when needed, should be informed by knowledge of the particular vulnerabilities of adopted children. It should not be assumed, for example, that a child adopted from a non-English speaking country at age six would naturally and independently recover from language deficits. Similarly, cognitive delays observed in a child adopted from foster-care need early rather than later attention. Teachers are in a position to observe educational problems first-hand, and can be advocates for children to encourage both parents and other school professionals to respond assertively and appropriately.

More Resources

We hope the information in this chapter has provided you with a good sense of the issues and vulnerabilities that adopted children bring to school, as well as some ways to start to build a classroom or school community that is inclusive and responsive to those needs. For those who are interested in learning more, there is a wealth of material available. In addition to the references used to prepare this chapter, the following publications and internet sites are excellent sources to learn more about adoption and schools.

Publications

Mitchell, C. *Adoption Awareness in School Assignments: A Guide for Parents and Educators.* (Order online: http://www.tapestrybooks.com/product.asp?pID=716&cID=271)

Schoettle, M. (2005). *Safe at School: A Manual for Teachers, Educators, and School Counselors*. Silver Spring, MD: Center for Adoption Support and Education (CASE). (Order online: http://adoptionsupport.org/)

Wood, L. and Ng, N. (Ed.) (2001). *Adoption and the Schools: Resources for Parents and Teachers*. Families Adopting in Response (FAIR). (Order online: http://www.fairfamilies.org/

Internet – Specific to Schools

- "Adoption and Schools" provided by *Adoptive Families* magazine. http://www.adoptivefamilies.com/school/index.php
- "Adoption in Schools" provided by the Child Welfare Information Gateway https://www.childwelfare.gov/adoption/adopt_parenting/school/
- "Back To School: A Guide To Making Schools And School Assignments More Adoption-Friendly" in the *Adoption Advocate* provided by the National Council for Adoption. https://www.adoptioncouncil.org/images/stories/NCFA_ADOPTION_ADVOCATE_NO27.pdf

Internet – General Information about and Resources for Adoption

- Tapestry Book Store http://www.tapestrybooks.com/default.asp
- The Adoption History Project http://darkwing.uoregon.edu/~adoption/index.html
- The Evan B. Donaldson Adoption Institute www.adoptioninstitute.org/

CONFLICT OF INTEREST

The authors confirm that they have no conflict of interest to declare for this publication.

ACKNOWLEDGEMENTS

Declared none.

REFERENCES

Barratt, S. (2012). Adopted children and education: the experiences of a specialist CAMHS team. *Clin. Child Psychol. Psychiatry, 17*(1), 141-150.
[http://dx.doi.org/10.1177/1359104511403559] [PMID: 21852321]

Beverly, B.L., McGuinness, T.M., Blanton, D.J. (2008). Communication and academic challenges in early adolescence for children who have been adopted from the former Soviet Union. *Lang. Speech Hear. Serv. Sch., 39*(3), 303-313.
[http://dx.doi.org/10.1044/0161-1461(2008/029)] [PMID: 18596288]

Brodzinsky, D., Schechter, M., Henig, R. (1992). *Being adopted, the lifelong search for self.*. New York: Random House.

Harwood, R., Feng, X., Yu, S. (2013). Preadoption adversities and postadoption mediators of mental health and school outcomes among international, foster, and private adoptees in the United States. *J. Fam. Psychol., 27*(3), 409-420.
[http://dx.doi.org/10.1037/a0032908] [PMID: 23750523]

Henry, M.J., Pollack, D. (2009). *Adoption in the United States: A reference for families, professionals, and students.*. Chicago: Lyceum.

Herman, E. (n.d.). *Timeline of adoption history.* Retrieved 12/11/13 from: http://darkwing.uoregon.edu/~adoption/timeline.html

Howard, J.A., Smith, S.L., Ryan, S.D. (2004). A comparative study of child welfare adoptions with other types of adopted children and birth children. *Adoption Q., 7*(3), 1-30.
[http://dx.doi.org/10.1300/J145v07n03_01]

Meacham, A.N. (2006). Language learning and the internationally adopted child. *Early Child. Educ. J., 14*(1), 73-79.
[http://dx.doi.org/10.1007/s10643-006-0105-z]

Melina, L. (1989). *Making sense of adoption.*. New York: Harper & Row.

Raleigh, E., Kao, G. (2013). Is there a transracial adoption achievement gap? A national longitudinal analysis of adopted children's educational performance. *Child. Youth Serv. Rev., 35*(1), 142-150.
[http://dx.doi.org/10.1016/j.childyouth.2012.09.019]

Smith, S.L., Riley, D. (2006). *Adoption in the schools: A lot to learn. (2006).*. New York City: Evan B. Donaldson Adoption Institute.

Tan, T.X., Yang, Y. (2005). Language development of Chinese adoptees 18-35 months old. *Early Child. Res. Q., 20*(1), 57-68.
[http://dx.doi.org/10.1016/j.ecresq.2005.01.004]

Tan, T.X., Marfo, K. (2006). Parental ratings of behavioral adjustment in two samples of adopted Chinese girls: Age-related *versus* socio-emotional correlates and predictors. *J. Appl. Dev. Psychol., 27*(1), 14-30. [http://dx.doi.org/10.1016/j.appdev.2005.12.004]

Tan, T.X., Marn, T. (2013). Mental health service utilization in children adopted from US foster care, US private agencies, and foreign countries: Data from the 2007 National Survey of Adoption Parents (NSAP). *Child. Youth Serv. Rev., 35*(7), 1050-1054.
[http://dx.doi.org/10.1016/j.childyouth.2013.04.020]

Taymans, J., Marotta, S., Lynch, S., Riley, D., Oritz, D., Schutt, J., Mallery, C., Embich, J. (2008). Adoption as a diversity issue in professional preparation: Perceptions of pre-service education professionals. *Adoption Q., 11*(1), 24-44.
[http://dx.doi.org/10.1080/10926750802291377]

Vandivere, S., Malm, K., Radel, L. (2009). *Adoption USA: A chartbook based on the 2007 national survey of adoptive parents.*. Washington, D.C.: The U.S. Department of Health and Human Services, Office of the Assistant Secretary for Planning and Evaluation.

Vonk, M.E. (2006). Children's understanding of adoption. In: Stolley, K., (Ed.), *The praeger handbook of adoption.* Praeger Publishing.

van IJzendoorn, M.H., Juffer, F., Poelhuis, C.W.K. (2005). Adoption and cognitive development: A meta-analytic comparison of adopted and nonadopted children's IQ and school performance. *Psych. Bulletin., 131*(2), 301-316.
[http://dx.doi.org/10.1037/0033-2909.131.2.301]

CHAPTER 10

The Clinically Anxious Student: Evidence-based Approaches to Assessment and Treatment

Stephanie Grace Prost and **Bruce A. Thyer***

Florida State University, Tallahassee, FL 32306, United States

Abstract: Although the primary focus of this text is not to provide a reference on mental illness conditions (see preface), this chapter is included for several reasons. First, anxiety disorders are the most common psychosocial diagnoses worldwide, making it a virtual certainty that anyone in the education profession will work with affected students during their career. Second, this chapter provides a foundation that will facilitate appreciation of the content in the succeeding chapter. Third, much of this material links to other chapters herein, and hopefully enhances the understanding that the information throughout the text is intimately and irrevocably interrelated. The psychosocial conditions described can impact individuals along a continuum ranging from impairing to life threatening. Following this discussion is a chapter discussing the intricacies-and necessity-of intervening in the school setting with an anxiety disorder largely unknown, yet not rare.

Keywords: Agoraphobia, Anxiety, Anxiety disorder, Body dysmorphic disorder, Nightmare disorder, Obsessive compulsive disorder, Panic, Phobia, Selective mutism.

INTRODUCTION

Members of the school system face unique opportunities and challenges when working with students with anxiety disorders. This chapter outlines the primary characteristics associated with anxiety, and common clinical diagnoses as delineated by the *Diagnostic and Statistical Manual of Mental Disorders* (5th ed.;

* **Corresponding author Bruce A. Thyer:** Florida State University, Tallahassee, FL 32306, United States; Tel: (850) 645-4792; Fax: (850) 644-9750; Email: bthyer@fsu.edu.

Raymond J. Waller (Ed.)

DSM–5; APA (APA), 2013). Further discussion of appropriate assessment and treatment options are presented, as well as indications for referral.

What is Anxiety?

Defining characteristics of anxiety disorders include excessive fears or feelings of anxiety. Though anxiety can be developmentally and situation-appropriate, the National Institute of Mental Health (NIMH) indicates that anxiety disorders develop when symptoms become difficult to manage and subsequently affect daily functioning for at least 6 months (APA, 2013; NIMH, 2014). Differentiation between feelings of fear and anxiety is primarily proximity-related, meaning, fear characterizes a response to a real *or* perceived *imminent* threat. Fear responses are further described by autonomic arousal and escape behaviors. In contrast, anxiety is considered a reaction to a *future* threat likely to elicit muscle tension and associated preparation for possible dangers.

An estimated 40 million Americans over 18 are affected by anxiety each year, with women 60% more likely to experience anxiety than men (NIMH, 2014). Further, approximately 8% of teens responding to a national survey reported having an anxiety disorder, with only 18% indicating they have received mental health care for their anxiety (NIMH, 2014). Anxiety, like other mental health conditions, has a multi-systemic etiology. Interactions between environmental conditions, familial and genetic precursors, and individual characteristics shape the likelihood of an individual developing an anxiety disorder, with no specific antecedent considered the defining cause (NIMH, 2014). These states (*i.e.*, fear and anxiety) are likely to overlap, however, they remain distinct. Additionally, the use of avoidance and escape behaviors may help to reduce fear and anxiety in some individuals (APA, 2013).

Resource	http://www.nimh.nih.gov/health/publications/anxiety-disorders-in-children-and-adolescents/index.shtml

Anxiety Overview: Common Clinical Diagnoses

The *DSM-5* outlines 11 specific anxiety disorders, each with unique characteristics and many with other distinguishing elements subject to further description (*e.g.*, phobia specification, onset) by a qualified mental health clinician (APA, 2013). Several additional conditions (*e.g.*, body dysmorphic disorder, nightmare disorder) are also highlighted due to their increased prevalence in student populations.

Anxiety Disorders

The *DSM-5* indicates that distinguishing among the various anxiety disorders is linked to the object or situation that induces fear or anxiety. Further, though the 6 - month period is considered a guideline for anxiety disorder duration, reduced criterion for duration may be considered with adolescent and child populations. Careful consideration by a qualified mental health clinician, keeping cultural context in mind, can help to determine if the fear or anxiety is considered developmentally appropriate or warrants intervention. Diagnosis of anxiety disorders is only made after assuring substance or medication use is not the primary cause of the fear or anxiety *and* that an additional mental health condition cannot account for the excessive fear or anxiety reactions.

Separation Anxiety Disorder

The primary source of fear and anxiety in separation anxiety disorder (SAD) is removal from the person to whom the individual is attached that exceeds the individual's developmental stage. Symptoms of separation anxiety disorder often present in early childhood, but can persist throughout the life course. Criteria for diagnosis require at least three of several characterizing reactions including recurrent distress or persistent and excessive worry:

- **when separated from major attachment figures,**
- **of possible harms that may befall the attachment figure (*e.g.*, disasters, morbidity, mortality), or**
- **of experiencing a future event (*e.g.*, being involved in an accident, morbidity, mortality)**

that would result in separation from the attachment figure. Refusal to go out and away from the attachment figure, persistent and excessive fear of being alone, and repeated nightmares regarding separation from the primary attachment figure are also possible demonstrations of SAD. Additional somatic complaints such as vomiting, aches, and nausea may also result when separated from the attachment figure or separation is possible.

As previously noted, shorter periods for children should be considered when determining if the presence of fear and anxiety warrants a clinical diagnosis. For separation anxiety, at least 4 weeks of symptom occurrence that affects important areas of functioning such as social or academic progress is required. Estimated 12-month prevalence rates for separation anxiety disorder among adults over age 18 ranges from about 1.0-2.0%. In contrast, 6-12 month prevalence rates are closer to 4%. Adolescent 12-month prevalence rates are similar to that of adults over the age 18, estimated at 1.6%. Clinical samples of children demonstrate equal presentations of separation anxiety disorder in both genders whereas community dwelling samples indicate increased frequency occurring in females.

Selective Mutism

Individuals with selective mutism may speak in some situations (*e.g.*, with immediate family members) but fail to speak within situations when it is expected (*e.g.*, school). Individuals are unlikely to initiate communication nor to reciprocate when spoken to. The consistent absence of speaking affects performance and achievement negatively within educational, occupational, and/or social situations.

Further, the mutism lasts at least four weeks but is not restricted to the first few weeks of school or other new environment. Care must be taken to assure that the mutism is not a reflection of an underlying communication disorder or other mental health condition. Selective mutism is rare in community dwelling populations with no epidemiological studies having been completed regarding childhood prevalence. Some studies have indicated cross-sectional prevalence of 0.03-1.0% across various settings with little evidence pointing to gender or racial disparities.

Specific Phobias

Phobias present as persistent or excessive fears or anxieties about a specific situation or thing that are out of proportion to the assumed danger of the situation or object. Reactions to the fear or anxiety-provoking object or situation may present differently in children (*i.e.*, crying fits, clinging behaviors) than adults. Individuals experiencing phobic reactions will avoid the object or situation actively. These responses must persist for at least 6 months while simultaneously causing significant distress in day-to-day functioning such as in social, academic, or occupational settings. Similarly to other anxiety disorders, clinicians must assure that phobic responses are not better explained by other mental health conditions. Several specifiers for specific phobia exist including:

- **animal (*e.g.*, spiders, dogs),**
- **natural environment (*e.g.*, hurricanes, heights),**
- **blood/injection/injury (*e.g.*, needles, surgical procedures), and**
- **situational (*e.g.*, airplanes, bridges).**

Among anxiety disorders, specific phobias can be considered relatively common with 12-month prevalence rates ranging from 7-9%. Estimates for European countries illustrate similar prevalence with relatively lower rates seen in Asian, African, and Latin American countries. Rates among adolescents ages 13-17 are markedly higher with an estimated 16% of community dwelling youth experiencing a specific phobia. Further, females are twice as likely to have specific phobias when compared to males.

Social Anxiety Disorder

One specific phobia, social phobia, is also known as social anxiety disorder. This condition is highlighted by excessive or persistent fear or anxiety related to specific social situations where the individual perceives increased levels of public scrutiny. Similarly to other anxiety disorders, presentation of social anxiety disorder may appear differently in children when compared to adults. Children experiencing social phobia must demonstrate fear or anxiety in situations involving their peers; not just in the presence of adults. Further, children may be more likely to cry, throw tantrums, or cling to others in social situations. Primary cognitions said to be associated with social anxiety disorder include concerns regarding public embarrassment or fear of rejection.

Thoughts of possibly offending others may also occur. Situations that provoke anxiety are avoided by the individual or faced with great trepidation. In parallel to many of the other anxiety disorders, the *DSM-5* indicates symptoms must persist for at least 6 months, though shorter time frames are appropriate for adolescents and children. These reactions to social situations must be out of proportion with the actual threat and symptoms must cause significant distress so as to affect important areas of functioning across social, academic, or occupational systems. Again, careful assessment should be completed to assure the social phobia is not associated with another mental health condition or the effects of a substance or medication.

Resource	http://www.childmind.org/en/health/disorder-guide/social-anxiety-disorder

Prevalence rates for social phobia in the United States hover around 7% for children, adolescents, and adults, with lower estimates seen throughout the world. Despite similar prevalence rates across genders in clinical settings, females have higher rates of social anxiety disorder in community samples, with greater prevalence disparities being found in child and adolescent age groups. Normative shyness is a consideration when examining differential diagnoses; however, the distinguishing characteristic of persistent, excessive fear or anxiety of social situations that impairs day-to-day functioning should shed light on individuals who are struggling with standard social settings and those who may require additional supportive services.

Panic Disorder

The highlighting feature of panic disorder is the persistent experience of unexpected panic attacks. Panic attacks, common in many mental health conditions and anxiety disorders, are defined as "an abrupt surge of intense fear or intense discomfort that reaches a peak within minutes" (APA, 2013, p. 208) alongside at least four additional characteristics stemming from either a calm or anxious state. These include:

- **palpitations or accelerated heart rate,**
- **sweating,**
- **trembling,**
- **dyspnea,**
- **chest pain or discomfort,**
- **feelings of choking,**
- **nausea,**
- **dizziness,**
- **temperature flux,**
- **sensations of numbing or tingling,**
- **derealization (sensations removed from reality),**
- **depersonalization (sense of being detached),**
- **feelings of loss of control, or**
- **fear of dying.**

In addition to the presence of such attacks, the month following an attack must include both a persistent concern that an additional attack may occur and the development of behaviors thought to reduce the risk of having an additional attack (*e.g.*, avoidance). Panic attacks should not be a result of substance or medication use or other medical conditions. Further, panic attacks should not be better explained by other mental health conditions such as phobias or obsessions found in specific phobia or obsessive-compulsive disorder, respectively.

European nations and the United States share similar 12-month prevalence rates of around 2-3% in adults over the age of 18, as well as in adolescents.

Except for American Indians, racial and ethnic minorities are less likely to experience panic disorder when compared to their non-Hispanic white counterparts. Much lower 12-month prevalence rates are seen in Asian, African, and Latin-American countries, peaking at approximately 0.8%. Females are twice as likely to experience panic disorder as compared to males and can be seen in younger populations as early as 14 years old. Panic attacks are uncommon in children, however, and gradual increases in prevalence are seen as puberty emerges, specifically in females.

Agoraphobia

Individuals with agoraphobia nearly always experience fear or anxiety regarding at least two specific real or imagined situations including using public transportation, being in open or enclosed spaces, being in crowds, or being outside or home alone. The level of fear is variable dependent upon proximity and the likelihood of the situation occurring and may manifest as a limited-symptom or full panic attack. As a result of the fear provoking situations, the individual will avoid the situation (cognitively, behaviorally) and may end up homebound. If the situation is unavoidable, the person with agoraphobia will endure the experience with intense fear or anxious responses that are disproportionate to actual danger posed by the situation. Individuals may believe they would be unable to escape or that help would not be available if needed.

Hence, persons faced with agoraphobia often require companionship when engaging in activities that may involve the feared situation. The situational fear or anxiety must persist for at least 6 months, be associated with clinically significant distress that impinges upon the individual's functioning, and not be accounted for by another mental disorder. The duration criterion should be considered a framework that allows for flexibility, however. Further, if an additional medical or somatic complaint is present, the fear or anxiety must be considered excessive. Care must be taken to determine if the fear provoked is, in fact, disproportionate to the situation because of cultural relevance. Older adults may also justify the excessive fears or anxieties by citing age-related constraints.

Concerns with self-medication of anxieties should be noted. It is also possible that severe agoraphobia risks restricting individuals to their residence and also can foster dependence on others for basic needs. Approximately 1.7% of adolescents and adults contend with agoraphobia each year with females being twice as likely to experience symptoms as their male counterparts. Prevalence peaks in late adolescence and early adulthood, with initial onset most often before 35 years; of age. Clinical features of agoraphobia remain stable throughout the life course, though variability does exist regarding fear provoking situations and associated cognitions over time.

The course of agoraphobia is chronic and progressive and has been found to be stable across cultural groups. Other mental conditions have been known to complicate remission including depressive and personality disorders, as well as substance use and other anxiety disorders. Co-morbidity with other anxiety disorders is common and depressive and substance use disorders are often secondary to agoraphobia. Some concerns exist regarding symptom reporting in children. Assessments should include multiple sources (parents, teachers), as a result. Adolescent males may be particularly unwilling to divulge anxieties—a required consideration for members of the school community.

Generalized Anxiety Disorder

The primary characterizing feature of generalized anxiety disorder (GAD) is excessive worry or anxiety about any number of activities, events, or situations that occurs more often than not over a period of at least 6 months. Individuals with GAD have difficulty controlling the excessive apprehensive expectation or anxiety associated with at least three of the following symptoms: restlessness, fatigue, difficulty concentrating, irritability, muscle tension, or sleep disturbance. The experienced anxiety or worry must further be associated with clinically significant distress that affects an individual's ability to function in social or occupational capacity. Further, individual symptoms are not attributed to substance use, other medical conditions, or other mental health disorders.

Similarly to the previously mentioned anxiety disorders, GAD responses are considered excessive or disproportionate to the actual danger threatened by the provoking activity, event, or situation. Worries and anxieties related to these encounters impact individual daily functioning in social or occupational tasks and are most often age-appropriate and developmentally restricted. Adults may be more inclined to worry regarding tasks associated with job performance, finances, or the health and well-being of dependents. Children and adolescents, in contrast, may experience anxiety or worry regarding performance (academic, extracurricular) and competency. Differentiating GAD from normal worry or anxiety hinges upon the:

- **frequency,**
- **intensity, and**
- **duration of symptoms.**

Worries in persons with GAD are excessive and impact daily functioning. Further, GAD symptoms may not require a precipitating factor, and are pervasive and distressing.

Individuals with GAD may also experience somatic complaints related to muscle tension including:

- **trembling,**
- **shaking,**
- **twitching, or**
- **aches and soreness, as well as,**
- **sweating, and**
- **gastroenterological complaints.**

Prevalence rates for GAD are similar to many other anxiety disorders and hover at around 1% for adolescents and 3% for adults in the United States. In contrast, the 12-month prevalence for GAD in other countries typically ranges between 0.4% and 3.6%. Cultural variation should also be considered as GAD symptoms may present primarily as cognitions or behaviors for some groups or may not be understood as excessive. Age of onset for GAD is variable, though the median age of onset is 30 years, later than most anxiety disorders.

Symptoms of GAD fluctuate in frequency, intensity, and duration throughout the life course, though full remission is uncommon. Co-morbidity with other anxiety and depressive disorders is common whereas co-occurring substance use, conduct, neuro-developmental/cognitive, and psychotic disorders are less common. It is important to note that children with GAD need only have one of the aforementioned six symptoms associated with anxiety or worry. Further, early life manifestations may be reduced to an anxious temperament.

Children and adolescents experiencing GAD may be excessively preoccupied with other concerns such as punctuality or catastrophes in addition to school performance. These youth may appear overly perfectionistic, require excessive reassurance regarding performance, and consistently seek approval. Increased impairment and co-morbidities are associated with early life presentation of GAD symptoms. As with other anxiety disorders and mental health conditions, special care must be taken to properly assess GAD in children and adolescents so as to reduce over-diagnosis and unnecessary intervention.

Substance/Medication-induced Anxiety Disorder

The primary clinical feature of substance or medication-induced anxiety disorder is panic attacks. However, these experiences must have developed shortly after, during, or in response to withdrawal of substance or medication use. The substance used must be capable of producing such an effect. Further, the panic attack must not be better accounted for by another anxiety disorder. Exclusions should also be made if panic attacks occur solely during the course of delirium. The panic attacks or excessive anxiety must also cause significant distress in social or occupational function. The diagnosis of substance or medication-induced anxiety disorder should not be given if the signs and symptoms pre-date the use of substances or medications or if the symptoms persist over time (greater than one month).

Intoxication with several classes of substances is associated with panic attacks and excessive worry and anxiety. These include:

- **alcohol,**
- **marijuana,**
- **caffeine,**
- **hallucinogens,**
- **inhalants, and**
- **stimulants.**

Withdrawal from alcohol, opioids, sedatives, hypnotics, anxiolytics, and stimulants are also associated with panic and anxiety. A wide variety of other substances including many anesthetics, bronchodilators, heavy metals, and toxins (*e.g.*, carbon monoxide, gasoline, paint) are known to evoke panic and anxiety symptoms. Prevalence in the general population is very rare (.002%), though rates are higher in clinical populations. Assessment using toxicology screening, may be warranted in an effort to secure an accurate diagnosis.

Anxiety Disorder due to Medical Condition

Similarly to many of the other anxiety disorders, the primary presenting feature of anxiety disorder due to a medical condition is the presence of panic attacks or excessive anxiety. However, the panic attacks or anxiety are a direct result of another medical condition. The panic attack or anxiety must not be better explained by another anxiety disorder or mental health condition or occur within an episode of delirium. The resulting experience must further be associated with clinically significant distress across social or occupational functioning. History, physical examination, and laboratory findings are often necessary to establish the causal order of the medical condition and subsequent anxiety. Attention must be paid to whether the medical condition has been previously associated with anxiety prior to providing such a diagnosis.

Many medical conditions are associated with anxiety including disorders of the endocrine system, cardiovascular disorders, metabolic dysfunction, and respiratory illnesses. Prevalence rates are unknown but may cluster with specific conditions (*e.g.*, asthma, hypertension). Development of anxiety disorders due to a medical condition follow disease progression and often predicate the use of diagnostic markers to establish temporal precedence.

Obsessive-Compulsive Related Disorders

Obsessive-compulsive related disorders are often closely related to anxiety disorders and are characterized by the persistent presence of either obsessions or compulsions. Obsessions are recurrent unwanted or intrusive cognitions, urges, or images. Most individuals indicate obsessions cause anxiety or distress. Individuals often attempt to suppress the cognitions, urges, or images—neutralizing the impact with other thoughts or behaviors. Compulsions are those behaviors or mental acts an individual feels compelled to complete in response to an obsession. Many compulsions are further qualified by strict rules or protocols that must be adhered to. Compulsions are performed to reduce risk of further anxiety, but are unlikely to be realistically related to the feared event or situation.

Many of the obsessive-compulsive disorders are found to overlap in affected individuals and clinicians should screen accordingly. It is important to note that the cognitions and behaviors contained in obsessive-compulsive related disorders are different from developmentally appropriate preoccupations and rituals due to their excessiveness and impact on individual distress and daily social and occupational functioning. Obsessions and compulsions are often time consuming—requiring an hour or more of an individual's day.

Though variations exists, several common themes are found in obsessive-compulsive related disorders including recurrent cleaning, preoccupation with symmetry and organization, persistent taboo thoughts, and harm. Obsessive and compulsive disorders are not attributable to any physiological substance or medical conditions and should not be better explained by another mental health disorder. Clinicians should specify the level of insight (*i.e.*, good/fair, poor, absent/delusional) and the presence or previous experience of tic disorder. It is important to note that children are likely less able to articulate the aims of obsessions and compulsions, though compulsions are more easily observable than obsessions.

Obsessive Compulsive Disorder (OCD)

Individuals with OCD must experience either obsessions, compulsions, or both. Obsessions are those thoughts, urges, or images that individuals experience as anxiety provoking (*i.e.*, not pleasurable) and involuntary. Persons with OCD attempt to resolve obsessions by avoiding triggers, using suppressive thoughts, or performing compulsions. Compulsions may provide relief from distress but are not performed for pleasure. As previously noted, obsessions or compulsions must be time consuming and cause clinically significant distress or impairment in social or occupational functioning though some variability is common (*e.g.*, 1-4 hours per day).

Varying themes are common across cultures, though United States and international 12-month prevalence rates of OCD are similar (1.1-1.8%). Mean age of onset is 19.5 years, though approximately one quarter of cases start by age 14.

Males have an earlier age of onset than females (25% of males experience onset prior to 10 years of age), however females are more likely to have co-occurring tic disorders. Onset is most often gradual, though acute presentations have also been noted. Further, childhood and early adolescent onset cases are associated with lifetime OCD.

Several factors have been associated with OCD in children and adults including:

- **temperament (*e.g.* greater internalizing behaviors, increased negative emotionality),**
- **stressful/traumatic events (*e.g.*, physical/sexual abuse),**
- **infectious agents (toxins), and**
- **genetic or physiological precursors.**

The consequences of OCD are significant and typically include reduced quality of life and social or occupational impairment. For instance, early onset of OCD can increase risk of developmental difficulties as a result of the restrictions imposed by the obsessions or compulsions (*e.g.*, reclusiveness from social situations). Remission rates are low due to frequent co-occurrence with other mental health conditions. Appropriate assessment and treatment may be helpful in reducing the risk of chronicity, though most individuals experience waxing and waning of symptoms. Suicidal thoughts are common in approximately half of individuals with OCD; attempts are made in roughly 25% of those with OCD.

Body Dysmorphic Disorder

An additional disorder, body dysmorphic disorder, concerns preoccupation with perceived physical defects (real or imagined) that may or may not be visible to others. Individuals may feel ugly, asymmetrical, abnormal, or deformed in one or many areas. Repetitive behaviors (*e.g.*, mirror checks, excessive grooming, plucking, shaving) and cognitions (*e.g.*, social comparison) are required. Preoccupations must be time-consuming (often 3-8 hours) and considered intrusive or unwanted. Individuals with body dysmorphic disorder experience significant distress in social or occupational functioning. The preoccupation with appearance is not better explained by another mental health condition (*e.g.*, eating disorder).

Additional specifiers include muscle dysmorphia (preoccupation with muscular size or proportion) and degree of insight (good/fair, poor, absent/delusional). Muscle dysmorphia is most common in males and many will work out or diet in an attempt to rectify the perceived flaw. Insight, as previously noted, can range from good (*e.g.*, understanding the preoccupation is unfounded) to absent/delusional (*e.g.*, completely convinced flaws are accurate).

As a result of these preoccupations, individuals with body dysmorphic disorder are faced with:

- **excessive anxiety,**
- **social exclusion, and**
- **low self-esteem.**

Many may seek elective procedures to enhance appearance and may become violent or legally retaliate with clinicians when results are dissatisfying. Prevalence rates for adults in the United States are higher than many other OCD related conditions and range from 2.2%-2.5% in males and females, respectively. Males are often preoccupied with genitals and muscle formation, whereas females are more likely to experience co-morbid eating disorders. However, rates are higher in dermatology patients (9-15%), cosmetic surgery patients (7-8%), orthodontic patients (8%), and patients seeking oral or maxillofacial surgery (10%). Body dysmorphic disorder has been observed internationally and often reflects cultural and societal norms (prevalence rates range: 1.7%-1.8%).

Mean age of onset for body dysmorphic disorder is 16-17 years, with the most common age of onset between 12-13 years; an important consideration for members of school settings. Many consequences of body dysmorphic disorder exist and are closely associated with the impaired social and occupational functionality including missing school or work, dropping out of school, inabilities to foster and maintain social relationships, and reduced quality of life. Severe cases have been associated with psychiatric hospitalization, becoming homebound, and suicide attempts. Those individuals with age of onset prior to 18 years of age are more likely to commit suicide, experience co-morbid mental health conditions, and have gradual progression than those who develop body dysmorphic disorder after 18.

Major depressive disorder is the most common co-morbidity of body dysmorphic disorder, though social anxiety disorder and substance-related disorders are also observed. Childhood abuse and neglect and genetic factors have been associated with the development of body dysmorphic disorder. Progression of body dysmorphic disorder is often chronic though timely, appropriate use of research-supported treatments has been shown to foster improvement.

Sleep-wake Disorders

Individuals facing sleep-wake disorders experience disturbances regarding the timing, frequency, and quality of their sleep. Sleep-wake disorders are often co-morbid with other mental health conditions such as anxiety, depression, and cognitive changes. Recurrent complaints regarding sleep have also been associated with subsequent mental health conditions and substance use. Multi-systemic or multidimensional assessments are central to identifying co-occurring physical or mental health concerns in individuals with sleep-wake disturbances.

Though the *DSM-5* classification of sleep-wake disorders includes a wide variety of conditions, this chapter will focus on a parasomnia: nightmare disorder. Parasomnias are characterized by experiences of abnormal physical or physiological reactions associated with sleep, sleep stages, or transitions. Prevalence rates of nightmare disorder are highest in school-aged children and adolescent populations; an important consideration for members of school communities.

Nightmare Disorder

Also known as sleep terror disorder, nightmare disorder is a parasomnia condition characterized by several diagnostic criteria. Most importantly, nightmare disorder requires the recurrent experience of well-remembered, dysphoric dreams. Dysphoria includes any number of negative emotive responses including anxiety or fear. Dreams most often revolve around the threat of survival and security.

The extended dreams most often occur within the second half of a sleeping episode (*i.e.*, REM sleep) wherein the dreamer will awaken and quickly become alert and oriented. These sleep disturbances cause clinically significant stress for an individual's social or occupational functioning and are not attributed to another mental health or substance/medication use. Further, other conditions (if present) cannot fully account for the extended, recurrent dysphoric dreams. Nightmare disorder is further specified regarding diagnostic association (*i.e.*, with associated non-sleep disorder, with other medical condition, with other sleep disorder), duration (*i.e.*, acute, sub-acute, persistent), and severity (*i.e.*, mild, moderate, severe).

The *DSM-5* describes nightmares as extended, elaborate life-like dreams that cause dysphoria. Individuals experiencing nightmares often note they are forced to avoid or cope with disastrous situations or imminent danger in their dreams; some nightmares also revisit previous traumatic experiences ("replicative nightmares"). Factors associated with increased early sleep REM (*e.g.*, jet lag, sleep fragmentation) may preclude nightmares earlier in the sleep stages. Upon awakening, individuals experiencing nightmares may contend with continued dysphoria and have trouble returning to sleep. Difficulty returning to sleep may predicate sleepiness during waking hours. In addition, persons with nightmare disorder may experience sweating, tachycardia, and rapid breathing. It is important to note that individuals with nightmare disorder are at an increased risk of suicidal thoughts and behaviors even when gender and mental health variables remain constant.

Nightmares typically develop between ages 3 and 6 and reach peak prevalence sometime between late adolescence and early adulthood. Between 1.3% and 3.9% of responding parents with preschool children indicated their child nightmares "often" or "always." These rates increase between ages 10 and 13 for males and females. Female adolescents, however, are likely to experience nightmares throughout early adulthood (ages 20-29) whereas males are not. Adult prevalence of at least monthly nightmares is approximately 6%; in contrast, frequent nightmares range from 1%-2%. Few individuals experience life-long nightmares, though some may persist beyond peak prevalence.

Several factors are associated with increased risk of nightmare disorder including childhood trauma. Further, children exposed to acute or chronic stressors are unlikely to spontaneously remit from nightmare disorder. Temperamental characteristics such as personality disturbances or frequent experiences of adverse events may also be problematic in the development of nightmare disorder. As previously noted, some environmental characteristics have been found to be associated with frequent nightmares including fragmented sleep, jet lag, and irregular sleep-wake cycles. Genetic precursors have also been associated with nightmare disorder and other parasomnias.

Differential Diagnoses

As previously noted, many anxiety disorders and obsessive-compulsive related disorders must occur exclusive of other mental health conditions. Differentiating these disorders from other co-morbid conditions can be difficult. However, clinicians must strive to correctly identify diagnostic features to prevent under- and over-diagnosis and to assure appropriate treatment. For instance, resistance to change (including leaving familiar environments) is common in autism spectrum disorders.

As a result, care must be taken to assure that persistent or excessive worry is not attributed to another mental health condition. Communication diagnoses such as early onset fluency disorders may be exhibited by selective mutism and should not be considered an anxiety disorder. Phobic responses have also been associated with reminders of previous traumatic experiences (*i.e.*, post-traumatic stress disorder) and are not restricted to expressions of fear and anxiety. Primary differentiation for children and adolescents should account for developmental stage, cultural context, and previous experiences.

Appropriate Assessment and Treatment of Child and Adolescent Anxiety

Assessment of Anxiety in School-aged Children and Adolescents

A common theme in the assessment of anxiety disorders is assuring excessive fear and worries are not accounted for by other mental or physical health conditions or as a result of substance or medication use. Further, the anxieties must be associated with significant, clinical stressors on social or occupational functioning often for a period of at least 6 months. Additional considerations must be made when assessing anxiety in children and adolescents. To begin, many of the signs and symptoms of anxiety disorders manifest differently in younger populations. Nervous or worried behaviors may present as somatic complaints rather than experienced as cognitions. Children may be especially unable to describe their thoughts or feelings yet may present with persistent stomach or headaches or indicate their "heart beats fast" (Silverman & Ollendick, 2005).

Further, assessment must consider childhood and adolescent development stage. Worries about starting at a new school, fleeting fears of academic performance, and anxieties over personal and social relationships are ubiquitous in school-aged children and adolescents (Silverman & Ollendick, 2005). Clinicians, therefore, must determine whether fears and anxieties are developmentally appropriate or have become maladaptive (Cooley & Boyce, 2004). Assessment should also consider cultural values and norms. Assessments should be completed in a manner that is culturally context-specific so as to reduce risk of pathologizing normative thoughts or behaviors in children and adolescents. For instance, the common concept of "saving face" in many Asian cultural groups may be observed as excessive preoccupation with academic or social performance for school-aged children and adolescents who identify with an Asian heritage (Kim & Cain, 2008).

Modes of assessment in childhood and adolescent anxiety are varied. The most commonly used methods include:

- **standardized clinical measures or rating scales,**
- **structured and semi-structured interviews, and**
- **direct observation.**

Rating scales are known for better performance regarding internal consistency and test-retest reliability. These features allow for greater ease in establishing concurrent validity with other established measures. Many standardized scales have been tested with both community and clinical populations of childhood and adolescents with anxiety, which allows for the construction of normative data. These normative values prove helpful when attempting to delineate whether thoughts, feelings, and behaviors should be considered appropriate or perhaps, clinical in nature (Silverman & Ollendick, 2005).

Clinical structured and semi-structured interviews are the most common tool used in clinical child and adolescent anxiety assessment. Interviews allow clinicians the opportunity to identify and quantify signs and symptoms of fear and anxieties in children and adolescents. However, diagnostic interviews have been associated with increased risk of errors and variance regarding inter-rater reliability and diagnostic precision (Silverman & Ollendick, 2005).

Direct observations prove beneficial when assessing school-aged children and adolescents because of reducing errors associated with testing and response bias. Observations can be helpful for identifying and further quantifying specific anxiety or fear-related symptoms. However, some concerns exist regarding long-term stability or reliability of direct observations. Direct observations of childhood and adolescent anxiety, however, are most often used in experimental settings and little evidence has been established regarding their validity in real-world settings (Silverman & Ollendick, 2005).

Members of the school and family systems can use observational techniques alongside explicit instructions and established criterion to provide mental health professionals insight regarding a child or adolescent with possible anxiety. This important information helps mental health professionals to make appropriate, thoroughly informed decisions regarding assessment and treatment.

Resource	http://www.aboutourkids.org/articles/anxiety_checklist_parents

Treating Anxiety in School-aged Children and Adolescents

Many considerations must be made when determining the most effective means of treating anxiety in child and adolescent population. The consequences of untreated anxiety in child and adolescent populations are varied. When anxiety disorders in children and adolescents remain unchecked, risks of developing co-occurring mental health diagnoses increase (Cooley & Boyce, 2004). Social and occupational functioning may also be threatened if adequate assessment of childhood and adolescent anxiety are not completed in a timely manner. Long-term consequences of untreated clinical anxiety include social restriction, suicidal thoughts, and self-injurious behaviors (APA, 2013; Barrett, Dadds, & Rapee, 1996).

Pharmacological

A recent meta-analysis provides initial findings related to the use of pharmacological interventions for pediatric populations (<18 years). The synthesis of over 20 studies including approximately 2,500 childhood and adolescent participants indicated that treatment responses were significantly greater for those participants randomized to medication groups than those within placebo groups in 14 studies. Most of these studies utilized selective serotonin reuptake inhibitors (SSRIs) and no evidence *via* controlled studies was demonstrated for the use of benzodiazepines. It is important to note, however, that medication was not tolerated as well as placebo prescriptions as indicated by high dropout rates due to adverse drug effects (Ipser, Stein, Hawkridge, & Hoppe, 2009).

Behavioral and Lifestyle

Additional treatment options for children and adolescents include behavioral or lifestyle interventions. Most behavioral interventions involve some use of cognitive behavioral therapy (CBT) aimed at increasing exposure to the feared or anxiety provoking object or situation (Silverman & Ollendick, 2005). These strategies may often involve family members of the child or adolescent, as well. For instance, results from a clinical trial using three groups (CBT, CBT + family based treatment, wait-list control) with children aged 7 to 14 ($n = 79$) with clinical anxiety demonstrated greater improvement with CBT conditions over the control group. Further, significant added benefits and therapeutic gains were noted in the groups using family treatment alongside standard CBT (*e.g.*, reduction in avoidant-type solutions, decreased self-reported fears).

It is important that children and youth who are referred for treatment of a presumptive anxiety disorder receive treatments that have been demonstrated to be effective for that specific disorder. The treatment for Social Anxiety Disorder is much different from that of OCD. It is incorrect to assume that generic or non-specific office-based psychotherapies will be of much benefit to youth with respect to their anxiousness.

Verbal psychotherapy may provide other benefits, such as providing emotional support, or lead to insightful awareness, but by themselves, these do not usually result in a reduction in fears or anxieties. School workers should also be aware of the existence of a large number of pseudo-scientific treatments that may be provided by licensed mental health care workers, and diligently enquire as to the research-based foundations of the assessment methods and treatments offered to referred youth (see Pignotti & Thyer, 2015; Thyer & Pignotti, 2015).

Any form of psychosocial therapy intended to help a child cope with or reduce their experiences with an anxiety disorder should be accompanied by systematic efforts to evaluate the possible effects of treatment with that particular individual. This is most commonly done through a research method known as single-subject research designs, widely taught within educational, psychological and social work degree programs (see Thyer, 2015).

When to Refer Students

Most of the conditions discussed in this chapter have included a diagnostic criteria related to distress in domains of social or occupational functioning. As a result, members of the school community (teachers, guidance counselors, administrators) are primary sources of information regarding possible impaired functioning.

Although in this chapter we have made reference to the use of the *DSM-5* as a scheme to diagnosis children and youth, we do so with an acute awareness of the limitations of this important document. Teachers and other school personnel need to be aware that the *DSM-5* is not a listing of medical diseases with demonstrable organic pathological origins. Although the *DSM-5* does contain some biologically based conditions, such as Down's syndrome, it is not justifiable to assert, as does the *DSM-5*, that biological conditions that affect psychological or psychosocial functioning result in mental disorders. Many of the *DSM-5*'s diagnoses have poor or unknown reliability and validity. It is a useful tool, but only to be employed with foreground knowledge of its limitations (Thyer, 2014).

CONFLICT OF INTEREST

The authors confirm that they have no conflict of interest to declare for this publication.

ACKNOWLEDGEMENTS

Declared none.

REFERENCES

APA. (2013). *Diagnostic and statistical manual of mental disorders.* (5th ed.). Arlington, VA: American Psychiatric Publishing.

Cooley, M.R., Boyce, C.A. (2004). An introduction to assessing anxiety in child and adolescent multiethnic populations: challenges and opportunities for enhancing knowledge and practice. *J. Clin. Child Adolesc. Psychol., 33*(2), 210-215.
[http://dx.doi.org/10.1207/s15374424jccp3302_1] [PMID: 15136184]

Ipser, J.C., Stein, D.J., Hawkridge, S., Hoppe, L. (2009). Pharmacotherapy for anxiety disorders in children and adolescents. *Cochrane Database Syst. Rev., 3*(3), CD005170.
[http://dx.doi.org/10.1002/14651858.CD005170.pub2] [PMID: 19588367]

Kim, E., Cain, K.C. (2008). Korean American adolescent depression and parenting. *J. Child Adolesc. Psychiatr. Nurs., 21*(2), 105-115.
[http://dx.doi.org/10.1111/j.1744-6171.2008.00137.x] [PMID: 18429840]

National Institute of Mental Health (NIMH). (2014). *Anxiety disorders.* Retrieved from: http://www.nimh.nih.gov/health/topics/anxiety-disorders/index.shtml

Pignotti, M., Thyer, B.A. (2015). New Age and related novel unsupported therapies in mental health practice. In: Lilienfeld, S.O., Lynn , S.J., Lohr, J.M., (Eds.), *Science and pseudoscience in clinical psychology* (2nd Ed.., pp. 191-209). New York: Guilford.

Silverman, W.K., Ollendick, T.H. (2005). Evidence-based assessment of anxiety and its disorders in children and adolescents. *J. Clin. Child Adolesc. Psychol., 34*(3), 380-411.
[http://dx.doi.org/10.1207/s15374424jccp3403_2] [PMID: 16026211]

Thyer, B.A. (2014). The definition of mental disorder found in the *DSM-5*: Too much and too little. *Mental Health and Social Work, 42*(4), 21-33.

Thyer, B.A. (2015). Evaluating school social work. In: Allen-Meares, P., (Ed.), *Social work services in schools.* (7th ed., pp. 297-326). New York: Pearson.

Thyer, B.A., Pignotti, M. (2015). *Science and pseudoscience in social work practice.*. New York: Springer Publishing Company.

CHAPTER 11

Social Anxiety Disorder in Schools: The Example of Paruresis

Steven Soifer* and **Wendi Albert**

University Of Memphis, Memphis, TN 38152, United States

Abstract: Anxiety disorders affect more members of the global community that any other psychosocial phenomena. Their voluminous impact is not limited to adults; anxiety disorders substantially influence the quality of life of many children and adolescents as well. This chapter diverges in format and intent from previous chapters in that the goal herein is to provide the reader with some of the applied difficulties that can emerge when attempting to intervene in the school setting. This chapter is not built upon the weight of empirical inquiry that defined previous chapters—indeed, that weight of evidence does not exist for the following topic. In order that the reader can appreciate the functional impairment that can be associated with anxiety disorders, a discussion of one type social anxiety disorder is reviewed. Then, in an attempt to illustrate the school effects related to what is perhaps the most common anxiety disorder most have never heard of paruresis and how it results in considerable distress as well as significant intervention challenges. The reader is strongly encouraged to exercise imaginative projection into the complications associated with this disorder in the school environment. Finally, a treatment protocol developed by the senior author is presented for the purpose of conveying the importance of school involvement.

Keywords: Anxiety, Cognitive behavior therapy, Parcopresis, Paruresis, Psychogenic urinary retention, Shy bladder syndrome, Social anxiety disorder, Social phobia.

INTRODUCTION

Social anxiety disorder is one of the most commonly occurring mental health

* **Corresponding author Steven Soifer:** University Of Memphis, Memphis, TN 38152, United States; Tel: 901-67--2615; Email: sdsoifer@memphis.edu

issues in youth (March & Albano, 1998), with prevalence rates of 8% (Miller, Gold, Laye-Gindhu, Martinez, Yu, & Waechtler, 2011; Neil & Christensen, 2008). However, epidemiological studies in the United States found that only 5.4% of those with social phobia sought treatment (Lipsitz & Schneier, 2000). This chapter includes a review of the literature on social anxiety disorder and social phobia disorder in children, including a discussion of implementation of evidence-based interventions to treat anxiety disorders in school settings. A detailed description of the diagnostic criteria for social anxiety disorder, barriers to treatment, and a rationale for increasing purposeful mental health programming in schools are also discussed.

The DSM-IV-TR and DSM-V use the terms "social phobia" and "social anxiety disorder" interchangeably to describe clinical impairments due to the overwhelming feeling of fear, and therefore, both terms were used in reviewing the literature. Following this literature review, we will examine a specific social phobia – paruresis or shy bladder syndrome – among children and adolescents, the environmental considerations and influences of the school for children with paruresis, encouraging the reader to reflect deeply on the functional impairment that paruresis - a condition defined by such situational specificity (attempting to urinate in the presence of other people), can have on quality of life.

Literature Search Strategy

This literature review consists of systematic reviews, meta-analyses, other evaluations of the literature, experimental and quasi-experimental designs, and case studies with children and adolescents as participants, reported in English language, published in peer-reviewed journals. Keyword terms included: social phobia, social anxiety, anxiety disorder, anxiety, anxious, intervention, treatment, assessment, school*, classroom, youth, children, adolescent, cognitive behavioral, and CBT. Searches were conducted from 1977-2014 on the following databases: ERIC, ScienceDirect, PsycInfo, Education Full Text, Social Work Abstracts, SAGE, Project Muse, JSTOR, Wiley, and Social Sciences Abstracts. Unpublished literature was not included in the review.

Social Anxiety Disorder/Social Phobia Disorder: Overview

According to the American Psychiatric Association (2000), as cited by Kearney (2005), social anxiety disorder is defined as a "severe, irrational fear and avoidance of social interactions and/or situations that involve performance before others, evaluation by others, and possible negative consequences such as embarrassment" (p. 2). The key factors in diagnosing social anxiety disorder as a clinical syndrome is *the degree* to which the fear inhibits everyday functioning *and the extent* to which the individual is distressed by having the fear (Lipsitz & Schneier, 2000).

The diagnostic criteria for social anxiety disorder is different in children than adults in that the anxiety must occur in peer settings and not just during interactions with adults (Spence, Donovan, & Brechman-Touissant, 2000). These authors described how the fear or anxiety may be expressed by children in crying, tantrums, freezing, clinging, shrinking, or failing to speak in social situations. According to Hudson and Rapee (2000), as cited by George (2008), social anxiety usually appears after 8 years of age, when individuals have developed the ability to anticipate negative evaluation from others and they begin to experience associated feelings of self-consciousness. This age of onset is not firm, however, and earlier onset can occur. Social anxiety disorder may manifest as school phobia, which is a common, and conspicuous display of anxiety in schools in which children experience severe anxiety regarding the idea of attending school and therefore may leave early or refuse to attend completely (Hudson, & Rapee, 2006).

Symptoms and Risk Factors

Socially anxious children and adolescents exhibit various symptomology that involves fear of negative personal evaluation and avoidance of social situations. Symptoms inhibit, among other outcomes, academic success, and eventually can even result in increasing long-term health risks. The tasks of adjustment and school functioning are immeasurably more difficult for anxious youth and can be manifest or be exhibited through:

- **truancy,**
- **repeating grades, and**
- **decreased likelihood of graduating**

compared to students without an anxiety disorder (Mychailyszyn, Mendez, & Kendall, 2010; Lipsitz & Schneier, 2000).

Biedel, Turner, and Morris (2000) found that younger children with excessive social anxiety might exhibit oppositional and school refusal behaviors, while adolescents tend to report more alcohol and substance abuse. Children with excessive social anxiety have chronically elevated heart rate levels (Kramer, Seefeldt, Heinrichs, Tuschen-Caffier, Schmitz, Wolf, & Blechert, 2012) and are at a greater risk for suffering from higher levels of dysphoria, depression, and other mood disturbances (Biedel *et al.*, 2000). Biedel and colleagues (1999), as cited by Kearney (2005), reported that 60% of youth with social phobia had concurrent mental health diagnoses. Of the described population, 30% had a comorbid diagnosis of:

- **generalized anxiety disorder,**
- **ADHD, or**
- **a simple (specific) phobia (such as paruresis).**

Risks associated with anxiety in children often include:

- **emotional difficulties,**
- **parental anxiety,**
- **difficult family circumstances,**
- **interpersonal problems,**
- **traumatic and stressful life events, and**
- **school problems (Tomb & Hunter, 2004).**

Obstacles to Treatment

Although few children and adolescents seek treatment for anxiety disorders, evidence suggests that social anxiety disorder in children is not necessarily a transient problem from which young people will recover without some form of treatment (Spence *et al.*, 2000). Unfortunately, there are a significant number of potential barriers families may face in seeking treatment, examples of which may include:

- **cost,**
- **time constraints,**
- **availability of qualified therapists, commitment, and**
- **logistical challenges (Essau, Conradt, Sasagawa, & Ollendick, 2012).**

Further, adolescents may be hesitant to pursue mental health services due to concern of being labeled "abnormal" (Fisher, Masia-Warner, & Klein, 2004; Masia-Warner *et al.*, 2011). Some research suggests that income status may not determine whether or not a family seeks treatment for the youth. For example, a study of 36 students with social anxiety disorder conducted by Masia-Warner, Fisher, Shrout, Rathor, and Klein (2007), revealed that only 11.1% of adolescents had ever sought treatment, despite all study participants being from a middle-class background.

School-Based Services

In order to facilitate access for children needing services, school-based programs have been suggested by many and are, of course, a theme of this text. School-based programs, whether part of the formal, universal school curriculum or as after-school activities and services, may decrease many of the difficulties families face in seeking treatment in the community, including:

- **time,**
- **location, and**
- **transportation challenges (Neil & Christensen, 2009).**

A school-based intervention would be particularly apropos for effectively treating anxiety disorders because school, among the most prominent means of social engagement for most children, is often where social anxiety manifests (Mennuti, Freeman, & Christner, 2006; Fisher, Masia-Warner, & Klein, 2004). In addition, schools are uniquely situated to utilize a systems approach that involves:

- **peers,**
- **family members,**
- **school staff, and**
- **community members,**

which could positively influence treatment outcomes (Mennuti *et al.*, 2006). For example, natural peer interaction provides an opportunity for children with social phobias to practice social exposure and skills, as well as to benefit from peer modeling (King, Heyne, & Ollendick, 2005). On the other hand, there may be some pitfalls related to school-based treatment services such as, for example, stigma and labelling (Dadds & Spence 1997).

Assessment

Currently there are some assessment tools available possessing clinical utility which, utilized in conjunction with clinical interviews, are helpful in identifying youth with elevated anxiety symptoms. For social anxiety symptoms, Mennuti *et al.* (2006) noted that the Social Phobia and Anxiety Inventory for Children (SPAI-C) and the Spence Children's Anxiety Scale are useful as screening tools. Other assessment tools include the:

- **Behavior Assessment System for Children (BASC-2),**
- **Child Behavior Checklist (CBCL),**
- **Conner's Comprehensive Behavior Rating Scale (CCBRS), and**
- **Beck Anxiety Inventory for Youth (McLoone *et al.*, 2006).**

According to Deluty and DeVitis (1996), teachers can play an integral role in identifying social anxiety disorders amongst children by:

- **gathering data,**
- **providing feedback on student's reactions to stressors, and**
- **contributing behavioral observational information concerning student's current psychological status.**

Offering a dissenting caveat, McLoone *et al.* (2006) contended that behaviors associated with excessive anxiety might not be readily identified by teachers, whose attention may be more likely oriented to externalizing behaviors. Best practice involves, however, including teacher reports used in conjunction with other sources of data including assessment instruments such as those listed above.

Interventions

Even though most children and adolescents in schools do not suffer from anxiety disorders, all students may benefit from school-wide programs that reduce stress and anxiety and promote mental health. Such programs, when designed to be flexible for example, accommodating school calendars and working around student schedules produce the most benefit. An example of an intervention designed to be a universal program promoting mental health of students is the FRIENDS program.

The FRIENDS program, which has been endorsed by the World Health Organization, utilizes a cognitive-behavioral, school-based curriculum demonstrated to have numerous mental health benefits, in addition to preventing and treating anxiety disorders (Essau *et al.*, 2012). It was designed to be used with elementary, middle school, and early high school students. It incorporates peer support and modeling, and includes programming for circumventing negative stigmatization (McLoone *et al.*, 2006). The effectiveness of the FRIENDs approach is supported by several outcome studies. For example, in a study conducted by Lowry-Webster, Barrett, and Dadds (2001), 75% of the children who were classified as at-risk for developing an anxiety disorder in the intervention group were no longer considered at-risk at post-intervention.

Resource	http://www.who.int/mental_health/evidence/en/preventionof_mental_disorders_sr.pdf

Coping Cat has also been utilized to educate children and adolescents how to identify, regulate, and cope with anxiety symptoms. With this intervention, students develop their own plans for gradual exposure to people, places, and things they fear employing cognitive-behavioral techniques (Tomb & Hunter, 2004). Leaders use social reinforcement to encourage and reward the students, and the students, in turn, are encouraged to reinforce their own successful coping skills. A modified version of Coping Cat, the Coping Koala program, also has studies suggesting its efficacy in reducing anxiety symptoms in children.

Resource	http://www.preventionaction.org/what-works/coping-koalas-%E2%80%93-it%E2%80%99s-called-contingent-reinforcement

For some students, a more intensive, targeted intervention may be necessary to curb anxiety and improve student success. For example, Skills for Academic and Social Success (SASS) was developed as a cognitive-behavioral school-based intervention for adolescents in high school with a social anxiety disorder (Fisher *et al.*, 2004). Components of SASS include:

- **psychoeducation,**
- **realistic thinking strategies,**
- **social skills training,**
- **exposure exercises, and**
- **a focus on relapse prevention (Masia-Warner *et al.*, 2011).**

Miller *et al.* (2011) modified the (SASS) program, incorporating the flexibility discussed above to positive effect. In order to work within the school's schedule, sessions were reduced from 12 to 10, with session duration lasting one hour as opposed to forty-five minutes. Paired t-tests revealed significant differences from pre- and post-assessment on both self-report measures of symptoms of anxiety, $t\ (23) = 4.20$, $p<.001$, and anxious avoidance, $t\ (23) = 2.81$, $p=.01$. Masia-Warner *et al.* (2007) likewise reported improvement of participants after SASS implementation. Following a 12-week attention controlled trial, 59% of their study's intervention group no longer met criteria for social anxiety disorder. An advantage of the SASS program is that it coalesces the participation of teachers, parents, and peers of socially anxious youth, to provide psychoeducation on social anxiety, such that all those involved can derive benefits (Fisher *et al.*, 2004). A final example, the Cool Kids program, is an anxiety treatment program administered to small groups of children who are either at high-risk or are already manifesting symptoms of excessive anxiety using techniques including:

- **psychoeducation,**
- **cognitive restructuring,**
- **graduated exposure, and**
- **assertiveness skills training**

to reduce anxious symptoms (McLoone *et al.*, 2006).

Therapeutic Components of Intervention

In terms of effectively reducing the anxious thoughts and feelings children and adolescents may manifest, cognitive behavioral treatments have the most empirical support. For example, Neil and Christensen (2009) conducted a systematic review of 27 randomized controlled trials describing 20 individual programs, school-based prevention, and early intervention programs for anxiety. Cognitive-behavioral therapy (CBT) techniques were components of the majority (78%) of the programs reviewed with positive effects. CBT has substantiating evidence that it reduces anxiety *via* delivery modalities including:

- **group interventions,**
- **parental involvement, and**
- **early intervention for children with mild to moderate symptoms (Bernstein, Layne, Egan, & Tennison, 2005).**

Therapeutic elements fundamental to CBT programs used to treat anxiety disorders include cognitive restructuring and graduated exposure. McLoone *et al.* (2006) described cognitive restructuring as teaching children to identify their anxiety-producing thoughts, researching evidence of the accuracy of those thoughts, and using this evidence to challenge and replace maladaptive thoughts. This cognitive technique can be modified based upon age and cognitive abilities (Spence *et al.*, 2000). Graduated exposure involves breaking down an anxiety-provoking situation into less threatening steps that a child can master incrementally, conceptually like progressing up the steps of the ladder (McLoone *et al.*, 2006).

It is best to incorporate parental/caregiver involvement so that the treatment strategies can be practiced and reinforced at home. While intervention for mental health conditions is often thought of as an individual and therapist endeavor, social anxiety is a phenomenon that not only is amenable to group intervention-group intervention may be preferable. Biedel, Turner, and Morris (2000), for example, argued that a group format is more useful and effective for the treatment of anxiety disorders than individual therapy because the group setting creates more opportunities for social exposure tasks as well as providing a means of peer modeling and support (King *et al.*, 2005).

Summary

Although the majority of children with mental health challenges do not receive the services they need, among those who do, schools are well positioned to be the primary medium of service provision. School-based interventions are appropriate for effectively treating anxiety disorders in children and adolescents because:

- **often the anxiety is manifested in school settings and around school issues,**
- **school service provision reduces many barriers families face in seeking treatment, and**
- **school can provide an affordable, accessible, and manageable locus of intervention.**

Although few universal programs have been thoroughly investigated, intensive programs exist that reduce symptoms of students with functionally impairing social anxiety. CBT, like other best practice interventions, typically involves multiple components and is tailored to:

- **individual needs,**
- **preferences,**
- **treatment goals, and**
- **cognitive abilities.**

CBT interventions, emphasizing learning and skill acquisition, are a natural fit for a school environment and have the most empirical support. However, the problem of excessive, functionally impairing anxiety has yet to be resolved for all people or all conditions.

Paruresis: The "Secret" Social Phobia

Paruresis, or shy bladder syndrome, is one form of social anxiety disorder that children and adolescents can suffer from but which is rarely recognized and is, in fact, largely unknown. The best estimate available of the number of people in the US that suffer from this social phobia is 22 million, or about 7 percent of the population (Kessler, Stein, & Berglund, 1997). Based on US census data, this would mean of those between the ages of 5-21, there are about 5 million potential sufferers (http://quickfacts.census.gov/qfd/states/00000.html) in this largely school-aged group.

It is possible that the number could be higher. There is anecdotal information that one-half of public school children avoid using the school bathroom (http://projectclean.us/). The reasons, of course, are more complex than just undiagnosed paruresis, as other factors such as germ phobias and school bullying in the bathrooms no doubt account for some of this avoidance. Nevertheless, clearly a substantial percentage is explained by paruresis, and there is little awareness by teachers and school officials of the problem.

Before undertaking a discussion of treatment strategy, it is necessary to give the reader a clearer understanding of what paruresis is and the environmental context of the disorder (Soifer *et al.*, 2001). This is important since a significant number of cases of paruresis in younger sufferers appear to be caused by environmental variables related to school restrooms and restroom use procedures. While education practice has responded to much that has been learned about *teaching* children over decades of practice, inquiry, and investigation, at least one domain in the school environment bears striking similarity across decades--little has changed within the *school restroom* environment since one of the authors (Soifer) was a public school student in the 1960s.

What is Paruresis?

Paruresis, also referred to as shy bladder or shy bladder syndrome, is a DSM V social phobia under the category 300.23, and involves "fear [of] and avoid[ing] urinating in public restrooms when other individuals are present" (APA, 2013, p. 203). It affects men, women and children in equal numbers, based on the limited data available (Stein, Torgund, & Walker, 2000). Descriptively, for those with paruresis, being in a public restroom when others are present is an anxiety-inducing situation. All anxiety disorders involve physiological responses, and paruresis is no exception.

In persons with paruresis, part of the physiological response is that the bladder neck muscle "freezes up" or spasms. The person with paruresis, as a result, cannot urinate regardless of the desire or attempt to do so. This inhibitory response is not volitional (which is a common myth), and the person *cannot* urinate, regardless of urgency of the need, for a period of minutes to hours to even days, depending on the person and the situation. In rare cases, psychogenic urinary retention is the result. The inability to urinate may result in the need to be catheterized, as would be the case if the sufferer had a physical blockage present in the urinary tract. In addition to learning history and environmental influences, there is most likely a genetic component associated with this disorder, as is the case in many mental health issues (Soifer *et al.*, 2001).

Resource	International Paruresis Association http://paruresis.org/

While the typical age of onset for social phobia is around puberty and many cases of paruresis fit this pattern the onset can be significantly earlier. The youngest age of onset, based on personal clinical practice experience (Soifer) is three, and the latest incidence of initial symptomology involves individuals of over seventy. Some people with paruresis have a co-morbid anxiety disorder, but at least 75% of one online sample did not (Hammelstein & Soifer, 2005). There is a dearth of data on incidence for children, except for a survey done online of children with selective mutism. In this sample, one-half of responding parents said their child also suffered from shy bladder syndrome (http://www.selectivemutismcenter.org/aboutus/whatisselectivemutism).

Finally, it should be noted that there is a bowel equivalent to paruresis, which is called shy bowel syndrome or parcopresis. This condition usually does not tend to present a problem of the same significance in the school setting, since children could have a bowel movement before school and/or when they got home after school (Chalabi, 2008).

Literature on Paruresis and Children

There is little written on the topic of paruresis, and virtually none of the existing data has focused on the school setting, especially from a treatment point of view. This lack of research tests the bounds of imagination since school is the setting most likely associated with negative effects for children and adolescents for social phobias. Prevalence rates for college students have been studied, though findings range widely. Malouff and Lanyon (1985) concluded from a college questionnaire that 7% of the responding population suffered from paruresis. Williams and Degenhardt (1954), who coined the term paruresis, surveyed college students and found that 14% suffered from the disorder. Rees and Leach (1975) reported prevalence rates for paruresis of 25-50% among male college students (n=190) and 20-25% among female college students (n= 113).

Finally, Gruper and Shupe (1982) reported a correlation between body shyness and paruresis, and reported that almost one-third of their sample of 90 male college students had a significant degree of urinary hesitancy around others.

Some case study results are available. Khan (1971) treated a 9 year old boy with severe urinary retention, reporting positive short-term effects. Glascow (1975) treated a 21 year old male college student, and after some trial and error, helped him with the problem using fluid loading and prolonged exposure. Stams, Martin and Tan (1982) treated an 8 year old boy with paruresis successfully using drug therapy and positive reinforcement in the form of money. Nicolau, Toro, and Prado (1991) treated a 13 year old girl using CBT combined with family therapy.

Caffaratti *et al.* (1993) discussed the treatment of a young girl, and erroneously noted that the disorder is uncommon in adults and even less common among children. Bosio, Mazzuchelli, and Sandri (1996) discussed how a 3 year old boy with urinary retention was treated by a team of professionals, though treatment of 5 years' duration, an excessive amount of time was reported. Jaspers (1998) successfully treated a 16 year old male using CBT, reporting that medications held little hope for people with this problem. Finally, Kroll, Martynski, and Jankowsi (1998) treated a 14 year old girl with psychogenic urinary retention using a combination of pharmacological and medical techniques. While these chronicles offer preliminary conceptual assistance for clinicians, their value is tempered by the inherent methodological weaknesses of case study reports.

Assessment and Diagnosis

Although there are now assessment tools for assistance with diagnosing paruresis, these tools, with few exceptions, are developed for use with adults (Deacon *et al.*, 2012; Gibbs, 2004; Hammelstein & Pietrowsky, 2005; Soifer, 2010; Soifer *et al.*, 2001). For example, the Liebowitz Social Anxiety Scale (Heimberg *et al.*, 1999) includes the item "urinating in a public bathroom," rated on a 4 point Likert scale for both fear and avoidance (low to high).

One scale mentioned in the literature - Spence Children's Anxiety Scale (SCAS) - contains an indicator about shy bladder: "I feel afraid if I have to use public toilets or bathrooms" (Essau, Muris, & Ederer, 2002).

In addition, an assessment tool for adolescents, the Kutcher Generalized Social Anxiety Disorder Scale for Adolescents (K-GSADS-A), uses a 4 point Likert scale with response options ranging from never to severe: "Using a public toilet facility or urinating (sic) in public" (Brooks & Kutcher, 2004). These are among the few options available for assessment of children with paruresis at the time of writing.

Treatment Protocol

The following described treatment protocol was formulated by one of the authors (Soifer) and has been adopted by a small number of other therapists. For adults, treatment for paruresis is relatively straightforward, defined, and substantiated by a small body of supporting evidence. The treatment protocol for children was developed from clinical practice beginning with a 9 year old boy with autism and a 13 year old girl, and was adapted from work with numerous adults.

The basic treatment protocol involves between 8-12 individual sessions using CBT techniques. This includes *in vivo* gradual desensitization or exposure, cognitive techniques such as decatastrophizing, and some elements now associated with Acceptance and Commitment Therapy (ACT). Not uncommonly, some form of adjunct drug therapy is used, either with the Selective Serotonin Reuptake Inhibitors (SSRIs), benzodiazepines, or both (Soifer, Himle, & Walsh, 2010). Service delivery occurs in weekend workshops involving a group of people suffering from paruresis (usually 5-20, mostly adult men). The time devoted to talk therapy in the group setting is roughly equivalent to an average of 10 typical therapy sessions for those who seek individual treatment. Applied practice is done throughout the duration of the weekend (Soifer, 2013).

Overall results for both the individual and group treatment have been excellent, though these results were collected in the absence of experimental controls. In one descriptive study (Soifer, Himle, & Walsh, 2010), data from 101 participants in shy bladder weekend workshops collected between 1997-2003 showed significant improvement for many of the participants following the workshop. Benefits were maintained at a one-year follow-up.

Working with children, in particular those in elementary and middle schools, presents some singular challenges. The first problem is how to know whether a child has paruresis. There is a pervasive lack of awareness concerning this issue among the lay public that likewise affects many professionals. In fact, it may be the least recognized social phobia in childhood. Moreover, many people are hesitant to discuss psychosocial concerns, and clinical experience suggests that people are often especially reluctant to discuss paruresis.

Once a child has been diagnosed with paruresis, several things must happen. Among the top priorities is that school officials need to be notified, and some accommodations for the child must be provided. In fact, failure to provide a student with accommodations may place the school at risk of a lawsuit under the new *Americans with Disabilities Act as Amended* (ADAAA), though to date, we are unaware of such a lawsuit having been brought under either the old ADA or the new ADAAA against a public (or private) school. Next, a treatment plan must be developed. Ideally, this plan will have at least two components. The first is treatment in the home environment, which should be relatively easy to implement (it is *not* recommended to do treatment in an office setting). The second component, when feasible, occurs in the school setting and is much more challenging to implement.

Great creativity and flexibility is needed in the treatment of children with paruresis. While it might seem intuitively uncomplicated to work on this issue, years of clinical experience suggests otherwise. Anecdotally, most clients have pursued multiple avenues of assistance and express exasperation with *every* single previous provider seen, either in the medical or mental health fields. As an example of poor advice clients have received, several have reported being told to "drink until you pee." Not only is it bad advice, but in the case of someone with severe paruresis, following this advice can actually make the problem worse. In such cases, this recommendation can place a sufferer at risk of hospitalization for medical intervention such as catheterization.

The in-home treatment protocol for children consists of first developing a behavioral hierarchy that catalogs the child's difficulty in using the bathroom at home. While it is possible that he or she has no difficulties at home, it is highly unlikely. The hierarchy should be developed to consider environmental factors such as:

- **ambient noise (bathroom fan on/off or TV on high or low in the background);**
- **whether the bathroom door is locked, just closed, or open; and**
- **whether the interventionist is paying attention to the client or something/someone else (listening to see if client is going or not, reading the paper, talking on a cellphone).**

Intervention begins at home and continues until the child is able to urinate with the therapist outside a potentially open bathroom door in the home. When this has been accomplished it is time to implement phase 2 of the treatment plan – in the school itself. The first phase of treatment in the home typically takes 4-8 sessions, depending on the severity of the paruresis.

The school treatment plan, as mentioned before, is often more challenging. First, the therapist is going to need to secure full cooperation and participation from school personnel, though such initiatives may be met with significant resistance. Second, even with cooperation, the school must demonstrate flexibility in allowing the therapist to work with the child, which may involve difficult logistical arrangements, such as:

- being in the school when it is empty (before or after school hours),
- absolute commitment to protecting the privacy of the child, and
- providing reasonable accommodations for the child during the day (for example, using the teachers' bathroom for privacy purposes and alerting teachers to this fact).

The child with paruresis is going to need virtually no one around (except the therapist, of course) to practice using the bathroom(s) in school. Otherwise, the school protocol is similar to the home protocol; that is, consideration of the key environmental factors causing the problem (proximity, visual and/or auditory cues, someone waiting) and working along the behavioral hierarchy through *in vivo* graduated exposure methods until anxiety reduction occurs. For example, the therapist might start down the hallway from the bathroom, placing him/herself there, and asking the client to go into the bathroom.

The first step in desensitization may be simply entering the bathroom itself. Then, after doing this, s/he might try urinating in the stall, then (if the client is male) at a urinal when the therapist is outside the restroom, and continued progression through the hierarchy. This all presupposes the client has done fluid-loading, that is, maintained hydration so that the physical need to urinate occurs. The ultimate goal may be somewhat variable, but a reasonable treatment goal to consider:

- **if the student is a girl, the therapist will want to get to the point where she is in the next stall, outside/or the occupied stall door, talking with the client (e. g. asking the client if she is done because the therapist needs to use the toilet);**
- **if the student is a boy, and there are urinals present in the bathroom, the goal might be for the therapist to be standing at a urinal adjacent to the client (also talking to the client as he relieves himself).**

It typically takes an additional 4-8 sessions to get to this point, depending, again on the severity of the paruresis. In addition, as this therapy is occurring, the student should be practicing during the week during school hours, beginning presumably in the teachers' bathroom and then proceeding to use the school public bathroom, following the behavioral hierarchy constructed for this purpose. School officials will need to make such accommodations as giving the student a hall pass to use the public bathroom whenever s/he needs to.

Environmental Considerations

Anecdotal reports from children and adolescents are suggestive that the origin of a significant number of cases of paruresis is in school, and a majority involve bullying in the school bathroom. Typically, such bullying manifests as verbal abuse from peers. Some, however, involved children exposed to physical abuse situations – such as an attempt by peers to open or even break down a stall door (if there were stall doors) to shoving or trying to shove a boy into a urinal while he is trying to urinate. Due to the current paucity of data, it is impossible to determine how many children begin school with paruresis and how many begin school and develop paruresis. Supervision of school restrooms could assist with problems such as bullying, but, ironically, could exacerbate the suffering of a student with paruresis from other causal mechanisms.

The reader may question what responsibility the school should have in the therapeutic needs of a student with paruresis. At least part of the answer to that question might begin with effects of paruresis on school behavior and engagement so common that they could be presumed, including:

- **in advanced paruresis, children aggressively avoid going to school (this can be misconstrued as school phobia, especially if the child has told no one about the problem),**
- **being late to classes (so s/he can use bathrooms when few, if any, are in them),**
- **behavior problems in the classroom (to be "expelled" from the class so s/he can actually use the bathroom under pretense), and retaining urine all day, which is detrimental to school performance can result in serious physical outcomes.**

Finally, it should be remembered that paruresis in many children appears to ensure as a consequence of adverse events that occurred in school restrooms.

CONCLUSION

Inclusion of a discussion of paruresis may seem somewhat esoteric. It certainly involves a clinical phenomenon about which little empirical information was conveyed to the reader, when there are innumerable mental health conditions about which much information could be disseminated. However, this example was included with intent, because it may serve as the best example of how a situationally specific mental health condition can have global effects on functioning and quality of life.

Paruresis, a term with which few people are likely familiar, involves an anxiety disorder occurring from the attempt to urinate when others are present, resulting in the inability to urinate, even if the need and desire are present. It is very common for school programming to regiment access to the restroom as a scheduled, group activity. Many schools likewise restrict access to restrooms at other times. The reader is encouraged to consider the effect that the inability to void urine for the entire day would have on a child in school, as well as the effect this inability would have on the student's capacity to concentrate, for example, on abstract mathematical concepts. Once evident, there is no reason to presume the problem will either mitigate or disappear over time unless effective intervention occurs.

Paruresis restricts what, for most people, takes but few minutes from and often carries little import for the typical day, thus making the restricted need to toilet the focus of the sufferers' day. A student with shy bladder experiences a significant amount of suffering, both physical and emotional, though the limited evidence available in addition to clinical experience suggests that this suffering is highly unlikely to be communicated to others for several reasons, not the least of which is embarrassment. The suffering that occurs is not due to the ill intent of school personnel. However, if you will pause to reflect for a moment, consider the divergent outcomes that could occur for a student suffering from paruresis in a school functioning under a regimentation to follow directives or else approach to human development, in contrast to a school committed to the promotion of health mental and physical of the people in that school community. The level of suffering experienced by our imagined student with paruresis is likely to be dramatically different.

CONFLICT OF INTEREST

The authors confirm that they have no conflict of interest to declare for this publication.

ACKNOWLEDGEMENTS

Declared none.

REFERENCES

American Psychiatric Association. (2013). *The Diagnostic and Statistical Manual of Mental Disorders* (5th ed.). Washington, D.C.: Author.

Bernstein, G.A., Layne, A.E., Egan, E.A., Tennison, D.M. (2005). School-based interventions for anxious children. *J. Am. Acad. Child Adolesc. Psychiatry, 44*(11), 1118-1127. [http://dx.doi.org/10.1097/01.chi.0000177323.40005.a1] [PMID: 16239860]

Bosio, M., Mazzucchelli, S., Sandri, S. (1996). Psychogenic urinary retention in childhood. A severe case treated by an integrated global approach. *Minerva Pediatr, 48*(3), 117-120. [PMID: 8766678]

Brooks, S.J., Kutcher, S. (2004). The Kutcher Generalized Social Anxiety Disorder Scale for Adolescents: assessment of its evaluative properties over the course of a 16-week pediatric psychopharmacotherapy trial. *J. Child Adolesc. Psychopharmacol, 14*(2), 273-286. [http://dx.doi.org/10.1089/1044546041649002] [PMID: 15319024]

Caffaratti, J., Pérez Rodríguez, S., Garat, J.M., Farré, L. (1993). Acute urinary retention of psychogenic cause in a girl. *Actas Urol. Esp, 17*(6), 367-370.
[PMID: 8368103]

Chalabi, B. (2008). *Shit doesn't happen: Lifting the lid on shy bowel.* Bristol: U.K. Kall Kwik Ltd..

Dadds, M.R., Spence, S.H., Holland, D.E., Barrett, P.M., Laurens, K.R. (1997). Prevention and early intervention for anxiety disorders: a controlled trial. *J. Consult. Clin. Psychol, 65*(4), 627-635.
[http://dx.doi.org/10.1037/0022-006X.65.4.627] [PMID: 9256564]

Deacon, B.J., Lickel, J.J., Abramowitz, J.S., McGrath, P.B. (2012). Development and validation of the shy bladder scale. *Cogn. Behav. Ther, 41*(3), 251-260.
[http://dx.doi.org/10.1080/16506073.2012.658852] [PMID: 22452544]

Deluty, R.H., DeVitis, J.L. (1996). Fears in the classroom: psychological issues and pedagogical implications. *Educ. Horiz, 74*, 108-113.

Essau, C.A., Conradt, J., Sasagawa, S., Ollendick, T.H. (2012). Prevention of anxiety symptoms in children: results from a universal school-based trial. *Behav. Ther, 43*(2), 450-464.
[http://dx.doi.org/10.1016/j.beth.2011.08.003] [PMID: 22440079]

Essau, C.A., Muris, P., Ederer, E.M. (2002). Reliability and validity of the Spence Children's Anxiety Scale and the screen for child anxiety related emotional disorders in German children. *J. Behav. Ther. Exp. Psychiatry, 33*(1), 1-18.
[http://dx.doi.org/10.1016/S0005-7916(02)00005-8] [PMID: 12389796]

Fisher, P.H., Masia-Warner, C., Klein, R.G. (2004). Skills for social and academic success: a school-based intervention for social anxiety disorder in adolescents. *Clin. Child Fam. Psychol. Rev, 7*(4), 241-249.
[http://dx.doi.org/10.1007/s10567-004-6088-7] [PMID: 15648278]

George, C. (2008). Solution-focused therapy: strength-based counseling for children with social phobia. *J. Humanist. Counsel. Educ. Dev, 47*(2), 144-156.
[http://dx.doi.org/10.1002/j.2161-1939.2008.tb00054.x]

Gibbs, R. (2004). *A summary of results from the Australian-based Global Internet Paruresis (Shy Bladder) survey conducted in 2004.* . Retrieved from: http://www.paruresis.org/research_results_RGibbs.htm

Glascow, R.E. (1975). *In vivo* exposure in the treatment of urinary retention. *Behav. Ther, 6*, 701-702.
[http://dx.doi.org/10.1016/S0005-7894(75)80198-5]

Gruber, D.L., Shupe, D.R. (1982). Personality correlates of urinary hesitancy (paruresis) and body shyness in male college students. *J. Coll. Student Person, 23*, 308-313.

Hammelstein, P., Pietrowsky, R., Merbach, M., Brähler, E. (2005). Psychogenic urinary retention ('paruresis'): diagnosis and epidemiology in a representative male sample. *Psychother. Psychosom, 74*(5), 308-314.

[http://dx.doi.org/10.1159/000086322] [PMID: 16088269]

Hammelstein, P., Soifer, S. (2006). Is "shy bladder syndrome" (paruresis) correctly classified as social phobia? *J. Anxiety Disord,* *20*(3), 296-311.
[http://dx.doi.org/10.1016/j.janxdis.2005.02.008] [PMID: 16564434]

Heimberg, R.G., Horner, K.J., Juster, H.R., Safren, S.A., Brown, E.J., Schneier, F.R., Liebowitz, M.R. (1999). Psychometric properties of the Liebowitz Social Anxiety Scale. *Psychol. Med,* *29*(1), 199-212.
[http://dx.doi.org/10.1017/S0033291798007879] [PMID: 10077308]

Jaspers, J.P. (1998). Cognitive-behavioral therapy for paruresis: a case report. *Psychol. Rep,* *83*(1), 187-196.
[http://dx.doi.org/10.2466/pr0.1998.83.1.187] [PMID: 9775678]

Kearney, C.A. (2005). *Social anxiety and social phobia in youth: Characteristics, assessment, and psychological treatment.* New York: Springer.

Kessler, R.C., Stein, M.B., Berglund, P. (1997). *Social phobia subtypes in the National Co-morbidity study.* Boston: Department of Health Care Policy, Harvard Medical School.

Khan, A.U. (1971). Psychogenic urinary retention in a boy. *J. Urol,* *106*(3), 432-434.
[PMID: 5097203]

King, N.J., Heyne, D., Ollendick, T.H. (2005). Cognitive-behavioral treatments for anxiety and phobic disorders in children and adolescents: a review. *Behav. Disord,* *30*(1), 241-257.

Krämer, M., Seefeldt, W.L., Heinrichs, N., Tuschen-Caffier, B., Schmitz, J., Wolf, O.T., Blechert, J. (2012). Subjective, autonomic, and endocrine reactivity during social stress in children with social phobia. *J. Abnorm. Child Psychol,* *40*(1), 95-104.
[http://dx.doi.org/10.1007/s10802-011-9548-9] [PMID: 21800016]

Kroll, P., Martyński, M., Jankowski, A. (1998). The role of psychogenic factors as a cause of urinary retention in a patient with lazy bladder syndrome. *Wiad. Lek,* *51* (Suppl. 3), 102-105.
[PMID: 9814116]

Lipsitz, J.D., Schneier, F.R. (2000). Social phobia. Epidemiology and cost of illness. *Pharmacoeconomics,* *18*(1), 23-32.
[http://dx.doi.org/10.2165/00019053-200018010-00003] [PMID: 11010601]

Masia-Warner, C., Fisher, P.H., Ludwig, K.A., Rialon, R., Ryan, J.L. (2011). Adapting treatment of social anxiety disorder for delivery in schools: A school-based intervention for adolescents. In: Alfano, C.A., Beidel, D.C., (Eds.), *Social anxiety in adolescents and young adults: Translating developmental science into practice* (pp. 281-296). Washington, DC: American Psychological Association.
[http://dx.doi.org/10.1037/12315-015]

Masia Warner, C., Fisher, P.H., Shrout, P.E., Rathor, S., Klein, R.G. (2007). Treating adolescents with social anxiety disorder in school: an attention control trial. *J. Child Psychol. Psychiatry,* *48*(7), 676-686.
[http://dx.doi.org/10.1111/j.1469-7610.2007.01737.x] [PMID: 17593148]

Masia Warner, C., Fox, J.K. (2012). Advances and challenges in school-based intervention for anxious and depressed youth: identifying and addressing issues of sustainability. *School Ment. Health, 4*(4), 193-196. [http://dx.doi.org/10.1007/s12310-012-9087-8] [PMID: 23227130]

Masia-Warner, C., Klein, R.G., Dent, H.C., Fisher, P.H., Alvir, J., Albano, A.M., Guardino, M. (2005). School-based intervention for adolescents with social anxiety disorder: results of a controlled study. *J. Abnorm. Child Psychol, 33*(6), 707-722. [http://dx.doi.org/10.1007/s10802-005-7649-z] [PMID: 16328746]

Malouff, J.M., Lanyon, R.I. (1985). Avoidant paruresis. An exploratory study. *Behav. Modif, 9*(2), 225-234. [http://dx.doi.org/10.1177/01454455850092006] [PMID: 4004731]

McLoone, J., Hudson, J.L., Rapee, R.M. (2006). Treating anxiety disorders in a school setting. *Educ. Treat. Child, 29*(2), 219-242.

Mennuti, R.B., Freeman, A., Christner, R.W. (2006). *Cognitive-behavioral interventions in educational settings: A handbook for practice.* New York: Routledge.

Miller, L.D., Gold, S., Laye-Gindhu, A., Martinez, Y.J., Yu, C.M., Waechtler, V. (2011). Transporting a school-based intervention for social anxiety in Canadian adolescents. *Can. J. Behav. Sci, 43*(4), 287-296. [http://dx.doi.org/10.1037/a0023174]

Mychailyszyn, M.P., Mendez, J.L., Kendall, P.C. (2010). School functioning in youth with and without anxiety disorders: Comparisons by diagnosis and comorbidity. *School Psych. Rev, 39*(1), 106-121.

Neil, A.L., Christensen, H. (2009). Efficacy and effectiveness of school-based prevention and early intervention programs for anxiety. *Clin. Psychol. Rev, 29*(3), 208-215. [http://dx.doi.org/10.1016/j.cpr.2009.01.002] [PMID: 19232805]

Nicolau, R., Toro, J., Perez Prado, C. (1991). Behavioral treatment of a case of psychogenic urinary retention. *J. Behav. Ther. Exp. Psychiatry, 22*(1), 63-68. [http://dx.doi.org/10.1016/0005-7916(91)90036-5] [PMID: 1918394]

Project CLEAN. (2015). Retrieved from: http://projectclean.us/

Rees, R., Leach, D. (1975). The social inhibition of micturition (paruresis): Sex similarities and differences. *J. Am. Coll. Health Assoc, 23*(3), 203-205. [PMID: 1127183]

Soifer, S.D. (2013). Overcoming the secret of shy bladder in a group weekend workshop. In: Grobman, L., Clements, J., (Eds.), *Riding the mutual aid bus and other adventures in group work* (pp. 113-116). Harrisburg, PA: White Hat Communications.

Soifer, S., Himle, J., Walsh, K. (2010). Paruresis (shy bladder syndrome): a cognitive-behavioral treatment approach. *Soc. Work Health Care, 49*(5), 494-507. [http://dx.doi.org/10.1080/00981381003684898] [PMID: 20521209]

Soifer, S., Zgourides, G.D., Himle, J., Pickering, N.L. (2001). *Shy bladder syndrome: Your step-by-step guide to overcoming paruresis.* Oakland: New Harbinger.

Spence, S.H., Donovan, C., Brechman-Toussaint, M. (2000). The treatment of childhood social phobia: the effectiveness of a social skills training-based, cognitive-behavioural intervention, with and without parental involvement. *J. Child Psychol. Psychiatry, 41*(6), 713-726.
[http://dx.doi.org/10.1111/1469-7610.00659] [PMID: 11039684]

Stams, U.K., Martin, C.H., Tan, T.G. (1982). Psychogenic urinary retention in eight-year-old boy. *Urology, 20*(1), 83-85.
[http://dx.doi.org/10.1016/0090-4295(82)90547-7] [PMID: 7112807]

Stein, M.B., Torgrud, L.J., Walker, J.R. (2000). Social phobia symptoms, subtypes, and severity: findings from a community survey. *Arch. Gen. Psychiatry, 57*(11), 1046-1052.
[http://dx.doi.org/10.1001/archpsyc.57.11.1046] [PMID: 11074870]

Tomb, M., Hunter, L. (2004). Prevention of anxiety in children and adolescents in a school setting: The role of school-based practitioners. *Child. Schools, 26*(2), 87-101.
[http://dx.doi.org/10.1093/cs/26.2.87]

Williams, G.W., Degenhardt, E.T. (1954). Paruresis: A survey of a disorder of micturition. *J. Gen. Psychol, 51*, 19-29.
[http://dx.doi.org/10.1080/00221309.1954.9920203]

U.S. Census Bureau. (2015). *State and County QuickFacts.* Retrieved from: http://quickfacts.census.gov/qfd/states/00000.html

CHAPTER 12

Reversing the Outcomes for US Military Families: From Resilience to Risk during a Protracted Armed Conflict

Amy E. Cox and **Raymond J. Waller***

Troy University, Troy, AL 36082, United States

Abstract: Historically, US military families have shown themselves resilient against numerous risk factors of potentially significant consequence. However, involvement in the longest armed conflict in US historyoften referred to as the war on terror-and concurrent policy changes for service members-has eroded the protection of resiliency for many military families. This chapter concludes the text by discussing these changes, the effects observed on contemporary military families, and confers important considerations for school mental health promotion for the huge student demographic from a military family. A brief summary of this volume is also provided.

Keywords: Combat, Deployment, Family supports, Military, Posttraumatic stress disorder (PTSD), Secondary trauma, War on terror.

INTRODUCTION

It may be tempting to assume that children in military families, due to the nature and potential familial consequences of a martial career, have borne a burden of stressors beyond the scope and imagination of most families, and that these stressors have been an underpinning of undesirable outcomes for children in military families. While military families may have endured an unfair burden for the current and perhaps previous US engagements, many people will be surprised

* **Corresponding author Raymond J. Waller:** Troy University, Troy, AL 36082, United States; Tel: (334) 983-6556 Ext. 1438; Email: rjwaller@troy.edu.

to know that, historically, being a member of a military family has not resulted in clear evidence of detriment to the functional capacity of these families. Indeed, though military life can impose compelling challenges, military families have proven highly resilient. For example, though military families relocate at a much higher rate than other families and though frequent moves can have an adverse effect, these moves have not only failed to impose harm, they may have served to *strengthen* children in military families (Kelley et. al, 2003). Succinctly, military families, despite the potential stressors of military life, do *at least* as well as other families on a wide range of investigated outcomes (*e.g.* Eastman, Archer, & Ball, 1990). Or they did.

The circumstances of the US involvement in the conflict often referred to as the war on terror- the longest military engagement undertaken by the US armed forces-has changed the risk burden for many military families. Where resilience historically occurred, hazard has overtaken many. This chapter elucidates some of the changes that have transpired which may be associated with decreasing resilience of military families, variables research suggest can help to buttress these families, and confers suggestions for schools in promoting mental health for their student members of military family units.

Current Status of US Military and their Families

The challenges placed on military families with the conflicts in Iraq and Afghanistan are numerous and complex and have changed the functional outlook for many military families. They have, in many cases, left the professional community with a dearth of empirical evidence to rely upon in guiding policy and practice. Part of the changing outlook for military families may have emerged because the concept of war is so different than it has been in the past, and scant data exists to address the change. The current conflict is of a type of conflict sometimes referred to as extra-systemic wars, which are defined as conflicts between at least one state (*e.g.* the US) and one nonstate (*e.g.* Al Qaeda) actor engaged in conflict transcending recognized borders (Simpson, 2006).

With the war on terror creating the "longest war in United States history" (Lester & Flake, 2013, p. 122), it is a given that our military members and their families will shoulder the brunt of this millstone as it relates to family functioning within the body politic. Although this is typically the case, the current conflict is unprecedented in placing the encumbrance directly and primarily on military families. While the general public is often encouraged to directly ignore the national status of conflict by political leaders, indirect encouragement for nonmilitary citizens to focus on matters other than armed conflict occurs in daily activities in the form of the absence of larger societal sacrifices observed during previous conflicts such as rationing of goods, growing victory gardens, or increases in domestic tax rates (*e.g.* Victory Gardens, n. d.; Rumbaugh, 2013).

An additional distinction of the current conflict is that it lacks a defined enemy and has no delineated end point, making it in some ways more comparable to 'the war on drugs' than a previous armed engagement (Raz, 2006).

Fig. (1). By Artist: Morley Size: 27"x 19" Publication: [Washington, D.C.] Agriculture Department. War Food Administration. Printer: U.S. Government Printing Office - http://www.art.unt.edu/ntieva/pages/about/newsletters/vol_15/no_1/WarPosterImages.htm, Public Domain, https://commons.wikimedia.org/w/index.php?curid=2030283

New Paradigm, New Scope

There are over two million children with a parent in the military on active duty or in the Guard/Reserves. An additional two million children have a parent that is a combat veteran. Learning how the current conflict affects individuals and families will help create programs and policies that can better meet service member's needs during this difficult time in our history, and resonates outward to the programming needs of every school.

Resource	http://www.militaryfamily.org/

DEPLOYMENTS

New Paradigm, New Stressors

Separation is not a new reality for military families. Military members are called to be estranged from their families due to deployment, being sent on unaccompanied tours or short or extended temporary duty assignments (TDY), or even enduring self-imposed disconnection so that children can finish out a school year before following the armed forces member to a change of duty station transfer (Lester & Flake, 2013). One of the historic strengths of military families has been their ability to adapt successfully and meet lifestyle changes unswervingly.

However, family separation begins to take on a new meaning during times of war. Combat stress adds psychosocial factors beyond separation during deployment, not the least of which are the supplementary stresses of ongoing threat of physical or mental harm to the service member(s) as well as the possibility of their death (Cozza, Chun, & Polo, 2005). Changes in military protocol imposed during the war on terror augment the risk burden further. For example, Lester and Flake (2013) stated that the length and frequency of deployments in the past decade have increased, while the time allowed between deployments has decreased. They found that rotation cycles observed historically allowed 18 to 24 months between deployments during peacetime; current practice may only allow the service member six months between wartime deployments. These frequent deployment cycles have been linked to numerous negative outcomes such as increased rates of divorce among sailors and marines (Link and Palinkas, 2013), which is not surprising since this frequency of cycling essentially has a service member in a perpetual cycle of deployment.

Resource	http://www.militaryonesource.mil/

Stages of Deployment

While it may be popularly presumed that deployment is a defined event beginning at a date of separation and ending with a date of reunion, this view fails to appreciate the emotional and logistical upheaval the process entails. A more comprehensive conceptualization is offered by Sheppard, Malatras, and Israel (2010), who described a five phase deployment model (as cited by Pincus, House, Christenson, & Adler, 2001) which includes:

- **predeployment,**
- **deployment,**
- **sustainment,**
- **redeployment, and**
- **postdeployment.**

The predeployment stage references the timeframe from the notification of deployment orders to the date of the service member's physical departure. This period is a flurry of activity where the military member balances family, departure arrangements, and work preparations. The deployment stage begins at the date of departure and includes roughly the first month of deployment. New routines, responsibilities and communication patterns are established during this time. The sustainment phase includes the time in between the first and last month of deployment. This period of time is about maintaining the new roles and life schedules implemented in the deployment stage.

The redeployment stage is the last month of deployment and is marked by homecoming preparations. The final stage is postdeployment , which begins the day a service member returns home and lasts for approximately three to six months. Lester and Flake (2013) described this as the *honeymoon* stage since it can be filled with feelings of joy and relief at the safe return of their family member. Unfortunately, the emotional elevation and expectations family members often feel are unrealistic and unsustainable, and the honeymoon can become a difficult readjustment or, in some cases, a nightmare, exacerbated by the experience of initial elation.

Systems of Support are Needed for all Family Members

Some support systems are potentially available to many service members and families during the deployment cycle including:

- **family,**
- **school,**
- **religious organizations, and**
- **local community programs.**

It is becoming ever more apparent how imperative it is that every member of the military family have ready means of information about and access to a good network of support. Without the positive impact of such a support system, military families can be severely affected by disenfranchisement and an additional burden of stress they need not-and should not-bear. Family members without adequate supports run increased risks of suffering from numerous psychosocial symptoms including:

- **depression,**
- **anxiety,**
- **loneliness,**
- **sleep disturbance, and more,**

all of which are be compounded during wartime deployments (Link & Palinkas, 2013).

Resource	http://www.defense.gov/home/features/2012/0212_familysupport/

Misinterpreting Needs of Military Families

Popular conjecture concerning stressors experienced by contemporary military families is likely to be myopic and to overlook many dynamics imposing risk discussed above, despite those risks being pervasive, largely inevitable, and potentially severe for families with deployed members. Thoughts and concerns of people lacking military experience may instead vault to assumptions relating to posttraumatic stress disorder (PTSD) being the primary concern related to a returning military service member. Though PTSD is indubitably a risk incurred by combat veterans, it is certainly not universal. However, the potential impairment associated with this response to trauma is so momentous, and the probability of secondary consequences to other family members of affected individuals so elevated, it would be negligent not to discuss the phenomenon and its' impact on family members.

Posttraumatic Stress Disorder

The *Diagnostic and Statistical Manual of Mental Disorders, Fifth Edition* (DSM V) states that PTSD involves four main symptom clusters after experiencing, witnessing, or learning of a traumatic event (American Psychiatric Association, 2013). These four symptom clusters are:

- **re-experiencing,**
- **avoidance,**
- **persistent negative alterations in cognitions/moods, and**
- **changes in autonomic arousal.**

There may be combinations of these symptoms. There are new additions to the diagnostic criteria included in the current DSM regarding recognizing PTSD in children ages six and younger. PTSD symptoms usually develop within three months of the trauma exposure.

Military members imperiled by combat are at risk of developing PTSD, and combat veterans have contributed to the development of the DSM concept and understanding of PTSD. The first edition of the DSM, available post-World War II, branded the results of combat exposure a "gross stress reaction" that was listed under the larger heading of "transient personality disorder" (APA, 1952, p. 40). Dohrenwend, Yager, Wall, and Adams (2013) stated that the diagnosis of PTSD was first introduced in the third edition of the DSM, following observations of the toll of the Vietnam War on veterans. They described how this disorder was "a novel syndrome of intrusive, avoidance/numbing, and arousal symptoms as the distinctive psychopathology following exposure to traumatic stressors" (p. 1).

Risk Factors for Developing PTSD

Out of the 50-60% of Americans subjected to a traumatic event during their lifetime, 8-20% of them will develop PTSD (Hoge, Austin, & Pollak, 2007). Hoge and others (2007) identified certain contributory rudiments that predicted these 8-20% and grouped them into three sections:

- **pretrauma,**
- **peritrauma, and**
- **posttrauma.**

Pretrauma includes risk factors that are present prior to trauma. Peritrauma involves the effects of experiences surrounding the trauma event. Posttrauma describes what is experienced after the traumatic event (see Table **1**).

The most potent risk factors by order of magnitude are:

- **lack of real perceived social support,**
- **subsequent life stress,**
- **trauma severity,**
- **adverse childhood, and**
- **low intelligence (Hoge *et al.*, 2007, p. 141).**

Table 1. PTSD Risk Factors.

Pretrauma	**Peritrauma**	**Posttrauma**
lower educational levels	magnitude of stressor	perceptions of social support
neurodevelopmental delays (speech, motor skills, *etc.*)	immediate reactions to stressors (safety fears)	life stressors
lower intelligence	dissociation	continued threat to safety
history of mental disorders		
female gender		

The DSM-5 (APA, 2013) identifies additional risk factors serving as pretraumatic diatheses, including:

- **temperamental (*e.g.*, anxiety, depression, obsessive-compulsive disorders),**
- **environmental (*e.g.*, socioeconomic status, ethnicity, family dysfunction), and**
- **genetic/physiological (*e.g.*, age, genotype).**

Examples of PTSD Risks Particularly Applicable to Deployment or Combat

Peritrauma risk factors may impact military personnel specifically when, for example, a service member is personally involved in harming a civilian or prisoner (Dohrenwend *et al.*, 2013). Losses associated with the trauma (*e.g.*, financial) and ongoing negative circumstances and occurrences after the trauma are examples of posttrauma risks (American Psychiatric Association, 2013). An idiosyncrasy of the war on terror is that one of the more effective weapons used against deployed service members is the IED (improvised explosive device). These contrivances can be associated with developing PTSD, but are also associated with causing traumatic brain injury (TBI). In fact, as many as half or more returning veterans with PTSD likewise have either comorbid TBI or TBI and chronic pain (Cifu *et al.*, 2013). IEDs themselves may prove to be among the tactical differences that could play a role in manifesting PTSD because these devices are operationally disguised to appear to be anything besides what they actually are, often typical roadside objects or refuse. This could mean that some returning veterans experience triggers of the combat experience any time they are in a moving vehicle, although a causal link has yet to be established (*e.g.Jones et al.*, 2014)

The consequences of PTSD are severe and have far reaching influence in a person's social life, family functioning, financial circumstances, and even recovery for wounds or adaptation to physical abilities. Therefore, identifying these risk factors early can be a significant step for mitigating and, hopefully at some future date, preventing PTSD.

Resiliency Factors

Hoge and colleagues (2007) simply described resiliency factors as characteristics useful for protecting oneself. They often seem to be diametrically oppositional variants of risk factors. Resilience is defined as being a positive response to stress and difficulties such as:

- **commitment,**
- **challenge, and**
- **sense of control, where**

commitment encompasses one's ability to frame life circumstances into an important and meaningful experience, challenge relates to one's ability to reframe difficult events as opportunities for growth, and control refers to one's ability to take control and be the driver of their own fate and future, regardless of obstacles.

Much research emphasizes the importance of *family supports* (Herzog *et al.*, 2011; Hoge *et al.*, 2007; Lester & Flake, 2013; Lester *et. al*, 2010; Link & Palinkas, 2013). Perhaps the strongest indicator for resiliency in children and adults is determined by how *social support is perceived* by the individual. Hoge *et al.* (2007) referenced the example of a fire fighter-also a potentially trauma-related vocation. If a fire fighter perceives herself as having active, positive support from her family, friends, employer, and union, then the risks of trauma related psychological duress are reduced. This can also be said of children. Children with warm, stable support systems have a greater prospect of being protected from experiences of misfortune (Lester & Flake, 2013).

Techniques of coping with adversity can be an indicator for whether or not an individual will be more resilient to experiencing PTSD. Good coping skills can obviate exposure to trauma. For example, coping styles that are proactive or optimistic rather that pessimistic tend to lower the risk for PTSD (Hoge *et al.*, 2007).

An initiative urged by many researchers and practitioners is identification of diatheses and risks associated with PTSD, such that *a priori* selection can divert those service members likely to manifest PTSD away from the most traumatic events. Dohrenwend and colleagues (2013) summarized this view thus:

> If the goal is to reduce rates of highly chronic war-related PTSD, as we believe it must be, then the positive interaction of severity of combat exposure and vulnerability... points to the need to keep the more vulnerable soldiers out of the severe combat situations (p. 14).

Assuming the sophistication to accurately make such determinations accurately is developed, it begs a critical subsequent question for military families: is it not correspondingly important to identify family members with similar risk profiles in order to protect the family unit as well? In other words, if diatheses are identified as predictive of more deleterious effects on family members of certain veterans, should that information be used to prioritize some service members to less dangerous assignments in order to protect the family? These questions are independent of the ethical debate that would ponder systematically and volitionally placing some people at greater risk of injury and death in order to prevent the psychosocial harm of another person.

Irrespective of the presence of protective factors, combat exposure is a potent risk factor associated with the development of PTSD, with approximately 30% of combat veterans manifesting symptoms (Noteworthy Briefs from the Field, 2008). A recurring finding in combat-related PTSD is a correlation between the *dose* (or amount of exposure) to combat and both the development and intensity of symptoms (Xue *et al.*, 2015), with higher doses a correlate of worse outcomes. The consistency of this finding calls into serious question the practice of multiple combat deployments. A related finding of note is that prognoses for PTSD treatment are better for civilian than for military personnel (*e.g.* Bradley, Greene, Russ, Dutra, & Westen, 2005). This finding could certainly suggest that combat is qualitatively more dangerous than other events associated with PTSD; if true, this could further insist upon an imperative policy initiative that does not require-or in fact forbidding-multiple deployments be allowed.

ADDITIONAL COMPLICATIONS FOR RETURNING SOLDIERS AND FAMILIES

Physical Injury

Another difference between previous US conflicts and the wars in Iraq and Afghanistan is the mortality rate post-injury (Link & Palinkas, 2013). Today, more service members survive serious injuries incurred in the arena of combat than has been the case historically. While saving lives and the return of an injured loved one is something to be celebrated, their return is often fraught with mixed and complicated emotions as well as functional life changes. The effects of injuries can reverberate throughout the family, though Link and Palinkas suggested "physical injuries are associated with family dysfunction only insofar as they are associated with psychological distress and family disruption" (p. 384).

Responding to an Injured Returning Family Member

After notification of the injury of a loved one, Cozza and others (2005) indicated it is essential for children to be prepared for what to expect. Information should be shared with children based on what is appropriate for their developmental and cognitive capacity. Parents regularly strive for balancing a marginal line between sharing too much and sharing too little information, with many parents likely deciding to share a limited amount of information so that the children are not overly apprehensive. As these researchers stated, though, "clinicians have challenged assumptions that such "secrets" could be adequately kept, emphasizing that older youngsters usually have some awareness that something significant has happened" (p. 375). Reasoned honesty may be the best policy. Conversely, in the event of an injury involving significant harm such as disfigurement or amputation, Cozza and colleagues advised that "graphic exposure can lead to pointless and problematic anxiety" (p. 375) in children.

Dekel and Goldblatt (2008) noted that children who have lived a good portion of their lives with a healthy, uninjured parent may have different responses to an injured parent than might other children who have lived with a parent who has had a disability their entire life. Many children, it should be noted, are resilient and handle difficult situations such as injury to a parent with unconditional love and support.

To minimize parental impact of injury or functional capacity on children, expectations should be addressed regarding imminent life changes. For example, children may be uprooted to either accompany the military spouse to the hospital treating the injured service member or sent to reside with extended family members or friends while care is received. Missing school and activities can be difficult for children, enhancing the importance of rapidly establishing a new supportive community if their primary social network is displaced. Therapist assistance can be helpful in supporting families facing these issues. Of particular importance is that parental response to life changes and stresses can be a robust mediating factor impacting children's responses (Gil-Rivas, Silver, Holman, McIntosh, & Poulin, 2007), meaning that the coping skills and responses of parents strongly influences coping ability in children.

Resource	http://www.health.mil/

Parental PTSD

Findings reported by Dekel and Goldblatt (2008) revealed the intuitive-that returned Vietnam veterans with PTSD were more likely to have a negative impact on their children than veterans without PTSD. They reported children with a parent returning from Vietnam who *did not have* PTSD had lower rates of:

- **behavior/emotional issues,**
- **depression, and**
- **anxiety**

than children of veterans with PTSD. Of the harmful symptoms most robust in conveying risk to children, numbing symptoms among returning parents with PTSD was deemed to have the largest deleterious effect on parent-child relationships.

Familial Transmission of Trauma

There are many detriments of wartime military service to family members that can affect their physical, emotional, and mental wellbeing, with PTSD representing a serious potential outcome. It should be noted that the effects of PTSD are not necessarily restricted to the returning service member. Herzog, Everson, and Whitworth (2011) noted that "immediate family members of combat-exposed soldiers with high levels of post-traumatic stress disorder (PTSD) are at risk for developing secondary traumatic stress" (p. 459). Link and Palinkas (2013) defined secondary traumatization as the transfer of PTSD symptoms to a veteran's partner (or other member of the family) *via* details of the veteran's wartime service experiences or distress.

Secondary traumatic symptoms are very similar to PTSD symptoms and include "avoidance of thoughts, behaviors, emotions and intrusion of unwanted cognitions and images that reminded the spouses of negative experiences of their Iraqi war deployed Soldier" (Herzog *et al.*, 2011, p. 468). However, depression and anxiety, not PTSD, are the most prevalent symptoms experienced by spouses.

Intergenerational Combat Exposure

Lester and Flake (2013) reported that some of the first studies investigating effects on children due to parental wartime deployments began with World War II. Those studies found that the process of reintegrating the service member into their family unit was distressing for all involved. Dekel and Goldblatt (2008) found similar difficulties with reintegrating World War II and Vietnam veterans, additionally finding "that Vietnam veterans whose fathers had participated in World War II developed higher emotional distress than Vietnam veterans whose fathers had not been exposed to combat" (Dekel & Goldblatt as cited by Rosenheck & Fontana, 1998a p. 284). This may be an additional circumstantial finding which demands reconsideration of allowing or requiring multiple combat rotations.

Having a Child with a Disability

Children with special needs may add stress to remaining caregiver(s) during the deployment of a different parent. Lester and Flake (2013) estimated that there are more than 100,000 children in military families that have special needs and concerns. A prior chapter (2) provided a thorough dialogue on disabilities, and there is no need to repeat that material. However, Waller (2014) discussed the basics of helping children with disabilities better cope with deployments. He offered a series of easy to implement strategies that could have significant effect cumulatively. His suggestions were to make sure to always consider the child's developmental needs and communicative capacity when conversing. Incorporate multiple means of communicating whenever possible.

Humans frequently limit themselves to oral communication. Visual prompts can be particularly useful in extending learning. For example, teaching the geographical details of a deployment including visual tools such as maps and globes with locations marked. Mark off calendar days as an aid to help understand the timeframes associated with the deployment. Some families have utilized calendars or beginning with a jar of M&Ms™ containing a number of candies matching the number of days deployed and make a ritual of having one each day to help count down the days until the deployed parent will return. When age appropriate, encourage journaling to help a child record and clarify their feelings. Journals can also be of assistance with making notes about discussion topics for the deployed caregiver when they next communicate. Journals can be audio recordings if writing skills preclude a written record. Create videos of the deployed service member as a way of providing the child with a means of 'keeping the deployed caregiver present', or for times the child is particularly missing them. Proactively engage all family members in the deployment process, which can help prevent unpleasant surprises as well and may obviate anxiety by virtue of ongoing discourse and processing. Monitor the outcome of this final strategy, since it could heighten anxiety in some children instead of lessen it.

Mothers in the Military

There has been an increase in the number of military women with children deploying to combat arenas such that the war on terror has involved more deployed mothers than any conflict in national history. Since the 9/11 terrorist attacks *via* hijacked airliners in the US, women represented 15 to 20 percent of active duty and reserve service members (Goodman *et al.*, 2013), and more than 40 percent of these women have children. With the increasing number of women deploying, it makes sense that more attention needs to be focused on the unique circumstances surrounding mothers in the military. For example, children of deployed mothers failing to adapt well to the separation experience suffer from:

- **behavioral problems,**
- **depression,**
- **sadness, and**
- **separation anxiety**.

Economic Distress

Deployment can result in financial stresses for a military family through many avenues of added expenses such as additional childcare needs. Military spouses are often financially disaffected in that their rate of pay is frequently and significantly lower than nonmilitary spouses in similar jobs-creating an additional source of stress for many family groups (for a discussion on the breadth of issues associated with military spousal employment, we suggest Schwartz, Wood, and Griffeth, 1991). The effect of a history of working well below competitive pay standards can render the military spouse as less employable than contemporaries or unable to support a household if the deployed service member does not return capable of previous wage earning capacity.

Reluctance to Access Mental Health Services

Negative stigma associated with seeking behavioral health services seems to inundate the military culture and the military family. Many military members and spouses fear the negative ramifications they might experience from senior command if family members access mental health assistance because, as

Goodman *et al.* (2013) pointed out, consuming certain behavioral services obligates mention in command reports. Practices such as this requirement could be perceived, justifiably or not, as institutional bias against the seeking or accepting mental health services. Service members themselves often show clear disinclination to pursue such help as well. For example, in a large national survey of veterans of the war on terror identified as having PTSD, fewer than half had ever sought treatment (Schell & Marshall, 2008). Indeed, other findings reported that nearly 50% of veterans of the war on terror append such stigma to mental health services that they are confident that accessing such services would be detrimental rather than helpful because they would view themselves so poorly for seeking treatment (Elbogen *et al.*, 2013).

Injury after Deployment

Although it is unclear why, returning combat veterans are at an increased risk of involvement in a fatal injury than are veterans with no history of combat deployment. Most of these fatal injuries involve car accidents (Kang & Bullman, 2001). A substantially smaller number of fatal injuries following deployment, though a number that is nonetheless tragically and unacceptably high, involves self-infliction (suicide). Prior to the onset of the war on terror, the suicide rate was lower for military personnel than civilians. Since the onset of conflict it has risen radically, while the suicide rate among the civilian population has remained stable (Katel, 2011).

Death

The current conflict has resulted in significant loss of life despite advances in military field medicine mentioned above. As of February, 2015, the US Department of Defense reported 4,412 total deaths in Operation Iraqi Freedom (OIF) and 2,216 total deaths in Operation Enduring Freedom (OEF). Cozza *et al.* (2005) noted that children impacted by a parental death "are at a higher risk for developing psychiatric disorders or other behavioral or emotional problems" (p. 376), further suggesting that it is reasonable to surmise that children of soldiers could suffer compounded psychological repercussions due to the possible "intentional and aggressive nature of these deaths" (p. 377). In addition, children are disposed to incur greater risk for pathological reactions when the surviving parent is emotionally unavailable to care for or provide support, or if she handles loss in ways that model poor coping (Pfefferbaum, Noffsinger, Wind, & Allen, 2014).

Military spouses have been judged "highly influential in determining child adjustment" (Lester *et al.*, 2010, p. 3); the spouse can be regarded as a positive or negative "conductor" for how their children react or adjust to family changes. The health and resilience of a child is strongly influenced by not only the condition or symptoms (*e.g.*, PTSD, injury, aggressiveness) of the service member but by the responses and coping of the military spouse.

A Note Concerning the National Guard/Reserves

National Guard and Reserve members can be at additional risk from wartime combat deployments. Such pressures can emerge from procedural or cultural variances with active service members. They may deploy with a unit other than their own, eliminating the consistency and comradery typical in active duty units. Many Guard and Reserve members do not live near a military installation and must leave behind family members that will not receive or have not been acculturated in the benefits of military personnel or military community support system (Sheppard *et al.*, 2010). National Guard and Reserve units have been depended on heavily for deployment support in recent wars, which sometimes burdens those families that are not in geographical areas of high military support beyond what might be experienced active duty service members. Lester and Flake (2013) reported some of these families may also feel more alone and have fewer friends due to lack of individuals with common or relatable experiences and emotions.

WHAT CAN SCHOOLS DO TO PROMOTE MENTAL HEALTH?

Before discussing school interventions, it might be useful to have feedback from military spouses regarding strategies they have found useful in helping their families cope with deployment of a service member.

Guidance from Military Spouses

One of us (Cox) is an active member of the United States Marine Corps Officers' Spouse Group in a geographical area in which a large military contingent resides proximate to a substantial military installation. Responses from this spouse group were solicited for feedback *vis a vis* positive and helpful ideas that they had incorporated and found useful with their children in the event of deployment spouse. We concede that this information was not collected adhering to standards of rigorous methodology, nor was that the goal.

Note that many of these suggestions can directly or, with modifications, be incorporated in the classroom setting as well.

All of the responses were provided by female spouses of service members.

Nine out of twenty three responses identified FOCUS (Families OverComing Under Stress) as a great resource for them during deployments, especially with their older children. FOCUS is a program that teaches resiliency to military families, and, based on the feedback offered, does so with efficacy.

Resource	http://focusproject.org/home/

Additional suggestions for families with older children during deployment include using a map that tracks the path and location of their deployed parent.

Numerous suggestions were offered for younger children as well. Among the most frequent was daddy dolls. Daddy dolls are created with cloth and stuffing and have the image of their deployed parent on them. Some include voice recordings so that children can hear their parent's voice telling them special messages, such as 'I love you'.

Kisses from daddy can be done, for example, with a jar of chocolate kisses that provide children with a visual measure of when their deployed parent will return. In addition, it gives children the enviable task of eating a piece of chocolate each day until their deployed parent returns, thereby engaging thoughts and discussion of the deployed caregiver on a daily basis.

Many spouses advised acquiring a good selection of books for children to help them understand deployments and how to cope with feelings related to missing their deployed parent.

Implementing date nights was a recurrent suggestion, wherein children get to have a special date each week with the at-home parent.

Suggestions made by the group that could be appropriate across ages included video exchanges, skype, and email with the deployed parent.

Relating to financial stress deployment can cause, respondents also stressed the importance of searching the area for special deals and discounts for military families. One respondent stated they were given free membership to the YMCA, which provided fun opportunities for keeping children busy. It also provided the opportunity for the at-home spouse to exercise, which has many benefits, not the least of which is reducing stress levels. Some spouses coped with long deployments through prayer time with their children and with the deployed spouse.

Additional advice provided by the group was to keep a positive attitude, because their attitude was instrumental in regulating the attitudes of children. Starting an open dialogue with children as soon as deployment news is received seemed to benefit one family, as did allowing their children to know it was okay to be sad, angry, or lonely.

Thus, the reader can observe significant confluence between the research findings and suggestions with the practical responses given by military spouses.

School Mental Health Promotion: Special Topics, Special Challenges

In order to promote mental health for your students *from* military families, there is one indispensable task you must undertake-you must track the ongoing status of your students *in* military families. If there is a cornerstone upon which school mental health promotion rests, it is empathy. Empathy, like a muscle, will grow if exercised and will atrophy if not. There is no condition of homeostasis. Proactively monitor the wellbeing of your students.

If empathy rests upon a pedestal, the beams supporting it in the school setting are community and climate . These two concepts have been discussed in multiple chapters so will not receive elaboration here. However, we would like to tender one final resource. It was developed by the UCLA Center for Mental Health in Schools, a priceless resource in its' own right. This chapter has discussed numerous risk and protective factors, but has repeatedly stressed the magnitude of one protective factor: a strong, proactive, accessible, mutually engaged system of support-what might alternatively be called a *community*. For readers eager to build or strengthen your school (in relation to its' larger) community, we suggest the following exemplary.

Resource	http://smhp.psych.ucla.edu/pdfdocs/guides/schoolcomm.pdf

CONCLUSIONS

Due to the nature of military life during wartime service, military children are inherently at risk emotionally and psychologically. Deployment cycles during wartime service cause disruptions in routines and family roles. Sheppard *et al.* (2010) aptly stated that "an important first step in assisting military families is to increase understanding of the effects of deployment on child and family outcomes" (p. 606). The goal of this chapter was to provide greater understanding. With greater understanding, appropriate steps can be taken incrementally to improve the lives of military families. In order to make *needed* changes, we should advocate for *informed* changes. The only viable means of being informed is by continually developing and accessing the scientific knowledge base. Optimally, the knowledge base should also influence *policy* in reconsidering recent changes that have occurred to the detriment of military families. This seems like a justified expectation. It is, after all, policy makers who wield the authority to commit service members to the field of conflict.

School professionals and affiliated professions are likely to discover that their primary pragmatic domain of intervention is in serving as, building, and strengthening resiliency factors for students in military families and for students presenting other special challenges. If this effort is pursued, we will be promoting mental health for all students. We all face special challenges sometimes. Many areas of clinical practice have already confronted the realization that risk factors are unfortunate and undesirable, but, at the level of clinical intervention, are often beyond the reach of individual intervention. Consider the example of poverty as a risk factor: unless you directly subsidize those affected by this risk from your own resources, there are limitations to your breadth of intervention options. This also resides within the purview of policy makers. Rather than limited options for directly targeting risk factors, we can have significant influence in expanding and strengthening protective factors. Opportunities for expanding protective factors, especially of increasing the support structure of the school community, are virtually limitless, bound primarily by a lack of imagination.

Mental health promotion in the schools might be likened to the difference between mainstreaming and inclusion (see chapter 2). At first glance, they might appear to have the same meaning, but, with greater understanding, it becomes evident that they are entirely different concepts. Part of the difference is attitudinal. As previously noted, the military parent's attitude plays a significant role in establishing the military child's attitude. It could be extrapolated that the school professional's attitude is a potent influence on the school child's attitude, which could all be directed towards supporting mental health and mutual support. At last count, we believe that includes everyone in the school community.

CONFLICT OF INTEREST

The authors confirm that they have no conflict of interest to declare for this publication.

ACKNOWLEDGEMENTS

Declared none.

REFERENCES

American Psychiatric Association. (1952). *Diagnostic and Statistical Manual of Mental Disorders. Washington, DC: American Psychiatric Publishing American Psychiatric Association. (2013). Diagnostic and Statistical Manual of Mental Disorders.* (5th ed.). Washington, DC: American Psychiatric Publishing.

Bradley, R., Greene, J., Russ, E., Dutra, L., Westen, D. (2005). A multidimensional meta-analysis of psychotherapy for PTSD. *Am. J. Psychiatry, 162*(2), 214-227.
[http://dx.doi.org/10.1176/appi.ajp.162.2.214] [PMID: 15677582]

Bureau of Medicine and Surgery. *Families OverComing Under Stress.* Retrieved from: http://www.focusproject.org/home

Cifu, D.X., Taylor, B.C., Carne, W.F., Bidelspach, D., Sayer, N.A., Scholten, J., Campbell, E.H. (2013). Traumatic brain injury, posttraumatic stress disorder, and pain diagnoses in OIF/OEF/OND Veterans. *J. Rehabil. Res. Dev., 50*(9), 1169-1176.
[http://dx.doi.org/10.1682/JRRD.2013.01.0006] [PMID: 24458958]

Cox, A. (2015). *USMC Officers' Spouse Group.* [Online forum comment]. Retrieved from: https://www.facebook.com/groups/USMCOSG/10155188054095304/?notif_t=group_comment

Cozza, S.J., Chun, R.S., Polo, J.A. (2005). Military families and children during operation Iraqi freedom. *Psychiatr. Q., 76*(4), 371-378.
[http://dx.doi.org/10.1007/s11126-005-4973-y] [PMID: 16217632]

Dekel, R., Goldblatt, H. (2008). Is there intergenerational transmission of trauma? The case of combat veterans' children. *Am. J. Orthopsychiatry, 78*(3), 281-289.
[http://dx.doi.org/10.1037/a0013955] [PMID: 19123747]

Dohrenwend, B.P., Yager, T.J., Wall, M.M., Adams, B.G. (2013). The roles of combat exposure, personal vulnerability, and involvement in harm to civilians or prisoners in Vietnam war–related posttraumatic stress disorder. *Clin. Psychol. Sci., 1*(3), 223-238.
[http://dx.doi.org/10.1177/2167702612469355] [PMID: 25309830]

Eastman, E., Archer, R.P., Ball, J.D. (1990). Psychosocial and life stress characteristics of Navy families: Family Environment Scale and Life Experiences Scale findings. *Mil. Psychol., 2*(2), 113-127.
[http://dx.doi.org/10.1207/s15327876mp0202_4]

Elbogen, E.B., Wagner, H.R., Johnson, S.C., Kinneer, P., Kang, H., Vasterling, J.J., Timko, C., Beckham, J.C. (2013). Are Iraq and Afghanistan veterans using mental health services? New data from a national random-sample survey. *Psychiatr. Serv., 64*(2), 134-141.
[http://dx.doi.org/10.1176/appi.ps.004792011] [PMID: 23475498]

Gil-Rivas, V., Silver, R.C., Holman, E.A., McIntosh, D.N., Poulin, M. (2007). Parental response and adolescent adjustment to the September 11, 2001 terrorist attacks. *J. Trauma. Stress, 20*(6), 1063-1068.
[http://dx.doi.org/10.1002/jts.20277] [PMID: 18157889]

Goodman, P., Turner, A., Agazio, J., Throop, M., Padden, D., Greiner, S., Hillier, S.L. (2013). Deployment of military mothers: supportive and nonsupportive military programs, processes, and policies. *Mil. Med., 178*(7), 729-734.
[http://dx.doi.org/10.7205/MILMED-D-12-00460] [PMID: 23820345]

Herzog, J.R., Everson, R.B., Whitworth, J.D. (2011). Do secondary trauma symptoms in spouses of combat-exposed National Guard soldiers mediate impacts of soldiers' trauma exposure on their children? *Child Adolesc. Social Work J., 28*(6), 459-473.
[http://dx.doi.org/10.1007/s10560-011-0243-z]

Hoge, E.A., Austin, E.D., Pollack, M.H. (2007). Resilience: research evidence and conceptual considerations for posttraumatic stress disorder. *Depress. Anxiety, 24*(2), 139-152.
[http://dx.doi.org/10.1002/da.20175] [PMID: 16892420]

Jones, N., Thandi, G., Fear, N.T., Wessely, S., Greenberg, N. (2014). The psychological effects of improvised explosive devices (IEDs) on UK military personnel in Afghanistan. *Occup. Environ. Med., 71*(7), 466-471.
[http://dx.doi.org/10.1136/oemed-2013-101903] [PMID: 24436060]

Kang, H.K., Bullman, T.A. (2001). Mortality among US veterans of the Persian Gulf War: 7-year follow-up. *Am. J. Epidemiol., 154*(5), 399-405.
[http://dx.doi.org/10.1093/aje/154.5.399] [PMID: 11532780]

Katel, P. (2001). 23). Military suicides: Is the military doing enough to help soldiers cope? *CQ Researcher, 21*, 781-804.

Kelley, M.L., Finkel, L.B., Ashby, J. (2003). Geographic mobility, family, and maternal variables as related to the psychosocial adjustment of military children. *Mil. Med., 168*(12), 1019-1024.
[PMID: 14719629]

Lester, P., Flake, E. (2013). How wartime military service affects children and families. *Future Child., 23*(2), 121-141.
[http://dx.doi.org/10.1353/foc.2013.0015] [PMID: 25518695]

Lester, P., Peterson, K., Reeves, J., Knauss, L., Glover, D., Mogil, C., Duan, N., Saltzman, W., Pynoos, R., Wilt, K., Beardslee, W. (2010). The long war and parental combat deployment: effects on military children and at-home spouses. *J. Am. Acad. Child Adolesc. Psychiatry, 49*(4), 310-320.
[PMID: 20410724]

Link, P.E., Palinkas, L.A. (2013). Long-term trajectories and service needs for military families. *Clin. Child Fam. Psychol. Rev., 16*(4), 376-393.
[http://dx.doi.org/10.1007/s10567-013-0145-z] [PMID: 23828635]

Noteworthy Briefs from the Field. (2008). Increased risk of PTSD symptoms in combat-exposed military personnel. *Psychiatric Dispatches-Primary Psychiatry, 15*, 25-26.

Pfefferbaum, B., Noffsinger, M.A., Wind, L.H., Allen, J.R. (2014). Children's coping in the context of

disasters and terrorism. *J. Loss Trauma, 9*(1), 78-97.
[http://dx.doi.org/10.1080/15325024.2013.791797] [PMID: 24683315]

Raz, G. (2006). *Defining the war on terror. All Things Considered.*. National Public Radio.

Rumbaugh, R.R. (2013). *A tax to pay for war. The New York Times.* Retrieved from: http://www.nytimes.com/ 2013/02/11/opinion/a-tax-to-pay-for-war.html?_r=0

Schell, T.L., Marshall, G.N. (2008). Survey of individuals previously deployed for OEF/OIF. In: Tanielian, T., Jaycox, L.H., (Eds.), *Invisible wounds of war: Psychological and cognitive injuries, their consequences, and services to assist recovery.* (pp. 87-115). Santa Monica, CA: RAND Center for Military Health Policy Research.

Schwartz, J.B., Wood, L.L., Griffeth, J.D. (1991). The impact of military life on spouse labor force outcomes. *Armed Forces Soc., 17*(3), 385-407.
[http://dx.doi.org/10.1177/0095327X9101700304]

Sheppard, S.C., Malatras, J.W., Israel, A.C. (2010). The impact of deployment on U.S. military families. *Am. Psychol., 65*(6), 599-609.
[http://dx.doi.org/10.1037/a0020332] [PMID: 20822199]

Simpson, E. (2006). *An empirical investigation of hybrid wars, strategy, and war aims.*. Conference Papers-International Studies Association.

Solomon, Z., Kotler, M., Mikulincer, M. (1988). Combat-related posttraumatic stress disorder among second-generation Holocaust survivors: preliminary findings. *Am. J. Psychiatry, 145*(7), 865-868.
[http://dx.doi.org/10.1176/ajp.145.7.865] [PMID: 3381934]

Victory Gardens. (n.d.). *Farming in the 1940s.* Retrieved from: http://www.livinghistoryfarm.org/ farminginthe40s/crops_02.

Waller, R. J. (2014). *Children in military families: Challenges and possibilities.* [PowerPoint slides].

Xue, C., Ge, Y., Tang, B., Liu, Y., Kang, P., Wang, M., Zhang, L. (2015). *Casualty Status.* [PDF file]. Retrieved from: http://www.defense.gov/news/casualty.pdf

SUBJECT INDEX

C

F

G

H

I

K

L

M

Made in the USA
Monee, IL
12 September 2026

62975273R00217